Philip Freeman

**The principles of divine service**

An enquiry concerning the true manner of understanding and using the order for

Morning and Evening Prayer

Philip Freeman

**The principles of divine service**
*An enquiry concerning the true manner of understanding and using the order for Morning and Evening Prayer*

ISBN/EAN: 9783337260484

Printed in Europe, USA, Canada, Australia, Japan

Cover: Foto ©Andreas Hilbeck / pixelio.de

More available books at **www.hansebooks.com**

# THE PRINCIPLES OF DIVINE SERVICE.

AN ENQUIRY CONCERNING

THE TRUE MANNER OF UNDERSTANDING AND USING THE ORDER FOR

## MORNING AND EVENING PRAYER,

AND FOR

## THE ADMINISTRATION OF THE HOLY COMMUNION

IN THE

## ENGLISH CHURCH.

BY THE LATE

### PHILIP FREEMAN, M.A.

VICAR OF THORVERTON, CANON AND ARCHDEACON OF EXETER, AND EXAMINING CHAPLAIN TO THE LATE LORD BISHOP OF EXETER.

---

### VOL. I.—MORNING AND EVENING PRAYER.

Stare super antiquas vias.
Σπάρταν ἔλαχες· ταύταν κόσμει.

CHEAPER RE-ISSUE.

Parker and Co.
6 SOUTHAMPTON-STREET, STRAND, LONDON;
AND BROAD-STREET, OXFORD.
1889.

Printed by Parker and Co., Crown Yard, Oxford.

# NOTICE TO THE CHEAPER RE-ISSUE.

THE present edition of this work will, it is hoped, by the reduction made in the cost of the volumes, place it within reach of a larger number of students of our Church's Ritual.

The writer desires to acknowledge, with the most humble gratitude to ALMIGHTY GOD, the degree of favour and acceptance which his humble labours have met with at the hands of the English Church. He has also the happiness of knowing that in one diocese, at least, of the Sister Church of America, unanimity on some important points has been brought about by an appeal to the transcript here attempted of the mind and usages of the Primitive Church.

THE CLOSE, EXETER,
   *Nov.* 14, 1870.

TO THE

CLERGY AND LAITY

OF THE

ENGLISH CHURCH,

AND OF

THE CHURCHES IN COMMUNION WITH HER,

THIS ATTEMPT

TO ELUCIDATE HER

OFFICES OF PUBLIC WORSHIP

IS WITH ALL HUMILITY

INSCRIBED,

BY THEIR AFFECTIONATE BROTHER IN CHRIST,

THE AUTHOR.

# PREFACE.

The end for which all things exist, and especially such as are rational and spiritual, is, by universal confession, that they may serve to the glory of Almighty God by duty and praise. In knowledge of Him, moreover, and in union to Him, stands the life of Christian men, and the means of their perfection. And in their seeking Him, once more, by ways of His appointing, lies the condition of their finding Him, and in Him all that they need. To maintain these relations, and carry on these great transactions, between Heaven and earth, is one purpose for which the Church was founded. Nor can any study be much more interesting than that of the mode in which she has been used to do this in time past, or in other parts of the world; any more important to us than that of the forms of such service existing at the present hour in the Church to which we belong.

It has not pleased God to reveal to us in all particulars, but only in large and general outlines, *how* He will be served. It has therefore from time to time been found necessary to expound, and in particular instances to vindicate, the ways in which, in the Churches of God, this duty of Divine Service has with more or less of variety been discharged. Nor has such at any time been deemed an unfitting employment for those who have received a charge to care for the discipline, as well as the doctrine, of Christ's Church.

In putting forth a treatise on these momentous subjects, designed to educe the general principles of Divine Service, or Christian Ritual, with an especial view to the interpretation of our own, I desire to adopt with all humility the words of a thoughtful divine on a similar occasion:—" The only ends at which my desires did aim in this work, were first and principally the Glory of God, which is the supreme cause of all causes, the main end of all aims, intended by good men or angels. The second, subordinate to this, was to give satisfaction to my longing desires of discharging my duty to the Church my mother, by doing her such service as I was able, in setting forth the true worship of God, and in maintaining the faith professed by her. The third was to give an account that I had not altogether spent my best days in waking dreams, or wandering projects, or private ends [a]."

I can hardly hope that in a work embracing, with somewhat of detail, two subjects of such proverbial difficulty and perplexity as the Israelitish sacrificial system, and the ritual of the Christian Church, I have altogether avoided errors, whether in matters of

[a] Dr. Thomas Jackson, Dedication of his work on the Creed, book ix., to Charles II.

fact, or in deductions from them. But I trust that in no case are they such as to invalidate the leading conclusions at which I have arrived as the result of these investigations: viz., 1, that, amid much of practical depravation and short-coming, an essential harmony and oneness of principle has pervaded the Service of God's Church in all times and lands; and, 2, that the Church of this country, through her Services, is in full accord with this universal mind of the Church; and more especially, as in her doctrine, so also in her ritual, when rightly conceived and acted up to, is not furthest removed from the mind and method of Apostolic days.

ISLE OF CUMBRAE,
*Whitsuntide*, 1855.

# CONTENTS

## OF VOL. I.

### INTRODUCTORY CHAPTER.

The Services of the English Church imperfectly understood. Causes of this. No *rationale* of them put forth at the revision of 1549. (p. 1—4.) The want not fully supplied by Hooker, (4—7); or Sparrow, Comber, &c., from their neglecting the old Offices, (7—11); or by Palmer, who does not fully investigate their effect on our present forms, (11—18). Objections to having recourse to the older Offices for explanation, answered, (18—27). Plan of the work, and *résumé* of points in the Morning and Evening Services illustrated in this volume, (27—33).

## PART I.

### CHAPTER I.

#### ON THE EARLY AND PRIMITIVE FORM OF DAILY SERVICE.

SECT. I.—This inquiry mainly historical. Paramount claims of the historical method. Cautions in applying it. (34—36.) Occasional change a universal law of the Church's Ritual, (36—39). Two great epochs of change, three great eras, of English Ritual, (39, 40). The Daily Offices brought hither by St. Augustine, *not* the Roman, (41). Prevailing erroneous notions as to the primitive times, viz. 1. that they had no other service than the Eucharist; 2. that they had the Eucharist daily. Causes of these misconceptions. (42—46.)

SECT. II.—The present Ordinary Offices of East and West derived from the same primitive source, (46—48.) The Offices, in their earliest known phase, chiefly nocturnal. Yet not derived from the Eucharistic, but co-existent with it from the first. (48—51.) Direct notices of it in early writers, why scanty. Reference to Ignatius, Philo, Justin Martyr, Tertullian, Hippolytus, Origen, Cyprian, Arnobius, Basil, Chrysostom, Cassian. (51—59.)

SECT. III.—Primitive forms of Ordinary Worship likely to be derived from those of the Temple and Synagogue, (59—62). General resemblance, accordingly, of the service described by St. Basil, 4th cent., to the Temple service, (62, 63). The existing Eastern Daily Offices, again, correspond in a general way with St. Basil's account, (64); and also, in details, with the services, 1, of the Synagogue, (64—67); and, 2, of the Temple, (67—69). Minor correspondences. Eastern Daily Offices, like the Jewish, devoid of lessons from Scripture. Saturday, or the Sabbath, a festival in the East. (69—72.) Illustrations of the Western Offices from the foregoing. Penitential introduction to the primitive Eastern Office a warrant for that of the English Church: analogy for it in the West also. (72—75.) The Venite, in some form, universal in East and West; with what differences, (72—78).

SECT. IV.—The probable contents of the primitive Daily Offices further examined. Two sources of information: 1. Apostolic Constitutions,—a second error of Bingham's, in deferring too much to them. 2. The existing Eastern Offices. Grounds for assigning an early date to their main contents; viz.: that the later Western schemes of service (in fifth and sixth centuries) were derived thence. (78—81.) Brief sketch of these schemes. Proofs of their Eastern derivation. (81—86.)

SECT. V.—Eastern Daily Offices, why neglected, as a means of illustration, by Western ritualists. How much of the Eastern Offices of primitive or very early date. Primitive scheme:—TWO OFFICES: 1. *Nocturno-matutinal*; 2. *Evening*. (87—99.) Table of Nocturns Office. (90.) Reasons for thinking it primitive. Midnight character. (Hymn of the Bridegroom's coming.) Accordance with Christ's precept, (St. Mark xiii. 35); with St. Basil's account of night-service in the fourth century. Psalms used as Lessons. (91—94.) "Songs of degrees," as used in this Office; and elsewhere in East and West. (94—96.) Western Offices, in what points indebted to Eastern Nocturns. Name and number of "Nocturns." Creed; Lord's Prayer; both probably of primitive daily use in the East. (96—100.) Hymns; their antiquity; responsory character. Te Deum; origin of it. Confession and Absolution. Litany. (100—106.) Table, comparing this office with our Matins. (106.) Remarks:—Doxology to the Lord's Prayer, peculiar to us among Western Churches. Eastern form of it. Our General Thanksgiving.

SECT. VI.—The ancient Nocturnal and Morning Offices followed each other without any interval: so Tertullian, St. Basil, and present Eastern Offices, (109—113). Table of contents of the Eastern Morning Office, (112). Benediction before the Psalmody. Origin and meaning of "Jube Domine, benedicere," before lessons in the West, (112—115); of "O Lord, open Thou," &c., (115—117). Six Psalms at the early Morning Office, in East and West; half penitential, half jubilant, (118—120). The Western Antiphon, its origin and purpose; how far a loss in our present Offices, (120—123). Eastern Psalm and Canticle scheme, in this Office, the origin of the Western Matins scheme of Psalms, Lessons, and Canticles, (123—129). The Lauds Psalms, &c., (130). Beauty of the Eastern Morning Office: indications of its date. (130—133.)

SECT. VII.—Table of contents of Eastern Vespers, (133). Resembles Nocturns and Matins conjoined. Hymn of "Joyful light," &c., (134—136). The Western Vespers follows this model as to, 1, general structure; 2, number of Psalms; 3, the *Capitulum*. Origin and intention of this, (136—141); and of the Western Collect, viz. from Eastern prayer-like hymns adapted to the Gospels. Derivations of *Collect*. (141—147.) Date of Eastern Vespers. Ceremony of entrance of the Gospels, with hymn following, the prototype of Western daily reading of Scripture. (147, 148.)

Remarks on the foregoing:—1. Primitive existence of other services than Eucharistic; 2. *Two*, or at most three, such services daily; 3. Ancient ideal of Church Service as a whole,—weekly Eucharist, daily prayer, (148—152); 4. Later Western Ritual derived from Eastern; mistakes of Western Ritualists from not acknowledging this; 5. Elements of primitive Service, —Praise, Meditation, Prayer, Confession; these preserved in our own, (152—157); 6. Our Services compared with those of the "Evangelical Church;" with that practically used in the Roman, (157—161).

# CHAPTER II.

## ON THE THEORY OF THE CHURCH'S ORDINARY WORSHIP.

SECT. I.—Various theories respecting it, (162—166). Deeper inquiry necessary. The Incarnation and priesthood of Christ. Twofold aspect of His actions, according as His Priesthood is taken fully into the account or not. (167—171.) Correspondent twofold aspect of the Christian estate: viz. 1. Renewal; 2. Oblation in, participation of, Christ:—imparted in Baptism and the Eucharist respectively, (171—178).

SECT. II.—The two Sacraments differ not in degree only, but in kind. Hence the greater solemnity of the Eucharist, from its peculiar relation to the Sacrifice of Christ. (179—184.) Infant Communion unnatural, (185). This solemnity points to less of frequency, and to necessity for a lower kind of service. Sunday and festival celebration the ancient rule accordingly. (185—192.) Daily Communion of later introduction; synchronized with decay in general discipline, (193).

SECT. III.—The Christian life possesses two aspects: 1. As a state of renewal in Christ; 2. Of priesthood in Him:—these being the development of the position given by the two Sacraments, (194—199). Public Worship an exercise more especially of our priesthood in Christ, (199). Results of this view. Harmonious operation of Eucharistic and Ordinary Service. Argument for retention of Daily Service; for restoration of Weekly Communion, (199—206). True view of priesthood, lay and clerical. Both truths must be firmly held, as of old. (207—211.) Contents of Ordinary Offices in part Baptismal, but in a still greater degree Eucharistic, (211—215).

## CHAPTER III.

### ON THE STRUCTURE AND CONTENTS OF THE ANCIENT ENGLISH OFFICES.

SECT. I.—Retrospect. The Eastern Offices, why so much dwelt on in ch. I., (p. 216—221). The survey of them resumed. Prime: its late origin; contents. Western Prime founded on it. Origin of our third Morning Collect. Third hour. Sixth. Ninth. Compline. The invention of it wrongly ascribed to St. Benedict. Its contents. Western Compline a mere abridgment of it. (222—228.) Origin of "Lighten our darkness." These Offices originally private. Expediency of adopting them entire, as public Offices, considered. Their doctrinal aspect. (228—233.)

SECT. II.—Obscurity of early Western ordinary Ritual. Probability that it was mainly identical with Eastern. Opinion of Grancolas to that effect. Sketch of its probable contents in this country and elsewhere. (234—241.) Later Western schemes,—French, Spanish, Milanese, Roman, English. By whom originated? Not by Pope Damasus; or St. Benedict. Probably by CASSIAN, chiefly. (241—245.) The ENGLISH and ROMAN Ordinary Offices quite *distinct*, though closely akin. Proofs of this. (245—249.) Cassian's qualifications for originating both rites. Hence CASSIAN and ST. LEO *probably co-originators of the Roman rite;*—CASSIAN *alone of the English;*—both *on the old Western basis*. Cassian's rite brought to England by St. Augustine. (249—254). *Résumé*. Western ordinary Ritual universally indebted to Eastern. The great Western Revision in fifth and sixth centuries a precedent for the English in the sixteenth and seventeenth. (254—259.)

SECT. III.—Spirit of the old English Offices, (see tables below, pp. 288, 289). Not appreciated by ritualists generally, (259—262). Character of Matins; of Lauds; of Prime. Review of spirit of these three Offices. (262—269.) Spirit of Tierce, Sext, Nones; of Vespers; of Compline. Genius of East and West compared. (270—274.)

## CHAPTER IV.

### ON THE STRUCTURE AND SIGNIFICANCE OF THE ORDER FOR MORNING AND EVENING PRAYER.

SECT. I.—The present English Offices, the only form in which the ancient ritual really survives. (275—281.) Threefold aspect of them: 1. Eucharistic; 2. Structural. (281—287.) TABLES, exhibiting the structural connection of the present with the old Offices. (288, 289.) Plan of evolution of our Morning Office. The old ideas and spirit, as well as the old order, preserved. Illustration of this from the revision made of the Primer. Suggestion in case of further revision. (290—299.) Evening Office similarly evolved. (299—303.) 3. Representative aspect of the Offices. Compensates for their brevity. Musical mode of service. (303—307.)

SECT. II.—General view of our present Offices. The old Confession and Absolution first placed before Matins by Quignon. Our Absolution founded on the latter. (307—313.) But cast in a different mould, after an existing reformed Service. Was an adaptation of the old *private* form of Absolution. (313—318.) Doctrine of Absolution. Eastern illustration. Our Confessions based on old *private* forms in use in the English Church. Large citation in it from Rom. vii. (318—322.) Sentences and Exhortation borrowed from the old English Lenten Capitula and Homilies. In what light to be viewed and used. (322—327.)

SECT. III.—Rationale of the Lord's Prayer, as a summary of the Office. The opening Versicles, &c. The Venite. Its twofold aspect. Substitution of anthems on Easter-day. (328—331.) The Psalms, an instrument, 1. Of praise; but also, 2. Of knowledge. Spirit of the old Offices, how preserved in them. Antiphons; how far the principle of them practically survives with us. Our Psalm-cycle more free and varied than the old. Eucharistic aspect of the Psalms. (331—337.)

SECT. IV.—The Lessons, primarily, supply topics of praise. The reading of Scripture at large vindicated on this ground. The old system compared with ours. (337—341.) Long Scripture-lessons a primitive usage, (341—344). Ethical and spiritual effects of them, (344—347). The Sunday and Festival Lesson-cycle. Loss of the ancient Benedictions. Eucharistic aspect of the Lessons. (347—350.)
The Canticles; their design. The Te Deum, how based on Scripture. Analysis of it. (350—355.) The other Canticles, (355—360).

SECT. V.—The Creed. Its position; its design twofold, as summing up of doctrine, and basis of prayer. "The Lord be with you," &c. Short Litany. Lord's Prayer; its different design here and at the beginning of the Office. (360—364.) The Petitions; their origin: how related to the Collects following. The First Collect; its deep Eucharistic connection. The Second: its design explained from the old Offices. The Third, traced to the East, and thence explained. (364—371.) The Intercessory Prayers; their counterpart found in the old Offices. Structure of Western Prayers. Pleading of Christ's merits peculiar, now, to the West. The invocations, an act of praise. Reference to the Holy Trinity. (371—374.) Longer prayers used in the East than West. Defence of this kind of prayer. Prayer for the Queen's Majesty; its grandeur: earthly titles in prayer ancient and commendable. Eastern parallel. Eucharistic aspect of Collects and Prayers. (374—378.) Design of the General Thanksgiving. Litany; how to be used. Prayer of St. Chrysostom; origin and significance. The Benediction, an old English Sunday feature; Apostolic; Eucharistic.

## CONCLUSION.

RE-AWAKENED energies of the English Church. After doctrinal principles, ritual to be considered. Proportion to be observed between Eucharistic and Ordinary Worship. Apostolic ideal, anciently realized. Later departure from this. Grievous inequalities of privilege for different classes. (381—384.) The English Church urged to strive for the recovery of the Apostolic standard. Her facilities for it. Such an aim not unworthy; nor visionary. Methods for bringing back weekly Communion. Non-communicating attendance contrary to primitive usage. (384—389.) Increased efficiency of our Ordinary Worship universally desired. Real condition of this question. Revision,—if any,—what direction the previous inquiry would suggest that it should take. Reasons for conservatism drawn from the same source. (389—392.) Projects of revision:— viz. 1. Rectification. The small amount aimed at not be set against the risk. The Proper Lessons. 2. Retrenchment. No necessity for this; but only for resolving, in practice, the present Offices. 3. Additional Offices. Real existing facilities. (392—396.) The present no adequate crisis for change. Due knowledge and use of the old Services the thing really needed. Causes of present desuetude of them as a whole. Want of due training of the clergy. Two reasons for restored continual services peculiarly pressing on the English Church. (396—398.)

# THE PRINCIPLES OF DIVINE SERVICE.

## INTRODUCTORY CHAPTER.

"Enquire, I pray thee, of the former age, and prepare thyself to the search of their fathers... Shall not they teach thee, and tell thee, and utter words out of their heart?"

THE work which is now very humbly tendered for the acceptance of the English Church, has been written under the earnest conviction, that the real nature of her existing Offices of Public Worship has been but very imperfectly investigated hitherto; and that they are in consequence neither correctly understood at the present day, nor used in their full and proper meaning.

This assertion is not made lightly. And that there is no such antecedent improbability in it as might at first sight appear, the following considerations may serve to shew.

It must be borne in mind, that when these Services first received, in the sixteenth century, the shape in which for the most part we still possess them, no explanation was put forth of the design of the several parts, or of the relation which they bear to each other; nor any statement made of the great principles upon which the use of such Services is based, and their structure regulated. The Revisers of the Offices doubtless took it for granted that these things were understood, and needed not to be recapitulated by them; more especially as the old Services would stand that generation in the stead of exponents, to a great degree, of the revised ritual. All that they did, therefore, was to prefix a very brief and general account of the grounds there were for a Revision, and of the objects chiefly aimed at in it [a].

It is indeed probable that they had themselves but an imperfect perception of the entire nature of the forms which, after thus revising them to the best of their power, they handed down. While they necessarily trusted in a measure to their own instinctive perceptions of what was fitting in the matter of Divine Worship, they also in a great degree yielded themselves up, in the exercise of a wise humility, to such provisions and arrangements as they found existing and long established, where no strong reason appeared for departing from them. And it is doubtless owing to their having thus joined to an eminently practical tone and temper, a high degree of deference to the judgment of the Church in past ages, that the Services, as revised by them, have retained their hold on the English mind ever since;—a period of three hundred years. For they have within them that which answers, on the one hand, to the practical desire, nowhere more strongly felt than in this nation, for intelligible as well as devout and worthy forms of worship; and, on the other, to its no less characteristic reverence for that which is fixed, time-honoured, and venerable.

But it is obvious that it would have conduced much, even at the time, to the full appreciation of the

[a] Preface to the "Book of Common Prayer," &c., of 1549: now placed after the Preface of 1662, and entitled "Concerning the Service of the Church."

Services, had some competent interpreter taken in hand, first, to explain and place on record the nature of the old Services, with a view to perpetuating just conceptions of so much of them as was retained unaltered; and, secondly, to unfold the principles on which the revised forms had been abridged or developed out of the old. For want of such a contemporaneous and quasi-authoritative exposition of facts and principles, the Church might very conceivably, in the lapse of time, drift away from a correct apprehension of the Services she had inherited.

But, it may be asked, though the Revisers themselves have not performed this part of interpreter towards their own work, have not others, at various times, supplied the deficiency?

Now in the first place, as regards the old Services, they were (as will be pointed out more fully hereafter[b]) in reality very imperfectly understood at the time of the revision, even by professed Ritualists. The Church of the West, including that of this country, had possessed them for at least a thousand years; but the works in which they were expounded missed of apprehending their true nature and intention, and that, too, in many most important respects. Add to which, that on the ancient Offices of the English branch of the Church in particular,—which differed in some not immaterial points from those of the Western Church generally,—no special commentary or rationale seems to have existed.

Next, let it be remembered how long a time elapsed, after the remodelling of these Services in the sixteenth century—(a period long enough, indeed, as the event proved, for the knowledge of them in their older form

[b] See below, ch. i. s. 7, and ch. iii. On the Ancient English Offices.

to have passed, for the most part, from men's minds) —ere there arose any professed commentator upon their structure and contents, or before any endeavour was made to fix the ideas, and unfold the mind belonging to them. Some noble materials towards such an undertaking were for the first time thrown together in an irregular way about fifty years after. Of this kind was the vindication of our Services by Hooker[c] from the objections of Cartwright and others. Such again were the few and fortuitously preserved notes of Bishop Andrewes[d]. The former of these great men, especially, has searched deep into the principles upon which many of the great elements of Divine Service and Worship, contained in our Offices, are based; and thus vindicated their general character, as well as many details of arrangement and expression. And these profound searchings and eloquent vindications will never be equalled or superseded on their own ground, and as far as they go. But the range of Hooker's comments was greatly narrowed by his controversial position. Where his opponents objected, he defended; but beyond this the nature of his work did not call upon him to enter into the matter or order of the Services. And again, the effectiveness of his championship, even on such points as he has occasion to treat of, is greatly impaired by one very material defect in the appliances which he had at command for dealing with the subject. With the older Offices of the English Church there is little or no appearance of his having been acquainted: whereas these, as must be evident from what has been already

[c] Laws of Ecclesiastical Polity, B. v. ch. 18—49. The fifth Book of Hooker's great work was not published till 1597.
[d] See Nicholls on the Prayer-book.

said, were likely in many points to be the best if not the only clue to the real character of the existing Services. And it is not too much to say that even Hooker's magnificent panegyric on the use of Psalms[e] might have received new features of beauty and truth, and his profound exposition of the matter and structure of our collects and prayers[f] have rested on still more immoveable foundations, had he viewed both these subjects through the medium of those grandly-conceived Offices, and by the light of those great ritual principles of structure and arrangement, which were the inheritance of this branch of the Western Church.

To take a single example:—the peculiar type, in which the Church's prayers are for the most part conceived, having been objected to by his adversaries, especially their being "cast in short petitions," (meaning apparently the collects,) Hooker ably defends them, as well by ancient precedent, as by the reason of the thing. The approval of such forms by St. Augustine, and the helpfulness of them to quicken and sustain devotion, furnished him with a very sufficient ground of defence;—though, indeed, it seems probable that St. Augustine was speaking not so much of collects or prayers, as of versicles and responses. But however this be, surely there was much, very much more, that might have been said; much, too, that is really indispensable to an adequate conception and appreciation of these ancient forms of address to Almighty God. The immense antiquity of the very collects themselves, and not merely of the form in which they are conceived, might for example have been effectively pleaded. Most important and weighty,

[e] L. E. P., B. v. ch. 37, 39.     [f] Ib., ch. 31, 35.

again, is their connection with the Office for the Holy Communion; as is also that condensation into them of whole tracts of Scripture, to which they perhaps owe their name, and which invests them with such singular interest and value, as the Eucharistic thoughts —derived from Scripture and digested into prayer— of holy men in days of unfathomed antiquity. It is evident that until these, and such-like high claims on our veneration and devout use are adequately set forth on behalf of our Offices, we have but a very partial knowledge either of what they are, or of the value that we should set upon them. So again, the mingling of Lessons with prayers might have been based upon other grounds besides those of pleasing and profitable variety. The peculiar character of the Canticles, as responsive to the Lessons, and of the Litany, viewed as anciently designed to precede the Holy Communion;—the different purpose to which the Lord's Prayer is intended to be used in the different positions in which it occurs;—these are grounds of defence, and topics of just eulogy, which an acquaintance with the older forms of the English Church would naturally have suggested. Still, after all, Hooker remains to this day our best, because our profoundest commentator on the Services of the Church. He it is who, beyond all others, has, in various particular instances, based the Church's practice on the unassailable foundations of sound Christian psychology. The *general* "Principles of Divine Service," in a word, have by none, either before or after him, been so truly or so eloquently expounded.

Another wide and dreary interval of sixty years separates Hooker from the next generation of Ritualists,—the school of Sparrow [g] and L'Estrange; who were thus removed by more than a century from the period of the Revision. These, with their successors Comber, Nicholls, Wheatley, Bennet, Bisse, and others, were professed expounders of the origin, contents, and nature of our Ritual. Yet, strange as it may seem, they are hardly less regardless than Hooker himself of the one source from which, beyond all others, the Services would be likely to receive pertinent illustration. It is true, these learned writers were not altogether unacquainted with the older Offices of the Western Church; and they occasionally, though comparatively seldom, refer to them. But their line of comment, as all who are acquainted with them are aware, runs almost exclusively in the direction of the writings of the Fathers, the Councils, and the Holy Scriptures; or again, in that of the successive alterations of detail which have taken place in the Services since the original Revision in 1549. Now illustration of this kind, though doubtless valuable and indispensable, fails to touch the question of the plan, scheme, or theory upon which the Services are framed. It misses altogether, unless by chance now and then, of expounding their true, because historically ascertainable, *rationale*. For this the commentators ought obviously to have had recourse to the older forms; and, if necessary, to earlier forms still, in which they in their turn had originated. This, however, they never dream of doing, but offer instead conjectures of their own, or of their predecessors, as to the nature of this or that element of service or order of parts;

[g] Bp. Sparrow's "Rationale," the first work of the kind, was published in 1655. L'Estrange's "Alliance of Divine Offices" in 1659 (Preface to 4th Edit. 1846).

or fetch remote illustrations from obscure corners of antiquity. All this is really beside the mark, when the true solution of such queries lies before us,—as for the most part it does,—in the older Offices of the English Church.

The truth is, that these writers entertained so strong a distaste, and with it so entire a contempt, for whatever had been done or used in the middle ages of the Church, that the last thing likely to enter their minds, was to seek counsel or guidance of Services belonging to that period, however much they might take warning by them. They assumed, as a matter of course, and without much inquiry, that the changes made in 1549 amounted to nothing less than the composition of an entirely new set of Services out of the materials of the old, selected and recombined at pleasure on altogether a different plan and principle. The former structure was deemed by them to have been absolutely pulled down, before the new one was erected. Whereas nothing is more remarkable in the original Preface to the revised Services, already referred to, than the utter unconsciousness which it manifests on the part of the Revisers, *of having done anything more than revise.* Certain things taken away,—a certain fusing and consolidation of parts or elements heretofore disjointed and broken up,—certain provisions for securing that the Psalms and Lessons should be really and thoroughly *used,* and not skipped for the most part, as in time past,—and the turning of the whole into English;— this was their entire idea of what they had done. They expected the people and Church of the day to accept the Services as essentially, and for all practical purposes, the same Services, revised; and, what is more, as such the Church and people manifestly did accept them. So clear were the Revisers on this point, that Cranmer, (as Jeremy Taylor has recorded,) offered to prove that "the order of the Church of England, set out by authority by Edward the Sixth, was *the same that had been used in the Church for fifteen hundred years past*[h].

And, on the closest scrutiny, it is found that this estimate and representation of their work is thoroughly borne out by facts. If by compiling or composing a Service is meant making an *ad libitum* combination of the ideas and elements previously contained in it, or adding new ones, then it is strictly true that they neither compiled or composed anything. Some elements or features, doubtless, they rejected; others they expanded. *But the exact order of such elements or parts of the old Services as they retained, they preserved inviolate,* both in the Daily Services and in the Communion Service; *and that without a single exception.*—For the proof of these assertions the reader is referred to the following pages.

Our commentators of the 17th and 18th centuries, however, persist, as has been said, in viewing the men of the 16th as "composers" and "compilers" in the largest sense[i]. Thus Wheatley—(to name an

[h] Jer. Taylor's Works, vol. vii. p. 292.
[i] Even the Preface to the latest Revision in 1662, though put forth by men who were not unaware either of the fact or of the importance of our ritual connection with earlier ages,—such as Cosin, Sanderson, Pearson, Thorndike, and others,—has not kept clear of these incautious and incorrect expressions. It commences with the words, "It hath been the wisdom of the Church of England, ever since *the first compiling*," (meaning evidently the Revision in 1549,) "of her publick Liturgy, to keep the mean," &c. The enemies of the English Church have not been slow to avail themselves of these *obiter dicta;* which, however devoid of weight against the facts of the case, have greatly contributed to foster the prevailing opinions as to the time from which our Services date.

author whose work embodies all the preceding ones, and exercises, in many respects not undeservedly, a very wide influence on the prevailing conceptions of our Offices)—was indeed professedly not unaware of the real state of the case. Yet, after once admitting it, he ignores it throughout the rest of his book. Indeed the account which he gives of the old Offices is so singular, as to lead to a suspicion that he had never even looked into the Daily Services;—with the Communion Office he appears to have had a better acquaintance. Who could recognise, in the following description, Offices of which at least three-fourths consisted *not of prayers at all*, but of Psalms and Holy Scripture? "Before the Reformation the Liturgy was only in Latin, being *a collection of prayers* made up partly of some ancient forms used in the primitive Church, and partly of some others of a later original; accommodated to the superstitions which had by various means crept by degrees into the Church of Rome, and from thence derived to other Churches in communion with it, like what we may see in the present Roman Breviary and Missal." He proceeds, however, to characterize the Revision itself as correctly as can be desired; as follows: "When the nation in King Henry VIIIth's time was disposed to a reformation, it was thought necessary to correct and amend these Offices; for *it was not the design of our Reformers,* (nor indeed ought it to have been,) *to introduce a new form of worship into the Church, but to correct and amend the old one*[k]." Yet after this he constantly speaks of "compiling" and "composing"; nor does he anywhere, that I am aware of, refer to the old Offices of the English Church as furnishing a clue to the structure of her present ones:

[k] Wheatley, Introd., p. 22.

his sole standards of appeal are the 1st Book of Edward VIth, the Apostolic Constitutions, and the ancient Liturgies of the Eastern Church. Such stray allusions as he makes to the Western Offices at all are in a condemnatory tone throughout.

Within the last few years, Ritualists of another stamp, and possessed with a juster idea of the exigencies of the case, have risen up to remedy, in a measure, the leading defect of all previous works bearing upon the Services of the English Church. Attention has at length been forcibly and not unsuccessfully drawn towards the one quarter which had so long and so unaccountably been left unexplored, and from which alone a true idea of them can be obtained. The publication of the "Origines Liturgicæ[1]" of Mr. Palmer is likely on this account to prove an epoch in the ritual literature of the English Church, only second in importance to that which was marked by the appearance of the Fifth Book of the Laws of Ecclesiastical Polity. Nor is it possible to speak of that work without rendering a deserved testimony to the perfect mastery which it exhibits over the vast range of ritual learning embraced by it, and to the clearness with which the results of the author's observation are set forth. There, as is well known, every part of our present Offices for Public Worship is, in common with the rest of the Book of Common Prayer, referred to its proper place in the older Offices. Other writers have followed in the same track. Mr. Maskell has published the old Communion Offices of the Eng-

[1] "Origines Liturgicæ, or Antiquities of the English Ritual," by the Rev. W. Palmer, M.A. For a compendium of Mr. Palmer's view of the ancient Liturgies, see Tracts for the Times, No. 63.

lish Church (according to the Uses of Salisbury, York, &c.) in the original Latin[m], arranging them in parallel columns, with a preface and notes; besides that his "Monumenta Ritualia[n]" contains a fund of interesting matter, tending to illustrate our existing ritual from that of the middle period of the Church in this country. The old Daily Offices, according to the Salisbury Use, have also been in part reprinted in the original, with brief but elaborate notes[o]. Some account of the existing Roman daily offices, with translated specimens, had some years since been given to the world[p], and may serve to give the English reader an idea of the old arrangements. And now, at length, has appeared a careful translation of the "Sarum Psalter[q]," (including a considerable part of the Offices, but not the Lections or Lessons,) largely illustrated from contemporary sources, and from the Uses of the other Dioceses.

Thus have the proper materials for the elucidation of our Offices of Public Worship been at length in a great degree rendered accessible; and also, to a certain extent, applied to purposes of illustration.

It might not unreasonably be supposed that these works, Mr. Palmer's more especially, must have exhausted the subject, and left little, if anything, to be done by others. But though Mr. Palmer, while leaving hardly any field of antiquarian investigation untrodden,

---

[m] "The Ancient Liturgy of the Church of England," &c., by Rev. William Maskell. 2nd Edition, enlarged.

[n] Monumenta Ritualia Ecclesiæ Anglicanæ, 3 vols.

[o] Portiforii Sarisburiensis Fascic. I. (Psalterium et Propr. Advent.) Leslie, Lond. 1842-3. The work is out of print.

[p] Tracts for the Times, No. 75.

[q] "The Psalter, or Seven Ordinary Hours of Prayer, according to the Use of Sarum," &c. Masters, 1852.

has also paid especial attention to this one in particular, it must be confessed that the principal thing that needed to be done with reference to it is exactly that which he has left untouched. He has, indeed, carefully specified throughout, as has been said, the place which the successive features of our Services occupied in the older forms; and where any change or substitution has been made, has justified the arrangement —on the whole, felicitously—by precedents drawn from the ritual of other Churches. The entire collection, so to say, of ritual specimens embodied in our Offices has thus been labelled and registered; and the place of each in our own or other ancient collections can be ascertained. And this is a great gain; and one for which the student of our Services cannot be too grateful.

Wherein then, it will be asked, is this work deficient as an exposition of those Services? I answer, first, in that it nowhere sets forth as a whole, in a lucid and connected view, in what degree, and with what modifications or developments, the old order and contents have been preserved in the remodelled Offices. From its failing to exhibit such a general *conspectus* as this, the work is not nearly so satisfactory or convincing as it might have been made. We do not rise from it with the impression that the parentage of our present Services, taken as a whole, can be successfully and legitimately traced to those which preceded them. When some particular feature or portion is noted as having been retained from the old forms, the circumstance has rather the air of a satisfactory incident, than of guaranteeing any real identity between the old and the new. The impression which the fact makes upon us is further weakened by its generally coming hand in hand with a variety of accidental correspondences,—for, such for the most part, they necessarily are [r],—fetched from remote sources, such as the Apostolical Constitutions, or the ancient Liturgies of Syria or of Armenia. Mr. Palmer has not perhaps intended to attach the same weight to these more remote coincidences, as to those which lie nearer home: but the prominence given to them has certainly had the effect of leading many to the conclusion that our present Offices are a mere mosaic or conglomerate; consisting of excellent materials indeed, but those totally unconnected, and more or less incongruous,—*undique collatis membris*. That they can claim anything like so close and peculiar an affinity with the early English Offices as in reality they may, is what few perhaps gather from the mixed company in which they are here exhibited.

Indeed, as regards our Communion Office, Mr. Palmer has in one place distinctly pronounced that "it resembles, in form and substance, rather the ancient Gallican, Spanish, Egyptian, and Oriental Liturgies," than the type which prevailed throughout Western Christendom at the time of the Revision: the *expressions* only of our Ritual being traceable in part to that type, in part to the Liturgies just mentioned. This statement, I do not hesitate to say, conveys an altogether erroneous impression. The

---

[r] It is probably a correct observation on the whole, that "there is no reason to suppose" the Revisers of our Offices "to have been intimately acquainted with the formularies of the Eastern Church. (Neale, Gen. Introd., p. 388). The Liturgy of St. Chrysostom had, however, been already translated into Latin, by Ambrosius Pelargus, and afterwards by Erasmus: hence, probably, the "Prayer of St. Chrysostom" (see below, in loc.) found its way into our Services. Other Eastern Liturgies were printed in 1560. Vide Renaudot, Lit. Or. Præf., p. 4.

order, form, and substance of our Communion Office, as at first revised, are *those of the English variety of the old Western Office, and of no other in the world;* with only the omission of some features, and the development of others. And though subsequent revisions produced some alterations of form and order, these tended to assimilate the Office, *not* to those indicated by Mr. Palmer, but to another and more primitive type which can be shewn to have preceded them [s].

But this is not the only or the chief thing which Mr. Palmer's work has left still to be done. It was no part of his design to elicit *the spirit and meaning* either of the old Offices or of the new. More especially he has made no attempt to *penetrate and to state the true nature and character of the old Offices,* but has contented himself with a very brief and general account of their contents [t]. It does not seem to have occurred to him that this, after all, was the great thing to be done in the matter. It is satisfactory, of course, to know that we use to a great extent the same substance and order of services as our fathers did; but it would be a further and a more important boon, if we could ascertain what *was the mind of those services;*—what are the conceptions that pervade them, when rightly understood;—whether their form and substance were dictated by any profound and true ritual ideas, which we perchance have at the present day lost sight of;—and how far such conceptions and ideas may be deemed to have passed on to us with the Services themselves. Such a life-like catching of the inner mind of our elder

[s] See below, Part II., chapter on the Primitive Form of Liturgy.
[t] Orig. Lit., Part I. ch. i. Introd.; and ch. iii. init.

Ritual were worth a thousand mere satisfactory correspondences of detail.

This then it is, that is perhaps above all other things needed in order to a full and correct apprehension of the present Services of the English Church,—viz. a careful statement and exposition of the nature, purpose, and spirit of her older Offices. Such a statement will accordingly be attempted, as a substantive and indispensable part of this Inquiry. And this, again, will be applied as a key to unlock the general nature and character of our Offices as at present constituted.

Though indeed, not the general spirit only, but the details too of the old Services, have yet to be thoroughly examined and estimated, as a means of appreciating the corresponding features in our present forms. Even in this department, Mr. Palmer has done no more—it hardly fell within the scope of his work to do more—than indicate the quarter whence light may be obtained. Antiquity—English antiquity more especially — has, hitherto, after all, been rather appealed to in justification of details, than resorted to for explanation of their meaning. Here, too, the specimens have been labelled, but not analysed. We know whence our good things come; but we are not much better informed as to what they are worth. What is the resultant, to the spiritual eye, of such and such a history and antecedents proved to belong to this or that part of our Offices; with what character and meaning they come invested to us in consequence; and with what mind we are accordingly to use them;—these are practical questions which have yet to be asked and answered.

To make such assay then,—to investigate and express the value and significance of the several *parts* of our Services, aided mainly, though not exclusively, by the facts of their previous history, their old placing, and obvious intention,—will be another object of these pages.

Some admirable efforts of this kind, bearing upon both the general character and the details of the Services, will be found in Comber's well-known "Companion to the Temple".ᵘ His general conception of the structure of the Daily Offices in particular, though unaided by reference to the older forms, is in the main singularly correct. But then, for want of such reference, his *rationale*, in common with that of Sparrow and his other fellow-ritualists, is in a great measure mere random and guess-work, and in that proportion, of course, both unconvincing and unsuccessful. What still needs to be done is to combine the sounder and better directed antiquarianism of the later, with the religious and reflective tone of the elder school of our Ritualists. It is not enough, on the one hand, to ascertain the history and antecedents of each part of our Services; nor, on the other, to make reflections, and offer suggestions, as to the manner of understanding and using them, which may or may not be in harmony with their real intention. Such comments, to be thoroughly to the purpose, must be based on correct historical and antiquarian knowledge.

On the whole, it cannot be denied that, even without travelling out of the field of illustration we have been hitherto speaking of, there is a wide range of questions, both general and particular, either imperfectly handled, or not handled at all, by previous

---

ᵘ See more especially his analysis of the "Venite."

writers on our ritual. The condition of what may be called the literature of our Offices is not unlike that of philosophical literature in the days of Bacon. When we "enter into a view and examination, what parts of that learning have been prosecuted, and what omitted[x]," we find that though "the great quantity of books makes a show rather of superfluity than lack," whole departments of illustration, nay, the *summa rei* itself, the principal and prerogative source of information, has been lying all but untouched the while.

The writer is aware that at the point which he has now reached in unfolding the nature of his work, he is liable to be met by an objection, seriously and earnestly entertained by many, to the whole line of illustration referred to. The old Offices of the English Church, in common with those of Western Christendom generally, were, it is commonly and most justly conceived, in many ways corrupt. The Preface to the first revised Services confesses as much; and so does every Minister of the English Church at the present day by declaring, at his ordination, his unfeigned assent and consent to the entire Book which contains both this Preface, and other statements of like tenor[y]. But it is further assumed, not unnaturally perhaps, that the services were corrupt to such a degree as to render them altogether useless, or worse than useless, as exponents of the mind of our present Offices. It is partly as sharing in this view, that our ritualists, from first to last (as has been pointed out)

---

[x] Advancement of Learning, Bk. II.
[y] e. g. the declaration subjoined to the Communion Office in 1662, and Articles XXV. and XXVIII.

have either ignored the old services altogether, or have contented themselves at most with a dry register of the points in which we are indebted to them. They seem to have assumed it as an axiom, that we could not possibly learn anything from the old conceptions or the old order; that both the whole and the several parts—however valuable and fit for our use when duly resolved and re-combined—must, considered as occurring in the old formularies, be radically and incurably vicious; and that therefore it was needless, if not actually undesirable, to make any inquiry into them.

Now it is surely a question worth asking, whether the old Services, though confessedly corrupt, were so in such a sense, and to such a degree, that they must needs be summarily rejected as witnesses or informants in this weighty inquiry as to the true sense of our present Services?

The writer is anxious not to be misunderstood. With the corruptions in question he has not the smallest sympathy. It is on the contrary matter of astonishment to him that any person, jealous for the honour of Almighty God and for the purity of the Christian faith and worship, should think it necessary to speak tenderly, or to be silent altogether, upon the debasing superstitions which have for so many hundred years disgraced both the theory and practice of the greater part of Western Christendom. A systematized Saint-worship, saddening enough to contemplate at the time when our Offices were first revised, has since then received fresh developments of a very awful character, until it treads, to say the least, upon the very verge of polytheism. And again, a direct idolatry, paid to various objects of sense, received at that time, and continues to receive still, the sanction, more or less formal and distinct, of the Roman branch of the Church. And the real difficulty, in truth, which must sometimes press itself on a religious mind, is how a communion which sanctions and adopts such fearful derelictions of the first principles even of natural religion, can be held to retain the being of a Church at all. It is one thing, however, fearlessly to pronounce, in accordance with truth, justice, and judgment, upon the moral and spiritual quality of an action, and quite another to undertake to decide upon the doer's standing in the sight of God. We have no commission to give judgment of award upon a Church or Churches, certain of whose actions and principles we may nevertheless be bound unequivocally to condemn. We may trust that it takes much to destroy the being of a Church, as it does, by God's mercy, hopelessly to destroy a soul. And I conceive that we may on the whole be well content to endorse the judgment and views, at once firm and charitable, adopted in this matter by those who, in revising our Ritual, defined not amiss for us our position in this respect also. We need not fear to say, on the one hand, with the men of the 16th century, that there were in the old Offices and ways — how much more in their later development, — "many things, whereof some are *untrue*, some are uncertain, some vain and superstitious [z];"—with those of the 17th, that "the sacramental Bread and Wine," e. g., "*may not be adored*, for that were idolatry to be abhorred of all faithful Christians [a];" knowing the while that a great portion of the Christian world does so adore them. And on the other hand, we may

[z] Preface to the Book of 1549.
[a] Rubric at the end of the Communion Office of 1662.

consent no less, with the men of both periods, to give to the " Churches of Jerusalem, of Alexandria, of Antioch, and of Rome," the name and the place of Churches, albeit " they have erred even in matters of faith [b]."

Faithfully, though charitably, to take up this position appears, indeed, to be the duty with which the Church of the English succession is peculiarly charged. Whatever part may, in God's providence over His Church, be allotted to other branches of it; whatever the truths or aspects of the truth, if there be any such, which are more especially confided to *their* keeping; *she* must not fear to be true to the part so distinctly assigned to her, as *the only communion now on the face of the earth, which, together with the ancient principles of sacramental truth and apostolic regimen, upholds the absolute and exclusive unity of the object of Christian worship.*

But while we do well to be faithful in our own generation to this responsibility, we shall on the other hand act most unwisely, if, in pursuing an investigation like the present, we throw aside without inquiry, on the ground of their temporary association with corrupt features of worship, the older Services of our Church. Conceivably, no doubt, they might have been so penetrated with those elements of unsoundness, and vitiated by them, as to be valueless for our purpose. But the question whether they are so is simply a question of fact, to be settled, like others of the same kind, by inquiry. And so it is, that on examination, these elements are discerned to have occupied a very small portion either of the Daily or Com-

---

[b] See Note A.

munion Services strictly conceived; apart, that is, from additions sanctioned by custom only, and not by the written "use" of the Church: so that they are really and discernibly separable from the whole; forming no part of its proper idea, and capable of removal without any prejudice to it.

Thus, as regards the ancient Daily Offices, the remark which has been made upon them as used in the Roman Church at the present day, is even more applicable to them as they existed in our Church at the time of our English Revision. "These Invocations do not enter into the *structure*" of the Offices; they are so placed that they "might easily have been added, as e.g. was the case with our own Thanksgiving[b]." "This is what occurs to us to observe," the writer proceeds, "on the first sight of these Invocations, &c.: but we are not left to a conjectural judgment about them; their history is actually known, and their recent introduction into the Church Services distinctly confessed[c]."

Again, as to our ancient Communion Office, a position which has been frequently maintained before is further confirmed in the following work, chiefly by a comparison of all ancient Communion Offices with each other; viz. that the parts of it which are commonly appealed to as furnishing evidence for corrupt doctrines or practices, are either palpably modern, and perfectly separable from the genuine Offices, or have been utterly misunderstood and perverted from their

---

[b] Tracts for the Times, No. 75.

[c] The only features of this sort which can claim any sort of antiquity, are an Invocation in the Prime Office, which Gavanti says is of great antiquity; and those contained in the Litany, which seem to be correctly ascribed to S. Gregory, at the beginning of the seventh century, Vide L'Estrange on the Litany, ch. iv. p. 146.

true acceptation, and therefore needed not to be rejected, but only brought back to their proper use[d].

But others, again, may think it undesirable to draw attention to the older Offices of our Church, not on account of their association with corruptions in worship, but rather because of the imposing grandeur, and in many respects the æsthetic beauty, of their structure and contents. It may be said, that the contemplation of these will only cause, in the minds of members of the English Church, dissatisfaction with our present simpler and more unpretending ritual; nay, more, that such dissatisfaction has already, as a matter of fact, been one cause of secessions from among us.

The answer to this objection—which, it must be admitted, is a plausible one—is, that by universal admission, the best mode of meeting a difficulty is, as a general rule, to look it fairly in the face; and that though there are some exceptions to this rule, in the present instance, at any rate, there is no alternative. The spirit of inquiry in matters religious and ecclesiastical, which, whether for good or evil, is a characteristic of this age, has already led to the republication in a great measure of these Services, either as objects of ritual study, or as contributions to devotional literature. The inquiry and the publicity which is deprecated, already exists. The time is gone by for any concealment of the history and antecedents of our present Ritual: and it is by fair and candid exhibition of its earlier phases, joined to adequate

[d] A striking exemplification of both kinds of corruption is pointed out in Part II., chapter on the Primitive Form of Liturgy. The elevation of the Elements in the Eucharist, as now practised, in order to their adoration, is (vide Bona in loc.) modern; while the ancient and undoubted elevation, later in the Service, was demonstrably designed for a totally different purpose.

representation of the entire circumstances which justified, and even required, a revision, and that too of no partial or hesitating character;—by demonstrating the unpractical character, proved by the experience of ages, of the older Offices, considered as public Services;—it is only by such means as these that any anxiety that may be felt for a return to the older forms can be unanswerably met. And accordingly it will be pointed out in these pages, that many other considerations, besides those of the abstract beauty or merit of the Offices, had to be taken into account at the time of the Revision, and must be so still in answer to any reactionary demands or tendencies.

Though this, indeed, is not all. The same process of inquiry which lays open to us the imposing structure of the mediæval Offices, also reveals to us a yet earlier stage of their history, and phase of their existence, towards which (though in some sort accidentally) they re-approximated, as the result of the Revision in the 16th century. So that the revised Offices were in reality a return, in point of general form, of duration, and of practicability, to the dictates of an early and an Oriental simplicity; while at the same time they are pregnant, under that simpler exterior, with all the finer and profounder elements of the later Western devotion. On this account the English Office-book is in reality peculiarly rich in the ritual spoils of time, and in the devotional experience of every clime and every age of the Church. While parting with much that was nobly elaborated, the work of the 16th century abounded in solid compensations for whatever of outward magnificence it laid aside, and would have been less truly great, had it been less fearlessly executed.

Thus much seemed necessary to be said in reply to some not unnatural but really ill-founded objections, which might be conceived to lie against one of the principal lines of illustration adopted in this work.

Whoever then shall be found willing, in a spirit of calm inquiry, neither too mistrustful of the past, nor too regretful for it, to ask after the mind of our Church's ancient Services, as one means of ascertaining that of her existing Ritual, will, it may be safely promised, be rewarded for the search. He will find in them "Principles of Divine Service" of no ordinary depth and beauty; principles, too, which have been faithfully conserved and handed down, as to all primary and essential points, in our present Services.

And one great principle in particular it will be the aim of the writer, chiefly by the help of the older Offices, to bring out prominently as a key to our existing Services,—viz. the Eucharistic principle; or, in other words, the idea, rightly apprehended, of the Holy Communion.

In the light of that idea he will have occasion to consider, first of all, our Daily or Ordinary Services. It will be seen that their structure and contents are, in virtue of their substantial identity with the Offices of earlier periods of the Church, closely connected with ancient and primeval Eucharistic conceptions, and can only be correctly apprehended or adequately used by viewing them in that connection.

So, again, our Office for the Holy Communion itself will find, after all, the best interpreter and exponent, both of its structure and of its particular features, in the older Communion Office of the English Church. Only, that Office must be taken and understood, not in the inadequate and often most corrupt sense which the commentaries and glosses of the middle period of the Church have fastened upon it, but in that true one which is thoroughly substantiated by its early history, and by comparison of it with the ancient Offices of all other Churches.

There is another deeply interesting department of research into which we shall find ourselves led, in turning to our older Offices as a source of illustration. We shall light upon certain most ancient, and to all appearance primitive, ways of converting Holy Scripture to purposes of Divine Service. These admirable methods, by which the Scriptures were in very early times, in the West more particularly, made the basis, the materials, and the vehicles of the Church's devotion,—and that too by no shallow or surface application, but in accordance with the profoundest conceptions both of them and of the Christian life, —are so little apprehended at the present day, or thought of in connection with our forms of service, that they cannot fail, when properly exhibited and applied, to cast altogether a new light upon them.

And yet more when we *combine* the light derivable from these two sources of illustration,—viz. the ancient and proper conception of the Holy Communion, and the ancient methods of devotion on the basis of Scripture,—do we find them exercising a perfectly transforming effect on the meaning of those Services, with the letter of which we are so familiar. What the saying of Psalms was to them of old time; or what of Collects, or even of the Lord's Prayer; or what the reading and hearing of Scripture;—we can only then understand, when we have thoroughly learned to enter into the Eucharistic and other devotional ideas which prompted and fashioned the forms of worship which we have inherited. But when we have duly mastered these, we shall, if we are wise, be prepared to adopt and act upon them, in lieu of those less profound, as well as less just conceptions of our Offices, which we have hitherto been content to rest in.

It will be seen, from what has now been said, with what degree of fitness, and in what sense, one of the mottoes placed upon the title-page of this work has been adopted. "To stand in the old paths,"—to be faithful to ancient, early-adopted, and often primitive conceptions and ways, in the matter of Divine Service,—is the course which these pages are designed respectfully yet earnestly to recommend to the members of the English Church, as the main thing to be done, if we would arrive at a correct apprehension and appreciation, as well as attain to a full and sufficient use, of our Offices of Public Worship. This watchword has indeed, as far as words go, been taken up, almost without exception, by others who have written on the subject. But, as has been shewn above, they have not been faithful to it. They have not ventured to claim kindred with the one stock of ancient ritual to which ours more immediately belongs. Through lack of knowledge, or of courage, or of due appreciation of what was wanted, it has been the practice to slur over the intermediate links which alone unite our Services, by a real continuity of essence and spirit, and even of form, with the ritual and mind of early days.

It is high time that this mode of dealing with them, which is happily as unnecessary as it is unworthy, should come to an end. Let us, by all means, take our stand upon the antiquity of our Ritual. Only it must be no less earnestly urged and maintained, that there is but one way of doing this. It cannot be done by ignoring the facts of the process by which our Services reached us. It is not by throwing down the ladder that connects us, ritually, with antiquity, that we can best prove our descent from it, or our coincidence with it. There is but one way of being true to our Service-book; and that is, to take it for what it is, and for what they, who first handed it over to us in its revised form, believed it with all their hearts to be. It is an old Book. Its elements, its method of service, its conception, and its order, are all old,—older than any other institution in this country;—some of them as old as the days of the Apostles themselves. Let us not be afraid to look it in the face, in its earlier lineaments. Let us try to understand it as it was, that so we may the better understand and use it as it is.

It is not meant to be affirmed that this is *all* that is needed. There are portions of our existing Offices which cannot be completely interpreted by reference to the old forms and ideas. The first Revisers of them, though they never in a single instance, that I am aware of, departed from the established order and sequence of such portions as they retained, did in various instances modify, or even give fresh development to, the old elements. This is a circumstance of which we derive no conception from Mr. Palmer's too general statement, that our Offices for Morning and Evening Prayer are "*an abridgment* of the ancient Services," (Pt. I. ch. i.). An abridgment, on the whole, it doubtless was; but it was in some respects a signal development,—e. g. in the department of lections or lessons from Holy Scripture, and in that of the Canticles responding to them. The methods according to which they were thus modified or developed, must of course be considered in themselves, without that direct assistance towards forming a just conception of them, which in other cases we derive from the older forms. Even here, however, we can generally discern ancient and received forms or methods of service, to which they had recourse. Thus the Exhortation, Confession, and Absolution, prefixed to the Daily Offices by the original Revisers, when they put them forth for the second time in 1552, have been commonly deemed to lie open, beyond other parts of the Service, to the charge of novelty. But the truth is, that they are all, though in different degrees, distinctly traceable to methods and formulæ then received, and familiar to the English Church of that day [d]. So, again, the particular versicles and responses which they substituted for the older series after the short Litany and Lord's Prayer, are those which had been long in use in the English Church every Sunday and Festival, as a part of the Bidding Prayer [e].

Subsequent Revisions, as is well known, went still further in the direction of remoulding the old features, and sometimes, though instances of this are not numerous, adding new. Some, which have the appearance of being altogether new, are in reality legitimate and intelligible expansions of the corresponding older elements. Of this kind are, e. g., the addition of intercessory prayers to the Morning and Evening

[d] See below, ch. i. s. 2, and ch. iv.      [e] Ch. iv.

Office, and a substitution, in the Communion Office, of a Confession based on the Commandments, for another form which formerly occupied the same position, and which the first Revisers had left out altogether.

In the structure of these parts of the Services there is, of course, more room for the exercise of individual judgment, than where the intention is for the most part defined for us by the older forms. Nor does the writer by any means undertake to say that he has always been able to form correct conclusions as to the view to be taken of these, any more than of the ancient Services. He has in all cases stated the facts and reasonings on which his conclusions are grounded, that others may judge for themselves. But having done this, he has not scrupled to offer practical suggestions, based on the views he has arrived at: not as desiring to exclude other interpretations, but as deeming those which he has adopted to be at least probable; and as conceiving that it is far better that the members of the Church should be provided with some definite notions, upon which they can act, of the Services prescribed for their use,—even at the risk of some degree of incorrectness of theory,—than that they should entertain mere vague and pointless conceptions about them. Let others, by all means, bring forward views which they deem more correct; none will more gladly than the writer welcome any that are better grounded than his own: and let the collective wisdom of the Church supply in due time, if it be thought needful, a more authoritative interpretation.

The writer's views on the subject of any further Revision of the Church's Offices will be found embodied in the chapters bearing upon the Revision of the 16th century, and on the capabilities of the present Services.

It only remains to state briefly the plan of this work. The First Part, contained in the First Volume, treats of the Daily Offices: the Second Part, occupying the Second Volume, of the Office for the Holy Communion. A chapter will be found, early in the First Volume, on the general theory of the Church's Ordinary Worship; more especially as to the relation in which it stands to her Eucharistic Worship:—an important subject, which the writer had nowhere seen treated with the attention which it seems to deserve. The Second Volume opens with a chapter carrying on the same subject by an investigation of the theory of Eucharistic Worship. These two chapters are of the nature, therefore, of a distinct Treatise, more or less complete, on the entire Theory of Christian Worship and Service.

The following are some of the chief points in which the prevailing conceptions about our Ordinary Offices have appeared to the writer to be erroneous, and to be capable of correction, either by referring to the ancient forms and ideas, or from other considerations.

I. The general structure and design of our Morning and Evening Services, and of the Litany; concerning which great vagueness of view prevails: while various opinions, more or less conjectural, have been propounded by different writers. More particularly, the relation in which they stand to the Office for the Holy Communion.

II. Among the details of the Services, the following points:—

i. The origin, structure, and design of the introductory part, which has been in various ways misunderstood and undervalued.

ii. The sense in which the Lord's Prayer is to be understood and used at the commencement of the Service.

iii. The *full* conception according to which the Psalms, forming the first great division of the Service, are to be used; and especially the relation of this act of worship to the corresponding action in the Holy Communion.

iv. The full idea under which reading and hearing of Holy Scripture, forming the second great division of the Service, is to be conceived of; and the analogy between this part of the Office, and certain features of the Holy Communion.

v. The design of the Canticles, considered as responsive to the Lessons.

vi. The true conception of the third and last division of the Service, commencing with the Creed; and its correspondence with one of the aspects of the Holy Communion.

vii. The light in which the Creed, occupying the position that it does, is to be viewed and used.

viii. The idea under which the Lord's Prayer occurs for the second time in the Service, and in what sense it is to be used in consequence.

ix. The exact origin and probable design of the Versicles which accompany the Creed and the Lord's Prayer.

x. The true nature of *Collects,* as distinguished from other Prayers; and the purpose and effect of introducing the current Eucharistic Collect into the Morning and Evening Office.

xi. The origin and peculiar character of the Second and Third Collects.

xii. The idea with which the intercessory Prayers, the general Thanksgiving, &c., were added to the Offices at the later Revisions; the general structure of these Prayers; and other particulars respecting them.

A similar *résumé* of the points touched upon in the Communion Office, may most conveniently be reserved to the commencement of the Second Volume.

# THE
# PRINCIPLES OF DIVINE SERVICE.

## PART I.

---

### CHAPTER I.

ON THE EARLY AND PRIMITIVE FORM OF DAILY SERVICE.

#### SECTION I.

---

"And he shewed me a pure river of the water of life, . . . proceeding out of the throne of God and of the Lamb. . . And on either side of the river was there the tree of life, which bare twelve manner of fruits . . . and the leaves of the tree were for the healing of the nations."

---

THE Church of England, in common with all other branches of the Church Universal, recognises two kinds of Divine Service[a], or Public Worship, and possesses certain accredited Offices for the performance of them. The Celebration of the HOLY COMMUNION, or EUCHARIST, is by universal consent the supreme act of Christian worship and service. Distinct from this, though nearly allied to it, is the more Ordinary kind, known to us by the name of COM-

---

[a] This, though commonly supposed to be a modern term, is the ancient phrase (*Servitium Divinum*), peculiar to the English Church, for the act of public worship. Vid. Rubr. Sar. ante Mat. fol. 3, 4.—The latter rubric shews that *Servitium* was applied to the Eucharist. See Preface to the Prayer-book, "Concerning the Service of the Church." Cf. S. Aug. Civ. Dei, x. 1. "Λατρεία Græce, Latine interpretatur Servitus ea qua colimus Deum."

MON PRAYER[b]. The existence of both these kinds of Service from the earliest ages of the Church[c], their general theory, and the relation in which they stand to each other[d], are points which will be discussed as part of the Inquiry, which it is the purpose of this work to institute, concerning the right manner of understanding and using the Offices now appointed for the performance of public worship in the English Church.

That inquiry is, indeed, far from being a new one. Of the labours, accordingly, of preceding writers on the subject, I have spoken at some length in the Introductory Chapter. I endeavoured at the same time to state clearly to what extent, and in what department of inquiry more especially, there still appeared to be room for an attempt like the present. I shall venture to assume some acquaintance on the part of the reader with the more important information contained in the works referred to, and now generally accessible, either in the originals or in more popular manuals[e].

The particular field of research, it may be remembered, to which we seemed to be more especially invited by the fact of its having been hitherto but imperfectly investigated, was that of the actual *history*

[b] Original title of the "Prayer-book," 1549:—"The Book of the Common Prayer, and Administration of the Sacraments, &c., of the Church, according to the Use of the Church of England."

[c] See below, sect. 2—6.

[d] Vide Part I. chap. ii., and Part II. chap. i., on the Theory of the Church's Ordinary and Eucharistic Worship.

[e] See Berens, Watson, and others, on the Prayer-book. A valuable compendium of this kind has lately appeared, entitled "A History of the Prayer book, with a Rationale of its Offices," by the Rev. F. Procter (Macmillan, Cambridge). It is an epitome of almost all hitherto existing information of the kind requisite for following out the line of inquiry here attempted.

of our Offices, viewed as conducting us to their original and real intention. And surely this is, in all reason, the *first* thing to be done in a matter of the kind. The *first* question to be asked about the Services of the Church is not so much, What are we enabled, by the exercise of our own ingenuity, to make of them? as, What is the meaning which properly attaches to them? What sense and acceptation belongs to them in virtue of the facts of their origination? Portions or features there will in all probability be, after all, upon which this method of inquiry throws but an imperfect light; and upon these we must form the best judgment that we can. But the historical inquiry, it cannot be too strongly urged, ought to precede all others.

Two cautions only, it is conceived, will be necessary in applying this historical method, so to call it, to the elucidation of these Services. The one, that we be careful to interpret the older provisions for Divine Service in no narrow or confined sense; looking rather to the principles involved in them, than to the particular forms in which these were embodied. The other, that, while we give to the original and proper intention of the Services, so far as it is ascertainable, the first place, we exclude not such other secondary and subordinate, or it may be even co-ordinate senses and applications, as they are capable of.

When then we set ourselves in earnest to ask, What are these Services which the English Church possesses? whence did they come? by whom were they composed? and in what sense were they intended to be taken and used? we find that these are questions which are far from admitting of a very plain and simple reply. In the case of every Church on earth, and emphatically in that of the Church of England, much consideration, and not a little of historical research, are required, ere we can give a full and adequate answer to such inquiries. In no instance, that we are acquainted with, does the Church's Ritual resemble a clear and undisturbed pool, exhibiting unaltered the features of primitive and Apostolic service. Rather is it, in all cases, to be likened to a river, having its source indeed in the heart of the Primitive Church, but which has experienced, from time to time, various accessions or diminutions, and presents accordingly, at different points in its course, a very different aspect. Thus did the Liturgies or Communion Offices of the Eastern Churches undergo, as is well known, several material revisions [f] and alterations, even within what may be called the historical period of their existence; while there is reason to believe [g] that even the earliest phase, under which they are known to us, resulted from a serious modification of their primary forms. The Eastern Offices for ordinary worship also received considerable expansion at about the same period [h]. Thus too were the ordinary Offices of the Churches of the West—the Roman, the Spanish, the French [i]—completely reorganized or replaced in the course of the fifth and following centuries; while their Communion Offices were all modified at an early period, and most of them in later days abandoned for a different form of service.

[f] Vide Palmer, Orig. Lit., Diss. on Primitive Liturgies.
[g] See Part II., ch. on Primitive Liturgy.
[h] See Part I. ch. iii.
[i] Vide Palmer, Orig., 4th ed. p. 218, &c.; and infra, Part 1. ch. iii.

This is not the place for entering into any extended discussion of the phenomenon thus presented by the rituals of all known Churches, of having undergone more or less of alteration, and so possessing a history. Suffice it to say, that it has all the appearance of a Divine provision for securing to the Offices of the Church in different lands the enrichment or adaptation which from time to time they needed.

These changes have in some cases,—as in the fourth and fifth centuries in the Eastern Church, under Basil and Chrysostom; and in the fifth and sixth under Gelasius and Gregory, in the West,—issued spontaneously from the bosom of the Churches themselves. They may then be viewed as occasions on which the Holy Spirit, working through the mind of the ecclesiastical rulers of the day, moulded the ritual of such Churches to His own high purposes.

At other times the change or substitution has proceeded from without, and has been more or less violent in its character; taking place, mostly, under a certain degree of protest on the part of the particular Church whose previous ritual was so altered or superseded. So was it, probably, in those various instances in which the ritual of Constantinople was substituted for those of other Eastern Churches, e. g. for that of Antioch, or Alexandria; and, more certainly, when that of Rome was made to replace the older offices of Spain and of France. But even in these cases it may be well to bear in mind that— distasteful to natural feeling, and in our human judgment to be deprecated, as such externally imposed changes of ritual are—it was a substitution, after all, of one Apostolically originated line or family of Offices for another; and that the change doubtless conferred some benefits, as well as entailed some loss, on the Churches which were the subjects of it. To which may be added, that in some instances, and probably in all, the old national customs and modes of service exercised a sufficient sway to modify in some degree the newly received forms, and thus maintain a continuity between them and the ritual which they superseded;—the result being a commingling, in however unequal proportions, of two previously distinct streams of ancient ritual. Though, in fact, there was often sufficient affinity between the older and the newly introduced forms, to render the change less serious than at first sight it might appear.

The history of the English Church exhibits a marked instance of each of the two kinds of ritual change which have just been spoken of. In one instance, we see her ancient and probably primeval ritual superseded from without by Offices belonging to a different stock or family; in another, we have a revision from within, and by her own deliberate act, of her then existing Services. I speak, of course, of the introduction of certain Offices into this country at the end of the 6th century; and of the Revision of them, again, in the middle of the 16th.

Thus then there are — beginning with the first planting of Christianity in Britain—three great cardinal events and epochal dates in our Church's ritual history; forming the commencement of as many ritual eras or periods, discriminated from each other, as we shall find, by certain broad features and characteristics. Other minor changes, no doubt, took place in the course of the periods marked off by these events; but nothing that can for a moment be compared to them in point of importance, at least for our present purpose.

The *first* of these periods extends, probably, from Apostolic times to the arrival of St. Augustine in England in the year 597.

The *second* extends from the arrival of St. Augustine to the authorization of the "Book of the Common Prayer and Administration of the Sacraments and other Rites and Ceremonies of the Church, after the Use of the Church of England," in 1549.

The *third* extends from the year 1549 to the present day.

There is indeed nothing novel in the distribution into periods here made. But it has perhaps not been sufficiently realized that *the whole science of English ritualism is reducible,* for all practical purposes, *to the correct apprehension of the three events by which these periods are ushered in.* To have mastered them in their entire character, is to have obtained the true key, the leading clue to the right understanding of our present Offices.

It must be here observed, however, that the history of the two kinds of Divine Service—the Eucharistic and the Ordinary—is, as will appear in the sequel, widely different throughout; so much so, that they must be treated of separately, if we would form a distinct and a just conception of them. Deferring then, in accordance with this necessity, no less than with the plan of the present work, all consideration of the Eucharistic Offices, let us proceed to inquire into the history and condition of the Offices of Ordinary Public Worship, during the first of these periods which have been indicated. This is necessary on two accounts;—as well that we may understand the probable condition of the Church in this country, as to its forms of Ordinary Worship, during that period, as in order to our knowing the earlier history of those Offices which first reached us at the end of the sixth century.

As regards the latter point indeed, the well-known circumstances of St. Augustine's mission to this country may seem at first sight to render this inquiry in part a superfluous, and for the rest a hopeless one. St. Augustine, it may be thought, would be certain to bring with him the Daily Offices of the Church of Rome at that time, with at most some slight modification:—and much beyond this we cannot, it is generally conceived, hope to know; the early history of the Roman, as of all other Western ritual, being confessedly very obscure[k].

But in the first place it is capable, as I conceive, of demonstration, that what St. Augustine introduced was not, strictly speaking, the Roman Daily Offices at all, but only a kindred, though very closely allied member of the family or stock of offices to which the Roman belonged[l]. And in the next place, the history of that entire family, including both the Roman variety and our own, is perfectly ascertainable, and may be traced up with clearness and certainty to very early, and probably to Apostolic days[m]. The truth is, that these offices, which have ever since prevailed in the Western Church, had at that time been but very recently received into it. And *their* history may be plainly read in the ritual annals of the countries from whence they came. It is the ritual history of the Western Churches themselves,—that of Rome not least,—previous to their receiving their comparatively newer formularies, that

[k] So Grancolas, Hist. Brev. i. 27. Mr. Palmer (ubi sup. p. 214—217.) traces the Roman offices to the sixth century, but no further.
[l] Vide infra, ch. iii. init.
[m] Vide infra, sect. 3—6, and ch. iii.

is so obscure; though even this, including the early history of Daily Offices in our own Church, may by a careful attention to ascertained facts be in a measure cleared up.

Strange questions have been raised as to the existence of any other kind of worship in the early Church, than that which takes place in the celebration of the Holy Communion. The opinion indeed that there was none such, may be said to be the popular belief, in this country at least, at the present day. Whereas it must, on a little consideration, appear incredible, and all but impossible, that such should have been the case. This opinion rests mainly, in truth, upon another mistaken supposition, viz. that the Holy Communion, or Eucharist, was celebrated in the earliest ages every day. The entire fallacy of this view is proved in a subsequent chapter[n] of this volume, to which the reader is referred. It may suffice to say here, that while many excellent writers, speaking in a rhetorical way, (as, for example, Sparrow and Jeremy Taylor,) have asserted or assumed the fact of ancient daily celebration, the view has been abandoned as altogether untenable by those who, like Fleury, Cotelerius, and Bingham, have examined for themselves. And with it, the idea that the Church had at the first no other Service than the Eucharist falls to the ground also: unless we are prepared to say that she utterly neglected, as a Church, the duty of perseverance in prayer, and that the Christians of the first century systematically adopted the custom of meeting together for the worship of God but once a-week.

But it is alleged that men well versed in antiquity,

[n] Ch. ii. on the Theory of Ordinary Worship.

such as Bingham, have acquiesced in this conclusion. This however is only an instance of the way in which the *dicta* of learned men are first carelessly quoted, and then pass from mouth to mouth without inquiry. Bingham was by far too well informed to make such a wholesale and improbable statement. His brief section° on this subject is couched in very cautious language, and leaves the matter, to say the least, entirely open.

Another cause of the general adoption of this opinion has been, that a too conventional and comparatively modern conception of what constitutes Church worship has been applied to the early Church. It is by no means essential to Church worship, of the strictest kind, that the people of a whole neighbourhood should be gathered into one assembly. Wherever there was a presbyter and but "two or three" to join in worship with him, there, doubtless, it was held, were the sufficient elements of Church worship. And this will abundantly account for the absence of any mention of the more ordinary kind of Church worship in the record preserved by Pliny in the first, and by Justin Martyr in the second century. The Service which naturally was dwelt on in both these instances, to the exclusion of all minor ritual,

---

° Christian Antiquities, XIII. ix. 1. vol. iv. p. 353. He entitles this section, "*No certain rule* for meeting in public, except upon the Lord's Day, in *times of persecution*, for the first two ages." The utmost that this can be taken to mean, is that the services which otherwise took place were in times of persecution intermitted or uncertain, except on Sundays. All that he adduces for proof even of this, is that Justin Martyr mentions no public assembly but the Sunday Eucharist; "whence learned men have concluded," (he quotes, however, no one but Cotelerius,) "that in his time the Church observed no other days of solemn assemblies." The true explanation of Justin Martyr's silence is given presently.

was the celebration of the Eucharist. This was the great Christian event, occurring, (as both writers evidently imply,) as a general rule, but once a-week; attendance upon which was the very badge of a Christian. And there seems to have been a peculiarity in the customs of the Church of the first two or three centuries (arising from the fewness of numbers in a diocese), which had the effect of giving a singular and overwhelming prominence to the Eucharistic service. It was this,—that the Bishop was commonly the celebrant at the Holy Communion; the priests, deacons, and laity—in a word, the whole body of the faithful within the diocese—being present. This is evidently the idea of Eucharistic celebration which St. Ignatius, writing in the beginning of the second century, has before his eyes in various passages of his Epistles. Thus too Clemens Romanus, in the first century, assumes the celebration to be a general gathering of this kind [p]:—"To the high priest," he says, (that is, the Bishop,) "his proper part in the service is assigned; and to the priests and Levites (i. e. deacons) theirs: the lay person is bound by rules applying to laymen. Let each one of you join in the Eucharist in his own order," &c. Now all this, while it exactly agrees with Justin Martyr's account in other respects, goes far to explain why he says nothing, in his Apology, of that secondary kind of service, which, being conducted probably for the most part by single presbyters, ministering to small bodies of the faithful, exhibited in altogether an inferior degree the great features of the Christian polity and worship. This view differs but little from that which Bingham, after all, acquiesces in, viz. that Justin

[p] Clem. Rom. Ep. I. ad Cor. c. 40, 41.

Martyr's silence as to Church assemblies on weekdays "is a negative argument against them, *unless perhaps some distinction may be made* between the *general assembly* of both city and country on the Lord's day, and the *particular assemblies* of the city Christians (who had better opportunities to meet) on other days: which distinction we often meet with in following ages." The exception would of course include such "country Christians" as had a presbyter among them.

On the whole, we may conclude that no presumption against the existence, in early times, of other Church Services than the Eucharistic can be grounded upon the silence either of Pliny's informant, or of Justin Martyr in his Apology. Nor, considering, first, the exceeding scantiness of ecclesiastical writings in the first two or three centuries, and next, the subordinate character of these services, would it be at all surprising if no mention of them were found within that period. This however is far from being the case. It has been contended with much ability and learning [q], that footsteps of such services are to be found in various early writers. The cause has indeed suffered by the attempt which has been made to prove the primitive existence of the minor Church Services during the day; which certainly were of later introduction as public offices. Spurious authorities have also been alleged, such as the writings of Dionysius the Areopagite; while genuine passages bearing upon the subject have been overlooked. There is, in reality, no lack of adequate testimony, both of a general and of a particular kind. Justin Martyr himself, in another of his works, bears no doubtful

[q] Bona Div. Psalmod. i. 2—4.

testimony to the kind of service which his silence in the Apology has been thought to disprove. We shall find, in short, in the case of Ordinary Church worship no less than of Eucharistic, a primitive fountain-head, having its seat in the very bosom of the Apostolic Church, and thence parted into several streams for the spiritual nurture of all the nations of the earth.

## SECTION II.

*"Why doth one day excel another, when as all the light of every day in the year is of the sun? By the knowledge of the Lord they were distinguished: and He altered seasons and feasts. Some of them hath He made high days, and hallowed them, and some of them hath He made ordinary days."*

NOTHING can at first sight be much more dissimilar than the earliest and the latest phases which the ordinary services of the Church at large have assumed;— beginning with the simple, and, though doubtless orderly, yet apparently free and unconfined, devotions of the Upper Chamber at Jerusalem, of which we obtain glimpses through the Apostolic writings; and ending with the complex and minutely regulated Offices which have now prevailed for many hundred years alike in the East and in the West. And these Eastern and Western Offices, again, differ so materially from each other, that it has been concluded, and that by no mean judges, that there is absolutely no connection between them; that "the Oriental rites" of ordinary service are, as to their derivation, "perfectly distinct from those of the Latin Churches'." The truth is, however, first, that the

r Palmer, vol. i. p. 218.

ordinary and non-eucharistic worship of the Church was, as it should seem, far more organized, even in Apostolic days, than we are apt to suppose; and secondly, that the Offices of the East and West are both alike developments, though on different principles, and with characteristic variations as to structure and contents, of the earlier and simpler form of the Eastern rite.

The changes wrought upon what seem to have been the primeval Offices,—more especially in their progress towards the West,—are indeed often very great; but the links by which the successive forms assumed by them cohere are certain and decisive. It would, indeed, be surprising if it were otherwise. For it was by no means the temper or disposition of the Church of the first few centuries to originate altogether new Services, but, at the utmost, to develope out of the old;—to retain at least some large and prominent features, serving to identify the altered service with that which preceded it. And the real difference between the courses adopted by the Eastern and Western Churches in the matter of their ordinary Offices of Divine Worship would seem to be this. The Orientals have adhered to the particular stock or family of Offices originally possessed by them, and have developed them in strict accordance with their proper laws and principles, not admitting any foreign influence to bear upon them. The consequence is that, as has been well observed, "the accounts which we have of the Eastern Offices in writings of the third, fourth, and fifth centuries all appear to agree most singularly," as far as they go, "with the existing Greek Offices[s]." The Western

[s] Palmer, ubi sup. p. 225.

Church, on the contrary, did, in the course of the sixth century in some Churches, (as, e. g. in the Roman),—at a later date in others,—admit certain Offices *new to them*, to the rejection, or serious modification, of their older ones; those Offices being derived from Eastern sources.

When then we turn our eyes towards Christian antiquity, to ascertain what the particular aspect or form of its acts of ordinary worship is likely to have been, the first point that strikes us is, that as the Eucharistic Service at the first was certainly nocturnal, the Ordinary Service, or the chief occasion of it however, would not improbably be so too. The same reasons would to a great degree hold good in both cases. Partly the fear of persecution, and partly the habit of nocturnal meeting for the Eucharist[1], would be likely to recommend the hours of the night for the more ordinary act of Christian worship.

It is in perfect accordance with this conjecture, that the earliest hints we have of the nature of the Church's ordinary service points to the existence of nocturnal or ante-lucan assemblies for that purpose.

The learned Bingham has unfortunately involved this matter in no small degree of confusion; and that in various ways: chiefly by representing certain services, used from an early period in particular Churches on the Wednesday and Friday in each week, to have been the first steps or rudiments of a secondary kind of worship, which thus by degrees came to be used daily. Whereas those services were in truth no other than the Eucharist itself, which in the Church of Africa by about A.D. 200, and by the third or fourth

---

[1] See Part II., chap. on Primitive Liturgy.

century in some other parts[u], had come to be celebrated on those days, with the addition, as it seems, of private devotions of considerable length. In the Egyptian Church they had no celebration on these occasions, but used only the earlier part of the Eucharistic Service; exactly as was ordered for those same days in the First Book of Edward VIth, and is still permitted on Sundays and festivals in the English Church. But all this was of the nature of Eucharistic, or quasi-eucharistic service, with private devotion superadded to it. It was a perfectly distinct thing from the ordinary non-eucharistic worship of the Church.

Dismissing, then, these erroneous conceptions, let us inquire what the nature of the early Church's Ordinary Service really was. Now that there were in the *fourth* century certain *nightly services* in constant use throughout the Churches of the East, there is no doubt whatever. It also clearly appears from writers of that date, that those services were by no means peculiar to the clergy, but were genuine and public Church Services. Thus St. Basil (circ. 370.) says, in a passage of the utmost importance for our present purpose,—"The customs which now prevail among us are consonant with those of all the Churches of God; for with us the people come early, while it is yet night, to the house of prayer," &c. St. Chrysostom speaks of the poor continuing in the church "from midnight till morning light." And Cassian, a writer of the early part of the fifth century, assures us that "this kind of devotion was most carefully observed by many secular persons, who, rising early,

---

[u] Tertullian de Jejun. xiv.; Bingham, xxi 3; xiii. 9. 2.

before day, consecrated the first-fruits of all their actions and labours to God [v]."

Thus fully did the nocturnal services of that period, (i. e. in the fourth and fifth centuries) when the Eucharist was no longer celebrated by night, but in open day, answer to the idea of ordinary or daily Church Services. The only question is, how and where did they originate? or how far back may we carry them?

Now, were the opinion tenable that the earliest ages had celebration of the Eucharist every day, it would be very natural to conclude that they had been substituted for that Service when it was transferred to the daylight hours; or rather were a sort of residuum which remained when the main stream of the Church's devotion had been drawn off into another channel. According to this supposition, then, the *non-eucharistic* services of this and the following centuries owed their being to the transference of the Eucharistic ones at some time in the first three ages, and had not co-existed with them from the beginning. Such is the view with which Mr. Palmer (assuming apparently the continual celebration) has suggested; viz. that "when persecution ceased, although the Christians were able to celebrate all their rites, and did administer the Sacrament, in the daytime, yet a custom which had commenced from necessity was retained from devotion and choice; and nocturnal assemblies for the worship of God in Psalms and reading still continued." And again: "As the nocturnal assemblies were first held for the purpose of administering the Eucharist, so when that Sacrament was celebrated at another time, the nocturnal

[v] Vide Bingham, vol. iv. p. 408.

service still retained the psalmody and reading of Scripture, which was always (?) the commencement of the Liturgy or Eucharist[x]." But as daily celebration was certainly not the primitive practice, the ordinary nocturnal services must be accounted for in some other way. Bingham, accordingly, while admitting that the nocturnal Eucharistic assemblies were but weekly, suggests that "the Church in after ages thought fit to continue them, *transferring them* (i. e. the assemblies, not the Eucharist,) *from the Lord's Day to all other days,* partly to keep up the spirit of devotion in the ascetics, and partly to give leisure and opportunity to men of a secular life to observe a seasonable time of devotion, which they might do early in the morning without any distraction[y]." This supposition is surely most improbable. No reason can possibly be assigned why the Church, on being allowed to hold her Sunday Eucharist in the daytime, should at that particular juncture institute for the first time, for every night in the week, a new service. That the eve or night before the Sunday or festival should continue to be observed with some kind of solemnities, as the remains of the old practice, would be perfectly intelligible; and in point of fact we find that it was so;—the days of celebration, we are told, "were commonly ushered in by pernoctations or vigils," which differed from the ordinary nightly service in being longer and fuller[z].

[x] Orig. Lit., p. 201, 206. It is an objection *in limine* to this theory, that the ordinary nocturnal Offices of the early Church did *not* involve any reading of the Scriptures; as will be shewn hereafter.

[y] Bingham, XIII. x. 12.

[z] Bingham, XIII. ix. 4, vol. iv. p. 360. The entire section is full of interesting illustrations of the nightly service on the eves of Sundays and festivals.

But whence, it must still be asked, came this weekday nocturnal service at all? And this one thing at least is clear, that it was perfectly independent of the transference of the Eucharistic Service to the daylight hours. It cannot have arisen out of that alteration; and it may perfectly well have co-existed from the first, as the week-night office, side by side with the ancient nocturnal celebration of the Sunday. Occupying, as became it, a far humbler position than that great rite, and aspiring, at the utmost, to run parallel with it on a far lower level; conducted too under many circumstances of inferiority, — by one or two presbyters, perhaps, instead of by the whole diocesan body of clergy; in small detachments, and with the attendance of but few (as compared with the Eucharist), even in cities,—it would be likely to obtain comparatively little mention in the slightly sketched accounts of early Christianity which have come down to us.

But though less prominent, and on that account less frequently alluded to, its existence is nevertheless, as was remarked at the end of the preceding section, abundantly vouched for. It must be borne in mind, that when once it comes to be distinctly understood and admitted that the Eucharist was not administered daily, many passages which have hitherto been supposed to refer to that ordinance, become evidence on behalf of service of a more ordinary kind. As when Ignatius, at the beginning of the second century, (A.D. 107,) exhorts the Church of the Ephesians "to pray without ceasing," and "to give all diligence to come together frequently," (or "in great numbers,") to give thanks and praise to God [a]; or bids the Mag-

---

[a] Ign. Ep. ad Eph. c. 13. σπουδάζετε οὖν πυκνότερον συνέρχεσθαι εἰς

nesians, "when they met together, to have one prayer and one supplication[b];" or the Trallians[c], "to abide in concord, and in their prayers with each other;" or urges Polycarp[d] to see that the Church's assemblies at Smyrna "were held more frequently," (or "more fully attended"). These passages are hardly capable of being referred to the celebration of the Eucharist, which was both pretty well fixed, as to frequency, to the Lord's Day, and was doubtless attended as a matter of course by every Christian. What room then was there for such exhortations as these, whether to greater frequency of services, or increase of attendance upon them? Whereas the frequency of the *ordinary* services may well have varied, more especially in the very earliest times. And in fact we shall see reason hereafter for believing, that though the nocturnal week-day service was probably all but universal from the first, there is far less evidence for the early prevalence of any other service. And that the attendance on these services, when they came to be fully established, was not universal, but rather (very much as with the daily services at the present day, and indeed in all ages of the Church) the habit of the more devout or leisurely,—we have the clear evidence of St. Chrysostom and Cassian in passages already referred to[e].

It is to be remarked, again, that inasmuch as the Eucharistic service, as far back as we can trace it, did

εὐχαριστίαν Θεοῦ καὶ δόξαν. Id. ad Polyc. 4. πυκνότερον συναγωγαὶ γινέσθωσαν. Pearson understands both places of "fuller assemblies." But see Jacobson *in loc.* In Eph. 13, the Eucharist need not be meant, probably is not; the context is general: and so Vet. Interp.

[b] Ad Magn. 7.  
[c] Ad Trall. 12.  
[d] Ubi sup.  
[e] Sup., p. 19.

not embrace [f], or only in the very smallest proportion, the singing of Psalms, while the ordinary services, so soon as we obtain a distinct view of them, consisted emphatically of Psalms and hymns, it follows that allusions in early writers to Church psalmody must as a general rule refer to ordinary services. Thus, e. g., Ignatius has the credit, whether justly or not, of having introduced the antiphonal mode of singing into the Church. This, then, so far as the tradition may be relied on, may be taken as an early evidence for ordinary worship.

Philo the Jew, a writer of the first century, in a well-known and curious passage[g], describes the devotions of certain persons at Alexandria, whom he calls Therapeutæ, "devotees," in terms very similar to those which St. Basil, as already quoted, employs about the ordinary nocturnal services of the Christians in the fourth century. It was thought by many ancient writers—Eusebius, Jerome, Epiphanius[h], &c. and has been maintained by learned moderns, as Goar[i] and Beveridge[k],—that these Alexandrians were no other than the first Christians, converted by St. Mark. On the fullest consideration, however, it seems necessary to conclude, with Valesius and Burton, that they were *not* Christians;—though it is singular that

[f] The Apostolic Constitutions indeed prescribe "the Hymns of David to be sung" among the lessons from Scripture before celebration; and Mr. Palmer speaks of this as a fact. But it has no countenance from antiquity. There are fragments of Psalms sung at the opening of St. Basil's Liturgy; and a single Psalm preceded the epistle in the Syrian Lit. of St. James and the Arm. (See also St. Augustine, below, p. 60.) A Psalm after Communion was also used in Lit. Rom. Arm., &c.
[g] De Vitâ Contemplativâ, ed. Mangey, vol. ii. p. 484.
[h] Vide Bingham, l. i. 1. Vales. in Eus. ii. 17. [i] Euchol., note, p. 22.
[k] Cod. Can. iii. 5. (See Coteler., Patres Ap.) Mr. Neale is content (Hist. of the East. Church, vol. i. l.) to follow Eusebius, &c.

Burton should question their being even Jews[1]. The chief, and indeed insuperable, difficulty is, that they combined, with their singing of Psalms and hymns, a bacchanal kind of dancing, which it is incredible that any body of Christians can have adopted. This, as they alleged, was in imitation of the songs and dances of the Israelitish men and women after the passage of the Red Sea. It seems most probable, on the whole, that they were a kind of Jewish monks. And there is strong reason for believing that they furnished in many respects the type of the subsequent Egyptian monasticism. For the Egyptian monastic devotions, as described by Cassian in the fifth century[m], while differing from the customs of the Church generally, accord in some marked respects with those of Philo's Therapeutæ. Thus they still observed, like Philo's ascetics, but two daily services, nocturns and vespers,—and these, too, differing widely from the common Eastern type,—when the rest of the Church had long had from three to seven offices. Philo, again, dwells much on the ascetics' reading and meditating on certain ancient books in their places of worship, as a part of their devotions[n]. And in Cassian's time, accordingly, the Egyptian monks, alone out of all the East, had from very ancient times had a lesson of the Old and another of the New Testament in their daily Offices; and spent all their time in meditating on the Scriptures.

Philo, then, cannot be cited as a witness to Chris-

---

[1] Eccl. Hist., vol. i. p. 22.   [m] See below, chap iii.

[n] He says they took nothing into their places of worship (οἴκημα σεμνεῖον, or μοναστήριον—the very term afterwards applied to the Christian ascetics' abodes) εἰ μὴ νόμους καὶ λόγια θεσπισθέντα καὶ ὕμνους, κ.τ.λ.

tian nocturnal worship in the first century. Nor indeed do the services described by him bear more than a general resemblance to the Christian services, such as we find them in St. Basil, &c. The week-day services were not strictly nocturnal at all, but took place *after* the rising of the sun. And the seventh-day night-service, as described by him, is hardly compatible with the Eucharist, since it seems to have been a mere series of musical exercises, more especially of Psalms;—which is exactly what the Eucharistic service was not.

Nevertheless, as a testimony *to early and late daily services* among the more devout sort of Jews, at about the Christian era, Philo's account is much to our purpose. Still more so is that which Josephus[o] gives of the Essenes,—a sect in many respects similar; viz., "that they used to rise *before the sun was up*, and offer to God certain prayers received from their forefathers." Nothing could be more natural than that the Jewish Christians (who have indeed by some been identified with the Essenes[p]) should take up, as a part of their new manner of life, what was thus familiar to the more devout among their own countrymen.

Our first direct witness therefore to the nightly services is no other than Justin Martyr, (circ. 150). He says that the philosophers contended, "that the Christians' praying as they did *through the whole night*, as well as by day, was inconsistent with their professed belief in the Providence of God[q]."

About twenty years later, Lucian, the heathen satirist, speaks of his coming into a religious as-

---

[o] Bell. Jud. ii. 12.  [p] Brücker, Hist. Philos., and Burton, p. 300.
[q] Dial. Tryph., init.

sembly, and of the officiating person's beginning his prayer with "the Father," and ending it with the "hymn of many names;" alluding doubtless to the Lord's Prayer, which was ended with a repetition, in the manner of a hymn, of the doxology addressed to Father, Son, and Holy Ghost[r]. Now certainly, according to the received notion that the Lord's Prayer did not occur (as probably it did not by the end of the second century) in that earlier part of the Eucharistic office to which strangers were admitted, this service could not have been the Eucharist. Reasons for believing that Prayer to have occurred in the primitive daily service will be given below.

Thirty years later, again, (circ. 200,) we find Tertullian using expressions which seem positively to identify the course of nocturnal and early morning service in his day with that which prevailed in St. Basil's time. He says there was a small clique of persons in the African Church, who would not kneel on the Saturday. "But we," he proceeds, "as we have received, on the day of the Lord's Resurrection (i. e. Sunday), and on that alone, abstain from that posture. But as to other times, who can hesitate to prostrate himself before God *on all days alike* (*omni die*) at *that first prayer with which we enter upon the light of day*[s]?" meaning doubtless the 51st Psalm, with which (as we know from St. Basil), the nocturns being ended, the morning office commenced at break of day. Further on, commenting on the practice of some Churches or persons, of following up the prayers with the Hallelujah and Psalms of praise, he calls prayer "the true sacrifice, which Christians as priests offer;" adding, "this victim, devoted with the whole

[r] Lucian, Philopatr. See the form below, sect. v. fin. [s] De Orat., c. 23.

heart, fed by faith, crowned with love, we ought *to lead up to the altar of God amidst Psalms and hymns*[t]." The whole passage is no doubt rhetorically conceived; but it has all the appearance of pointing to Church worship;—yet not to Eucharistic worship exclusively, as that was not a service of Psalms and hymns at all. On the whole, the best account that we can give of this passage is, that Tertullian had before his eyes in writing it the entire order of Sunday or festival service which prevailed when the Eucharist had been transferred to the daytime; a change which had certainly begun to be made in his time[u]. We seem to have the nocturnal service followed at break of day by matins, and the whole concluded and crowned with celebration of the Eucharist[v]. He also speaks of the obligatory morning and evening prayers, said apparently either in the church or at home.

It will not be necessary to pursue these testimonies much further. It may suffice to say that Hippolytus, bishop of Portus Romanus soon after Tertullian's time, (circ. 220,) speaks more than once of psalmody and singing of hymns, as a customary part of the Church's services[x];—that Origen[y], in the same century, in answer to a charge made against the Christians of using magical books in their services, declares that, on the contrary, what they used was the ordered or *prescribed prayers*, as became them, *day and night constantly;* thus testifying not to the services only, but to the books used in them;—and that St. Cyprian,

---

[t] Ib., c. 25. The Oxford translation (in the index) understands it of private prayer. But the case seems plain the other way.

[u] e. g. It was celebrated on Wednesdays and Fridays, as a part of the "stationary service."     [v] Ib.

[x] Hippol. de Consumm. Mundi, &c. Vide Bingham, vol. iv. p. 211.

[y] Ib., p. 215. See ib., p. 220, &c., for Cyprian and Arnobius.

and Arnobius, in a passage to be referred to hereafter, vouch for the practice of the third and early part of the fourth century in Africa.

Thus have we, from the apostolic Ignatius downwards, until we reach the explicit account of St. Basil, towards the close of the fourth century, a continuous stream of testimony to the prevalence of ordinary service. Thus did it please God to set from the beginning two great lights in the firmament of the Church, the greater and the less, to divide the light of her Eucharistic Festival from the comparative darkness of her ordinary days.

## SECTION III.

"Look unto the rock whence ye are hewn, and to the hole of the pit whence ye are digged. Look unto Abraham your father and unto Sarah that bare you."

In proceeding to speculate, next, on the character which the ordinary and non-eucharistic devotions of the first Christians would be likely to assume, we discern two models then existing, after one or other of which they might conceivably be fashioned: two sources from which their contents might not improbably be drawn. The one is the Eucharistic Rite itself; the other the Jewish Ritual.

I have already spoken of an hypothesis which would connect these services with the Eucharistic by representing them to have been a residuum of it; and though that view of them cannot be sustained, we might nevertheless not unnaturally look to find them framed after that greater service as a model, or borrowing their contents from it. And in such expectation we should be further encouraged by our knowing that the Church, in subsequent ages, largely enriched her ordinary ritual from time to time with features or portions of her Eucharistic Service. Nevertheless it must be confessed that, on examination of so much of the ancient ordinary services as we have reason for thinking to have been of primitive date, we find little that answers to this notion; at least in the ordinary services strictly so called. The additions made to the nightly services on Sundays, (or festivals,) when the celebration of the Eucharist was transferred to the daytime, had indeed, as might be expected, a eucharistic bearing, in the way of preparation for the rite. But in the services of other nights,—with a single exception, of which hereafter,—it is difficult to discern anything positively and essentially eucharistic, either in structure or contents. Of course, since the Eucharist, according to the ancient universal conception of it, embraces and exhausts all the possible elements of worship, there must necessarily be an affinity, and essentially and at bottom a connection, between it and any other Service the Church can offer. But the actual scheme of the primitive nocturnal services was conceived, to all appearance, after another idea.

As the Eucharistic Ritual of the early Church strikes its roots deeply into the old Israelitish sacrificial ordinances, and is framed in many respects upon them[z]; so, there is great reason for saying, did the primitive Christian worship of a more ordinary kind take its rise in those services of the Temple and the Synagogue, which had been superadded in the course of time, by

[z] See below, Part II., chapter on the Theory of Eucharistic Worship.

David, or Hezekiah, or Ezra, to the original letter of the Mosaic institution. So that while the staple elements of that institution passed on into the great realities of Christ's Offering of Himself, and into the supreme act of Christian service instituted by Him in especial connection with it, the more ordinary kinds of Jewish worship merged, in a parallel manner, into corresponding Christian action. Independently of the beauty, and the conformity to all analogy, of such a provision as this,—by which, as by so many other arrangements, the continuity between the elder and the later covenant would be secured,—a little reflection will shew that such was, even humanly speaking, the natural course of events [a]. The simple and yet all-including record, which holy Scripture has preserved to us, of the ritual of the Apostolic Church on and after the Day of Pentecost, while it distinctly recognises two kinds of service, the one Eucharistic, the other not, makes attendance on the ancient Israelitish ritual a not unimportant feature of the latter. "They continued stedfastly," it is first said, "in the Apostles' doctrine and fellowship, and in breaking of bread, and in prayers [b]." But this was not all. As a part of their non-eucharistic devotion, they also "continued daily with one accord *in the Temple*," in contradistinction to their "breaking bread in the house, or at home," (so it should manifestly be rendered ; see below, ch. ii.) And we have scarcely less evidence of the converts from among the Jews (at least) continuing to attend diligently upon the services of the *Synagogue*. For besides the frequent mention of the Apostles' resorting

[a] Eusebius (Eccl. Hist. II. 17.) recognises this probability; speaking of the early Christians of Alexandria as ἐξ Ἑβραίων, ὡς ἔοικε, γεγονότας, ταύτῃ τε Ἰουδαϊκώτερον τὰ τῶν παλαιῶν ἔτι τὰ πλεῖστα διατηροῦντας ἔθη.

[b] Acts ii. 42, 46.

thither, this seems to be clearly implied by Acts xv. 21; where the weekly reading of Moses in the Synagogues in every city is spoken of as a means of conveying to Jewish certainly, perhaps even to Gentile converts, the knowledge of certain fundamental precepts or dictates of religion. It would surely be natural, then, that when distance from the Temple, and other causes, gradually threw the Christian body entirely upon their own resources for their ordinary ritual, that ritual should bear some impress of the influences by which it had at the first been cradled and fostered.

And if we may safely—as, for reasons which will appear presently, I conceive we may—look upon certain features as having appertained to the nocturnal services from the first, then we certainly find unmistakeable proofs of paternity and derivation subsisting between the Temple and Synagogue[b] services and those of the primitive Church.

The earliest writer who gives us any detailed account of the latter, is, as we have already seen, St. Basil, in the fourth century. They consisted in his day of psalmody with prayers intermingled; the whole ushered in with a profoundly penitential confession. And of these Psalms, as we learn from him and other writers, the greater part were sung (to all appearance) continuously, and without selection; while others were fixed, and used constantly, as the 51st, with which the night-service concluded, and the 63rd, which followed shortly after in the morning office. The mode of singing was in part alternate, in part with

---

[b] Jahn, (Archæologia Biblica, §. 398,) a very matter-of-fact writer, entirely adopts this view. "It was by ministering in Synagogues that the Apostles gathered the first Churches. They retained also essentially the same mode of worship as that of the Synagogues; excepting that the Lord's Supper was made an additional institution," &c.

a leader; a response being made by the people at the close of each Psalm[c]. Now in all this there is a manifest resemblance, of a general kind, to the Jewish Temple service, such as we have reason to believe it existed in our Lord's time[d]. For it too consisted entirely of Psalms and prayers, the former making up the bulk of the service; and commenced with a penitential prayer. Moreover, some one Psalm was fixed, only varying with the day of the week; and the singing was alternate, or by way of response or burden.

And as St. Basil and others thus witness to a general resemblance between the service of his day and the ancient Jewish services, so through another source of information we seem to be certified both of the primitive date of this resemblance, and of the existence of yet other and closer correspondences. The existing daily Offices of the Greek Church, as has been well observed[e], answer with extraordinary fidelity in several particulars to the accounts given by writers of the third and following centuries of the Eastern Offices of that day. This fact, while it by no means assures us of—what, indeed, may easily be disproved —the equal antiquity of every particular of their present complicated structure[f], yet invests them with considerable value as witnesses on points about which there is concurrent evidence in favour of an early date. If these Offices have thus preserved certain of their features for 1500 or 1600 years, those features may

[c] St. Basil, Ep. lxiii. ad Neocæs. Bingham, XIII. x. 13; XIV. i. 11.
[d] See Prideaux, Connection, i. 6; Lightfoot, Temple Service, ix. 4; Bingham, XIII. v. 4.
[e] Vide Palmer, Orig. Lit., vol. i. p. 229.
[f] For the fullest, indeed the only full account of the daily Offices of the Eastern Church, see Mr. Neale's elaborate work, General Introduction to the History of the Eastern Church, vol. ii. pp. 830—941.

be, and probably are, older still. They may, for aught we know, be primitive. And if those features, why not others? such more especially as fall in with any otherwise probable theory.

Now the existing daily Offices of the Greek Church entirely answer, first of all, to the account given by St. Basil, and others, of the ordinary nocturnal services in their day. They are by name, and in their manifest design, nocturnal and early matutinal Offices. Such at least is by far the greater and the principal portion of them. They still, as in St. Basil's time, present the aspect of a great service of Psalms, with hymns and prayers intermingled. They still commence with a deeply penitential prayer. The Psalms are still sung for the most part continuously, with the addition of certain fixed ones. And among these fixed Psalms are the very same, used in the same part of the service, as in St. Basil's time. The manner of singing is still alternate, or with a response, resembling the Western antiphon[g]. Thus far then the Greek Offices of the present day thoroughly agree with those of the fourth century, and also, like them, exhibit features which tend to connect them with the Jewish Services.

But these Offices, on further examination, betray their origin still more clearly. The most solemn part of the service of the Jewish Synagogue at the present day (called "the eighteen prayers") is believed, on good grounds, to have been in use long before the Christian era[h]. Now the introductory part of the present Greek Offices, consisting of invocation, prayer

[g] Neale, p. 916, note h. Below, sect. vi.
[h] See Prideaux, Connection, Part 1. vi. 2, for a translation of these prayers. And compare ibid., viii. fin.

for pardon, invitation to praise, is plainly an epitome, only Christianized, of the first eight of the "eighteen prayers;" as may be seen upon comparison of them.

The authenticity of some of the eighteen prayers (from the 10th to the 14th, and the 17th) has been doubted of, as they seem to contain allusions to the destruction of Jerusalem. But these, it will be observed, are precisely the prayers with which the introduction of the Greek Offices has nothing in common; —a confirmation, in a manner, of the reality of the connection. The ritualist will be interested at discerning here the almost unquestionable origin of the famous "Trisagion" hymn. The common account ascribes it to Proclus, (A.D. 434,) but it is doubtless far older. A good judge is of opinion "that it is of exceedingly primitive use in the Church, and *probably Apostolic*[1]."

PART OF THE "EIGHTEEN PRAYERS" OF THE SYNAGOGUE[k].

1. Blessed be Thou, O Lord our God.

*Ans.* Blessed art Thou, O Lord, O King, our Helper, our Saviour, Creator and possessor of the universe, bountifully dispensing benefits.

2. Thou sustainest . . . all that live.

COMMENCEMENT OF THE EASTERN OFFICES.

Blessed be our God, now and for ever.

*Ans.* Amen. Glory be to Thee our God, heavenly King, the Comforter, the Spirit of Truth, who art everywhere, and fillest all things, Treasury of blessings, and Giver of life; descend and remain on us, O Blessed One, cleanse us from all impurity, and save our souls.

---

[1] Neale, p. 367. Vide ibid., p. 471.

[k] The translations here given are taken, with slight variations, from Prideaux, and Neale, p. 895. The numbers are those of the prayers.

| | |
|---|---|
| 3. Thou art Holy, | Holy God, |
| Thy Name is Holy, for a great King and a Holy art Thou, O God. | Holy and Mighty, Holy and Immortal, |
| [Comp. 2, " Thou, O Lord, art mighty for ever . . . Thou Lord of might."] | |
| 5, 6. Have mercy upon us, O our Father. | Have mercy upon us. Glory be to the Father, &c. |
| For we have transgressed; pardon us, for we have sinned. | O most Holy Trinity, have mercy on us; purify us from our iniquities, and pardon our sins. |
| 7. Look, we beseech Thee, on our afflictions. | Look down upon us, O Holy One. |
| 8. Heal, O Lord . . our infirmities. | Heal our infirmities. |
| For Thou art a God who healest. | For Thy Name's sake. |
| [O Lord, have mercy on us, 6, 16, &c.] | Lord have mercy (*thrice*). |
| "Our Father," " Merciful Father." | "Our Father," &c. " Lord have mercy ;" (*twelve* times). |
| 18. We will give thanks unto Thee with praise. | O come let us worship God our King. |
| Lord, Thou art the Lord our God. | O come, &c., and fall down before Christ our King and God. |
| Be Thy Name, O King, exalted and lifted up on high. | O come, &c. . . before Christ Himself, our King and God. |

These coincidences are, it is conceived, too close to be accidental. It will be seen that the order of topics is the same in the two cases, viz. 1. Acknowledgment of God, in various characters and attributes, and then (thrice) as " Holy." 2. Prayer for pardon, addressed to God as " Our Father." 3. Invitation to the act of praise. Only, in several ways, as might be expected, a Christian character is given to the whole by the acknowledgment of Christian doctrine; as in the expansion of the title of "Helper" into that of "Comforter," (i. e. Aid, Paraclete, Advocate,) Spirit of Truth, &c., who is invited to descend on the worshippers. The Jewish invitation to the praise of God, again, is beautifully translated into Christian language, reminding us of St. Paul's words, "Whom therefore ye ignorantly worship, Him declare I unto you." And though it may seem strange to us that a prayer of great length should be thus epitomized into a very short one, the fact is that such summaries were customary among the Jews[1], who seem to have possessed an epitome of these very "eighteen prayers," called "the Summary," or "the Short Prayer[m]," to be used by those who had not leisure to attend the synagogue. Nor is it improbable that the short form in the Christian Service was so used in early times, as to give opportunity to the people for a more extended acknowledgment of God and confession of sins; in accordance with what St. Basil says of their "making confession to God with labour and affliction and long-continued shedding of tears, and then at length, standing up from their prayers, betaking themselves to the singing of the Psalms."

One more link of connection between the Christian and the Jewish Services deserves to be mentioned. On the Sabbath-day, if we may rely on the accounts of the Talmudists, the two songs of Moses (Deut. xxxii., Exod. xv.) were sung at the offering of the

---

[1] See Lightfoot, Temple Service.

[m] Literally, "the Fountain." The form itself is not, it seems, in existence. See below, on the Lord's Prayer, which is shewn to be, probably, no other than a superior and divinely sanctioned summary of these same prayers.

morning and evening sacrifice respectively[n]. And in the Greek Services these two songs or canticles are still sung at the early morning Office; the latter on Sunday, and the former on Monday; the scheme being completed by the singing of the second song of Moses, and other canticles, (those of Hannah, Habakkuk, &c.) at the same service throughout the week[o]. This can hardly be a mere accident. It was of course natural that the song of triumph celebrating the passage of the Red Sea should be transferred to the morning of the Festival of the Resurrection, of which that event was so eminent a type. And it may possibly be an indication that this song had already, in Apostolic days, been adopted as a part of Christian worship, that St. John in the Revelation describes the triumphant saints as "standing upon the *sea of glass,* and singing the song of Moses *and of the Lamb.*" It is perhaps more remarkable still that the other song of Moses (Deut. xxxii.) was doubtless in some parts of the East—probably in Egypt—sung at morning service on the Saturday or Sabbath, as among the Jews of old: whence it passed over to the West, as a part of the early morning Office of that day[p]. Nor can it be well accounted for, on any other hypothesis than that of an early and a Jewish origin, that these Offices, and, to a certain extent, the similar Offices derived from them throughout the world, proceed upon the Jewish mode of reckoning the day. That the Vespers or Evening Service was considered the first

[n] Lightfoot, Temple Service, vii.; Bingham, vol. iv. p. 194.
[o] Neale, p. 834, note. Compare the lection at the Greek Lauds on Easter-Day: "This is the day on which God caused the children of Israel to pass over the Red Sea," &c. Ib., p. 883.
[p] Sabbat. ad Laudes, Regul. S. Benedicti; Brev. Sarisb., Rom., &c.: see below, p. 83.

Office in the twenty-four hours in the Greek system, appears from hence, that the 104th Psalm received the name of the pro-œmiac or *prefatory* Psalm from its being used at the beginning of the *Evening* Office, and so prefacing the entire services of the νυχθήμερον. The Book of Psalms, too, was begun, not as in the West, (mostly) on Sunday morning, but on Saturday at Vespers, as the commencement of the week.

Now it must, I think, be admitted, that the existence of these palpable correspondences, both of general character and of detail, between the Jewish ritual and the existing Greek Offices for ordinary worship, is a powerful argument in behalf of the antiquity and primitiveness of so much of the latter as the correspondence involves. For it is difficult, if not impossible, to assign any time, subsequent to the first days of Christianity, at which the services are likely to have received their elements or their shaping from such a quarter. Whereas at the beginning of things it was, as has been already observed, perfectly natural. And it may be added, that our discerning in them features, derived not from the Service of the Temple alone, nor from that of the Synagogue alone, but from both, viz., their general structure from the Temple, and their introductory part from the Synagogue, seems exactly to meet the case with which the Apostles would have to deal, in fixing the outlines of ordinary Christian Worship. The converts who had been brought up within reach of the Temple, and those who could only resort to the Synagogue, would both of them find, in such a Service, that which they had been accustomed to. There was, moreover, a recognised connection between the Temple and Synagogue services, they being offered at the same hours[q].

[q] Prideaux, ib.

And there is one very remarkable circumstance—(such at least it appears in the present day to Western Christians,) belonging to the Ordinary Offices of the Eastern Church, alike in early days, and at the present hour. I mean the absence of lessons—of the reading, that is, of Holy Scripture, for purposes of instruction and meditation, as distinguished from the singing of Psalms. Bingham[r] expresses great surprise at this phenomenon, as exhibited in the scheme of service given in the Apostolic Constitutions, and endeavours to reconcile what he supposed to be a discrepancy between them and other early authorities. So Mabillon[s] too quotes—but, like Bingham, thinks it incumbent upon him to call in question—Abbot Theodamar's similar assertion about the Roman daily Offices previously to the time of St. Gregory, viz. that they contained no lessons from the Scriptures. But the truth is, that there is no reason for doubting that the Apostolical Constitutions correctly represent, in this particular, the usage of early times. Basil, as we have seen, speaks of no other service than Psalms and prayers. It is true a host of passages may be alleged, from Justin Martyr downward[t], in proof that the Scriptures were variously read, according to the differing customs of the Churches: but on examination it proves that in all these cases it is, or at any rate may be, the Eucharistic Service that is spoken of. The only exception is that of Cassian, who is speaking of the monastic use of Egypt: and a canon of the council of Laodicea (circ. 360), which will be explained hereafter.

[r] XIII. x. 10; xi. 6.
[s] Liturg. Gallic. de Cursu Gall., p. 385. "Neque enim verisimile est nullas tunc in divinis officiis lectiones fuisse," &c.
[t] Bingham, XIV. iii. 2. See below, sect. vi. fin.

The Ordinary Greek Offices, to this day, are in like manner entirely devoid of lessons. A summary *allusion*[u], of a general kind, to the Epistles, is the nearest approach they make to the reading of holy Scripture, beyond the Psalms: and even this has obviously been borrowed, though probably at a very early period, from the Eucharistic Office. I speak of the regular daily Offices: in the morning Office on Sundays and Festivals, the Gospel is read[x]; and there were also lessons at Vigils.

Now this absence of lessons, except on Sundays, is exactly what would result from the Christian Ordinary Services having originated with those of the Temple and Synagogue conjoined. For in the former there was no reading at all[y], if we except the rehearsal of the Decalogue; while in the latter, the reading was indeed an important part of the service, but seems to have taken place, in the Apostles' time, on the Sabbath only[z].

[u] Called the prokeimenon, or preface; taken from the Psalms, and reflecting (on Sundays, &c.) the spirit of the Epistle (Goar, p. 25); but on the week-days fixed prefaces were used (Neale, p. 406, 901, where the week-day forms will be found). It was said at Vespers and at Sunday Lauds.

[x] It was, as would appear, by following out the idea of the "prokeimenon," that the *capitula*, or short lessons from the Scriptures, found their way into the daily Offices of the West. See below, sect. vii.

[y] The saying over of the Phylacteries, bearing the appointed texts, was to all appearance done by each one for himself.

[z] Acts xv. 21. "Moses of old time hath in every city them that preach him, being read in the synagogues *every Sabbath-day*." "Chez les Juifs, il n'y avait que le jour du sabbat qu'on lisoit," (Grancolas). Maimonides (ap. Prideaux, ubi sup.) speaks of two other synagogue-days, Monday and Thursday, in which the law was read, as well as on the Sabbath. But it would appear from St. James's words just quoted, that this was a later practice. That it was so is also indicated by there not being any portions of their own assigned to those days; *the portion for the coming Sabbath* was read instead, in two sections. This is curiously analogous to the rule for the Epistle and Gospel in the West.

Another peculiarity in the ways of both the present and the early Greek Church, which must be accounted for in the same way, is the high honour paid to the Saturday or Sabbath. Among both Greeks and Armenians, "Saturday is viewed (as it was in early days[a]) in the light of a second Sunday. The Liturgy (i. e. Communion) is then celebrated, even when on other days of the week it is not; and in the daily Office the hymns, &c. are varied, as for a day of peculiar solemnity[b]." So Bingham[c] considers that "the Greek Church received the day as they found it delivered to them by the Jews, among whom it was always a festival."

We may here pause for a moment to notice how the introductory portion of the ancient Greek Offices —if we may assume its antiquity on the grounds here alleged — illustrates or confirms the corresponding part of the Western Church's ritual, and of our own more especially.

Few parts of the existing Daily Services of the English Church have been more severely criticised, on the score of supposed novelty, and departure from the customs of the Church elsewhere, than the penitential introductory portion of them. And yet not only have we, as has been long ago pointed out, an unquestionable warrant for this, of a general kind, in the testimony of St. Basil already cited; but, on further investigating the introduction before us,— doubtless the very one to which he alludes, and probably Apostolic,—we are furnished with as full and exact a precedent as could be desired. Objection

---

[a] See below, chap. ii., on Ordinary Worship.    [b] Neale, Gen. Introd., p. 731; and see p. 919.    [c] XX. iii. 5.

has been made, and perhaps still oftener felt, first, to our having a set Confession at all in this position daily, and twice a-day; and next, to its being of so decided a character. To the latter objection we may safely leave the Church of St. Basil's day to reply. And in answer to the former, we have but to point to the Eastern Offices. Every day, and twice a-day at least,—before each of those Ordinary Services which correspond precisely in their nature and intention to our own,—has the Church of the East, probably from the very beginning, poured forth a profoundly penitential prayer, containing (as may be seen by recurring to it, p. 66.) a full confession of "sins, iniquities, and infirmities," and full acknowledgment of need of pardon and healing, together with many a "Lord have mercy upon us." In short, whoever will compare our form with the ancient Greek, or the still older Jewish prayer, will find the topics as nearly as possible the same, while the expression is greatly intensified.

Nor is this merely an interesting analogy and point of correspondence, fetched from a remote quarter, with which our Offices have no real connection. These Greek Offices are, on the contrary, as will appear hereafter, the lineal progenitors of our own: there is no fault or break in the series; however considerable the changes from time to time made, the continuity and the essential identity are perfect. So that the prefixing of a solemn and somewhat fully wrought out penitential introduction to our Offices at the revision of them in the 16th century, was simply the restoration of a primitive feature of them to its "ancient usual place." Not that the Revisers, probably, had the slightest knowledge what the introduction to the Greek daily Offices was, unless it might be that general idea of it which St. Basil has preserved. They acted instinctively on a principle which is indeed recognised throughout the West as in the East, only that the penitential element is not made so prominent. For in all Western Offices, the versicles preceding the nocturnal or matins Office are "O Lord, open Thou my lips, and my mouth shall shew forth Thy praise:" to which is added, "O God make speed to save me: O Lord make haste to help me." Now these versicles are manifestly portions, the one of the 51st, the other of the 70th Psalm, both profoundly penitential Psalms, and occupying, entire, a corresponding position in the Greek Offices. Besides which, in one widely prevailing variety of the Western rite, special provision was made for a penitential act in connection with the *Venite.* For it was ordered by the rubric that at the words "O come let us worship, and fall down and *weep*" (*sic,* after the Vulg. and LXX.) "before the Lord our Maker," all were "to fall down" accordingly[a].

But this preparatory portion of the Greek Offices seems also to bear witness to the immense and probably Apostolic antiquity of another feature common to the ordinary worship of the East and West alike; the use, namely, of the 95th Psalm, or of a portion of it, as an invitatory to the act of praise and worship. It will be observed that the Jewish and the early Christian Service alike follow up their more penitential part with the declaration of a desire and an

---

[a] S. Bened. ad Vigil. The injunction was doubtless borrowed from the Greek rite which enjoins three reverences (μετανοίας, v. Goar in voc.) to be made at the words of the invitatory, "O come let us worship, and fall down before," &c. Horolog. in loc.

intention of giving worship and praise to God. The Christian form expresses this in the very language, only with a Christian adaptation of the 95th Psalm; the Jewish, in terms evidently in part derived from it. (Thus: "For thou art the Lord our God"="For He is the Lord our God:" and "Be Thy Name, O King, exalted and lifted up on high"="A great King above all Gods.") It is possible, indeed[e], that this Psalm prefaced the entire Temple service, was thence abbreviated into the representative form in which it appears in that of the Synagogue, and so reached the Christian services of the Eastern Church.

However this be, we notice two points of difference between the Eastern and Western daily Offices as regards the *Venite*. In the East, the Psalm itself is not used, but only a threefold "invitation to praise," or "invitatory," based upon the first, third, and sixth verses of it. In the West, on the contrary, the Psalm itself seems to have been invariably used at full length: the invitatory, based, as in the Greek Office, upon the Psalm, being said at intervals[f]. And again, the form of the invitatory itself, unvarying in the East, was in the West almost infinitely diversified[g], according to the usages of different Churches, and the associations of different seasons and festivals.

Here then is a specimen—the first that meets us—

[e] See note B at the end of the volume.

[f] The manner of inserting the invitatory in the older Offices of the English Church is shewn in p. 122 of Leslie's Portiforium. The invitatory was not *always* used in the West. St. Benedict's Rule (cap. 9.) gives a permission to omit it; which some of the French orders availed themselves of on all week-days. The Cluniac order seems *never* to have used it. Vide Hæften, Disq. Monast., p. 713.

[g] An interesting collection of these variations will be found in p. 293 of the "Christian Remembrancer," No. 70, Oct. 1850. For the English forms see Transl. Sar. Psalt., p. 16.

of the way in which the West developed, both truthfully and beautifully, the simpler conceptions of the early Eastern Church. It should be added, however, that no variation of later times ever exceeded, and very few equalled, the Hebraic grandeur and simplicity (an indication of its primitiveness) of the Eastern invitatory, (vide p. 66). Neither did the Western invitatories always sound the note of *Christian* praise: e.g. the Roman form for the greater part of the year is, "Let us adore the Lord who made us." Those of the English Church—which were quite different—were more true to this idea.

Our existing Offices have certainly experienced a loss in point of ritual beauty and expressiveness, in having parted not only with the varied Western invitatories,—(the *practicability* of which, as of other like features, in a public and congregational service, has never yet been proved, and may well be doubted,) —but also in not having reverted even to the primary formula of the Greek Church, which doubtless served to impress the character of *Christian* praise on the whole psalmody of the Office and of the day. In other respects, the exhortation, "Praise ye the Lord," (the old "Alleluia,") answers the purpose of the regular invitatory [h], and was probably intended to do so, when, in the first Book of Edward VI., the *Venite* was ordered to be sung "without any invitatory,"— i.e. without any of the exact type which had been customary. The response, "The Lord's Name be praised," was added in 1662, and, though unlikely to have been so intended, completes the resemblance

[h] The Hallelujah is frequently recognised as an invitatory in ancient writers, e.g. St. Aug., "Nunc ergo *exhortamur* vos, ut laudetis Deum: et hoc est quod omnes dicimus, Halleluia, Laudate Deum." Serm. cli. de Temp.; Hom xi.: and Vide Bingham, vol. iv. p. 458.

to the regular Western invitatory, which was always responded to in terms of itself. It is also a return to the old Jewish and Greek commencement; viz. the Jewish; "Blessed be Thou, O Lord our God." *Ans.* "Blessed art Thou, O Lord:"—and the Greek; "Blessed be our God, now and for ever and ever." *Ans.* "Amen. Glory be to Thee our God, glory to Thee." (Vide sup., p. 65.) And, on the whole, the present English Office happens to reflect, with more accuracy than any other, the features of the Eastern introduction, as having, (see end of Section v.,) 1. Confession of sin; 2. The Lord's Prayer; 3. Portions of Ps. li., viz. vv. 3, 9, 15, 17, in the sentences and versicles, (the Greek Office has the whole Psalm next after the invitatory); 4. Glory be, &c.; 5. The *Venite*, with a quasi-invitatory, followed immediately by Psalms, no hymn intervening before them, as in the elder Western Offices, nor any antiphon accompanying them, but only the "Glory," &c.; which in the Greek Church, however, was only said at the end of all the Psalms[1], or of the three portions into which the psalmody (or, as in the Office before us, Psalm cxix.,) was divided.

Such are the links by which the introductory part of the Western Offices stands connected with the corresponding portion of the primitive Eastern ones; and, through that, with the ancient Jewish service of the Synagogue. Further proofs of the same connection will be amply given in the next division of this chapter. Enough has perhaps been said already to make good the position, that the humbler no less than the grander Offices of the Christian ritual were,

---

[1] So Cassian, ii. 18; Bingham, vol. iv. p. 406. The Roman Church seems also to have had this usage in early times. Ibid., p. 430.

as to their rudiments, derived from the Church of the Elder Covenant.

## SECTION IV.

"And it shall be in that day, that living waters shall go out from Jerusalem; half of them toward the Eastern sea, and half of them toward the Western sea."

THE *commencement*, then, of the ordinary or weekday services of the Church, in the earliest times, having been in all probability such as has been here exhibited,—let us next inquire what other features may, on tolerable grounds of evidence, be presumed to have belonged to them.

And here I must speak in very different terms of two sources of information, which appear to me to have been estimated hitherto in the inverse ratio of their deserts: the one, the Apostolical Constitutions (so called); the other, the existing Offices of the Eastern Church. The former of these has been far *too much* deferred to, and the latter far *too little*, in such endeavours as have been made to ascertain the outline or contents of the ancient ordinary Services of the Church. After the fullest consideration, I do not hesitate to avow it as my opinion, that the account of them given in the Constitutions is, taken as a whole, entirely factitious and untrustworthy. Elements of truth—in accordance with the practice of the compiler of that singular document [k]—it doubtless contains;

[k] For the latest and fullest estimate of the merits and demerits of the Apostolical Constitutions, see "Christian Remembrancer," 1854.

but it egregiously and palpably misrepresents the entire actual *status* of ordinary worship in the first two or three centuries. This would in itself be of little importance; but, unfortunately, Bingham (who is copied, word for word, by Wheatley[1] and others,) has given weight and currency to these representations by the degree of deference which he pays to the Constitutions in this matter. It becomes necessary, on this account, to point out that they can only be acquiesced in by utterly ignoring the concurrent testimony of all antiquity besides. For instance, who can credit,—after what we have seen of the general tone of the Church's services, as represented by St. Basil, in the fourth century, or with the knowledge that we have of the delight which she has in other ages taken, beginning with the very days of St. Paul, in multitudinous and protracted psalmody[m];— who, with this before their eyes, can credit that at any period in the second, third, or fourth century, (to give the widest possible range to the Constitutions,) *two* very short Psalms (the 63rd and 141st) were all that was sung in the morning and evening services? Bingham is naturally somewhat astonished at this, but labours to shew that it may possibly be reconciled with what we know from other sources[n]. But the truth is, that this is not the only inconsistency or absurdity (for we can call it no less) that appears in this scheme of service. It is further represented that this one Psalm was followed, morning and evening, by prayers for catechumens, penitents, &c., concluding with a benediction by the Bishop. Now in all this it is manifest that the concoctor of this imaginary "daily service"

[1] Wheatley, V. iii. 1, 2.   [m] Ephes. v. 19.   [n] XIII. x. 10; xi. 6.

has applied to the week-days what can only have had place in the Sunday services, and then only in the morning Office. The solemn expulsion daily of the various orders of persons who were not capable of being admitted to the Eucharist, when no celebration was about to follow,—and this repeated at the evening service,—is so absurd as to be absolutely incredible. And the uniform concluding benediction by the *bishop* is scarcely less manifestly borrowed from the same source, viz. the Sunday idea of service. The bishop's presence at the Eucharistic Service was indeed, as has been remarked already, almost a matter of course in early times; but this cannot, with any probability, be supposed to have extended in all cases to the daily Offices.

I conceive, then, that we may safely dismiss all further consideration of the Constitutions as evidence of the actual state of ordinary Church Service, as a whole, in early times. At the same time they will be found to confirm in various points, as if in spite of themselves, the views which we obtain from more trustworthy quarters.

In turning now to the other source of information alluded to,—the existing daily Services of the Eastern Church,—I must first explain on what grounds I venture to claim for them a far higher authority, as witnesses to ancient practice, than has been usually accorded to them.

In the first place, then, tenacity of ancient ways and customs characterizes, by universal admission, the Eastern mind[o]. And we have already seen that

---

[o] "Plebs rudis, antiqui ritus apprime tenax."—Goar, p. 26. Mr. Palmer (ubi sup.) says he has not observed any discrepancy between

from the third or fourth century down to the present day, certain features of the Eastern Church's ritual have been handed on without alteration. The question is, How far back may we, on good grounds, carry this changelessness in the matter of Church Service? And again, How much of the existing Eastern Services does it include?

Now it will be remembered, that the ground upon which the early and primitive antiquity of these Offices, as far as regards their *general character* and their *introductory portion*, seemed capable of being firmly based, was their correspondence, and all but identity, as respects these, with the ancient Jewish services. An entirely different, and, indeed, converse kind of evidence must be appealed to for the antiquity of other features and characteristics of them. It is because we can discern, not obscurely or doubtfully, that these Offices were to all *subsequent* ones of a kindred kind,—even to those whose antiquity we can trace the farthest back,—as a model after which they were framed, and an authority to which they deferred: it is therefore that we seem to be justified in assigning to them, or to certain features of them, however, an immense and indefinable antiquity. There are certain curious, and at first sight unaccountable phenomena in the various schemes of service drawn out in later times (i. e. in the fifth and sixth centuries) for the use of the Western Church, which are at once explained by turning to the Offices of the East. This is a kind of evidence which, from its nature, can be but partially and imperfectly unfolded at this stage of our inquiry. Nor, perhaps, can it be entirely appre-

---

the old Eastern Offices, as far as they are disclosed by the writers of the third and fourth centuries, and the existing ones.

ciated, except by such readers as already possess a somewhat full and accurate acquaintance with the Western ritual arrangements. Yet it may be well briefly to exemplify in this place, what will hereafter be made to appear more plainly, viz. that the Western forms of ordinary service, while differing one from the other more or less widely, are one and all manifestly subject to a law as to their structure, and draw upon a common source for their contents; and that in the Eastern Offices that law and that source are clearly discernible.

Let me first, however, explain somewhat more distinctly, though it can be but very summarily, what are the Western schemes of service to which I have just referred.

It is pretty certain, then, that in the course of the fifth and sixth centuries,—within a period extending from about A.D. 420 to 600, or later,—a scheme of ordinary or daily service (distinct from the Eucharistic) came to be very widely adopted in the Churches of Europe,—chiefly in those of Rome, Milan, and parts of France and Spain. How far it was purely an importation, or was grafted upon an indigenous stock of service already existing in each country, is difficult to determine. Upon this point we shall obtain some light by and bye. In either case, its adoption amounted to a vast reorganization of the previous daily ritual of those Churches. But besides the Churches, the monasteries also of Europe adopted a scheme of service in its main features the same. Who were the authors of these schemes we are only in part informed. It seems certain that JOHN CASSIAN, a Thracian, brought up at St. Jerome's monastery at Bethlehem, and ordained a Deacon by St. Chrysostom, was the first to introduce the leading principles of the new ritual into the Churches in the neighbourhood of Marseilles, where he was abbot of a monastery. He had visited the East, and Egypt, and has left an account of the devotions used in the monasteries of the latter. It is generally agreed that from that country the particular number of twelve Psalms, for the nocturnal services, was imported into Europe[p]. It may have found its way into Italy, however, at an earlier period, as Athanasius had founded a monastery at Aquileia, and the communications between Egypt and Italy were otherwise frequent. But it is not until the time of St. Benedict, circ. 530, that we can assign a definite date to any entire Western ritual. About the time that he drew up his scheme of service for the monastery of Cassino, the Roman, the Milanese, French and Spanish Churches (see Mabillon, Curs. Gall.) were completing theirs, differing in many particulars, but all of them, in common with St. Benedict's, adopting the following as their outline:—

1. Nocturns, al. Matins; properly a *night-service*, used before daylight, mostly with twelve Psalms read in course; and lessons more or fewer.

2. Lauds; an *early morning* service, generally joined on to the former at daybreak, with fixed Psalms, and Canticles.

3. Prime; a *later morning* service, with fixed Psalms.

4. Tierce; at 9 A.M., ditto.

5. Sexts; at 12 noon, ditto.

6. Nones; at 3 P.M., ditto.

7. Vespers, or *evening* service; with four or five Psalms read in course, and Canticle.

8. Compline; a service at *bed-time*, with fixed Psalms.

[p] Vide Palmer, Introd. p. 215. Cassian, Cœnob. Instit. For various opinions as to the birthplace of Cassian, see Milman, Hist. Latin Christianity, vol. i. p. 129.

And now to proceed with our proofs of the common derivation of all these schemes from the Oriental.

Do we observe then, in all of them, a remarkable anxiety to connect the 21st Psalm ("The King shall rejoice,") with the Sunday nocturnal service; which is accomplished in one case by *ending*[q], in the other by *beginning*[r], the psalmody with that particular Psalm? The reason of such anxiety is seen at once, when we find that this, with the 20th, was a fixed daily Psalm at the early morning office of the Oriental Church[s]; obviously on account of its being so well adapted to carry on, in a striking manner, the idea of the Invitatory repeated at the beginning of that service, by exalting Christ as the Great KING. It was familiar therefore, doubtless, to the whole East, and perhaps to the West also, as a Sunday Psalm more especially, (the attendance at the Sunday services being greater than on other days); so that the framers of the newer Western Offices did not venture to displace it, though it taxed their utmost ingenuity to include it in their new schemes. One of these schemes, it will be seen, has managed to retain the 20th as well as the 21st Psalm. In like manner, in one plan (St. Benedict's) the *third* Psalm is *prefixed* to the nocturnal office all the year round, while in the other it is *included* in the eighteen Psalms.

---

[q] Brev. Rom. Sarisb., &c. Dom. ad Mat. The eighteen Psalms for the Sunday nocturnal (i.e matins) office, in the Roman and old English uses, were from the first *to the twenty-first* inclusive; omitting Pss. iv. and v., and reckoning our Pss. ix. and x. as one.

[r] Reg. St. Benedicti Vigil. Dom. (and Bona, Div. Psalm. xviii. 3.) The twelve Psalms for the Sunday vigil (or nocturnal) office in St. Benedict's scheme, were *from the twenty-first* to the thirty-second, inclusive.

[s] Infra, sect. vi.

This arrangement, again, satisfied an old condition of morning psalmody: Psalm iii. having always had a place at the Eastern early morning office, as the *first* of a group of six Psalms. It will be observed that in these and other instances the Western framers drew freely upon the Eastern early *morning* office for their own "nocturns;" this having in fact become a morning office, only used before daylight.

So again, was it a universal rule throughout the West, (as Bona has observed, though he had no idea *why* it was so[t],) that the Psalms, so far as they were sung in regular order, should be spread over the night (i. e. matins) services of the week, in such a way as to be used *as far as the* 109*th inclusive, and no further?* No reason can possibly be assigned for so arbitrary a rule, but this,—that in the Greek office this was the *last Psalm*[u] at the early morning office of every day. It was manifestly placed there for the sake of its commencement, ("Deus laudem meam," "Hold not Thy tongue, O God of my *praise,*") praise or lauds being the key-note of that office. It had acquired, too, unusual prominence, by having certain hymns (*stichera*) varying with the day, sung between the verses of it. It had thus become inseparably associated with the *close of the nocturno-matutinal office,* and accordingly was preserved in the West as the conclusion of the *week's* nocturnal or matin psalmody, whatever might be the plan on which the preceding Psalms were dis-

---

[t] Bona, Div. Psalmod. xviii. 1. p. 861. "All nations of the Western Church agree in this, that they terminate the (week's) night services (i. e. the matins) with Ps. cix., and begin the day-hours with the 110th."

[u] Bona, p. 905.

tributed. Thus, in one scheme[x], the Saturday nocturns Psalms are from the 97th to the 109th; in another[y], the 101st to the 109th. So, once more, when Psalms were wanted to furnish forth or complete new offices for the 1st, 3rd, 6th, and 9th hours, which had not been originally hours for Church worship, the Western compilers borrowed the entire 119th Psalm for the purpose from the Greek nocturnal Office. In one of these schemes[z], it was arranged so as to be read through daily; in another[a], it was made to last two days; other Psalms being found for the rest of the week. As to the Greeks themselves, when they adopted these more novel day offices, they retained the 119th Psalm in its old place, and provided for them another selection of Psalms.

These instances, with others which will be adduced hereafter, abundantly prove that the Eastern daily offices were to the later Western ritual nothing less than the quarry whence the materials for its stately structure were hewn,—the fountain whence it drew its inspirations,—the law which, amid its widest diversities, and in its boldest developments, it instinctively recognised and obeyed.

I am content to have proved this for the present, of the *later* Western ritual; reserving for a future chapter the grounds there are for believing that the *earlier* forms in use in the West, took their rise, too, in the same primitive fount which has been here indicated.

[x] Brev. Rom. Sar. Sabb. ad Mat.
[y] Reg. S. Bened. ad Vig. Sabbat.
[z] Brev. Rom. Sarisb. &c., and Primam, quoted.
[a] Reg. S. Benedict. Domin. et Fer. 2ª. ad Tert. Sext. Non.

## SECTION V.

"In the night His song shall be with me, and my prayer unto the God of my life...... At midnight I will rise to give thanks unto Thee."

It may seem strange that so obvious a key to the intricacies of the Western Offices, as that which the previous section suggests, should never have been applied hitherto to their elucidation. This, however, is easily accounted for, when we consider that the few who, like Bona, had sufficient knowledge of Eastern ritual for the purpose, held it far too cheaply to imagine the possibility of the Western Offices being in any way beholden to it. Others, as Bingham, had a very slender acquaintance with the existing Eastern daily services. Goar has only commented on a small portion of them; nor, until the publication of a recent work [b], was anything like an accurate or intelligible account of them accessible to the English reader. Much less have they been laid under contribution, as the Eastern Communion Offices have, (by Renaudot, Palmer, and others,) in illustration of Western ritual.

We proceed to inquire *how much* of the present Eastern offices may be considered to possess a claim to antiquity. On this head, indeed, we cannot expect to arrive at any great exactitude; nor is it very important for our purpose that we should do so. Yet it may answer a good purpose to set forth, at this point in our inquiry, what we may reasonably

[b] The Rev. J. M. Neale's General Introduction to the History of the Holy Eastern Church. 2 vols.

presume to have been, from some very early time, the general outline of these offices. Those, more especially, to whom the study of ancient ritual is untrodden ground, and to whom the vastness and complexity of the later Western Offices presents a formidable appearance, may be not unwilling to contemplate them in this their earlier and simpler stage. We may also notice as we pass some of the points on which our own Offices, in time past or present, receive illustration from this source; thus relieving, it may be hoped, the dryness of merely antiquarian discussion.

Judging then by the existing Greek Services, combined with the evidence of antiquity, there were daily in the Christian Church, from immemorial ages, —that is to say, we know not how early,—*three* offices of ordinary worship, resolving themselves in practice into *two*. Of these, the first, probably, in point of antiquity, and, when viewed in conjunction with the office next succeeding it, in importance also, was the MIDNIGHT (τὸ Μεσονυκτικὸν) or NOCTURNAL OFFICE[c] proper; commencing at or after midnight, and extending to the dawn of day.

The second, following upon the first without any interval[d], was the EARLY MORNING OFFICE[e], (τὸ Ὄρθρον.)

[c] Bona, Psalmod. xviii. 13. Neale, Gen. Introd., p. 912. Goar, (Euchol., pp. 26, 46,) makes remarks on the office, but does not give it.

[d] Quotidiana laudum divinarum officia a vigiliis nocturnis *auspicantur* Græci. Μεσονυκτικῷ aliud officium ὄρθρος, sub adventu lucis persolvendum, *jungitur.*" The two corresponding offices in the Latin Church were avowedly continuous, probably from the earliest times. Vide Bona, Div. Psalm. iv. 5. 1.

[e] Goar calls it the Lauds Office; and so Neale, p. 913. But the name signifies a morning (or dawn) office, and nothing else. Bona calls it Matins, (and so King,) reckoning the latter part of it as Lauds; which is surely more correct,—only it leads to a confusion with the

The third in importance, though reckoned first in order by the Orientals, was the EVENING OFFICE, (τὸ Ἑσπερινὸν,) taking place not earlier than 6 P.M. of the preceding evening.

The leading characteristic of all these services, or rather of *both* of them, (for they may with propriety be spoken of as two[f],) was, notwithstanding a large infusion of the penitential element, and of prayers and litanies, that they were great offices of psalmody and hymns,—orbs of Divine Song, the greater and the less, ruling over the day and over the night. It was thus that, on ordinary days, the Christians of early times fulfilled, in the order in which they are given by St. Paul to the Ephesian Church, those two *great* precepts of Divine Service:—"Be filled with the Spirit, speaking to yourselves in Psalms and hymns and spiritual songs, singing and making melody in your hearts unto the Lord; giving thanks[g] always for all things to God and the Father in the Name of our Lord Jesus Christ;" and again, "Praying always with all prayer and supplication, and watching (ἀγρυπνοῦντες) thereunto with all perseverance."

Both these Offices, the NOCTURNO-MATUTINAL and the EVENING, contained certain *fixed* Psalms; while

---

Western Matins. The term adopted in the text, while correctly translating ὄρθρον, avoids this confusion.

[f] Goar fully recognises these two (the midnight + the morning, and the evening offices) as the *great* occasions of daily worship, even if there were others, from the earliest times. "Quotidianus Ecclesiæ usus, Patrumque antiquorum auctoritas, apostolicis institutis, scripturâ, et ratione fundata, Matutinum (vide sup. note d.) et Vespertinum Conventum solemniori apparatu ubique peragi ostendit." Euchol., p. 9.

[g] The term εὐχαριστοῦντες (Eph. v. 20.) doubtless includes, or even primarily intends, the Eucharist. Yet it cannot but include also these more ordinary devotions, by which the mind of Eucharistic praise and prayer was carried on through the week.

others, it is most probable, were sung in the order in which they occur in the Psalter, according as the time allowed. There is no reason to think that the arrangement [h] by which, in the Greek Church at the present day, the Psalms are generally sung through in the week, in addition to the fixed Psalms, is of greater antiquity than about the third or fourth century, since we find different rules about this prevailing in different Churches [i] at that period.

The earlier or midnight portion of the Nocturno-Matutinal Office commenced with the Introduction already described (p. 65), and proceeded thus:—

(*First Watch* [j], or *Nocturn.*)
Psalm li.
Psalm cxix. in three portions,
(each portion ending with "Glory" and Alleluia, thrice).
The Nicene Creed.
Trisagion (p. 66.) and "Most Holy Trinity," ib.
The Lord's Prayer.
Two midnight hymns, (p. 92).
Hymn of the Incarnation.
Kyrie eleison (forty times).
Prayer for grace and protection.
Ejaculatory petitions.

(*Second Watch*, or *Nocturn.*)
Invitatory, viz.
"O come let us worship," &c. (as p. 66).
Psalm cxxi. ("I will lift up mine eyes.")
Psalm cxxxiv. ("Behold now, praise.")
"Glory."
Trisagion, and "Most Holy Trinity."
The Lord's Prayer.
Hymns.
Kyrie eleison, (twelve times).
Remembrance of the departed.

[h] Neale, p. 856.
[i] e. g. in the Armenian. Vide Bona, Psalmod. xviii. 15.
[j] S. Benedict calls them Vigiliæ: Reg. c. 9.

Short thanksgiving hymn to the Trinity.
Dismissal benediction.
The Priest requests forgiveness from the people.
Litany.

In this simple and undoubtedly very ancient Service, there are several points worthy of observation.

It is, first of all, in name, and doubtless was originally in practice also, not a nocturnal merely, but a *midnight* Service. This, however little accordant with the general practice in subsequent ages, (even in St. Basil's time it had apparently ceased to be a μεσονυκτικὸν, and was only *antelucan*,) is thoroughly in the spirit of the very first age of the Church's being, when the expectation of her Lord's Second Coming was so vivid, and so closely connected with the midnight hour more especially. And of the existence, accordingly, of a habit of *midnight* worship in Apostolic times, we have an indication in the Acts of the Apostles; Paul and Silas, in the prison at Philippi, breaking out "at midnight" (κατὰ τὸ μεσονύκτιον) into "a hymn of praise and prayer to God," (προσευχόμενοι ὕμνουν τὸν Θεὸν, Acts xvi. 25; see also xx. 7). The title then of the Office furnishes a strong presumption for its primitiveness; for at what subsequent time, it may be asked, previous to the rise of monasticism in the third and fourth centuries, was an office for such an hour so likely to originate? The contents of it, again, clearly bespeak it a midnight office; as regards, that is to say, the *first* of the two "nocturns" into which it is divided; which is exactly the part which might be expected to bear this character. For the 119th Psalm was no doubt chosen for this among other reasons, that it alone, in the whole Psalter, speaks of the actual *midnight* hour as proper for devotion: "At midnight I will rise to give thanks to Thee," (v. 52); while it also refers to the "night" and the "night-watches" generally, (vv. 55, 148). But the very solemn hymns in the first nocturn are also of profoundly midnight character:—

"Behold the Bridegroom cometh in the middle of the night; and blessed is that servant, whom He shall find watching; but unworthy he, whom He shall find careless. Beware therefore, my soul, lest thou sink down in sleep[k], lest thou shouldst be given over to death, and be shut out from the kingdom; but be sober, and cry, 'Holy, Holy, Holy art Thou, O God . . . have mercy upon us.'

"That day, the day of fear, consider, my soul, and watch, lighting thy lamp, and making it bright with oil; for thou knowest not when the voice will come to thee that saith, Behold the Bridegroom. Beware therefore, my soul, lest thou slumber, and so remain without, knocking, like the five virgins. But persevere in watching, that thou mayest meet Christ with rich oil, and He may give thee the divine wedding-garment of His glory."

One thing more may be observed in connexion with this midnight office; viz. that, divided as it is into two parts, it seems, when taken in conjunction with the evening and the early morning offices, to carry out with great exactness the precept of our Lord: "Watch ye therefore, for ye know not when the master of the house cometh, at *even*, or at *midnight*, or at the *cock-crowing*, or in the *morning*." For so was the night at that time divided into four periods; —I. Ὀψεί, the evening, from twilight to 9 P.M.

[k] Μὴ τῷ ὕπνῳ κατενεχθῇς, ἵνα μὴ τῷ θανάτῳ παραδοθῇς: an evident allusion to Eutychus' sinking down in sleep at the *midnight* service at Troas, and being taken up dead: Acts xx. Comp. v. 7, μέχρι μεσονυκτίου; and v. 9, κατενεχθεὶς ἀπὸ τοῦ ὕπνου .. ἤρθη νεκρός.

II. Μεσονύκτιον, midnight, or the first watch, from 9 to 12. III. Ἀλεκτοροφωνία, (cock-crowing, or the second watch,) from 12 to 3 A.M. IV. Πρωί, morning till daybreak[1].

This service corresponds, again, very exactly in many particulars with St. Basil's account of the nocturnal service in the fourth century. We have, 1st, the penitential introduction; 2nd, psalmody following, (the hymns are mentioned by other writers); 3rd, prayers intermingled. Further, the psalmody is of two kinds, apparently corresponding to St. Basil's description. For he says that at one time, "dividing themselves into two choirs, they sing alternately, securing hereby at once due meditation on the Divine Oracles," viz. by listening in turns silently, "and also providing against distraction of their own thoughts," by having a part to perform themselves. All this agrees remarkably with the character of Ps. cxix., which is so emphatically throughout μελέτη λογίων, " a meditation on the Oracles" (the term itself, λόγια, occurs eighteen times, and an equivalent for it in every verse; μελέτη frequently, vv. 24, 47, &c.): while it also especially calls for the alternate method, to keep up the attention. Here too we see a probable reason, or at any rate a compensation, for the absence of Scripture Lessons in the Eastern daily Offices; this Psalm and others being used as a meditation no less than as praise.

St. Basil, again, says that at another part of the psalmody, they allowed one to begin, or rather lead, the singing, (κατάρχειν,) the others joining in at the close either of each verse, or more probably of each

[1] Jahn, Archæol. 101.

Psalm. Now of the two Psalms appointed for the second nocturn, one at least, the 134th, is especially adapted by its construction for this purpose; the last verse ("The Lord that made Heaven and Earth give thee blessing out of Sion,") being confessedly a response to the first three. It is further to be remarked, that these two Psalms are the first but one, and the last, of the well-known and kindred fifteen (cxx.—cxxxiv.) called "Songs of degrees," following next after the 119th, (which was sung in the first nocturn); and it is very conceivable that the rest of the Psalms of the group may have been used, more or fewer, as time permitted, to fill out the office. This supposition would bring the night service into yet fuller harmony with St. Basil's account; for he says, "Thus, with variety of psalmody, they carry on the night."

The modern practice, in this office alone, does not add any course of Psalms to the fixed ones. But the "fifteen Psalms" are used at Vespers during a part of the year, (from Sept. 20 to Christmas,) only substituting Ps. cxxxvi. to make up the number; Ps. cxxxiv. being omitted, as occurring in the night office[m]. This is the more striking, because it is an infraction of the ordinary distribution of the Psalms, and points perhaps to some such anciently prevailing habit as I have supposed, of using these Psalms as a group. And as the origin of their title of "Songs of degrees," according to the Jews themselves, is that they were "sung on certain steps" in the sanctuary, between the court of the men and women[n], we seem to have here another link between the Temple Services and those of the early Church. Another account derives the name

---

[m] Vide Neale, Introd. pp. 855, 6.     [n] Hengstenberg, Ps. cxx.

from their being sung in chorus by the Levites or priests, "not by the crowd of people, but by some distinguished persons, *who sung before the rest;*— they were sung, or at least begun, from a high place." (Luther, ibid.). This, again, which is perfectly reconcileable with the other account, singularly agrees with the view we have elicited, of the probable manner of saying these particular Psalms in the early Church. Hengstenberg, however, acquiesces in another view, viz. that these were songs sung by the pilgrims as they went up yearly to Jerusalem at the great festivals. They may have been so, and have been sung in the Temple besides. He remarks further, in terms singularly apposite to our present subject, that " Ps. cxxi. ('I will lift up mine eyes unto the hills,') was designed to be sung in sight of the mountains of Jerusalem, and is manifestly *an evening song* for the band of pilgrims, *to be sung in the last night-watch;*— Ps. cxxii. ('I was glad when they said unto me,') when they reached the gates of Jerusalem, and halted for the purpose of forming in order, for the solemn procession into the sanctuary; in which they used Ps. cxxxiv." We have here a very plausible account, at least, of the selection of these two Psalms, cxxi. and cxxxiv. (to the omission of Ps. cxx.) as the fixed Psalms for the second Christian nocturn.

On this view of Hengstenberg's, too, the singular and unique provision made about these fifteen Psalms in the present usage of the Greek Church, is seen to be most beautiful and appropriate. The only period of the year in which any long portion of the Psalms is *repeated* evening after evening is the *fifteen* weeks before Christmas Day. And the Psalms so distinguished are, as we have seen, no other than these "Pilgrim songs." The idea evidently is that the Church is then approaching week by week—a week for each song of degrees,—to the true Tabernacle and Temple which our blessed Lord by His Nativity "pitched among men." These Psalms are also said on week-days in Lent. The Western Church has inherited a precisely analogous usage. The fifteen Psalms were anciently said every day during Lent, and are still appointed for every Wednesday in that season. Their being thus used at *evening* in the Greek Church, while it is in exact accordance with Hengstenberg's hypothesis, may more immediately have arisen from their having been occasionally sung in the primitive night office, as suggested. The fitness of them, or of any of them, for that office, independent of any Jewish association, is manifest. "No one of them," observes Hengstenberg, "bears an individual character; all refer to the whole Church of God; finally, all bear the character of pensive melancholy. The fundamental thought in all is, the Providence of God watching over His Church."

These somewhat lengthened remarks on the possible origin of the certainly very ancient, and probably Apostolic psalmodical arrangements before us, will not, I trust, be thought misplaced. Nothing, surely, can be much more interesting or instructive, than to trace as far back as we can the details of a service which was unquestionably the *incunabula* and earliest stage of those which we possess at the present day.

For, to proceed with our comments on the Eastern Nocturnal Office, we cannot fail to observe in it the manifest germ of many subsequent arrangements in the Western Ritual. The division of the nocturnal service into two "nocturns," as they were sometimes called, both commencing, in a measure, in the same way, was doubtless connected with the ancient Jewish distribution of the night into "watches." It would also answer the purpose of allowing the worshippers to relieve one another. The nocturn idea was adopted in the most marked manner in the West. In the Benedictine scheme the "nocturns" are *two*, as in the Greek, with the addition of a third on Sundays. In the Roman and English use, on Sundays and Festivals, the nocturns are also three; though on ordinary days there is but one. And we may observe an indication of the two (or three) nocturns having ceased to be in reality distinct services, in there being no repetition, in the Western forms, of any portion of the commencement of the office.

The Psalms of the first nocturn in the Greek Office are immediately followed by the Creed and the Lord's Prayer. The generally received opinion [s], as to the date at which these formularies first began to be used in public worship, would go far to deprive this feature, at any rate, of the offices before us, of all claims to antiquity. In another part of this work [t], however, some reasons are given for believing that the concealment of the Lord's Prayer from the unbaptized, by excluding it from the earlier part of the Communion Office, was not of Apostolic, but of somewhat later date; and the occurrence in this office both of it and of the Creed, far from militating necessarily against its antiquity, may equally well, at least, be an evi-

[s] Vide Bingham, vol. iv. p. 465; v. 139. Palmer, Orig., vol. i. pp. 215—217. The considerations in the text seem to be a sufficient reply to Mr. Palmer's view. Bingham only proves the late admission of the Creed into the *Communion* Office.

[t] Part II., chapter on Primitive Form of Liturgy.

dence of its dating earlier than the introduction of that system of concealment. It would by no means be imperative, when that discipline came in, to eject these features from the scheme of the service, but only to veil them by using them silently; just as in the Eastern Communion Offices (in the Alexandrian more especially) the Lord's Prayer seems to have been concealed by a paraphrase. This, accordingly, I conceive to be the true account to be given of our finding the Creed and Lord's Prayer in the existing Eastern Offices. The Creed in the earliest times would of course be comparatively brief; but the rudiments at least of such a formula were certainly delivered by St. Paul to the Churches, (vide 1 Cor. xv. 1, &c.) and doubtless by the other Apostles. And it is almost inconceivable that the Churches of the East can have secured a correct, uniform, and universal acquaintance with the articles of the Christian faith, on the part of their members, in any other way than by using the Creed, from the time its very rudiments existed, in their public Offices. Now, in the way here supposed, they might perfectly well thus have used it, even during the prevalence of the catechumenical system. And this supposition will account, as perhaps nothing else can, for our finding the Creed and Lord's Prayer said silently, or under the breath, (except the beginning and the conclusion,) in the Western Daily Offices. Various fanciful reasons have been assigned for this practice"; but it is mani-

" Thus Durandus (ad Prim.), ingeniously enough: "The Creed is said in a low voice, but the conclusion aloud; to signify that with the heart man believeth to righteousness, and with the mouth confession is made unto salvation." But the "Myrroure" (a 15th century Commentary on the Hours; vide Maskell,) tells us it is because the Apostles' Creed "was made privily, before the faith was openly preached to the world." Transl. Sarum Psalt., p. 118. Equally good

festly a relic of the ancient system of concealment, and was most probably derived directly from this part of the Greek Offices. The ancient English Nocturnal Office has both the Creed and Lord's Prayer in exactly the position[x] which they here occupy, namely, immediately after the Psalms; only said by the choir, however, and privately, not as an actual part of the Office. The Roman use has not the Creed in the same position, but only the Lord's Prayer.

But the Creed and Lord's Prayer also occurred daily[y] of old in the body of the English Offices, as it still does; preceded by the *Kyrie e'eison, Christe eleison,* &c., in Greek, (said in the *English* Office *nine times,*) and followed shortly after by the "Trisagion," as in the Greek Office, — "Sanctus Deus, Sanctus fortis, Sanctus (et, Angl.) immortalis." And to this again succeeded (which is surely most remarkable), on certain occasions[z], and in the English Office only, the very Psalm (121st) which we find presently in the second Greek Nocturn.

One thing more we may observe about the Creed in the Greek Office, viz. that it followed immediately upon the great meditative Psalm (119th) which, as has been observed, stood the ancient Church, in some sort, in the stead of Lessons in their ordinary night service; while it precedes the Lord's Prayer, the prayer for protection, and other petitions. The latter arrangement is found, accordingly, in the Western Prime Office, (which was the chief office of prayer,

reasons for the silent use of the Lord's Prayer may be seen in Durandus, l. c.

[x] Brev. Sarisb. Rubr. ad noct. i. Mat. Dom. i. de Advent.

[y] viz. among the Preces, used at Prime all the year round (except on three days) in our Church; much more rarely in the Roman.

[z] viz. when there was a *Memoria,* or commemoration of a festival.

see below, chap. iii.) and survives in our own services. The former was, accidentally as it should seem, restored in the English Offices at the revision of them in 1549, by the Creed's taking its place immediately after the Lessons and Canticles.

The Lord's Prayer is followed, in both the Nocturns of the Greek Office, by hymns. The immense antiquity of the practice of singing hymns, and not Psalms merely, in the Offices of the Church, is well known. The term, though doubtless originally applicable to Psalms, and used with this latitude in St. Matt. xxvi. and 30, Acts xvi. 25, is evidently not identical with ψαλμὸς, since St. Paul enumerates both[a]. A hymn has been well defined as a "Song addressed to God[b]." Hence it came to be applied very early to *Christian* songs of praise, inspired or otherwise, as distinguished from the ancient Psalms; more especially to such as were addressed to Christ : though the term Psalm was also not unfrequently applied to these also. Philo, in the curious passage already referred to, says that the persons in the first century whose habits he describes, "did not only meditate, but also compose songs and hymns to the praise of God;" and that "in their night service, one of them would stand up and sing a hymn to God's praise, either newly composed by himself, or long ago by one of the old Prophets[c]." And as Eusebius (circ. 320) thought the Christians were meant, it is evident that in his time such hymns existed in the Church's nocturnal services, for it is of such services that Philo is speaking. In the next succeeding ages, as we have seen, they are mentioned together with Psalms, as a characteristic of the

[a] Eph. v. 19; Col. iii. 16.
[b] Ἡ εἰς Θεὸν ᾠδή. Vide Bona, Psalmod. xvi. 9. [c] Philo, ubi sup.

ordinary service of Christians. Hymns were duly retained in the newer forms adopted in the West in the fifth and sixth centuries; with this peculiarity, that the hymn, at nocturns, immediately followed the invitatory. It is probable that in this position it was originally no more than a metrical expansion of the invitatory. Such at least is obviously the character of the simple hymn, attributed to St. Gregory, which was universally used in the Western Sunday office during the greater part of the year[d]. In the case of ordinary hymns, the more natural and preferable arrangement appears to be that of the Greek Office, as placing the uninspired after the inspired. We can hardly regret therefore, that in the English Revision, the hymn (or anthem) was omitted in this position, and placed (in 1662) later in the Office; as nearly as possible in the position which it occupies in the Greek Office, and in the Western Lauds and Vespers.

Though indeed there is another light in which the hymns in the Greek Service may be considered. Taking the Psalms, more especially the 119th in the first nocturn, to be in one point of view (as St. Basil represents them) Scripture Lessons, read and meditated upon, we have in the hymns a sort of response to them; exactly such as the Te Deum, Benedictus, and Magnificat are to the actual reading of Scripture in the Western Offices. Nor is it at all improbable that the use of these particular hymns, of the Te Deum especially, as responsories to the Lessons, may have originated in the offices before us. It is certainly most

---

[d] Brev. Sarisb. ad Mat. from 1st Sund. after Trin. to Advent—(to 1st Sund. in October, Rom.):

"Nocte surgentes, vigilemus omnes,
   Semper in Psalmis meditemur, atque
   Viribis totis Domino canamus . . . .
   Ut pio Regi pariter canentes," &c.

remarkable that the two hymns following the 119th Psalm and the Creed in the Greek first nocturn, have much in common with the Te Deum[e]; as containing (p. 92) the invocation, "Holy, Holy, Holy," and as expressing, though in different ways, faith in the Incarnation, and the expectation of Christ's "coming to be our Judge." The two forms, the Greek and the Latin, are probably amplifications of the primitive elements which are common to them. The Saturday nocturns hymn of the Greek Church makes a yet nearer approach to the Te Deum; as it speaks of our "imitating on earth the Powers in Heaven, by crying aloud, 'Holy, Holy, Holy, art Thou, O God,' (comp. 'All the earth doth worship Thee . . . . To Thee all Angels cry aloud, the Heavens and all the Powers therein. To Thee,' &c., 'Holy, Holy, Holy,' &c.)"

Both portions of the Greek Office terminate with prayers; the latter has also a dismissal blessing, which seems to be properly the conclusion of the entire Service. Yet there follows, as if a sort of afterthought, a Litany, preceded by a request on the priest's part for the people's forgiveness; to which they respond by a reverence, and he sums up with a prayer of pardon for all. Now all this strikingly corresponds with another well-known feature of the Western Ritual. Towards the close of the Prime and Compline, and after a sort of dismissal benediction has been given,—"The almighty and merciful God bless and keep us all. Amen,"—the old English use prescribed, all the year round, (not, as the Roman, on certain days only,)[f] an interchange of ac-

[e] On the following up of Scripture lessons with the *Te Deum*, see further, below, sect. vi. fin., and note D at the end of the volume.

[f] Rubr. Brev. Sarisb. ad Prim. et Compl. (The only exceptions were the three days before Easter, and All Souls' day.) Brev. Rom., ib. This does not seem to have been in the Roman Offices at all when

knowledgment of sin, and request for intercession, between the priest and choir; after which the priest said an absolution, and then followed petitions and collects. This is doubtless derived, though with some variations, from—or from a common source with—the Greek ceremony;—which is a request of the priest only to the people for *their* blessing and forgiveness, in case (as it would seem to mean) he has, to their common loss, committed any error in the preceding service[g]; and the prayer for pardon or absolution is forthwith said by him on behalf of all. The Western form is a more distinct and comprehensive confession of *having sinned*, and is said first by the priest to the people, and then *vice versâ;* as is also the formula of praying for mercy: the priest summing up with a desire of pardon for all. So that the ceremony, as adopted and modified in the West, was evidently intended to be mainly official;—an interchange of acknowledgments between the persons officially performing the Service (for to them it is confined) of any imperfections in the discharge of their duties in the whole preceding services of the day. For it occurred towards the close of the *last* of those three offices, (Nocturns, Lauds, and Prime,) which were commonly taken together at the beginning of the day; and again in the last office at night, the Compline: and so was appropriately placed to answer this purpose. And it may have been as taking this view of it, as well as on ac-

Amalarius (9th cent.) and Durandus (13th) commented upon them. But of its having existed from the first in the *English* Office, together with other features of the Greek Nocturns (as e. g. Ps. cxxi.), which the Roman has not, there seems no reason to doubt.

[g] This view will account for what Mr. Neale remarks upon, (in loc.,) viz. the postponement of this rite to the end of the Greek Office. Compare the confession, &c., at end of Compline, below, ch. iii. sect. i.

count of its objectionable form, that our Revisers of 1549 omitted this feature altogether, considering it ill-adapted, as such, to be retained in a service which they pre-eminently designed to restore to congregational use. The intended range of the Western "confession and absolution" may well, however, have been wider than this, though this its ancient application was chiefly kept in view. It is commonly understood[h] as a confession of the sins of the night or day preceding: and in this character it was first removed by Quignon (1535) in his revision of the Roman Offices, to the beginning of the Matins; and also, (doubtless by following in his track,) on second thoughts, and after much modification, assigned the same position by our Revisers in 1552.

The Eastern night-office on Sundays is totally different from that of the week-days, which has been now described. This is entirely in accordance with the view adopted above, (section ii.) of the week-day night services having had a separate origination from those of the Sunday.

I have thus dwelt at some length on the nocturnal Eastern service, because of the extraordinary degree in which—considering its comparative brevity and simplicity—it illustrates, and indeed supplies the true rationale of various parts of the Western Offices; —of those of our own Church, both unrevised and revised, more especially. There is also, I conceive, considerable appearance of this part of the Eastern Offices having been far less altered or expanded than any other. Some features, indeed, as the hymns, are

[h] Bona, Psalmod. xvi. 20. "Ad Primam et Completorium...*generalis confessio* recitatur, ut quicquid *in nocte vel die* quocunque modo deliquimus, pœnitentiæ lavacro mundemus."

doubtless, in their present form, of later date. But, as compared with the Offices used at early morning, or at evening, the nocturnal Office is simplicity and primitiveness itself. Those obviously more recent arrangements[i], by which the manner of singing the Psalms in course (besides the fixed Psalms) is regulated, and the festivals of saints are commemorated with a vast variety and complexity of hymns[k], find no place in this, as in those other Offices. Whatever of expansion and enlargement, in short, the Eastern Offices, in the East itself, received in the course of ages, it fell (as was natural when the zeal for actual night services had somewhat declined) on those of the early morning and the evening, leaving the night Office comparatively untouched. This Office also contains, perhaps, a greater number of elements of Divine Service than either of the other two ancient Eastern Offices; viz. Psalms (both as an act of praise and as a lesson for meditation) and hymns; penitential confession, and a species of absolution; the Creed, and the Lord's Prayer; short petitions and set prayers; and a litany. Here, therefore, we discern, even in this short compass, those three great features of the Church's ordinary service, which the subsequent Western expansions brought out with ever-increasing distinctness;—praise, perception of divine mysteries and knowledge, and prayer:—corresponding to, and in a manner carrying on continually, through the whole contexture of the Christian life, the great acts of the Eucharist,—oblation, participation, and pleading.

[i] For these vide Neale, pp. 855, 897, 918. Compare the rubric at end of Midnight Office:—"Observe that the Office is to be sung thus all the week."

[k] Ibid., pp. 903, &c., 921, &c. Below, sect. vi. fin.

We may not unfitly conclude this section by exhibiting in one view the points of resemblance between the Greek nocturnal Office and our own Morning Service, or Matins. I am far, indeed, from attaching *first-rate* importance to this resemblance, striking as it is. There doubtless remain, after all, not a few points of dissimilarity; and some of the coincidences, as e. g. between the responsory hymns, may not be made out with any absolute certainty. I am aware, too, that if we take in the continuous psalmody which followed the Greek Nocturns uninterruptedly, the resemblance will then be, especially as to form, rather between the Greek services and the *unrevised* English Offices of Nocturns, (or Matins,) and Lauds. However, it must be confessed to be very remarkable, and to indicate no small degree of correct instinct in our Revisers, that they should have brought back our Offices to so near an essential and even circumstantial correspondence with their original and probably Apostolic phase.

In the following scheme, such features of our Office as have been removed from their proper place for comparison's sake, are indicated by brackets.

| *Eastern Nocturnal Office.* | *English Matins.* |
|---|---|
| First Nocturn. | |
| Benediction. | |
| Penitential prayers for absolution and cleansing. | Penitential sentences, confession, absolution. |
| Glory be, &c. | |
| Our Father, &c. (aloud). | Our Father, &c. (aloud). |
| For Thine is, &c. Amen. | For Thine is, &c. Amen. |
| Kyrie eleison, (12 times). | Penitential versicles, viz.: |
| [Greek Morn. Off., " O Lord, open Thou my," &c. | " O Lord, open Thou our," &c. |
| " And my mouth," &c.] | " And our mouth," &c. |
| Glory be, &c. | Glory be, &c. |

| *Eastern Nocturnal Office.* | *English Matins.* |
|---|---|
| Invitatory, from Ps. xcv., viz.: "O come let us worship God our King," &c. | Invitatory, "Praise ye the Lord." Ps. xcv., "O come, let us sing," &c. |
| Ps. li. | [Verses of Ps. li., in the sentences.] |
| Ps. cxix., in three parts. | Psalms, in course. |
| Glory be, &c., at end of each. | Glory be, &c., at end of each. |
| [On Sat., Pss. lxv.—lxvii. lxviii.—lxx.] | [At Evensong, Ps. lxvii., as a canticle.] |
| | [Ps. lxx. ver. 1, as a versicle and response.] |
| Alleluia, i. e. "Praise ye the Lord." | ["Praise ye the Lord," *before* the Psalms.] |
| [No Lessons, Ps. cxix. being used as a meditation.] | The Lessons. |
| The Creed (aloud). | The Creed (aloud). |
| "Trisagion," and "Holy Trinity," &c. | Short Litany to the Holy Trinity. |
| Our Father, &c. | Our Father, &c. |
| Responsory (?) hymns, one resembling the Te Deum, one of the Incarnation. | [Two responsory hymns, or canticles; viz., Te Deum and Song of Zacharias, (of B.V.M. and Simeon, Evens.)] |
| Kyrie eleison, (forty times). | Versicles and responses. |
| | First collect. |
| Prayer for grace to live well, and for aid against all perils. | Second, for grace to live well; and, Third, for aid against all perils. |
| Second Nocturn. | |
| "O come," &c., and Pss. cxxi., cxxxiv. | |
| Hymns, &c., as p. 90. | |
| Praise to the Holy Trinity for redemption. | Anthem. |
| | Intercessions, or Litany. |
| | Thanksgiving, chiefly for redemption. |
| Dismissal benediction. | |
| Request for pardon; absolution. | Dismissal benediction. |
| Litany. | |

I have only to remark on this comparative table, that even the minuter coincidences, or such as may have the appearance of being forced, are for the most part historically traceable, with great probability, to the influence of the Greek Office. Thus the "O Lord open," &c. was borrowed by the framers of the Western Nocturns (otherwise called Matins) from the Greek Morning Office. How Ps. lxvii. found its way into our Evensong from the Greek Night-office will be shewn hereafter. The first verse of Ps. lxx. came to us, as a versicle from the same service, *viâ* the schemes of Benedict, Cassian, &c. The Creed and Lord's Prayer I have ventured to mark as said *aloud* in the primitive times; since if the account rendered above of their occurrence in the Greek Office be correct, they doubtless were so said originally; as they are in the East at the present day.

The "For Thine," &c. (which is repeated at the end of the Lord's Prayer as an exclamation) was worth noting, because the rest of the Western Church has it not, as neither had ours until the Revision. Our latest Revisers (1662) restored it both here, and in the Post-Communion, as an act of praise; but not where the Lord's Prayer occurs after the Creed, nor yet at the beginning of the Communion Office; both positions being more or less penitential. In what sense this doxology is to be accounted a part of the Lord's Prayer, seems uncertain. It is rejected by the best critics from the text of St. Matt. vi. Of its Apostolic antiquity, however, as an adjunct to the Lord's Prayer, the Office before us, and the Eastern Communion Offices, doubtless afford strong evidence. It must be added that the Orientals in this Office, and generally, vary from us, in inserting

in the doxology the mention of the Holy Trinity.
"For Thine is, &c. . . Father, Son, and Holy Ghost,
now and always, and for ever and ever." Yet the
very ancient Liturgy of St. Mark has it in the form
which we use; and so has that of Armenia, which is
some evidence of the practice of the East about the
year 300, when Armenia was evangelized from Cæsarea. We are thus led to the conclusion that ours
is, at least, an equally ancient form of the doxology.
The "praise to the Holy Trinity for redemption,"
marked as corresponding to our Thanksgiving, runs
thus : " My hope is the Father, my refuge is the Son,
my defence is the Holy Ghost; Holy Trinity, Glory
be to Thee." The Litany with which the Greek
scheme concludes, possesses extraordinary interest
for the English Church. For *her* ancient Litany,
forming the foundation of her present one, exhibits,
in a greater degree than that of the Roman or any
other branch of the Church, the features and the
*ipsissima verba* of the Litany before us; as will be
shewn in the proper place. I proceed to speak of
the remainder of the ancient Eastern Offices.

## SECTION VI.

"Thou makest the outgoings of the morning and evening to sing."

It has already been explained, that the Offices with
which the ancient Eastern Church in part anticipated
and in part commenced the day, formed in practice
one continuous Service. The testimony of Tertullian
in the second century is scarcely less explicit than that

of St. Basil in the fourth, to the effect that the nocturns were carried on until the dawn of the day; and that then, at the breaking forth of the light (which takes place far less gradually in the East than with us) the Morning Office commenced with a particular prayer or Psalm, accompanied with peculiarly solemn and devout prostration. The only difference is that Tertullian speaks of "the *prayer* with which we enter on the light of day;" St. Basil, of "offering up at dawn the *Psalm*[1] of confession, each one taking home to himself the penitential words." The two statements are perfectly reconciled, if we understand the Psalm (51st) to have been said as a solemn prayer; exactly as it is once a-year in the English Church at the present day.

The existing Eastern Offices[m], on careful examination of them, are found to correspond entirely with these representations. In the *midnight*-office proper, indeed, there neither is, nor perhaps ever was, any singing, in addition to the fixed Psalms, of others taken continuously and in considerable number. The remainder of the gradual Psalms (cxx.—cxxxiv.) may indeed have been used at the second nocturn; as I have above ventured to conjecture. But this does not answer, after all, to the idea of prolonged and diversified psalmody which St. Basil presents to us, and which has been characteristic of the East in all ages.

There was doubtless, therefore, in St. Basil's time a provision for the singing of Psalms *ad libitum*, as regards quantity, in the interval, longer or shorter, between the nocturns office proper and the break of

---

[1] This certainly means Ps. li.: vide Bingham, vol. iv. p. 406.
[m] Vide Neale, p. 915; Horolog., p. 90; Goar, p. 39, 40.

day. And a perfectly analogous provision exists at the present day; a considerable number of Psalms being sung at the commencement of the Morning Office, and previously to that part of it which is proper to the daybreak or dawn. One third fewer are sung in summer than in autumn; a double number in Lent. The number of Psalms sung on each day is settled by a rule, varying with the season This prolonged psalmody concluded, the *Fifty-first* Psalm follows, as in St. Basil's time, with only a brief hymn intervening; and *then* succeeds that burst of Canticles and "Lauds Psalms," properly so called (viz. the 148th—150th,) which marks the opening of the day, and sends up from all created being the incense both of the Old and of the New Creation.

It will be seen, by the way, from this statement, how it came to pass that the framers of the Western Ritual put the continuous psalmody in their *nocturns* Office. For in truth it was difficult to say whether this grand constellation of psalmody belonged most to the night or the early morning[n]. It was perhaps traditionally inseparable from the Western idea of Nocturns. Other features of the Eastern Morning Office they adopted in their own.

The following table exhibits, in merely a general outline, the structure of the Greek Morning Office on week-days:—

Invitatory (as in p. 66).
Pss. xx., xxi.
Hymns (for victory, &c.)
Trisagion, &c. "Our Father," &c.
Penitential Litany, beginning with Ps. li. ver. 1.

[n] "Last in the train of night,
If better thou belong not to the dawn."

Benediction. ("Bless, Father," &c.)  "Glory to," &c.
"O Lord, Thou shalt open, &c.; and my," &c., (Ps. li. ver. 15).
Six Psalms, iii., xxxviii., lxiii., lxxxviii., ciii., cxliii.,
(with Antiphon at end of each).
Twelve Prayers, (meanwhile).
Litany.
Hymn.
Psalms sung in course,
(varying in number from *one* (119th) to *twenty-eight*).
Short hymns.

### Psalm li.

Canticle. Odes. (Magnificat before ninth ode).
Lauds Psalms (cxlviii.—cl.)
Litany, &c.
Benediction.

It will be seen that there is first a prefatory portion, analogous to that of the nocturnal Office, and differing from it chiefly in this, that it carries out *at once* the exhortation of the invitatory by means of Pss. xx. and xxi.; just as the West does at Matins by means of Ps. xcv.: and that in lieu of Ps. li. itself, which in the Nocturns immediately follows the invitatory, there is a penitential litany, beginning with Ps. li. ver. 1. The fitness of both Pss. xx. and xxi. to carry out the idea of the Greek invitatory, ("O come let us worship our God and King," &c.,) is manifest; —the one Psalm ending with, "Save, Lord, and hear us, O King of heaven, when we call upon Thee;" the other beginning with, "The King shall rejoice in Thy strength, O Lord." There are also three hymns, still pursuing the idea of these Psalms, by desiring blessing and victory for kings and people; then follows the litany aforesaid.

My reason for considering this as properly no more than a sort of vestibule to the Office, though in many respects it has more the appearance of being a substantive portion of it, is, that there are indications, shortly after, of the Office itself not having yet, strictly speaking, begun. But of the great antiquity of this portion of the Eastern Morning Office, we seem to have irrefragable proof in the remarkable deference paid to it, as has been already pointed out, by the framers of the Western Ritual; their psalmodical schemes being so contrived in all cases as to include one or both of these Psalms (xx. and xxi.) in the Sunday Matins Office.

The invitatory and two Psalms, then, together with the litany, answering the purpose of a half-joyful, half-penitential preparation for the Morning Office, the Service proper commences with the people's desiring the priest to give a blessing: "In the name of the Lord, give the blessing, father." This, we can hardly doubt, is the source from whence the form so universally used in the Western Ritual, before the Lessons, took its rise: "Jube, domine, benedicere." The exact meaning of this has been much disputed. The question is, whether it is addressed by the reader to God or to the priest. In the Roman use it is said in the former sense in private recitation of the service; in the latter in public. The English use apparently knew of no such distinction°;—it was taken, as this passage in the Greek Office seems to prove it ought, for a request to the priest that he would desire a blessing. The "jube" is only a recognition, in a somewhat strong form, of the priestly *power* or commission to invoke a blessing. The formula is best rendered, "Sir, desire God to bless us." But it is

° Vide Leslie's Portif. Sarisb., p. 5, and note, p. lii. Maskell, Anc. Lit., p. 111. The Transl. Sar. Psalt., p. 11, gives two renderings; both, probably, incorrect: "O Lord, bid a blessing;" "O Lord, bid him bless."

singular, that in the East the priest acceded to the request by blessing God; in the West, by blessing himself and the congregation. This is somewhat characteristic. For it is much more usual in the Eastern forms than in the Western, for man to lose himself in the thought of God, and in the pure joy of jubilant praise. The prototype of both kinds is to be found, however, in the blessing of Abraham by Melchisedec, the most ancient priestly benediction on record, (Gen. xiv. 19, 20): "Blessed be Abram of the Most High God; and blessed be the Most High God, which hath delivered thine enemies into thine hands." The Greek form of benediction in this place is (as in the case of the invitatory) unvarying, as follows:—"Glory to the Holy, and Consubstantial, and Quickening, and Undivided Trinity; always, now, and ever, and to ages of ages. Amen." To which some person appointed responds, "Glory to God in the highest, and in earth peace, good will toward men," (thrice).

The manner in which the Three Persons of the Holy Trinity are signalized in the blessing will be remarked: "Holy" referring to the Father; "Consubstantial," to the Son; "Quickening," to the Holy Ghost. The Western benedictions before the Lessons, (varying however with the season,) follow this type; being almost always conceived in reference to the Holy Trinity. Thus the first Salisbury benediction for Sundays was:—

"The Father eternal bless us with His continual blessing: God, the Son of God, vouchsafe to bless and help us: may the grace of the Holy Spirit illuminate our hearts and bodies."

There is of course, after all, this striking difference between the use made in the East and in the West of this kind of benediction; that in the one case it precedes a series of Psalms, in the other of Lessons. But here comes in what has been before remarked, viz. that to the Orientals the saying of Psalms was a meditation upon Scripture as well as an act of praise. Mr. Palmer[p] has pointed out this mode of using the Psalms, as occurring in some Communion Offices both of the East and West. Thus the Apostolical Constitutions seem to enumerate Psalms among the *Lessons;* though they are there ordered to be *sung.* So too we find St. Augustine[q] considering the Psalm as a Lesson : " We have heard the Apostle, the Psalm, and the Gospel; all the Divine *Lessons* agree;" and again, " We have heard the first Lesson from the Apostle, then *sung* a Psalm; after this came the Lesson from the Gospel; these *three Lessons* we will discourse upon." These passages exhibit the Psalms as used at once as a song and as a meditation; exactly as I have supposed the six Psalms to have been in this Office, and the 119th in the Nocturns. And that these particular Psalms in the Greek Lauds were viewed in some degree in this light, we seem to have an indication in the rubric prefixed :—" Then we begin the six Psalms, *listening with all silence and penitence.*" It is on the whole highly probable that we have here the origin, both of the ante-lectional benedictions of the West, and, in a measure, of the position assigned to the Lections or Lessons themselves; viz. in close conjunction and interweaving with the Psalms.

The fixed Psalms for the Greek Morning Office are,

[p] Vol. ii. p. 57. "It appears therefore that the gradual" (i.e. Psalm after the Epistle) "was anciently looked upon as a Lesson from Scripture even when it was sung."

[q] Serm. 165, 176, de Verb. Apost.

iii., xxxviii., lxiii., lxxxviii., ciii., cxliii. But before they were begun, was said that verse of Psalm li., which became universal in the West as a versicle and response preceding the entire psalmody and service of the day: "O Lord, Thou shalt open my lips, and my mouth shall shew forth Thy praise," (twice; St. Benedict has it *thrice*.) That it was derived to the West from the East we have this reason for believing, that its use in the Eastern Office is accounted for, not *merely* by its suitableness, but by its being closely connected with the penitential introduction, founded upon Psalm li., which has just preceded. It is the link between the confession of unworthiness to praise, and the praise itself; and in this light accordingly it is to be viewed and used, where it occurs in our Western forms. It *presupposes a penitential preface*, public or private, to have preceded the whole Office. And thus the introduction of such a preface into our Offices, at the Revision of them, is once more seen to be in thorough harmony with the archetypal form, from which the whole West alike has derived its daily services.

The commentators on the Western versicle and response have devised, as usual, a variety of ingenious reasons for their being thus prefixed to the Office. Thus, e.g. Durandus conceives that it is "because at Compline, the night before, we shut our mouths, commending ourselves to God, whom therefore we now desire to open them[r]." "The Myrroure[s] admonishes its readers, more to the purpose, that this verse is only said at Matins, that is, the beginning of God's service, in token that the first opening of your lips should be to the praise of God, &c."

[r] Dur. Rat., V. iii. 9.   [s] Transl. Sar. Psalt., in loc.

Similar ingenuity has been exercised to account for the singular number being used in the versicle, "O Lord, Thou shalt open *my* lips[t];" and, which is still more remarkable, in the response, though made by the whole choir or people, "And *my* mouth shall," &c. It sets forth, we are told, "that the whole body of the faithful have but one body and one soul[u];" or it is "in token that ye begin your praising and prayer in the name of holy Church, which is one and not many. For though there be many members, they make but one body[x]." These are no doubt excellent *ex post facto* reflections. But the same reasons would have required that the singular number should be maintained throughout the Office. The true account of the matter is simply that the singular number was used in this place in the East; and that for two reasons,—partly because it is so in the 51st Psalm, which so pervades this part of the Office; partly because it was to be said by some *one* person appointed thereto, as appears by the rubric[y]: "Then we begin the six Psalms, listening with all silence and penitence; and the appointed brother or hegumen saith, 'Glory to God,' &c. 'O Lord, open Thou my lips, and my mouth shall shew forth Thy praise.'" It should be added that the plural adaptation, introduced at our Revision, has a warrant in the Saturday nocturn hymn of the Greek Church: "O uncreated nature, Maker of all, open Thou our lips, that we may shew forth Thy praise," &c.

As to the Hexapsalmus, or set of six Psalms, which

---

[t] "Domine, labia mea aperies. R. Et os meum annunciabit laudem tuam."

[u] Durand., ibid.      [x] Myrroure, ibid.

[y] So Neale, p. 916. The Horologium (ed. 1738) does not specify by whom the versicle is said.

follows this exordium, it is in various ways remarkable for the influence it has exercised on the structure and contents of the Western Offices. The *number* of the Psalms first calls for our attention. It was most religiously adopted by Benedict in the scheme of psalmody which he drew up for the monastic devotions of the West. Borrowing, as has been already remarked, the "two Nocturns" of the Eastern nocturnal Office, he placed *six* Psalms in each; thus making up at the same time the famous number of *twelve* Psalms, which was a ruling provision in all Western nocturnal (or matutinal) psalmody. The English and Roman uses, while resolving the two Nocturns into one (on ordinary days), retained the same number of twice six, or twelve Psalms. This, however, may rather have been in deference to the twelve Psalms of the Egyptian monastic use; of which hereafter. It is remarkable, that during the singing of the three last of the six Psalms in the Greek Office, *twelve* prayers are at the present day appointed to be said by the priest; while in the Egyptian monastic scheme, as described by Cassian[z], each of the twelve Psalms was followed by a prayer said by him who led the Psalms;—indications these of a widely spread regard for the number twelve in the East, and not in Egypt only, in connection with the nocturnal psalmody.

The number of six Psalms[a] was also retained uni-

[z] Instit., ii. 8.

[a] The Sunday Lauds Psalms in the West were 93, 100, 63, 67, Benedicite, (Song of the Three Children), and 148—150, as one. The week-day (e.g. Monday's), 51; then 5, 63, Song of Isaiah, 148, 149, 150. The Benedictine, on Sundays, 67, 51, 118, 63, Benedicite, 148—150. On week-days, 67, (not antiphoned); then 51, three varying a canticle, 148—150.

versally in the Western Morning Office or Lauds; though the ritualists will have it that the number is *five*. On Sundays, the Pss. cxlviii.—cl. are to be reckoned, as they are always *called, one;* no doubt because they formed one group, under the name of αἶνοι, or Lauds, at the close of the Eastern Office. If these, on week-days, be accounted as *three*, the number of Psalms is still six; the 51st being viewed, as in the Greek Office, as preparatory. The canticle, it is agreed, in all cases counts as one.

The grounds for the selection of the particular Psalms in the Greek Office are not difficult to discern. Two of them, iii. and lxiii., are, by their contents, morning Psalms; and that as such they were appointed, appears from the choice made of a verse to be repeated at the end of each : " I laid me down and rose up again," &c., and, " with my spirit within me will I seek Thee early," &c. These accordingly passed also into the Western Offices as early Psalms. The 3rd, as we have seen, prefaces, in the scheme of Benedict, the nocturnal psalmody of each day; while in the English and Roman uses it is included in the twelve Psalms of the first Nocturn on Sunday. The 63rd again, one of those mentioned by St. Basil, is universally made a Lauds Psalm in the West; viz. on Sunday in the Benedictine, and every day in the other uses. Of the other four Eastern Psalms, one, the 103rd, is of thanksgiving character, and so allies itself with the two first mentioned; while three are profoundly penitential,—xxxviii., lxxxviii., and cxliii. Thus in these six Psalms there is a union, in equal parts, of thanksgiving and penitence; which in fact is the characteristic of this Morning Office as a whole. The early Morning Office, or " Lauds" of the Western

Church, has always preserved this same character; beginning on week-days (and on Sundays also in the Benedictine scheme) with the great penitential Psalm, the 51st; the rest of the psalmody being, except on Sundays, in about equal proportions, jubilant and penitential [b], just as it is in the Greek Office.

I must not omit to observe, that we seem to have the earliest and simplest form of the *antiphon*, in the repetition at the end of each of these six Psalms of some verse or other of the Psalm itself. Grancolas, indeed [c], considers the Western antiphon to have originated with the short prayers said by the Egyptian monks after each Psalm. And it is not improbable that this usage may have influenced the form of the more freely constructed antiphons, taken from other parts of Scripture than the Psalms, or composed on purpose, and often taking the form of a short hymn [d]. But in its proper nature the antiphon would seem to be some part of the Psalm itself, so selected as to express, as far as may be, the leading character, or some salient feature of it. This is exactly the nature of the Greek antiphons before us, as may be seen in the specimen given above, in the case of Pss. iii. and lxiii. The antiphon of these two Psalms is repeated twice, probably on account of their pecu-

---

[b] In Bened. we have 67 and 51, one of each kind, fixed; and in the successive days of the week, 5, 57, 65, 90, 92, ½ song of Moses, (to v. 22,) of one kind; and 36, 43, 64, 88, 76, 143, of the other. This is most probably the rationale of dividing the song; the other half forms the Saturday canticle. In the Roman and English we have 67 (fixed), and on successive days, 5, 65, 90, 92, jubilant; and 51 and 63 (both fixed), 43, 143, penitential; the proportions being less equal than in Bened.

[c] Histoire du Breviaire, tom. i. p. 201. And see Neale.

[d] The English (Salisbury) Use had a somewhat peculiar, and not very commendable, *metrical* antiphon, for the Sundays in the Trinity half of the year.

liarly matutinal character. Of Pss. xxxviii. and ciii., the last verse is adopted; of Pss. lxxxviii. and cxliii., the first verse[e]. Thus have we, in the brief compass of these six Psalms, specimens of the leading varieties of antiphons in after-times in the West; the most usual, and apparently the most legitimate being, 1, the last verse; 2, the first verse; 3, a verse from the body of the Psalm. Very often in the West the last verse is adopted, (apparently,) merely because it is such, and not from its fitness to express the mind of the Psalm. And when, as was the case in the principal services of psalmody, (the Nocturns or Matins and the lesser hours,) several Psalms which happened to come in succession were followed by a single antiphon, it is plain that the alleged and legitimate purpose of the antiphon was frustrated.

It follows from hence that the rejection of the antiphons by the English Church in the 16th century, (in which she was partly followed by the French in the 18th, 1726—1791,) was, as regards the ordinary psalmody, by no means the loss that it is often represented to have been, if any at all. The antiphons had for the most part, on Sundays especially, when there was but *one* antiphon to every *four* Psalms, ceased altogether to discharge the office for which they were originally introduced. And to have provided each Psalm with a strictly appropriate antiphon (setting aside the complexity of the system) would, however plausible it may sound, be in a great many instances absolutely impossible; the contents of

---

[e] St. Benedict's antiphons for Pss. 63, 88, 103, 143, are nearly the same, and quite in the same spirit, as the Greek ones. Ps. 88 also retains its place as a morning Psalm in Brev. Par.s. (Sat. Prime). On the removal of antiphons in the reformed Parisian and other French Breviaries, see *Ecclesiastic*, Jan. 1847 and 1854.

many Psalms being so varied. Nor, even if possible, would it be desirable. The freedom, fulness, and infinite variety of play, of which the Psalms are capable, and which they inevitably assume in the mind of the fairly informed member of the Church,—all this is surely most undesirably straitened and cramped by the imposition, in the shape of an antiphon, of one fixed and invariable sense.

The Western Church has, however, in another respect, developed with great beauty and power the simple antiphon idea of the East. Of the Psalms before us, *two* more especially are so antiphoned as to bring out their application to the morning hour; the rest, though expressive of the penitential aspect of the returning daylight, have more of the nature of a choral repetition or burden, consisting of the first or last verse. Following this hint, then, the Western Church has devised a vast variety of antiphons, according to the season or day; by means of which the key-note of the season, &c., was sounded, or intended to be so, at intervals during the psalmody. This was unquestionably a powerful instrument for imparting distinctness of expression to the Psalms. It reminded the worshipper, from time to time, what colour his devotions might fitly derive from the associations of particular seasons; it taught him what kind of instruction to be then more especially on the watch for in the Psalms. It is at such times that the absence of antiphons is felt to be a loss. Whether they could, consistently with congregational use of the Psalms, have been retained in our Offices at some special seasons, I do not undertake to determine. But were any of the methods of service, which were laid aside at our Revision, to be selected for restoration, I conceive that the antiphons, with this restricted application to special seasons and to Festivals, would possess a weighty claim upon the Church's consideration. A single antiphon, fixed for the season, and said before and after the entire psalmody of each day, would involve comparatively little complexity, and would greatly help to sustain the character of such seasons as Christmas, Lent, and Easter: during the last of which indeed, such a single antiphon was used.

It would carry us too far from our proper subject, were I to attempt to give the reader a detailed conception of the remainder of the existing Greek Office, which, after the recitation of the six Psalms, becomes exceedingly complicated. I shall only observe, therefore, upon the singing of the Psalms in course, which follows soon after, that the number of Psalms used is even greater than in the West; about fourteen on an average, at ordinary times, and sometimes as many as twenty-six at special seasons: the Psalter being generally sung through once, and sometimes twice, in the week [f]. The morning psalmody for each day falls under two great divisions, called *Cathismata*, (a third is added at special seasons); after each one of which three short hymns (or stanzas, rather) are sung, together with a "Glory," and a single line or verse from the preceding set of Psalms [g]. Each of these large divisions, again, is subdivided into *three*, (called *staseis*,) with the "Glory" alone at the end of each. Now here we seem to have the exact prototype of the

---

[f] The West preserved an almost solitary specimen of this multitudinous psalmody, in the eighteen Sunday Psalms of the Roman and English Matins; the Church of Milan had on occasion as many as sixteen; viz. on alternate Mondays: vide Bona, p. 899. The Church of Tours anciently had from fourteen to thirty Psalms at Matins in the winter season.

[g] Neale, p. 918. Paracletice in loc.

Western mode of treating the continuous psalmody, on Sundays and Festivals more especially; just as the hexapsalmus furnished the type of the manner of antiphoning single Psalms. For both the Roman and English uses [h] divide the Sunday or Festival psalmody into *three* large portions (called Nocturns); at the end of each of which is, 1, a "Glory[i];" 2, an antiphon, generally a single verse from the preceding set of Psalms; 3, a short hymn, consisting of a verse and response. Moreover, the first Nocturn on Sundays is subdivided into *three* sections, having in the English use the "Glory" at the end of each; not, as in the Roman, at the end of each *Psalm*. Both uses add an antiphon at the end of the subdivisions. On weekdays, when there is but one Nocturn, or large portion of Psalms, sung, its termination is of the same kind as that of each Sunday Nocturn. The Eastern stanzas are adapted by their contents to a different topic on each day of the week; e.g. on Sundays the Resurrection, on Wednesdays and Fridays the Cross, &c.; a refinement which the West has not followed; but its verses and responses vary with the season instead.

The canticles, which follow, (only preceded by Ps. li.,) are nearly the same as were used in the West: the songs, viz., of Moses, (Exod. xv., Deut. xxxii.), of Hannah, Habakkuk, and Isaiah, (ch. xxvi.), the prayer of Jonah, and half the Benedicite, on the successive days of the week; besides the fixed Magnificat and Benedictus, reckoned as one. The West has substituted the song of Hezekiah for Jonah's

[h] For specimens of the Western Psalm and lection system, see Tr. Sar. Psalt.; Leslie's Portifor. Sar.; Tract. 75; Bennett's Principles of the Prayer-book, Serm. 4; Procter's Rationale, p. 165.

[i] In the Spanish Church the "Glory" *followed* the responsory, &c., as it did in the East. IV. Concil. Tolet., c. xvi.; Bingh., vol. iv. p. 424.

prayer, and changed the appropriation of the other canticles to the several days. The appearance of the Magnificat among the *morning* canticles will be thought singular. But it is remarkable that the earliest trace we have of it in the West is in the *Lauds* Office of the Church of Arles, where it was ordered to be used by a canon of Cæsarius[j], circ. 506, probably after the model of the East, introduced by Cassian a century before. In the Armenian Church, however, it was used at Compline[k], the last *evening* service, *as well as* at Lauds; and it was thus, perhaps, that it found its way into the Western Vespers.

The canticles are accompanied by a certain series of hymns, called odes, generally nine in number, separated into three groups by a short litany after the third and sixth; but only three in the period of the year which precedes Easter. I mention this here, because there is considerable appearance of the *Lection or Lesson system* of the West, as regards Festivals more especially, having originated in a measure with this part of the Greek Office. These odes were, it appears, *called* lections by the Greek monks of the order of St. Basil settled near Tusculum, a few miles from Rome[l]; probably because the account, or *legend*, of any saint or martyr commemorated was read after the sixth ode; though indeed the odes themselves were often recitative or narrative. Now it is at least remarkable that the Western classification of Festivals was into feasts of *nine* or of *three lections*, the nine being also divided, with the Psalms which they ac-

[j] Mabillon, Curs. Gal., p. 406.
[k] Bona, p. 909. It is not used in Lent at Milan.
[l] Bona, p. 906. "Sequuntur deinde *lectiones* currentis diei, quas vocant canones, et constant novem lectionibus; quælibet autem lectio vocatur ode."

companied, into *three* groups, and the number of three lections being more peculiarly the festival usage of a particular season[m], viz. Easter. Again, before the *ninth* (or the third, if there were but three) of the Eastern odes, or lections, the Magnificat was said, and *after* it a hymn closely resembling, as far as it goes, the Te Deum[n]: "For Thee all the powers of the heavens praise; and to Thee, &c. Holy is the Lord our God; Holy, &c. Our God reigneth over all." Now the Te Deum was, as a general rule, the response[o] to the *ninth* lection (or to the third, if there were but three) on Sundays and Festivals in the West.

There are other points which complete the identification of the festival lection system of the West with the "odes" of the East. The lections or readings of the former are really subordinate, just as in the East, to the musical part of the scheme. For while the responsories, with their versicles, sung at the end of each lection, are fixed, the lection (on Sundays at least) might vary[p] in length, and *did* vary in different editions of the Offices. In the English use the series of *responses* was called a *historia;* and by this *historia*, —not by the lections, which were quite subordinate,— was the character of the week or day determined[q].

[m] The Eastern idea herein was to diminish the praise of a mournful season; the Western, to reduce the labour of a festal one.

[n] Compare Nocturns Office, supra, p. 66. And see note.

[o] The English use substituted it for the *repetition* of the ninth response; the Roman for the response itself. The Bened. had twelve lessons on Sundays and great festivals, with the Te Deum as the *invariable* response.

[p] Comp. Sar. rubric in some MSS., "Then let the clerk, (*clericus,*) *when enough at his discretion* has been read," &c. Arl. MS. Transl. Sar. Psalt., p. 48.

[q] e.g. Sar. Brev. Pica de Dom. i. Adv.: "Litera dom. A. Tertia Decemb. *tota cantetur historia* aspiciens;" i.e. "Let the whole of the nine lection responses set down for 1 S. in Advent, (the first of which

In short, when we examine the Western lection system, we find that it too was in reality a series of nine or three "odes" or singings, with a certain accompaniment of lections or reading. And these "lections," on saints' days, were not from Scripture at all. Those connected with the first *six* responsories were the life or record of the saint commemorated, (just as the legends in the Greek Office are connected with the *sixth* ode,) while the remaining three were parts of a homily on the Gospel for the day. The characteristic difference between the East and West in the matter was this; that in the West the *Psalms* were interwoven with the lection or ode system, each group in the scheme consisting of three Psalms and three odes, with their lections; and that the lections on ordinary days, and partly on Sundays, were from holy Scripture. But these peculiarities, too, were probably of Eastern importation. There is a well-known canon of the Council of Laodicea (held circ. 360), which enjoins that "the Psalms should not be sung uninterruptedly; but that after each Psalm (or singing[r], rather) there should be *reading*." It is difficult, and even impossible, to reconcile this with the ancient practice of the East generally, there being, I believe, no other trace in *Eastern* antiquity of this alternation of Psalms[s] with Scripture lessons. It has indeed

---

began with the word *aspiciens*,) be sung through." These are the famous "rules called the Pie." Vid. Procter's Rationale, Leslie's Portiforium, &c.

[r] διὰ μέσου καθ' ἕκαστον ψαλμόν. That the reading was meant to come, not between each Psalm, but each set of Psalms, is probable, because the design of the canon was to relieve the *tediousness* of the prolonged psalmody.

[s] St. Augustine (ap. Bingham, vol. iv. p. 423) is only speaking of the one Psalm used at the Communion Service.

been explained[t] of the division of the psalmody into *Cathismata*, as above, by means of a hymn sung at the end of each, which might *perhaps* be called "reading." But certainly, of *Scripture* being read at those pauses we have no Eastern example. Now though this particular canon does not prescribe of what kind the reading should be, the 59th of the same Council[u] forbids any other books than the Scriptures to be read in the church. It seems necessary, therefore, to suppose that this canon never came into force in the East beyond the exarchate of Ephesus, in which Laodicea was situated; and Mr. Palmer[x] has shewn that other provisions of this Laodicean Council bore reference to that district alone. The Church of Lyons, however, which the same writer proves to have derived its ritual from Ephesus, had by the year 499, and probably much earlier, adopted a scheme of lections in full accordance with these two Laodicean canons. For in an extant account[y] of the night-service preceding a Synod held in that year at Lyons, against the Arians, we find that there was (no doubt after the first set of Psalms[z]) a lesson from Moses, then Psalms sung, then a lesson from the prophets, then Psalms again, then a gospel; after which no more Psalms, but an epistle at some later period, probably in the Communion Office. Here then seems to be the earliest recorded instance of the alternation of Psalms with Scripture. It seems, too, that *three* sets of Psalms were sung, each followed by a lection,

[t] Balsamon, ap. Neale, p. 855.   [u] Mabillon, Curs. Gal., p. 400.
[x] Diss. Prim. Lit., sect. v.   [y] Mabillon, Curs. Gal., p. 399.
[z] Mabillon, without reason, supposes the lesson to have come first. But Grancolas (Hist. Brev., i. p. 55.) says: "Dans le premier (Nocturne) on disoit des Pseaumes, et on lisoit de Moïse," &c. But he incorrectly places a fourth set of Psalms before the epistle.

(which may or may not have been in three parts, and accompanied by responses). Now this is exactly what would result from adopting, together with the general Eastern custom of dividing the psalmody of the day into three *staseis* or parts, the Laodicean peculiarity of inserting Lessons of Scripture at the intervals. The Roman and English use, again, would result from combining the Lyonnese model with the Eastern ode scheme. I do not mean that it was necessarily through these channels (scil. the Ephesine and Gallican rituals) that the Western Psalm and lection system was perfected.; but in some such way it probably did originate. And hence descended to the English Church of the present day her still compound, though no longer involved system of Psalms, Lessons, and responsive canticles, woven together into one complex act of praise and meditation; an act that meditates still as it praises, and as it meditates, adores.

The *Ainoi*, or three last Psalms of the Psalter, celebrating (like the Benedicite, framed upon them) the *praises* of God in the name of all creation, are in a manner the crowning feature of the Eastern Morning Office. These Psalms are an invariable feature in the Western Lauds Office, which indeed derives its name from them; and they enjoy the peculiar distinction of being reckoned as one Psalm[a], the "Laudate Dominum de cœlis." The rest of the Greek Office, on ordinary days, consists of various short hymns, doxologies, and supplications. Of the various enrichments and amplifications which it receives on Sundays and Festivals, I have, for the most part, forborne to speak.

* So in the East the characteristic Psalms, cxli., cxlii., sung at Vespers, are reckoned as one piece, the Κύριε ἐκέκραξα.

The most important, to us, of these additions, is perhaps the "Morning Gospel," as it was called; *not* the same as afterwards followed at the Holy Communion. It was hence, probably, that on Sundays and Festivals in the West the Gospel[b] for the day, or the beginning of it, was read at Matins, with three lections out of a homily upon it.

Such then is the great Morning Office of the East; perhaps the most magnificent and most finely-conceived Office of ordinary worship which the Church has ever possessed. Owing to the embodiment in it (instead of in the Nocturns, as in the West) of the continuous psalmody, and, in a rudimentary form, of the lection system also,—as well as of the fixed and characteristic hexapsalmus, canticles, and lauds,—it exhibits a fulness and variety of contents to which the West at least can shew nothing comparable. It was doubtless well, and apparently even more true to the primitive ideal, than the present Eastern arrangement, to incorporate the mass of the psalmody with the Nocturns, as the Western framers did; for such seems to have been, even in St. Basil's time, the theory of the Offices. But the majestic ideal of the Eastern Daybreak Office was by that removal seriously marred and impaired. As it now stands, and probably has stood from an early period, it might well furnish the theme of a great oratorio. We have seen how, (p. 111) commencing with a brief prelude of praise, it presently subsides into the notes of profoundest penitential preparation. In the hexapsalmus the two elements of praise and penitence strive in finely-adjusted proportions for the mastery; and the same conflict is dis-

[b] In Reg. S. Bened. the entire Gospel was read, and four lections from a homily upon it.

cernible still, by the constitution of the Psalter itself, in the tide of continuous psalmody which follows. In the 51st Psalm—the penitential burst of confession prompted by the breaking forth of dawn—the sorrowful element obtains for a brief space the ascendancy; but it is immediately succeeded by the "songs" and "lauds," in which God's six days' work, once made and marred, is acknowledged as created anew by the Resurrection of Christ at the early morning hour: and thus the voice of a world redeemed to God rises at last in one chorus of unwavering and triumphant jubilation.

In endeavouring to form a judgment of the degree of antiquity which this Office, after deducting from it the confessedly later hymnal developments, can claim, we may observe, first, that with one or two exceptions, it is wanting in those close affinities with the Jewish Services which seem to stamp a primitive character on the *Nocturnal* Office in its actually existing form. On this account, I conceive that Office to be the oldest organized daily service in the world; a view which, if correct, greatly heightens the interest of those resemblances which we have detected between it and the existing English Daily Office;—only we must bear in mind that it was followed by a large addition of psalmody, to which we have nothing parallel.

But the Greek Morning Office also bears positive marks, besides this negative one, of a somewhat later origination. The precise and studied arrangements of the *six* Psalms; of the *twelve* prayers accompanying them; of the *two* sets of *threefold* groups of Psalms sung in course; of the *nine* canticles, and the *nine* odes framed with reference to them[c]; all have a

---

[c] "To a certain degree the character of the Canticles," respectively, "is impressed on all the Odes." Neale, p. 834, note.

highly artificial appearance. The *germ*, indeed, of some of these numerical dispositions may be discerned in the Jewish services: it is the full elaboration of them that discriminates this office from the nocturnal; which itself had the characteristically Jewish numbers of *twelve* and *forty* Kyrie eleisons[d]. The selection of the number six seems to have been suggested by that of the days employed in the Creation; to which event the Office in various other ways refers. For not only are the Benedicite and the three Lauds Psalms evidently appointed as summing up the praise of all created things, but the entire service varies with *the day of the week*, whereas the Nocturn Office is fixed except as to Saturday and Sunday. Besides which, the Psalms said in course, the hymns sung between the larger divisions of them, and the canticle, all change with the day, in a weekly cycle; as the single selected Psalm of the Jewish Temple Office, and perhaps other features of it, did. The twelve prayers might refer to the twelve hours of the day, as the ritualists tell us the twelve Eastern Kyries and the twelve Western Psalms do[e]. The nine canticles, and again the nine odes, divided into three groups of three, probably symbolised the Holy Trinity[f], or the nine orders of angels[g]. Now all this, though it may very well have arisen in extremely early times, (St. Basil perhaps alludes to the antiphons of the hexapsalmus,) yet bespeaks the second rather than the first age,— the secondary than the primary stage of formation,—of the Church's ritual. We seem to detect in it the first

---

[d] Supr., p. 66.
[e] Neale, p. 895, b; Durand., v. 3, 27.
[f] So Zonaras, ap. Neale, p. 833.
[g] Vide Bp. Andrewes' Devotions, 2nd Day, ad fin.; Neale, p. 469.

stirrings of a more ambitious and more systematizing spirit of development than that of apostolic days, when the constituents of the Temple or Synagogue Services sufficed, with comparatively little adaptation to Christian ideas, for the purposes of ordinary worship. We may perhaps discern the more organized Morning Office in the process of formation in the days of Tertullian (circ. 200) : for he speaks with commendation of those persons or congregations who shewed more than the ordinary diligence and zeal in their prayers,—evidently, from the context, Church prayers,—in that they wound them up with the " Hallelujah," or with Psalms of that kind ; i.e. jubilant Psalms, such as the Lauds, singing them responsively [h].

## SECTION VII.

*"It shall come to pass, that at evening-time it shall be light."*

THE simpler Evening or Vespers Office of the East may be dismissed with a less extended notice. Yet in one respect it possesses surpassing interest, viz. as the only one of the Eastern Daily Offices which, in its ordinary form, stands in an avowed relation to the Eucharist. Its contents are as follows :—

EASTERN VESPERS.

Introduction, as far as to The Invitatory, inclusive. } v. p. 65, 66.

---

[h] De Oratione, c. 27, ed. Routh. Similar views as to the comparative date of this Office will be found in Note E, extracted from " Palmer's Dissertations on the Eastern Communion."

Psalm civ. (The "Prefatory Psalm.")
Seven Prayers (meanwhile) "of the lighting of lamps."
"Glory," &c. Alleluia, (twice).
Litany.
Psalms (usually about seven) in course, in three parts.
"Glory," at end of each part.
Pss. cxli., cxlii., as one,
with Ps. cxxx. interwoven.
Ps. cxvii. ; Ps. cxxii. (set as a hymn).
"Prayer of Entrance," (viz. of the Gospels).
The "Entrance." "Wisdom: Stand up."
Evening Hymn to Christ as "Light."
The Prokeimenon (i.e. summary of the Epistle).
Intercession.
Litany and Prayers, for protection, &c.
Prayer of bowing down the head.
"Glory be, &c."
Canticle, "Nunc Dimittis."
Trisagion, "Holy Trinity," &c.
Our Father.
Thanksgiving for redemption (vide Nocturns, supr. p. 66).
Dismissal.

It will be seen that this Service reflects in miniature the features of the conjoint Nocturns and Morning Office, (pp. 65 and 111) only with such characteristic variations as serve to adapt it to the evening idea. The full penitential introduction and Invitatory, followed by a selected Psalm (civ.) of some length, and a second group of fixed Psalms further on, one of which (cxxiii., "To Thee lift I up mine eyes,") is a "song of degrees,"—all remind us of the Nocturns scheme. As for the continuous psalmody, St. Basil would probably have reckoned it a Nocturns feature; the subsequent ages a matutinal one. But the parallel, on the whole, lies rather between the Vespers and the Morning Office; the Invitatory being here *at once* followed by a Psalm of praise, (as there by Pss.

xx., xxi.;) during which, as during the hexapsalmus, is said a fixed number of prayers (seven), having reference to the *light*, and to the succession of night and day. Here too the number of fixed Psalms in one group (four or five) comes nearer to that of the Morning Office; for in the nocturns there were but two fixed Psalms in a group. But the capital feature of the resemblance lies in this: that as the Morning Office leads up through a finely-varied series of plaintive and jubilant psalmody to the *natural* dawn, considered as the memorial of the Creation and of Christ's Resurrection; so does the Evening Office, through a similar progression, to the bringing in of *artificial* light at the close of day; — the type and the remembrancer of the coming in of the True Light, "not of this world[1]," in the world's eventide, and of His giving Himself, also at the evening hour, for its salvation. Hence, after the chequered rise and fall of praise and penitence has subsided into the deeply penitential Psalm cxxx., "Out of the deep,"— as it did into Psalm li. in the Morning Office,—it culminates once more in the Psalm of praise of all nations (cxvii.), and in a hymn consisting of the words of Psalm cxxiii., "Unto Thee lift I up mine eyes," expressive of the profoundest expectation. Then with a suitable prayer takes place the "entrance" (a feature in the Eastern Communion Offices) as of the Gospels, considered as enshrining Christ Himself. Then after an exhortation to the acknowledgment and hearing of Him as present, ("Wisdom: Stand up,") bursts forth the triumphant "Hymn of the Evening Light,"—the Lauds of eventide,—at once giving thanks for the gift

---

[1] St. John viii. 23. Comp. i. 4, 5, 9.

of artificial light, and praising the True "Light that shineth in darkness," "in Whom is life, and the life is the Light of men."

"Joyful Light of the holy glory of the immortal Father, the heavenly, the holy, the blessed, JESU CHRIST; we, having come to the setting of the sun, and beholding the evening light, praise[k] God, Father, Son, and Holy Ghost. It is meet at all times that Thou shouldst be hymned with auspicious voices, Son of God, Giver of life; wherefore the world glorifieth Thee."

Then is read the *prokeimenon*, or summary of the Epistle. A litany of intercession follows, and a prayer "of bowing down the head," like those which in the East follow eucharistic consecration. Finally, the Nunc Dimittis, the Lord's Prayer, thanksgiving for redemption by Christ, and dismissal benediction.

The points in which the Western Evening Office (or Vespers) has taken the Eastern as its model, are for the most part sufficiently obvious. There is the same acknowledgment of this as being the second great Office in point of importance in the twenty-four hours[l], answering to the conjoint Nocturns and Lauds. Like Nocturns, it has a fixed number of Psalms, said continuously, and in about the Eastern proportion to those of Nocturns. Like Lauds, again, it has a canticle, collect, and *preces*. The number of Psalms read continuously was in general *five;* in St. Benedict's scheme, *four*. This difference probably resulted from reckoning or not reckoning the fifth Psalm (cxxiii.) in the Eastern scheme; it being, in fact, sung as a hymn in two parts[m]: or from counting Pss. cxli., cxlii.,

---

[k] Horolog., ὑμνοῦμεν: but St. Basil, αἰνοῦμεν.

[l] Durandus, in loc.

[m] Durandus (in Adv. vi. 2, 15) suggests various mystic reasons for the distinction between the monastic and the secular practice in this matter.

as two or as one. The memory of the selected Psalms in the Greek Office also survived in different ways in the Latin Church. Thus the verse for the sake of which Ps. cxli. was evidently chosen, ("Let my prayer be set forth as incense, &c. . . . an evening sacrifice,") furnishes the West with a verse and response at Vespers[n] nearly all the year round, at which incense[o] was used, as in the East. Again, the Roman and the English uses have adopted each a Psalm from this Office into their Lauds as an occasional feature, (the English into *Compline* also,) viz. cxxx. and cxxiii.

But above all, the strongly characteristic *prokeimenon* was preserved in the West, in the singular feature called the "Capitulum." There can, I conceive, be no doubt that such is the account to be given of the "short chapter," (as it is sometimes rather incorrectly called,) which peculiarly characterized the Western Vespers, though it was also introduced in the Lauds and other "hours." It is evidently not a mere text selected at random. In its proper nature it is nothing else than the *heading*, or commencement, by way of a *summary*[p], of the *Epistle* for the day. Accordingly, on the eve and in the evening of all the more notable Sundays and Festivals, it consisted of the first few lines of the Epistle. For ordinary Sundays and weekdays a fixed Capitulum was used. Now this is closely parallel to the Eastern usage. On Sundays and Festivals the *prokeimenon* (said at *Lauds*, however,) was

[n] Brev. Rom. Sar. ad Vesp. Dom. et Fer.
[o] Durand. in Vesp., sect. 3; Goar, p. 3.
[p] Bona: "The short reading from Scripture called by some *collectio*, *lectiuncula*, or *versiculus*, by St. Benedict *lectio*, is universally known as the *Capitulum*. The reason of the name is that the capitula are generally brief *summaries* of the Epistles in the Communion Office. The diminutive form refers to its brevity." Psalmod. xvi. 16.

the same "summary" as was prefixed to the Epistle at the Communion. On week-days the Vespers *prokeimenon* (there was none at Lauds) was a fixed, or rather arbitrary one, varying only with the days of the week. The West, therefore, carried out in the Vespers Office itself, just as the East did at Lauds, the idea of which the *prokeimenon* contained the germ; viz. that of projecting, so to speak, the mind of the current eucharistic Epistle upon the preceding ordinary Offices.

It may be objected that the two things are different: that the Eastern feature is a verse from the Psalms, with another responding to it; the Western, a portion of apostolic Scripture. But we have already seen that the lection system of the Western Nocturns is apparently to be identified with, and derived from, the Eastern Odes. And just so it is here. The parallel is complete. The Capitulum was, after all, but a single feature in connection with a complex piece of singing. In England it was followed (when it was a genuine Capitulum from the Epistle) by a responsory, exactly as the Nocturn lections were; and, in all uses, by a hymn, a verse and response, (generally one based upon Psalm cxli., "Let my evening prayer ascend," &c.) It results, therefore, that the Western Capitulum was properly, like the Eastern *prokeimenon*, an expedient for forecasting the Epistle for the Sunday or the Festival, by introducing a summary of it into the previous ordinary Service: which was in one case a suitable musical composition, generally from the Psalms; in the other, the first few lines of the Epistle, followed by such a composition.

It may be said, however[q], that if any part of the

---

[q] So Palmer, Orig. Lit., II. iv. 4; Neale. p. 406.

Western ritual corresponds with or represents the *prokeimenon*, it is the *gradual*; for this is a verse from the Psalms adapted to the Epistle, only following instead of preceding it: and Mr. Palmer thinks it may have been removed thither from its original position, before the Epistle. Nor is it at all improbable that the gradual may have been suggested by the *prokeimenon*, with which it has so much in common. But it lacks, after all, the peculiar characteristic of the latter; which is its serving as a link between the eucharistic and the preceding ordinary Office. The gradual was never so used; the Capitulum was: with its verse and response, it discharged the precise function of the *prokeimenon*.

It does not seem difficult to discern how it was that the *Epistle* more particularly came to be thus projected upon the ordinary weekly Offices of the Church, probably even in primitive times. The Epistles were from the first, and by the express tenor of some of them, designed to be recited in the churches[r]. And they would in the first instance be read, not exactly as Scripture, but as the living voice of apostolic authority and teaching. It is probable that as such they obtained a place in the Communion Office at an earlier period than the Gospels did; which may be the reason of the Epistle's universally taking the precedence. In the very earliest times, then, when as yet there were no Gospels to read, or the custom of reading them had not come in, the Epistle would be the only kind of "Scripture of the New Testament" which the Eucharistic Office had to lend to the ordinary Services. And the fact of our finding the Epistle, and nothing else, *constantly* com-

[r] Col. iv. 16; 1 Thess. v. 27.

memorated, and that too in the evening hour, which was primitively associated with the Eucharist, seems to furnish a strong presumption in behalf of the primitive date of the existing Eastern Vespers[a].

The English Church at the Revision nominally and in form rejected the *Capitulum* altogether;—a serious loss, indeed, had not the principle of it been essentially retained, and in one respect largely developed. First, as to the ordinary Capitulum. The principle of it clearly was, that at evening the apostolic teaching by means of the Epistles should be in some way brought before the mind; and so a touching memory preserved, not of that only, but of the original evening Institution, and time of celebration, of the Eucharist. And surely never was a traditional habit, justly dear to the Church, more faithfully developed, than when the single and almost unvarying verse from a single Epistle was expanded into the reading at large in the Evening Office, thrice in the year, of the whole body of the apostolic Epistles.

It is perhaps to be regretted that the Capitulum, in its Sunday and Festival aspect, was not retained in the Revision of our Offices. Its value, as impressing on the eve, by anticipation, the mind of the next day's Epistle, is considerable; nor does it appear but that

[a] It is an interesting circumstance, that the fixed weekly Capitulum at Vespers in the English Church was verse 5 of 2 Thess. iii. ("The Lord direct your hearts into the love of God, and into the patient waiting for Christ;") for, as is generally admitted, the Epistles to the Thessalonians were the earliest written of any, and they were specially ordered to be read in the Church, (1 Thess. v. 27; comp. 2 Thess. iii. 17). And it is at least conceivable that the habit, as at first formed, of thus commemoratively fulfilling the apostolic injunction at the ordinary Offices, passed over from St. Paul's favourite Church of Ephesus to Gaul, and so reached our shores. The verse of 2 Thess. iii. occurs in the Roman Prime as "a short lection."

it might, no less than the Collect, have survived without involving much of that complexity, their dread of which our Revisers sometimes carried to excess. Happily, in the Collect itself, such anticipative reference is in almost all cases, though less distinctly, involved. And in one respect our Revision has, accidentally, perhaps, but most effectively, restored a feature of this part of the ancient Greek Vespers to its original position and function. The *Nunc Dimittis* had a peculiar fitness in that Office, coming as it did after the celebration of the True Light, and the reading of the summary of the Epistle, and so giving thanks for the "Light to lighten the Gentiles." It was with some disadvantage, therefore, that it was allotted to Compline in the Western schemes; and with proportionate fitness that it was made to succeed, with us, the eventide reading of the Epistles.

The origin of the Western *Collect*[t], to which allusion has just been made, may be traced with almost equal certainty to the Eastern formularies. In the sense in which I now speak of it, it may be defined as a prayer for some grace or blessing in connection with the Epistle or Gospel for the day, or with both of them. But it is a further peculiarity of the Collect, that it is transferable, or communicable rather, to the ordinary Office of the day, including the eve. Now the *principle* of this kind of prayer, and of this particular application of it, may not only be clearly discerned in the Eastern ritual, but is there carried out with much greater fulness than in

[t] Mr. Palmer says, "If I were to hazard a conjecture on the origin of Collects, I should say that they were introduced from Alexandria," i.e. from its liturgy. (I. iii.) This may account for the Collect for the king, &c.; but of the Collect proper no Eastern *Communion* Office contains any trace.

the West. It is true that in their Communion Office the Orientals use no such prayer. The current and variable Epistle and Gospel are not allowed to colour the Eucharistic rite by being made the basis of a prayer introduced into it, but only by means of the *prokeimenon* hymn epitomizing the Epistle. The Gospel, the principal lection of the Office, is thus deprived of a function which we of the West expect to see it exercising almost as a matter of course, and as a part of our idea of it. But in compensation for this, it imparts its character, in a very great degree, at least on the more notable Sundays and on Festivals, to the preceding Vespers and Morning Office; to the latter more especially. The variable hymns at Vespers,—the "odes," the lection after the sixth of them, and the other hymns, at Lauds,—all give expansion in various ways to the theme of the Gospel[u]. Here, then, is the principle of the Collect, exhibited on a large scale. Further, not a few of these hymns are scarcely, if at all, distinguishable in character from our Collects. Take the following short hymns, introduced at Lauds on Easter-day:—

"Thou, O Lord, that didst endure the cross, and didst abolish death, and didst rise again from the dead, give peace in our life, as only Almighty."

"Thou, O Christ, Who didst raise man by Thy resurrection, vouchsafe that we may with pure hearts hymn and glorify Thee."

Here we have the invocation and petition, grounded upon the topic of the Gospel, which are the characteristics of the Western Collect. As a general rule, however, these hymns, &c., are not prayers, but acts

[u] For specimens translated at length, see Neale, p. 857—867, and 877—887; see also note D.

of praise and meditation; nor would it be very natural, or easy to be accounted for, that the Western ritualists should have given such prominence, by means of the Collect, to a somewhat occasional feature of the Eastern system. But there is one particular kind of hymn in the Greek Office, which, could we be assured of its possessing the requisite antiquity, would have a strong claim to be considered as the actual prototype of our Collects. It is called the *Exaposteilarion*; a name which has been variously explained, but seems to refer to ἐξαπόστειλον, "Send down from above," a characteristic word of frequent occurrence in these hymns: "the aim of which seems originally to have been a kind of *invocation of the grace of God*[x];" with the same reference, as in the other hymns, to the Gospel of the day. These more uniformly *prayer-like* hymns occur, too, very nearly at the close of the series at Lauds; so that to any one taking up the Service-books in which they are found[y], they would appear but little removed from the Epistle and Gospel, and might very well suggest the position which was assigned to the Collect in the Western Communion Offices. Add to this, that when there was a saint's-day *exaposteilarion* to be used, as well as a Sunday one, there was a fixed rule for the precedence of the latter in ordinary cases; while on some great Festivals, as e.g. in the coincidence of the Annunciation with Palm Sunday, the order was reversed, exactly as in the case of the Western Collects[z]. The Collect, too, was assigned

---

[x] Neale, p. 844. Comp. ibid., pp. 866, 885, 924.

[y] Viz. the Triodion, and the Pentecostarion, containing the proper ones. The ordinary ones are in the Octoechus.

[z] Neale, p. 924, note.

to the selfsame place in the Western Lauds and Vespers, as the exaposteilarion and other hymns occupied in the Eastern Lauds; viz. after the Capitulum (= the prokeimenon) and canticle[a]. These correspondences must be allowed to be very striking. The difficulty, however, as regards the exaposteilaria, is that the invention of them is commonly ascribed to a ritualist[b] of the tenth century. But it may be fairly conjectured that they existed in some shape already, and that he only brought them to greater perfection, or to their present form.

It is remarkable, in connection with what has now been said, that, as is generally agreed, we have no trace of Collects (in the sense here meant[c]) previous to the time when Cassian and others imparted to the Latin Church some acquaintance with the Eastern rites, circ. 420: Leo the Great, an early friend of Cassian's (440), and Gelasius (490), being reputed the first composers of them[d]. And whether they had the particular forms called exaposteilaria before them or not, it is, I conceive, by far the most probable account that can be given of the peculiar and somewhat complex phenomena belonging to the Western Collect, (phenomena which place it almost beyond the reach of any one's invention,) that the idea of it was in all respects derived from the consideration of the Eastern

[a] It was said also at the Prime and other hours in the English use. The Benedictine had it at the end of Nocturns.

[b] Constantine, son of Leo the Philosopher. Neale, ibid., vide Mosheim, cent. x.

[c] "Hæc distinctio adhibenda videtur: si præcise de collectis loquamur, quibus nunc utimur, verissimum esse reor earum primos auctores fuisse Gelasium et Gregorium: id enim omnes rerum Ecclesiasticarum Scriptores asserunt, et antiqua monumenta evincunt. Quod si breves orationes intelligimus," &c. Bona, Rer. Lit., ii. 5. 4.

[d] Bona, Psalmod., xvi. 17. 1; Grancolas, i. p. 22, &c.

system. We seem to see, compressed into the terse Collects of Leo, Gelasius, or Gregory, the more diffuse spirit of the numerous Eastern hymns. And thus they would be the very quintessence, so to speak, of the Gospels, on which the latter were founded. It is observable, too, that the earliest Sacramentary, or Collect-book, that of St. Leo, contains several Collects for each feast, sometimes four or five[e]; which is exactly what we might expect to find, on the supposition that he was compiling from the Eastern ritual. The only innovation made by the Western composers, and that a very natural one, was to incorporate the Collect, not with the ordinary Service only, but with the Communion Office itself. And they completed the scheme by means of the "gradual," "super oblata," "post-communion," and other hymns and prayers.

The derivation of the word Collect has, as is well known, been much disputed. It seems most probable that it is to be traced to two different conceptions[f], when it is applied to an ordinary prayer, and when it signifies the peculiar kind we are speaking of. In the former case, it is either from *colligere orationem*[g], the "summing up the prayers of the people;" or from an old name for the Church's assemblies, *Collecta*[h]. But the Communion Collect neither sums up any previous petitions, nor is it obvious on what particular account, though several might be imagined, it would be named from the "assembly." A ground

---

[e] Palmer, I. iii.

[f] Vide Bona, as above, note c.

[g] Cassian, ii. 7; Bingham, XV. i. 4. The minister's prayer at the close of some part of divine service, collecting and including the people's preceding devotions.

[h] Levit. xxiii. 36, Cœtus et collecta. Deut. xvi. 8, In die septimo quia collecta est Domini Dei tui. Comp. Tertull. de Fugâ, c. ult.

upon which this latter derivation for it might reasonably be based, is the following. The Sacramentary of St. Gregory provides two Collects for the Feast of the Purification; of which one was to be said "*ad Collectam* ad S. Adrianum," i.e. at the ordinary service at St. Adrian's Church, where they met first; the other, "ad Missam ad S. Mariam," to which they proceeded for the Holy Communion[i]. It appears hence, that in St. Gregory's time the ordinary Office, as distinguished from the Communion, was called *Collecta*. And it is very conceivable that a prayer which, though said also at Communion, had this as its characteristic, that it was designed to impart to the ordinary Service the spirit of the Eucharistic Gospel, would on that account be called the *Collecta*. This nomenclature would represent very accurately the Eastern principle. With this view accords, too, another name by which the current Collect seems to have been sometimes[k] called, viz. the *Benedictio*; it being the form in which the peculiar grace or blessing spoken of in the Gospel was invoked upon the attendants on the ordinary Service. (Compare, too, the Greek name, *exaposteilarion*.) But it may still be questioned whether the true reason of the name be not its *gathering out of* the Eucharistic Scriptures of the day the topics of a prayer or blessing; a derivation which has always been a favourite one with ri-

[i] Bona, as above.

[k] Viz. as occurring at the end of the Benedictine Nocturns. S Bened. Reg., cap. 11. "Et data Benedictione, incipiant Matutinos," is the last direction he gives for the Nocturns Office. Now certainly the monastic use has always had the Collect for the day in that place. This, therefore, must be meant. Mr. Palmer questions it, (Orig. Lit., I. i. 16,) but it is so taken by all the best commentators. Vide Haeften, Disq. Mon., p. 749.

tualists[1], and has at least the recommendation that it renders very accurately one great characteristic of the Collect.

I have only to add respecting the Greek Evening Office, that while, as an organized service, it has a less purely primitive air than the Nocturns; its structure being, like that of Lauds, though in a less degree, artificial: it nevertheless seems to bear a decided note of primitiveness in the *prokeimenon*, and in substance is probably apostolic. It may indeed even be thought, at a first glance, to favour the view of those who would represent the ordinary services as being the *reliquiæ* of the Eucharistic Rite. But though there is a visibly designed *parallel* between the Evening Office and the Eucharistic, it is plain that a parallel it is, and no more. There are in the Eastern Communion Offices two solemn "entrances;" the bringing in, that is, of the Gospels, and of the elements. It is the former of these alone (or rather a symbolical commemoration of it by the entrance of the Priest and Deacon, without the Gospels,) that occurs in the Vespers. Of the other there is no trace. The Presence of Christ, which is recognised by the admonition, "Stand up; Wisdom," is not that which is connected with the Elements, but His Presence as the Word or Wisdom of God in the Holy Scriptures [m].

---

[1] Bona, p. 859; Wheatley, in loc.

[m] The ceremony of the Entrance of the Gospels is as follows. After the prayer of entrance, "the holy doors are thrown open, and the Deacon precedes the Priest through the north door of the sanctuary, and so round in front of the holy doors, as in the little entrance in the Liturgy. When they are before the doors, the Deacon saith, "Sir, bless the holy Entrance;" Priest, "Blessed be the Entrance of Thy holy things (or Gospels) always, &c. Amen." Then the Deacon, standing within the doors, saith, "Wisdom; stand up." The Priest and

We have, however, in this ceremonial, a recognition of two things: viz. 1. (as in the Eucharistic "little Entrance") of the Presence of Christ with power in the public reading of Holy Scripture; and 2. of the close connexion between all such public reading, on ordinary occasions, and the Eucharist;—the hearing and meditation of Scripture being in truth a lower yet most real reception of Christ to purposes of divine wisdom and knowledge. The West did not adopt this Eastern ceremony into her ordinary Offices[n]. Yet she gave full effect to it in a highly practical form, by introducing the actual reading of the Scriptures, to a considerable amount, into her scheme of Services. The "prokeimenon" was developed into the "Capitulum;" the "Odes" into the lection system. The English Church at her great Revision gave yet fuller development to the lection element. And in assigning so eminent a place as she does to Holy Scripture in her ordinary worship, she acts entirely in the spirit of her Eastern prototype; translating, so to speak, into language suited to the age in which her lot is cast, the expressive symbols of a more dramatic antiquity.

———

ONE or two remarks are naturally suggested by what has been laid before the reader in this chapter.

Deacon go towards the altar, the doors are shut, and the choir sing a hymn to the blessed Trinity,—"Joyful light," &c. (as above, p. 136).

[n] The French Church retained it, in some places, in the Liturgy. Neale, p. 305.

1. One fact, then, which I conceive stands revealed and unquestionable, is that from the very beginning of the Christian Church another kind of service than the Eucharistic co-existed side by side with it, absorbing in no small degree the spiritual energies, and expressing the religious emotions, of the earlier ages. The importance of this fact,—combined with that of the weekly, or at any rate *festival*, character of Eucharistic worship, during the same period,—in its bearing upon the intended character and province of Christian Ritual as a whole, can hardly be overrated. For a view of the relations and entire harmony of operation subsisting between the Ordinary and the Eucharistic worship of the Church, the reader is referred to the next chapter.

2. A second point, which seems to be equally well ascertained with the former, is that in the earliest age, and down to about the fourth century, the Church thought it good to have in effect *two*—at the utmost they may be called *three*—solemn services of ordinary public worship in the day, and no more. At the last-mentioned epoch, she was induced[o], under the influence of the monastic system, or in emulation of it, to institute public service at other times; viz. the 1st, 3rd, 6th, and 9th hours, and late in the evening; seasons of prayer which had doubtless from very early, and some of them from apostolic times, been observed as a matter of private or household devotion. How far she in this respect acted the part of a wise householder, may surely now at least be questioned. The system, as a system of numerous daily Offices of public worship, prescribed for the use of the members of the Church, has been practically for hundreds

[o] See below, chap. iii. sect. i.

of years abandoned throughout Christendom. So far as the Offices survive at all, (and in the West it is but a fragment that does so,) *two* Services, by aggregation, or *three* at the most, testify ᵖ with no uncertain voice to the sound wisdom of the primitive and apostolic provision in this matter. The great Church of the West, moreover, had she but eyes to see it, has good reason, in the present degraded state of her ordinary worship, to rue the day when, in the shape of vastly multiplied, as well as complex and unvernacular services, she laid a yoke upon the neck of her children, which the event has shewn that they were not able to bear.

3. Next, let it be noted by such as look upon the ordinary Offices of the Church as a mere make-shift of later and less devout ages, and would substitute for them daily Celebrations, with or without communicants, that the first ages had not so received. The further we go back, the more intense do we find this token and expression of the Church's life, viz. watchfulness in offices of ordinary prayer. In such offices it was that at midnight at the first, and still in after days "very early, while it was yet dark," the Church rose to seek her Lord; only the more intensely, and with longer watching and prayer, "as it began to dawn towards the First Day of the week,"—that Day on which they looked, as of old, that He should "stand in the midst of them" by Eucharistic Pre-

---

ᵖ Neale, p. 891: "At present, however, there are in the Greek Church eight canonical hours; prayers are actually, for the most part, said three times daily: Matins, Lauds, and Prime by aggregation, early in the morning; Tierce, Sexts, and the Liturgy (Communion), later; Nones, Vespers, and Compline, by aggregation, in the evening." For the practice of the Western Church, see the end of this chapter.

sence; when He should "stand at the door and knock," and should "come in to sup with them, and they with Him[q]." The early Church's mind unquestionably was, to carry on the work of her weekly and Festival Eucharists by full and carefully adapted provisions of daily prayer. In them her eyes still looked backward, we may conceive, to past, as they certainly looked forward to approaching celebration. Evening by evening, probably from the very first, she recalled to mind[r] the great Evening Institution; and when the Eucharist itself was removed from the eve to the morning of the Lord's Day or Festival, she marked its approach by suitable variation of the preceding ordinary service. At the same time, the service which was to this extent made much of, aspired to no co-ordinate equality with the Eucharist. Causes which must exist to the end of time sufficiently secured its inferiority and due subordination. Already, in primitive days, ordinary service was quite another thing from Eucharistic; so much so, that it but feebly impressed the vision, or coloured the representations, of the chroniclers of early Christianity[s].

The corollary from these premises cannot be doubtful. The most legitimate endeavour of a Church emulous of apostolic practice,—the first axiom of Christian ritualism and apostolic polity and discipline,—is surely the restoration of weekly Celebration and Communion; the one as a matter of faithfulness as a Church, the other as the badge of Christian mem-

---

[q] This latter provision was extended to the eves of Festivals, as being days of Eucharist; while at very high seasons, as Easter, it is probable that celebrations were at a very early time more frequent.

[r] Viz. by the prokeimenon, "entrance" at Vespers, &c. Sup, sect. vii.

[s] See above, sect. i., ii.

bership. This, with occasional Festival opportunities, and not either daily Celebrations or daily Communions, (which it is questionable if the Church ever heard of until the third, or it may be the fourth, century,) was the ancient and primitive way of Service. And next, second only to this first and paramount obligation, the Church is bound to provide a humbler, yet not ignoble, sacrifice of morning and evening worship. In point of attendance, it is all but impossible—though no pains should be spared in making it do so—that this service should come up to the standard of the weekly Eucharist. There is no reason in the world, unless by the Church's fault, or their own, that need prevent Christians, as a general rule, from attendance on the latter; there are many that must shut out not a few from the former. To bring up, then, *every one* of her members, being of sufficient age, in the habit of weekly (and, if it may be, Festival) Communion, and the greatest possible number in that of daily Church worship; this, and no less, is the Church's bounden aim. I earnestly question whether much more than this, save in the peculiar case of the clergy, or at special times, comes within the ordinary design of our Lord for the members of the Mystical Body.

4. In the next place, enough has been disclosed in this chapter of the links by which the later Western ritual stands connected with the early Eastern formularies, to evince the certainty that the former owes its parentage to the latter. This is a fact, however, of which the expounders of the Western Offices, from Amalarius and Walafridus Strabo (in the ninth century) downwards, have not had the slightest conception. Blinded by a fond belief that all ritual must

have originated with Rome,—that she could not possibly be beholden, at any rate, to the despised Church of the East, for any part of her ecclesiastical system,— they have fallen into precisely the same error as we have had occasion to observe in the professed expounders (until lately) of our own Services. Leaving entirely neglected the one chief and prerogative source of information as to the *rationale* of their Offices, they have but guessed, not always very shrewdly, at the reasons of things; and have continually taken refuge in mystical ones, often absurd and puerile to the last degree. There is no possible objection to devout musings, or even fancies, as to the number, order, connection, and the like, of the elements of service which the Church has inherited. But it need not impose any undue restrictions on such meditations, but only guide them into channels where they may flow without risk of bringing contempt on the whole subject, though we should inquire somewhat after the historically ascertainable origin, laws, and principles of the Church's ritual. The true history of the ritual of Western Christendom has yet to be written; and, whenever it is written, it must surely be by having recourse to the materials and sources of information which have been here indicated.

5. It is natural to inquire, again, What great and guiding principles of Divine Service and Worship do we gather from the review of these early and (in part, at least) primitive forms? What is the ideal of ordinary Christian devotion which they exhibit to us? and how far are the existing ordinary Services of the English Church true to those principles and to that ideal?

And first,—not to enter now upon those Eucharistical principles which must lie at the root of all

Christian Service,—it is surely here represented that *to lose ourselves in the praise of God* is the peculiar joy and glory of the Christian estate. " Psalms and hymns and spiritual songs;" "singing and making melody in the heart to the Lord;" "giving thanks always for all things to God and the Father in the Name of the Lord Jesus Christ;" in one word, PRAISE,—is, according to these Offices, the ruling aspect of Christian devotion.—Next, the due nurture of the soul by meditation on the law of God, and on the great Christian verities, is, though less prominently, and by somewhat different media from those which were employed in later times, yet unquestionably designed in these Services. The twofold idea under which the 119th and others of the Psalms were anciently used, viz. as acts both of praise and of meditative learning, has been already pointed out. In the hymns also, and other addresses, the great subjects of adoring belief—such as the Incarnation, the Passion, the Resurrection and Glory of Christ, and His coming to judgment—are the ever-recurring topics. To these was added, at the Night Office, the Creed itself; besides that by the prokeimenon, or summary of the Epistle, very much as by our " First Collect," the Eucharistic teaching of the week or day was in a measure kept before the mind.—Thirdly, " Prayer and supplication for all saints," and " for all men; for kings, and for all who are in authority," and in order to "making our own requests known unto God," is the remaining great work proposed to be done in these Services.—And underlying all the rest,—laid as the basis of all at the commencement of each Service, and breaking out ever and anon afterwards throughout, more especially in the Morning daybreak Office, (which, as in the West afterwards, is half penitential,) — is the deep confession of sin and unworthiness, powerfully contrasting with the elevated tone of the Offices as a whole.

Our own Daily Services, whatever judgment may be formed of them as compared with those of the middle period of the Church, do certainly, both as to their elements and as to the proportion in which these enter into them, accord in a striking manner with the Services whose contents have just been sketched. I speak not now of details,—these have been touched upon before, and a more than sufficient correspondence elicited[t],—but of the *kind of things* that it is well for Christian men to do in public worship, and of the degree of prominence that they should give to them respectively. For with us, too, the burden, the staple of the Service, is, it may be confidently affirmed, and will be more fully shewn hereafter, Praise. "The greatest part of our daily Service consisteth," in the words of Hooker, "in much variety of Psalms and hymns[u]." But the position he intended to lay down may be affirmed much more broadly when we have grasped the true principles of our Service. From the Venite to the end of the Creed,—nay, to the end of the Office,—is, in one point of view, a continued act of praise; broken only by the introduction of the topics of it by means of the Lessons; carried on again, not merely by the anthem or hymn, but by the invocation and adoration of God under various attributes, with which every prayer commences, and many conclude; and crowned by a general act of thanksgiving, almost peculiar to us, though sufficiently countenanced[x]

---

[t] See above, p. 66.   [u] L. E. P., v. 43.   [x] See above, pp. 66, 134.

by ancient Oriental precedent. It is, indeed, much to be remarked, that the intercessory prayers and thanksgivings which conclude our revised Daily Offices, and which have on various grounds been objected to, possess at least this merit, that they exhibit many admirable specimens of that towering sublimity of address[y], and that joy in exuberant praise, which is characteristic of Eastern worship, and in which the Western ritual is comparatively very deficient. They restore, in a measure, the "exclamations" which occur so frequently in Eastern Offices. It is chiefly in the amount of her psalmody that our present Offices contrast unfavourably with those of the West, and yet more with the Eastern. This, in itself to be earnestly regretted, could it be avoided, is a result of the brevity of the Offices themselves. All that is here maintained is that the *proportion* of praise, in the entire Offices, is not inadequate; that this all-important element pervades their entire structure, and that the later revisions of them, more especially, tended to enlarge it. —With us, again, as with the Eastern Church, meditative learning and pondering of Holy Scripture goes hand in hand with praise, and is only second to it in consideration.—With us, prayer and intercession come in as a third element with these;—prayer no less deep and personal, and intercession no less wide and Catholic, at the least, than that which we discern in the Greek Offices.—With us, finally, the foundation of penitential confession is deeply laid at the commencement of *both* our Services, and characterizes their whole tenor to a degree which has called forth alike the scorn of enemies and the half regretful and apolo-

---

[y] See the Prayer for the Queen, and the Occasional Prayers.

getic admission of friends[z]. Surely, of one thing at least the English Church needs not to be ashamed, viz. of bearing in her ritual the marks of the Crucified[a]. With her, as with her ancient Eastern prototype, the "strength" of Praise is made perfect in the "weakness" of Confession.

Lastly, let us for a moment compare this Service, thus primitive alike in its ideal and its forms, with that which in modern times has been adopted as a substitute for it in two other Communions, each of which is, by persons differently minded, deliberately held up as a model for the imitation of the English Church. To speak first of the newest Communion of Western Christendom, the "Evangelical Church" of Prussia and other parts of Germany. The summary of their ordinary Service is as follows:—

> A Hymn.
> A Commencement Prayer (read at the altar-step).
> The Epistle *or* Gospel.
> A Hymn.
> The Lord's Prayer.
> The Sermon.
> "Church Prayer," (read from the pulpit).
> The Lord's Prayer.
> Benediction, (Phil. iv. 7).
> A Hymn.
> Benediction, (Numb. vi. 26).

[z] Vide Tracts for the Times, No. 86, on the comparatively penitential character of our Offices. It should be remarked, however, that the element of praise, though in many respects restrained, was in others enlarged and intensified at the Revision; more especially by appointing the Te Deum (or an equivalent) *daily*, and by the addition of the General Thanksgiving and the "exclamation" or doxology, "For Thine is," &c., by increasing the number of "Glorys," and omitting the *penitential* Preces after the Creed.

[a] "Now, journeying *westward*, evermore
   We know the lonely Spouse
  By the dear mark her Saviour bore
   Traced on her patient brows."—*Christian Year.*

It has been well observed that—

"This so-called Liturgy is wholly *un*-liturgical: it has no Creeds; no Psalter; no kneeling; no responses; no common or congregational supplications or thanksgiving. The prayers are mere book-exercises recited by the minister, and listened to by the people. No lessons are appointed to be read from the Bible. There is a Gospel *or* an Epistle in the morning, but no Scripture at all in the afternoon. The only parts of the service which exhibit real life, are the singing and preaching. The language of the formularies is wordy and diffuse, conceived in the flowing, periphrastic style which Baxter would have substituted for the English Liturgy."

Such is the service seriously recommended for the adoption of the Church of the Future. The ritual of England's future, at any rate, may it never be.

From the newest we turn to the most ancient Communion of Europe. We may at least look to find, in the ways of ordinary service prevailing throughout half Christendom, something to justify the confidence with which the practical system of that Communion, not least in the matter of ordinary worship, is held up to our imitation. Now, that in many parts of the continent attendance upon some kind of ordinary worship is far more extensively realized than in this country, is not questioned; nor can we too earnestly desire that we may so far be enabled to follow so good an example. But it is worth while to inquire what the service is which commands this degree of attendance. Now, first of all, it is *not* the anciently descended scheme of service that is thus attended. The following statement of a peculiarly well-informed writer, having now been on record several years without being called in question, may perhaps be taken fairly to represent the state of things in this respect throughout Roman Catholic Europe:—

"Yet of one thing, in conclusion, it seems proper to remind the reader, lest the glitter of so magnificent an array of sevenfold devotion should blind the eyes of any to the real state of the matter. Except in monastic bodies, the Breviary, as a Church Office, is scarcely ever used as a whole. You may go, we do not say from church to church, but from cathedral to cathedral, of central Europe, and never hear — never have a chance of hearing — Matins, save at high festivals. In Spain and Portugal it is somewhat more frequent; but there, as everywhere, it is a clerical devotion exclusively. But anywhere, as we had occasion to say in a previous number, 'to find in a village church a priest who daily recited his Matins publicly, would be a phenomenon.' Then, again, the lesser Hours are not often publicly said, except in cathedrals, and then principally by aggregation, and in connexion with Mass. Vespers is the only popular service; and that, in connection with 'Benediction,' seems to be put forward by English Ultramontanes as *the* congregational service of the Roman Church of the future. Our readers will remember that some time ago we made a statement, characterized by many persons at the time as 'startling,' that 'in no national Church under the sun are so many Matin Services daily said as in our own.' An Anglo-Roman priest shortly afterwards strongly remonstrated with us for certain other statements contained in the same number. But of this point he took no notice; and therefore, we may fairly presume, allowed its truth. We feel it only right to dwell on this, because, having had occasion in the preceding pages to enlarge with so much admiration on the Roman theory, we are bound not to shut our eyes to Roman practice [b]."

Let us next inquire what the service used *is*. And here, again, in preference to giving an estimate of my own of the condition and merits of the ordinary worship practically existing in the Roman Church, I shall quote the words of another. They will be recognised as those of an able layman of our own day, well qualified by information to speak on the subject, and not chargeable with want of breadth or catholicity in his sympathies. And as the passage to which I allude happens to sum up with remarkable accuracy the

[b] "Christian Remembrancer," No. 70, Oct. 1850. For some account of the present state of things, practically, in the East, see note II.

views expressed in this chapter, I shall make no apology for citing it at length:—

"Christian worship is derived from that of the old faith. The Jewish worship was, as all sects allow, of two kinds,—the more solemn rite of sacrifice, and the auxiliary offering of prayer and praise, and reading of Holy Scripture. The former confined at first to the Tabernacle, and then to the Temple; the latter common to the Temple and the Synagogue. The former, a thing which perished at the destruction of the Temple; the latter, a thing which continues to our own day. That Christian worship strictly follows this analogy is not a matter of such concurrent acceptation; and yet it does so. . . 'Opus Dei, quod singulis diebus, horis propriis ac distinctis, in Ecclesiis et Oratoriis celebratur, duplex est, Missa et Officium Divinum,' is the majestic commencement—majestic from its truth and simplicity— of the Rituale Cisterciense.

"In the primitive Church, the 'Opus Dei' was, as later, twofold; but it [afterwards] ceased to be vernacular, and, except in churches which were collegiate, (to use the most general word,) the Officium Divinum ceased to be necessarily collective; and nowhere, we feel we may speak generally, was it congregational. Then came the days of the Reformation, and the Roman Church, with a most deplorable deficiency of courage, would neither make the 'Opus Dei' in either branch vernacular, nor the Officium Divinum at all congregational. The congregational attendance at (not participation in the Office of) the Missa, the chief remnant of collective worship, was encouraged by the building of churches consisting of altar alone, and nave, and therefore unsuited to the Divine Office (i.e. ordinary service). The English Reformers went to work root and branch,— too much so, it might be said, in many particulars,—but, in principle, in a clear-sighted and decisive manner, by rendering both the Missa and Divine Office at once vernacular, collective, and congregational. In the Roman Communion things could not stop as they were; popular devotion craved for vernacular food. The result has been a singular system of compromise. On the one hand, the Mass, and the observances growing from it, 'Benediction' in particular, have almost exclusively occupied the churches; Vespers alone, as an authoritative service, out of the various divisions of the Divine Office, struggling for recognition. On the other hand, an irregular bundle of vernacular forms of worship, litanies, methodistical hymns, and modern prayers, &c. have accumulated, and are encouraged by authority as the playthings, so to speak, of the laity, who, it is assumed, cannot compass anything better; while the old and venerable *Officium Divinum*, the breviary services, are remanded to the mere private use of the clergy[e]."

Meanwhile, the English Church holds fast to a form of ordinary worship possessing, whatever its defects otherwise, one advantage which the rest of the Western Church has recklessly thrown away; viz. that of having come down to her in an unbroken succession from primitive days. Her foot, in this matter at any rate, is on the rock of apostolic practice and precedent: " her foundations are upon the holy hills."

[e] "Oratorianism and Ecclesiology." (By A. J. B. H.)

# CHAPTER II.

## ON THE THEORY OF THE CHURCH'S ORDINARY WORSHIP.

### SECTION I.

---

"Though He were a Son, yet learned He obedience by the things which He suffered; and being made perfect, He became the author of eternal salvation unto all them that obey Him; called of God an High-Priest after the order of Melchisedec."

---

THAT the Church of Christ has never been without some form of Ordinary Worship, in addition to the Holy Communion, is so probable in itself, and is countenanced by so many concurrent circumstances, that few perhaps will be found, on reflection, to deny the position altogether, though they may be unwilling to acquiesce in all the conclusions arrived at in the preceding chapter. And, at any rate, that the Church was guided, at a period not long after the first age or two, to the universal adoption of such services, none will be hardy enough to gainsay. " De Divinis Officiis," says the deeply-learned Mabillon, " quæ in Ecclesia Gallicana *jam inde a primis temporibus* obtinuerunt, breviter disseramus." And again: " Etsi in publicis fidelium conventibus, *jam inde ab Ecclesiæ nascentis exordio*, Psalmi aliæque preces recitatæ sint, tamen," &c. And once more: " Avariis divinorum officiorum modis, qui *tam in Oriente quam in Occidente a primordiis instituti sunt*, exordium ducimus."

Such was his impression, from his acquaintance, in a general way, with antiquity. And I believe it may be said without fear of contradiction, that, from Malabar to Ireland, no Church has ever yet been known to exist, which had not ordinary offices of some kind or other.

Here, then, an interesting and deeply important question arises, as to the position which this kind of service properly occupies in the Christian scheme, and the ends which it was designed (can we doubt, divinely designed?) to answer. It is indeed easy to assign a variety of motives and reasons for such services, all of which must be allowed their place, and which help to make up the sum total of their rationale. But if we inquire, as surely we ought, after the most elevated conception which we may allowably, and without trenching on the prerogatives of the highest kind of Christian Service, entertain of this lower form of it, the question is not so easily answered. The statements which are ordinarily put forth on the subject in our popular manuals, or even in treatises of greater pretensions, are seldom such as go to the bottom of the matter, or can, on any profound view of it, be deemed satisfactory. One favourite representation is, that in these acts of worship, i. e. in the use of the ordinary Offices of the Church, we discharge a duty of merely natural piety, with only such advantages as accrue to us from our better knowledge of God under the Gospel dispensation, and from the intercession of Christ, which we are privileged to plead. Thus, among commentators on the Church's daily Services, as used in the middle ages, Martene (echoing, for the most part, the language of his predecessors) is content to base the institution of such

Offices on the general duty incumbent on Christians, of continual prayer and service[a]. L'Estrange, an early commentator on our present Offices, goes back to grounds of natural religion in search of reasons for public prayer[b]. Sparrow, again, in his well-known work, falls back upon *à fortiori* arguments from the Law[c]. Neither does Hooker, when speaking of the Church's ordinary public Prayer, place it on such grounds as might have been expected from the profound manner in which he treats of the Sacraments; dwelling simply on the promise of our Lord to Christian assemblies, and on the prevailing power which would be likely to belong to the prayers of an aggregation of Christian men, as compared with those of an individual[d]. These representations are, indeed, as far as they go, to the purpose; and must have their place in any just and full view of the subject. But we may reasonably ask whether this is the whole truth? whether the whole case, so to speak, for ordinary Christian worship, is fully set before us here? and whether some broader and more distinctively Christian ground may not be taken for it?

And, accordingly, this kind of worship has by other writers, who have formed juster conceptions of its

---

[a] Martene de Ritib. Eccl., init.

[b] "As God is the first Principle and prime Efficient of our being, so that very being is obligation of the highest importance for us to defer Him the greatest honour." Alliance of Divine Offices, p. 23, ed. 1846.

[c] "Thus it was commanded under the Law, and certainly we Christians are as much at least obliged to God as the Jews were," &c. Rationale, init.

[d] "The service which we do as members of a public body must needs be accounted so much worthier than the other, as a whole society of such condition exceedeth the worth of any one. In which consideration unto Christian assemblies there are most special promises made." Eccl. Pol., V. xxiv. 1.

dignity and its province, being variously characterized as a means of union[e] to Christ, an effective act of communion with the Church, and of intercession with and for her; as the discharge, in a word, of an elevated spiritual function, such as cannot in any lower manner (as, e. g. by private or household worship) be so effectually performed. And surely we may safely reject such a view of it as would make it be no more than the expression of natural devotion,—the orisons, as it were, of the natural man,—only sanctioned and sublimed by Christian promise and privilege. But at the same time we must be equally careful lest we exalt it to a position, and assign to it powers, to which it can lay no claim. Be it what it may, how excellent soever within its own sphere and limits, it is not, after all, the Church's great, distinctive, and supreme act of Service. In the endeavour to assign to it such a place as will secure its observance on high Christian grounds, there is no little risk of claiming for what is confessedly a secondary mode of access to God, and of reception of Divine gifts, those privileges which belong to the Eucharist, and to that only. Indeed it must be said that ritualists and other writers have not been sufficiently careful to keep distinct the position and privileges of the Holy Communion on the one hand, and those of ordinary acts of worship on the other.

Thus, then, our present inquiry assumes the phase of a comparison and discrimination between the lower and higher forms of Christian Service and worship. The point for our consideration is, how comes this kind of service to be superadded to, and to co-exist with, the one principal and supreme act of Christian

[e] Vide Wilberforce on the Incarnation, chap. xii.

Ritual solemnly instituted by Christ Himself? Is it independent of the Eucharistic Rite, or supplementary to it? Does it, on the one hand, occupy a distinct ground of its own, a department of spiritual need altogether unprovided for in the Eucharist? And yet how can we conceive that that great act of Service, divinely ordained for the dedication and refection of man's nature, leaves any department of his being really undedicated or unprovided for? Or is this lower kind of service, on the other hand, purely ancillary to the higher; a branch proceeding from it; a tributary falling into it; and to be conceived of as always, and strictly, in subordination to it? This view, again, rigidly accepted, is by no means free from difficulty. Nor, I conceive, is it possible to attain to a satisfactory solution of the question before us, without taking a wider and more comprehensive view than might at first sight seem necessary, of the whole subject of the nature of Christian worship.

It has been well observed [f], that the Church's rites, even to her most ordinary ones, are based upon her deepest doctrinal mysteries. Accordingly, when Hooker would justify a particular kind of petition in our ordinary Church Service, he is carried by his subject into a consideration of the two Wills of Christ [g]; and again, in expounding the nature of the Sacraments, into the question of the two Natures in Christ [h], and their union in His one Person. An inquiry like the present, embracing, in outline at least, the entire subject of the Church's ritual action, may

---

[f] See a thoughtful sermon on "The Prayers of the Saints," by Archdeacon Smith, of Jamaica.

[g] Laws of Eccl. Polity, V. 48.

[h] Ibid., V. 50—57.

well be expected to lead us, in like manner, into the consideration of some one or more of the greater mysteries of the Gospel.

Now there are, as it would seem, two especial mysteries of the Christian religion, in the right understanding of one or other of which, or of both taken together, we may find the answer to most questions, concerning either ritual or practice, which can arise under that dispensation. These are, the INCARNATION, and the PRIESTHOOD, of CHRIST. In those two Facts, taking both of them in their widest sense, is summed up the whole of our Lord's operation on behalf of His Church; as well those actions of His by which the salvation of man was in the first instance wrought, as the processes by which He still carries on His great work until the consummation of all things.

In the INCARNATION of our Lord we may properly include, not only the fact itself, but all those effects and consequents of it, which, but for it, could not have taken place: such as His Nativity, and all the events of His Divine Childhood and Manhood; His Circumcision, Manifestation, and Presentation in the Temple; His Baptism and Ministry; His Fasting and Temptation; His Miracles and Teaching; His Agony and Passion; His Death and Resurrection; His Ascension, and Session at the Right Hand of God the Father, which continues to this hour.

The PRIESTHOOD of Christ, though most closely and intimately connected with His Incarnation, yet seems capable of being discriminated from it as a second and distinct step in His great work. The Incarnation was in order to the Priesthood, as one step may be in order to another, but did not properly involve it. Christ's "Body was prepared Him," in order that, like all other priests, "He might have somewhat to offer." "The Body" was assumed by one act, in order to its becoming by another "a Temple," the sphere and scene of awful sacrificial transactions. And the whole work of preparation and adaptation for becoming a Priest and an Offering was separated, in fact, from the act of oblation itself. First of all, those actions which we have included under the idea of the Incarnation, were done by the SON OF MAN, the second Adam, *as such;* by the new Head of the human race working out a perfect and acceptable obedience. And then the work thus done was, by a distinct action, offered to God the Father by the same Divine Person *as Priest.* True it is, that from the beginning of the great Economy or arrangement, (as they of old time used to designate the Incarnation, with its whole effects,) the idea of dedication and offering entered into every action of the obedient Sonship. In this sense, and to this extent, the offering must be conceived of as having begun from the very moment of the Incarnation[1] itself. But not till

---

[1] See Note F. Similarly, Dr. Jackson (Priesthood of Christ, IX. chap. iv. 3) says: "Betwixt a priest complete, or actually consecrated, and no priest at all, there is a mean or third estate or condition; to wit, a priest *in fieri,* though not *in facto,* or a priest *inter consecrandum,* before he be completely and actually consecrated." And again, ch. xi. 5: "During the time of His humiliation He was rather destinated than consecrated to be the author and fountain of blessedness unto us." This excellent writer has, however, involved himself in a difficulty, by insisting that Christ was not qualified to *act,* nor did act, as a priest at all, until after His Resurrection,—appealing to Heb. v. 8—10. But though the seal of the Father's acceptance of His Priesthood was finally set by His Resurrection, it is unquestionable that His offering of Himself upon the Cross was a proper act of Priesthood. It was at once the act by which He consecrated Himself for His Priesthood. ("For their sakes I sanctify Myself," St. John xvii.,) and by which He saved and sanctified the world, ("that they also may be sanctified").

the very close of His ministry in the flesh did our Lord solemnly, and by a set and suitable action, enter upon His Priesthood: "Then taking the dignity of the Priesthood, or rather, *then fulfilling in action also the dignity which He had always had*, He offered the Sacrifice for us[k]."

It is next to be observed that the actions of Christ consequent upon His Incarnation may be viewed either (1), as personal actions merely; or (2), in their bearing upon the salvation of mankind.

(1.) Let us view them, first, as personal actions merely. We shall find that they assume a very different aspect, according as we leave out or take in His priestly functions and operation.

Viewed apart from their connection with His Priesthood, they are simply actions of obedient Sonship, crowned with the reward of that obedience. The spectacle, as has been already said, is that of the second Adam accomplishing in Himself that perfect conformity to the Divine Will which the first Adam failed to exhibit. We behold a life of faultless obedience to God and entire love towards man, — of obedience unto death and love unto death,—crowned, as its reward, with glory and worship.

But this series of personal actions assumes a new character when it is conceived of not only as *done*, but as *offered*. And a distinct operation was provided in order to its being offered. Christ was not only conceived at the first of the Holy Ghost, and afterwards sanctified in all His actions by the same Holy Spirit, but was also at the last, through the same Spirit, sanctified (or rather "sanctified Himself") as an

[k] Hesychius, bishop of Jerusalem circ. 600. In Lev. c. 4, Bibl. Patr. tom. xii. p. 63, ed. 1677.

offering, (St. John xvii. 10). Not only *was* He " the Lamb of God," but He also, " through the eternal Spirit, offered Himself," as such, to God[l]. The action of His Priesthood supervened upon the proper action of His Incarnation[m]. What He was as Man, He offered as Priest. The obedient Sonship was sanctified and offered in the office of the eternal Priesthood. " Though He were a Son, yet learned He obedience by the things which He suffered; and having thus been made perfect," (consecrated, τελειω-θεὶς,) " He became the author of eternal salvation to all them that obey Him;" being then, and not till then, named or " *called of God an High Priest.*" Thus was the second Adam, even towards Himself, a second and a greater Aaron and Melchisedec[n].

(2.) But let us now consider the actions of our Lord, not in their personal character, i. e. in their relation to Christ's own Person, but in their bearing upon man's interests; as actions representative and potential, in which was wrought once for all, or out of which issues, by unceasing application, the salvation of mankind. We shall find the same duality of aspect appertaining to them, as we did when we were considering them as personal actions merely.

These mystically effective actions, if we leave out of view their connection with Christ's Priesthood, appear simply as great deeds of victorious re-creation; as the quelling, on behalf of mankind, in the Person of Christ, of the old enemies, Sin and Death; as the

[l] Heb. ix. 14.

[m] "The Priesthood is an accident, the Humanity or Manhood is the subject or substance that supports it." Dr. Jackson, Priesthood of Christ, p. 213.

[n] On the question whether, and in what sense, Christ was a Priest towards Himself, see Thos. Aquin., Summa, iii. 22, 4.

dying out and abolition of the old corruption, and the raising up of a new, perfect, and immortal manhood.

But the selfsame actions present themselves under quite another and an added aspect, if we take into consideration the Priesthood and its effects. We find another set of phenomena taking their place as co-efficients in the work of salvation. Conceivably, indeed, it might have sufficed the good pleasure of the Divine Will, and the exigency of the case, that by actions partaking of the former character alone—actions, that is, of a merely restorative and re-creative kind—the salvation of man should be effected. The utmost aspirations of heathen philosophies, whencesoever derived, had dreamed of nothing beyond such a reconstitution of human nature. Nor perhaps could unaided reason, even with the knowledge of the fact of the Incarnation, have attained to the conception of anything further. To restore to its perfection the original ethical condition of man; to place him in his primeval position of harmonious discharge of his relations to God, his fellow-man, and himself: this might well be thought to be all that God purposed concerning him, and might also seem capable of accomplishment through the medium of the Incarnate Word, *as* Incarnate, without the intervention of any further economy. And by some single rite, such as Baptism, it might further be imagined,—a rite, that is, capable of imparting the regenerative and reconstitutive effects of the actions of Christ, and guaranteeing the continually renewing assistances of the Holy Spirit,—the entire gift of salvation, in all its parts, might be conveyed to man.

The illumination of a special teaching,—a teaching directed towards the inculcation of a yet greater mystery, and towards the unfolding of a still higher destiny than that of mere renewal,—was, it should seem, necessary to prepare mankind for the apprehension of any further privilege as being in store for man. Accordingly, together with the mysterious necessity for Atonement, and closely interwoven with it, another great feature of human destiny had been all along intimated. This was the *acceptable oblation* of regenerated man to God by the Priesthood of Christ; and, together with this, the *power of acceptable offering of himself by man, in and through that Priesthood.* Such an intimation was clearly involved in the mysterious idea and practice of SACRIFICE. That idea and practice, undiscoverable, as it should seem, at least in all its bearings, by the mere reason[o], and forming no part of the mental heritage of man in his first estate, had been in the world coevally (in all probability) with the Fall, was familiar to the patriarchs, descended almost universally to the Gentiles, and was divinely expanded and reduced to detail for the chosen people of God. And when all the particulars of the teaching embodied in those old rites, whether patriarchal, Gentile, or Mosaic, came at length to be summed up and expounded in the priestly action of Christ, it was seen that the purport of it, as regarded man's position and functions towards God, was this; —that, besides the restoration of man to the image of God, (which of itself, indeed, required an act of priesthood for its accomplishment,) the Divine purpose included the setting on foot of certain new and bettered relations to Himself, on the part of the creature so restored. It was not to be deemed the goal of human attainment or perfectibility " to do justly, and to love

---

[o] See below, Part II., Theory of Eucharistic Worship.

mercy, and to walk humbly with his God;" or in whatever other way ethical completeness may be described. Such duties would indeed be indispensably necessary, but they would be taken up into a higher sphere. A new standing before God would now be provided for man, consisting in a capacity for acceptable oblation of himself to God, and for special and transcendent participation of God by him. The great saving actions of Christ were destined to include not only such a dying and rising again as would redound to the renewal and re-creation of man, but such a Death as was, by virtue of priestly operation, a perfect Reconciliation and Atonement; such a presentation of the risen and ascended Body as constituted It a perfect and acceptable Gift and Oblation to God. Henceforth man would be empowered and privileged not only to *do* that which was well-pleasing in God's sight, but also acceptably to *offer* it. That which henceforth he did in Christ, and as a member of Him, would through Christ have a real acceptableness with God, as a gift to Him, and as redounding to the actual increase of His glory. Henceforth he would be not only " a son," but " a priest unto God and his Father." For the exercise of this exalted spiritual function, and for the continuance and increase of his acceptableness in it, a special rite, over and above the Sacrament of his regeneration, would be provided. In that rite he would be privileged, as a priest unto God, (1), to present and to plead, in the way of memorial, the one Sacrifice of Christ, and with it to offer himself acceptably; and (2), sacramentally to eat and drink of the great High-Priest's Sacrifice of Himself.

And, exalted and mysterious as is the condition described in these terms, it may be remarked, that such an advance, in point of spiritual position and functions, is exactly what might be expected to accrue to man, as the result of a Divine Person's having condescended to enter into the *human* side of religions and ritual transaction, and of man's having been marvellously incorporated into Him. It could not be but that such a wondrous event should involve a greatly elevated ritual position towards God. It was in a manner likely that man would in his measure inherit a glorious priesthood, by his having been ingrafted into the very Body of a Divine High-Priest[p].

Now these considerations account for a very peculiar feature, for such it is, in the economy of our salvation: I mean the *duality*, and not the duality merely, but wide diversity, of the Christian Sacraments; the distribution into two several and very different gifts, the Baptismal and the Eucharistic, of the estate which we have in Christ. Such a distribution, and such diversity, is a natural result of the twofold aspect which the saving actions of Christ themselves possess. Those actions being, under one aspect, purely re-creative, or restorative; under another, sacrificial and oblationary; are imparted (as to the virtue of them) to the one purpose in one Sacrament, and to the other in the other. The Sacraments, the instruments of salvation, are fitted, in number and nature, to the twofold aspect of the one series of saving actions to which they owe their grace. Holy Baptism is so fashioned and empowered as to be the type and the instrument of simple re-creation and restoration; of the ethical readjustment which needed to be made, in order "to repair man that fell." The Holy Eucharist, again, is so fashioned and empowered as to be the type and

[p] See S. Aug. in note G, at the end of the volume.

the instrument of those sacrificial functions, both of oblation and participation, which form the crowning stage of man's exaltation in Christ. Renewal, in short, is but half the Christian's privilege; there is added the yet more marvellous and inscrutable mystery of his acceptable oblation of himself as a priest to God, and effectual participation, in the same character, of God. Baptism is the compendium and the instrument of the one privilege, the Eucharist of the other.

If it be asked how the selfsame series of actions of our Lord, as e. g. His Death and Resurrection, (and I conceive it to be of the last importance to maintain that it is the selfsame actions that operate in the two Sacraments,) are available to different effects in Baptism and in the Eucharist;—in the one to death unto sin and new birth unto righteousness; in the other, to sacrificial oblation and participation:—it might suffice to point to the analogy of the actions themselves, as done by our Lord, and considered as His personal actions merely. There is every appearance of their fulfilling, as personal actions, two distinct courses at one and the same time. The actions from the Nativity to the Ascension and Session go forward (under one aspect) as simply those of the Man Christ Jesus, or the WORD Incarnate, fulfilling a course of Divine Manhood. Yet all the time it is certain that the whole course was of the nature of a continuous sacrificial action, or possessed at least a sacrificial aspect: each act, as it took place, had its sacrificial position and character. Since, then, *the two aspects* of Christ's acts, though concomitant, are strictly separable, what should forbid but that the virtue of those actions should be derived and drawn off, in a corresponding manner, into two several channels: so that they should be present, in one rite, under one aspect, and to one purpose; and in another rite under another aspect, and to another purpose?

And there is yet another analogy to be found, in the undoubted truth of the perfect union of the Divine with the human Nature in the Person of Christ from the very Incarnation; combined with the equally undoubted difference of *degree* in which the lower nature was at successive periods penetrated, irradiated, and empowered by the higher. We might have concluded that so intimate a presence of the Divine Nature would at once, and from the first, have imparted to the human all the exaltation and all the powers destined for it. And yet, both in respect of growth and of official functions, the perfectioning process was gradual. "For as the parts, degrees, and offices of that mystical administration did require which He voluntarily undertook, the beams of Deity did accordingly either restrain or enlarge themselves [q]." Perfect God and perfect Man from His birth, yet not perfect as to the adolescence and illumination of His human Soul, until His maturity, (for "He increased in wisdom;") not perfect for the work of His prophetic office until His Baptism and Temptation; nor for His Priesthood until the eve of His Passion; nor for His universal kingly power as man until His Resurrection; He experienced by degrees and instalments the enabling powers of that Deity which, in point of presence and personal union, was never absent from Him. And if this was the case with respect to the imparting of particular effects of the Divine Nature within Him to His natural Body, Soul, and Spirit, may not the like well have place at this hour in the case of the mem-

[q] Hooker, Eccl. Pol. v. 54. Compare Moberly, Sayings of the Forty Days, p 32.

bers of His Body mystical? Here, too, the awful Gift may restrain or enlarge itself. The selfsame Person imparting Himself, with all His saving actions, in both Sacraments alike, may impart one while, and by one Sacrament, certain aspects and effects [r] of those actions; at another time, and by the other Sacrament, certain other aspects and effects of them. And it is, to notice this in passing, one incidental confirmation of this mode of viewing the Sacraments, that according to it those two holy ordinances, whatever other difference, or pre-eminence one over the other, they may present, are in this respect at least co-equal; that in both the whole Christ[s], with all His saving actions, is present: a consideration serving at once to secure equal honour to the two ordinances in which, and in which alone, our Saviour enters into entire union with us; and also to exalt them, at the same time, to an immeasurable superiority above all others claiming or possessing sacramental powers.

Baptism, then, in its proper and distinctive nature, —as discriminated, that is, from the Eucharist,—is the Sacrament of renewal and regeneration: being the admission of man into the virtue of Christ's saving actions *considered as renewing and re-creative*. The Eucharist, again, in its proper and distinctive nature, or as discriminated from Baptism, is the Sacrament of priestly or sacrificial oblation and participation: being

---

[r] Hooker, V. lvi. 15: "Christ is truly said more or less to impart Himself as the graces are fewer or more, greater or smaller, which really flow into us from Christ;" where he speaks, however, of ordinary spiritual growth, and does not touch upon the question now before us, whether the grace of all Christ's actions is imparted in *both* Sacraments. See ibid., s. 13.

[s] "Christ is whole in the whole Church, and *whole with every part of the Church, as touching His Person*, which can no way divide Itself, or be possessed by degrees or portions." Hooker, ibid.

our admission into the virtue of the same actions, *considered as priestly or sacrificial;*—as redounding to capacities for acceptable oblation, and for feeding upon Christ as an Offering. Not indeed that the two Sacraments, though thus discriminated from each other by strong distinctive differences, do not each partake, in a degree, of the characters and qualities more immediately and supremely pertaining to the other. Holy Baptism *does* confer a kind and degree of priesthood [t]. The holy Eucharist, again, is a signal and glorious instrument of renewal. Only, as there is a degree or kind of renewal proper to Baptism, which the Eucharist confessedly cannot give, viz. re-creation or regeneration proper,—the initiation of life in Christ to them that have it not: so is there a perfect and supreme degree of priesthood enjoyed and exercised in the Eucharist, which Baptism cannot bestow, and which they who are merely baptised cannot exercise: viz. the pleading of Christ's Sacrifice in the most prevailing form; supremely acceptable oblation of themselves in Christ, as "priests unto God;" and participation, to the purposes of transcendently intimate union, of the one Sacrifice [u].

[t] S. Cyril, Catech. Lect. xviii.

[u] Comp. Jer. Taylor, (Holy Living, IV. x. p. 266): "As the ministers of the Sacraments do, in a sacramental manner, present to God the sacrifice of the cross, by being imitators of Christ's intercession; so the people are sacrificers too in their manner; for besides that, by saying *Amen,* they join in the act of him that ministers, and make it also to be their own; so, &c. .... while in their sacrifice of obedience and thanksgiving they present themselves to God with Christ, whom they have spiritually received; that is, themselves with that which will make them gracious and acceptable." So Dean Jackson speaks of Eucharistic participation as being a consecration of Christians to a priesthood parallel to that of Aaron: "Whoso eateth shall live for ever; for he that truly eateth is consecrated by it to be a king and priest for ever unto God the Father." (Works, vol. viii. p. 378.) See further, note G.

## SECTION II.

"To whom coming, as unto a living stone, ye also, as lively stones, are built up a spiritual house, an holy priesthood, to offer up spiritual sacrifices, acceptable to God by Jesus Christ. By Him therefore let us offer the sacrifice of praise to God continually, that is, the fruit of our lips giving thanks to His Name."

THE views stated in the preceding section, besides their bearing upon our present subject, furnish an answer to several inquiries which can hardly fail to force themselves upon thoughtful minds in reference to the holy Sacraments. Such, for instance, as the question how there should be in both Sacraments an entire union to Christ, and yet the effects of the two Sacraments be different. For it might well seem, on a first view, that entire union to the same Person would always produce the same effects. And again, as to the real nature of the difference between the two Sacraments, and of the great pre-eminence, in point of awfulness and mysteriousness, universally accorded from the earliest times to the second Sacrament. It appears, from what has been said, that the difference is partly one of *degree* only, but that there is also a most important difference in *kind*. The Eucharist, under one point of view, and that its simpler and less transcendent one, is the making good and carrying on, by fresh supplies of the same kind of grace, of the renewal imparted in Baptism. Such is the account Hooker gives of the relation of the Sacraments to each other:—

"The grace which we have by the holy Eucharist doth not begin but continue life. . . . Life being therefore proposed unto all men as their end, they which by Baptism have laid the foundation and attained the first beginning of a new life, have here their nourishment and food prescribed for *continuance of life* in them [v]."

Now even under this aspect the Eucharist may, *in a certain sense*, be said to transcend Baptism; so immense is the spiritual advancement which it is capable of imparting. So much so, indeed, that the analogy of food can hardly be said to represent the fact adequately. Food is by no means such a plenary gift to the body as the Eucharist is to the spiritual being. Perhaps the nearest analogy which the natural life presents is that of *growth*, more especially that degree of it which transforms infancy into manhood. This is so real a *multiplication*, so immense an exaltation, in all its parts and powers, of the infantile life as at first imparted, as not altogether inadequately to typify the vast accessions to the first-imparted baptismal life, which the Eucharist is capable of bestowing. And this analogy, too, no less than that of food, is fully sanctioned both in the Old and New Testament; Christ being so constantly represented as the "*Growth*," (i.e. means of growth) of His people [x]. But still it must be admitted that it is only *in a sense* that the Eucharist, considered merely as a means of the continuance and growth of the spiritual life, can be said to be a greater gift than Baptism. After all, the great law of being must hold, that "the life is more than the meat." As the crowning marvel of creative power and love is the imparting to inert matter the mysterious principle of life, and of intel-

---

[v] Hooker, Eccl. Pol., V. lxvii. 1.

[x] Zech. iii. 8, vi. 12; Is. iv. 5; Jer. xxiii. 5; Eph. ii. 21, iv. 16; Col. ii. 19.

lectual and spiritual existence; insomuch that the subsequent maintenance and advancement of these powers is as nothing in comparison, (it is our blessed Lord's own estimate ʳ :) so, however great, in potency of virtue and fulness of measure, the spiritual sustenance and growth imparted by the Eucharist, it can never, considered *as* sustenance, really transcend in marvellousness the mysterious quickening bestowed by the spiritual new birth. At the utmost, there results a co-equality in point of power and mysteriousness between the two Sacraments, viewed as instruments of spiritual life and growth merely; for if one of them is greater in one point of view, the other is so in another. Great is Baptism, inconceivably great; for it is "a new creation:" and great too, inconceivably great, is the Eucharist also; for it draws out that, which in Baptism is once for all created, into infinity of increase, and eternity of duration. In a word, so long as we consider the Sacraments as operating *in pari materia* and *ex loco æquali*,—in the same sphere, and as it were on the same level,—as only different degrees or manifestations of the *same kind of thing*, viz. renewal,—we have no faculties for pronouncing whether of the two is the greater and the more mysterious. Whether the spiritual new birth at the first, or the eternal growth of the new being afterwards, is the more marvellous and excellent, who can with any confidence pronounce? Both are great deeps; whether of the two is the deeper, our line is too short to fathom.

Whence then that peculiar character of profoundest and most reverential awe, with which the Church ˢ

---

ʳ St. Matt. vi. 25.
ˢ Compare the greater awfulness of St. Paul's language in Heb. x.

from the earliest ages has invested the mystery of the Holy Eucharist? Or whence,—if participation in order to growth is, as so many suppose, the whole purport of the Eucharistic act,—whence the very large proportion in which all ancient Eucharistic Offices are directed to those other great topics of Oblation or Dedication, and Pleading? The view which represents the Eucharist as merely a means of making accessions, by way of growth, to the baptismal estate of grace, yields no account whatever of these great features in the ancient idea of the Eucharist. And yet some grounds there must be for this comparative estimate of the two Sacraments, which accords to the second a vast and unqualified pre-eminence over the first, both in point of solemnity, and also as an occasion for the discharge of certain spiritual functions of a Christian!

For though Baptism was held of old, as was fitting, in exceeding reverence; though it rightly enjoyed the lofty titles [a] of "New Creation," the "Anointing," the "Gift[b]," "Illumination," "Consecration," and the like, yet the language applied to it is still as nothing, compared with what is said of the Eucharist. This is spoken of in very early days, as "the awful, the tremendous, the unspeakable mysteries," "the hallowed, celestial, ineffable, stainless, terrible, tremendous, divine gifts[c]." The Eucharistic Presence of Christ, throughout the ancient Liturgies, or Communion Offices, is ever represented as something far

29, than in Heb. vi. 1; in which passages he seems to speak of profaning the two Sacraments respectively. See Note G.

[a] Vide Bingham, Eccl. Antiq., XI. l. 1—10. p. 399—411.

[b] Ibid., p. 412.

[c] Lit. St. James, (circ. A.D. 200, at latest). Neale, Gen. Introd., vol. ii. p. 611.

more awful and intimate than His Baptismal Presence; and warnings of proportionate solemnity have in all ages, after the example set by St. Paul[d], been used to deter men from partaking it unworthily. And this is of itself a remarkable circumstance, that those who have received the gift of new birth and spiritual life should be so solemnly warned of the danger of partaking, without certain special, and in a manner new, qualifications, of the means of sustaining that life. The qualifications for Baptism have ever been "repentance and faith." This faith is directed, (1) towards "all the articles" of the Creed; and (2) towards "the promises of God made in that Sacrament," viz. that it shall be effectual to "death unto sin and new birth unto righteousness," through the virtue of Christ's Death and Resurrection[e]. The requirements of our Church for Communion (justly representing, I conceive, the mind of the Church from the beginning) are still, as in Baptism, repentance and faith. But this faith is now specially directed towards right conceptions and due thankful remembrance of (1) the "*Sacrifice* of the Death of Christ," as such, and (2) of "the benefits which we receive thereby;" not towards His Death and Resurrection as re-creative and regenerative mysteries. All this surely bespeaks some further mystery as involved in the Eucharist, beyond the character which it possesses as a direct continuation and advancement, on the same level, of the baptismal gift of life. And the fact which it points to is doubtless that the Eucharist makes

---

[d] See above, note p. 181.

[e] See the end of the Baptismal Office: "That as He died and rose again, so should we who are baptized die from sin and rise again unto righteousness," &c. Compare Romans vi. 3—6.

us partakers more intimately, more directly, completely, and peculiarly, of an aspect of our Lord's actions into which Baptism but very partially and imperfectly admitted us. The Eucharist, over and above its powers for the maintenance of the baptismal life, admits us to a position and to functions awfully and mysteriously related to the most awful and mysterious of the characters and functions of Christ. Hence, then, the surpassing solemnity of the action, and hence the duties peculiarly assigned to it in the Eucharistic Offices. If Baptism possesses, as it does, "the shadow" of Christ's Priesthood, the Eucharist has "the very image" of it. If Baptism makes us in power, and *de jure*, "priests unto God," the Eucharist constitutes and exhibits us as such *de facto*, and in action. If Baptism makes us to be the spiritual Israel, God's children and sons, supernaturally gathered into One Body, and sustained by various lower effluxes of the priestly and sacrificial work of the Aaron of the heavenly sanctuary; the Eucharist introduces us to the inner privileges of priestly action and participation, the antitypes in some sort of those by which Aaron's seed was brought into a peculiar nearness to God, and partook of that bread of presence, and of those more eminent sacrifices, which were withheld from the rest. So much more intimate is the Eucharistic than the baptismal Presence, Eucharistic than baptismal Participation, of Christ; even as the Israelitish priests stood in a more awful nearness to the presence of God than the people, and as eating, e.g., of the sin-offerings was a more solemn and privileged act than eating of the ordinary peace-offerings[f].

[f] These illustrations cannot, perhaps, be pressed very closely in

These considerations seem, further, to throw some light on a point of much interest; the existence, namely, of Infant Communion in certain early ages of the Church, and its abeyance since throughout Western Christendom. That it was the primitive custom to give the Holy Communion to infants has been affirmed, but is absolutely devoid of proof; and there is a very strong presumption against it. Early vouchers for it are Tertullian and St. Cyprian; and it prevailed till perhaps the middle ages in the West, and is continued at this day in the Eastern Church. And were participation in certain consecrated things by a fit (or not unfit) recipient the whole matter, the analogy of Baptism would all but enforce the practice in question. But it is not so. To the full and proper Eucharistic act, a conscious act of oblation and presentation is indispensable. Now this cannot be discharged by unconscious, nor even by young, children. While, therefore, there is not a little to be said, at first sight, in favour of giving the Eucharist to infants, as being the Sacrament of growth, and the carrying on of the life imparted in Baptism,—we see that the practice is in some sort a putting asunder of things which Christ has joined together in His ordinance, by bringing those to it who can join but in a part of it, viz. the receptive; the very converse error to that by which the later Western Church has systematized *non-communicating* attendance on the Eucharistic offering. On this ground we may not only, I conceive, acquiesce in the disuse of Infant Communion, but also most seriously question its having been apostolic or primitive. The early zeal for the Holy Eucharist will

all particulars; but they may serve to give an idea of what is meant. Vide Levit. vi. 26.

abundantly account for a well-intended deviation from primitive order in this matter, even as soon as the days of Tertullian.

But let us now proceed to inquire what light we derive, from the considerations here set forth, upon the question before us, as to the true theory of the Church's ordinary worship contained in her Daily Offices.

Now in the first place, our observing that the Holy Eucharist, if we include all aspects of it, is of so sublime and transcendent a character, makes it reasonable or likely that there would be provided within the Church lower and simpler means of Divine worship and intercommunion. In proportion as the Eucharist is excellent and awful, admitting man to the very inner mysteries of his Christian estate, and so calls for the most intense concentration of his entire powers upon the discharge of his part in it; in that proportion is it unfitted to be the ordinary and continually applied, still less the exclusive instrument of spiritual intercourse between God and man.

This view, or so much of it as denies the every-day character of the Eucharist, will doubtless be exceedingly unacceptable to many persons in the present day. It is probably a growing opinion among members of the English Church, and those not the least learned or entitled to carry least weight in such a matter, that daily Communion, where it can be had, is the proper instrument of Christian perfection. The intended and normal condition of the Church is, they conceive, that there should be everywhere a daily Eucharist, and that all faithful persons should be daily communicants; or at any rate as many persons as possible. But, while I yield to none either in a deep sense of the lamentable infrequency of that celebration among us, or in the earnest desire that it might be, according to apostolic practice, weekly, at least, everywhere,—more constant or even daily, at some special seasons: I would at the same time no less earnestly protest against a view which has no standing-ground in apostolic or primitive usage ; and the attempt to carry out which can, as experience has shewn, only end in the depravation of the holy rite it is designed to exalt. Let us by all means do honour to God in all ways of His appointing; but let us not think to do so by straining His sacred ordinances to other purposes than those which they were designed to answer. Let us accept with teachableness the lessons on this point which are written for us, alike in the scriptural and apostolic, as in the post-apostolic, history of the Church.

Now looking to those lessons, and that history, I venture to affirm, 1st, that the Holy Eucharist is *in its proper nature* a festival thing; by which I mean a high, occasional, and solemn one, not every-day or common; and 2ndly, that in the very earliest, and surely the wisest and holiest age, celebration, though never less than weekly, was rarely more frequent than that ; *never*, that we know of for certain, (though at high seasons it may possibly have been so,) *daily;*— and that in these considerations, not in any *à priori* arguments as to the excellence of the rite, is to be laid the basis of a right estimate as to the frequency of celebration which is either to be expected or desired. *Sunday and festival celebration*, in a word,—a designation which leaves ample verge for diversity within certain intelligible limits,—may safely be affirmed to be, as a general rule, the prescript for the Church, and to exhibit with the greatest fidelity the true character and purpose of the Holy Eucharist. That the clergy may have occasion to celebrate much more frequently than this, publicly or privately, as a part of their ministrations to the people, is of course undeniable. And that this measure may be in different degrees exceeded by clergy and laity alike, even to the degree of daily celebration at particular times, is conceded also. But that whensoever and wheresoever this is the case, it is the bringing in a Festival, i. e. a high and solemn idea and character, into the common and average tenor of the life of Christians,—that it is the elevation of the Christian life into an uncommon condition of privilege, and one not designed for them as a general rule,—this I would affirm no less.

Such a view, I venture to assert, not merely the nature of the thing, but the practice of the Church in the earliest and purest ages, her sad experience in all later and less clearly-sighted ones, and certain of her disciplinary rules at all times, entirely fall in with. It is indeed commonly and inconsiderately said, and the saying passes from mouth to mouth without inquiry, that the first Christians communicated every day. Thus Jeremy Taylor frequently assumes this to have been the practice. (See, e. g., Worthy Communicant, p. 621.) So others :—

(Sparrow, Rat., p. 221): "In the primitive Church, while Christians continued in the strength of faith and devotion, they did communicate every day. This custom continued in Africa till St. Cyprian's time, &c. But afterwards the custom grew faint, and some upon one pretence, some upon another, would communicate once a-week." And Wheatly, chap. vi. sect. i.: "We find the Eucharist was always in the purest ages of the Church, a daily part of the Common Prayer."

The truth is, that there is not a shadow of evidence

that in apostolic times, at least after the very first Pentecostal inauguration of the Church, if even then, there was daily celebration of the Eucharist. The evidence is, on the contrary, entirely the other way. That there may have been immediately after the Day of Pentecost, such daily celebration, the well-known passage in Acts ii. 42, 46, no doubt affords a strong presumption. But even this must be allowed to be capable of another interpretation. All that is *certainly* affirmed by it is, that besides their daily attendance at the temple, the faithful did also at a house or houses, in contradistinction to the temple, (most probably in the upper chamber of the holy Institution,) "break bread." Whether the καθ' ἡμέραν, "daily," applies to the Eucharistic celebration as well as to the temple services, is a question for criticism, which I apprehend there is nothing in the passage to decide for us either way. On the whole, I conceive the improbability of new converts being thus admitted to a daily Eucharist to be very strong indeed. It is certainly at variance with all else that we subsequently gather on the subject. The manner in which the first day of the week stands out, from the Acts (ch. ii. 1.) to the Revelation, (i. 10,) especially for Eucharistic assemblies, (Acts xx. 7; 1 Cor. xvi. 2.) must be admitted. And though an ingenious and devout writer endeavours to shew that the celebration at Troas was twofold, one before, and one after, St. Paul's preaching [g]; the more probable opinion certainly is that which an ordinary reader derives from the passage. External evidence towards the close of the apostolic times comes in to prove con-

[g] Bp. Jolly, on the Eucharist, p. 160. Fleury (Mœurs de Chrétiens, iii. 14,) takes the ordinary view.

clusively that then, at least, weekly Eucharist was the ordinary rule[h]. The well-known letter of Pliny, manifestly describing the Eucharistic practice of Christians, from the mouth of one of them, represents it as confined to a certain day,—no doubt the Sunday. Justin Martyr's testimony (A.D. 150) probably recognises occasional celebrations on other days, but most distinctly gives Sunday as the rule. Tertullian (at the end of the second century) speaks of celebration *twice a-week*, besides, and on festivals. But St. Cyprian, 250 B.C., is the first who alludes to it as taking place daily. Thenceforward there is occasional mention of it as such, but nothing approaching to a proof that it was of universal prevalence; indeed, there is abundant proof that it was not. And the inference is irresistible, that if apostolic and post-apostolic Christians maintained the life of faith with far less than a daily Eucharist, it follows, 1st, that that rite in its primary intention, was, as has been said, a Festival, i. e. a high and solemn, not ordinary and every-day, thing; and 2nd, that, with this apostolic example before our eyes, it is at least a question (surely one which all but demands an affirmative) whether great moderation in multiplying of Eucharistic celebrations be not the part of

[h] Vide Bingham, XIII ix. 1, vol. iv. p. 353, (and Cotelerius, ibid.); also XV. ix. 2, p. 358; where the question of ancient frequency of celebration is fully discussed. The following are some of his conclusions:—"This frequency of Communion may reasonably be supposed to be, then, according to the known practice, once a-week, or every Lord's day. Roman Catholic writers, though somewhat concerned to prove ancient daily celebration, admit the same. So Cotelerius, as above. So Fleury (Mœurs des Chrétiens, iii. 39): "On offrait le sacrifice tous les Dimanches, et encore deux fois de la semaine;" speaking of the times of the first Christian Emperors. Again, i. 14, speaking of the primitive ages: "Chaque Eglise particulière s'assemblait le Dimanche. .... On s'assemblait aussi le Vendredi;" alluding perhaps to Tertullian's stationary days. So too Krazer, de Liturg.

Christian wisdom, not to say of apostolic conformity. Such, at any rate, seems to have been the view seriously entertained and acted upon in many parts of the ancient Church. The Church at large was slow to admit any innovation in the apostolic usage. This appears from an expression in the very ancient Eucharistic Office of the Alexandrian Church, the Liturgy of St. Mark intimating that celebration was confined to Sundays or Festivals. The first prayer in it (which I have elsewhere[i] given reasons for considering to be of primitive antiquity) contains the words, "And, we pray Thee, grant us to spend this *holy day*," &c. And in full accordance with this, again, we find, as an historical fact, that even in the ancient monasteries of Egypt "it was peculiar to Sundays and Festivals;" that, in addition to the daily Offices, "they met at the third hour for the celebration of the sacred Mysteries[k]." And, indeed, throughout the Church of Alexandria, so late as the end of the fourth century, the Eucharist was only celebrated on Saturdays and Sundays, both these days being reckoned as Festivals. For among the canons preserved by Timothy, bishop of Alexandria, (A.D. 380,) we find a restrictive injunction laid upon married persons, applying to those two days, based upon the ground "that upon them the spiritual Sacrifice is offered to the Lord[l]." The Armenian Church, again, an offshoot of that of Cæsarea in Cappadocia, founded by St. Gregory the Illuminator towards the close of the third century[m], has

---

[i] Vide infra, vol. ii., chap. on Prim. Liturgy. The date of St. Mark's Liturgy is believed to be about A.D. 200.

[k] Cassian, ap Mabillon, De Lit. Gall., p. 383. He writes in the fifth century, but is doubtless describing customs of long standing.

[l] Tim. Epist. Can., c. xiii., ap. Bingh. XIII. ix. 3.

[m] Vide Neale, Gen. Introd., p. 67.

to this day a most remarkable regulation, viz. that the Eucharist *may not* be celebrated *excepting on Saturday and Sunday*, or on great Festivals of our Lord or the blessed Virgin Mary. This probably represents, though perhaps it enforces too rigidly, the ordinary usage of the Church of Cæsarea at the time of St. Gregory aforesaid, which would thus accord with the Alexandrine usage just referred to. We find St. Basil, bishop of the same Cæsarea about seventy years after, testifying that they had Communion on *four* days of the week, viz. Wednesday and Friday, in addition to Saturday and Sunday[n]. The Church at large, again, by an almost universal provision, has declared her mind that the Eucharist is of the nature of a festival thing. Whence, otherwise, the rule that none should participate in the Eucharistic elements oftener than once in the same day? Why not twice or thrice a-day or even hourly? There is nothing in the world that can account for this prohibition on the part of the Church, but her strongly entertained mind that participation more than once in a day would evacuate the great rite of some important and indispensable feature. And what can that be? Its sacramental efficacy? Surely not. The reason manifestly is this: that in daily participation the Eucharistic act is carried to the utmost limit it is capable of, consistently with its character as the high Festival of Christianity.

I have only to add here on this subject, that the Church seems early to have rued having innovated upon the apostolic usage by the introduction of daily celebration. There is certainly a remarkable and ominous synchronism between this change and the grievous falling off of that primitive custom of *weekly*

---

[n] St. Basil, Ep. 289, ap. Bingh. ib. 3.

*reception* of the mysteries, which the Church has never yet been able to bring back as the badge of Christian membership. It is in the time of St. Chrysostom, St. Jerome, St. Ambrose, and St. Augustine, that we first find daily celebration to have obtained an extensive footing in the Church. The Churches of Constantinople and Carthage, of Rome and of Spain, now provided a daily Eucharist[o] for such as desired it; and these great Doctors are busied with settling a question, comparatively new to the Church, as to the expediency of such frequent reception. And it is at this very time that we also first hear, from the same writers, of Christian men, alike in the East and in the West, contenting themselves with Communion *once a-year;* which still remains as the allowed minimum in the Western Church, England only excepted. "If it be our daily bread," says St. Ambrose, "why dost thou then receive it once a-year only, as the Greeks have come to do in the East[p]?" This is a fact which we shall do well to ponder. I shall have occasion to return to it in connection with the duty of the English Church at the present day.

[o] St. Jerome, Ep. 50, 58; St. Aug., Ep. ad Jan. 118. Vide Bingh., XV. ix. 4.

[p] St. Amb., de Sacr. v. 4.

## SECTION III.

"And they shall bring all your brethren for an offering unto the Lord out of all nations, to My holy mountain, to Jerusalem, saith the Lord. And I will also take of them for priests and for Levites."

"That I should be the minister of Jesus Christ unto the Gentiles, ministering the gospel of God, that the offering up of the Gentiles might be acceptable, being sanctified by the Holy Ghost."

THE necessary existence of some kind of ordinary service follows as an obvious corollary from that ordained infrequency (comparatively) of the Eucharistic rite, which has been spoken of in the preceding section. The character, position, and functions, again, of such ordinary service, may be in a great measure deduced from the sacramental principles we were lately engaged in tracing, and of which we may now resume the consideration.

It was well said of old, insomuch that the saying has passed into what may be called an axiom of the Church, that "the Sacraments are the extension of the Incarnation." They are, that is to say, the instruments whereby (to use the words of St. Paul) "the Body of Christ increaseth with the increase of God[q]." "Christians are really, though mysteriously, incorporated into the incarnate Body of the Lord Jesus Christ, by virtue of their incorporation into that Church which is His mystical Body[r]." Thus is the mystical Body true to the qualities of a body in this

---

[q] Col. ii. 19; Eph. iv. 16.

[r] Serm. by Rev. C. T. Smith, ubi supra. So Hooker: "In Him, even *according to His Manhood*, we, according to our heavenly being, are as branches in that root out of which they grow." (V. lvi. 7.)

respect even, as well as in others, that it too "groweth," "until we all," the parts of that Body taken together, "come to a perfect man, to the measure of the full stature of Christ [s]."

But how are the Sacraments empowered to be "the extension of the Incarnation;" the *means*, that is, of extending it, so as that it shall include continually more and more members? The nature of this Divine Economy would seem to be as follows. There is in spiritual things, as in natural, causation. Christ's Sacraments produce their effects, not in the manner of a holy charm, in virtue merely of His promise *to* them, but as causes, by reason of His presence *in* them. For the natural Body of Christ, with all its wondrous doings and characters, was to be as a germ, no less than a type, to that greater mystical Body of His, which was to bear as a whole the impress of those doings and characters. And that the Body, as a whole, might be conformed to its type and exemplar, it was necessary that the several members and parts of it should be first so conformed, each one by itself. In order to this, then, the grace of the aforesaid actions and characters of the incarnate Word was gathered into those Sacraments which were destined to be the instruments of the entire Body's growth. The instruments of ingrafting were no rude or random ones, but worthy of the Divine Artificer of this new masterpiece of creation, the mystical Body of the incarnate WORD. They were so fashioned as to contain within them, by an especial fiat of the Divine Will, the virtue of those actions and characters of the WORD made flesh, in conformity to which the bettered estate of man was to consist. It is therefore that they are instruments of power to

[s] Eph. iv. 13.

ingraft into Christ's Body, and to produce conformity to His likeness, because they are themselves replete with the virtue and potency of His Person and actions[t].

The Sacraments then being of this nature; thus epitomizing, so to speak, the Person and actions of the Lord Jesus Christ, in order to convey the virtue of them: the Christian life was to be the development of these sacramental compendia into suitable action; that so out of a sacramental conformity imparted once for all, might grow an actual or acted conformity. (Conversely, of course, the Sacraments are the concentration of the Christian life into certain intensified and all-including formulæ.)

In this consideration is to be found the true answer to every question concerning Christian practice and duty. As our natural duties as men arise from the position in which, as men, we find ourselves placed,—duties, domestic, patriotic, or international,—so do our supranatural duties and functions, as Christians, arise from the nature and particulars of the estate into which, as Christians, we are admitted. As no man knows what are his rights and duties as a citizen, otherwise than by consideration of the constitution under which he lives; so, of what we are, or what bound or designed to do, as Christians, we can form no idea, but by re-perusal of that twofold charter which has admitted us to the privileges of the spiritual kingdom. The Sacraments, therefore, are really fundamental to the whole matter. To them, and through them to the Person and actions of Christ, the grace

---

[t] Rom. vi. 3—5: "Know ye not, that so many of us as were *baptized into Christ Jesus*, were baptized *into His Death?* Therefore we *are buried with Him by baptism* into death... If we have been planted together in (rather, *made to partake of the nature of*) the likeness of His Death, we shall also [partake of the nature of] His Resurrection."

whereof they embody and convey, we must look. Whatsoever is involved or implied in *them, that* is our position, and thence flows our business and calling as Christian men. The Sacraments describe and set out to us, how compendiously soever, the duties of our Christian estate and citizenship. It is in full accordance with this statement, that the Epistles, especially St. Paul's, are mainly directed, as will be seen on careful consideration of them, to *unfolding the duties of Christians, arising out of the position given them by the Sacraments*[a];—a truth which, had it been duly borne in mind, would have done away with all suspicion of any possible rivalry or contrariety between the true doctrine of the Sacraments and that of the written Word; or of any incompatibility between zeal for the one and implicit reverence for, and submission to, the other.

But the Sacraments are twofold. Do they then, it may be asked, respectively set out to us two different lines or classes of duties? Not so; they do but exhibit the selfsame duties under two different aspects; following herein, it will be perceived, the analogy of that one series of actions of our Lord, whose twofold aspects they respectively embody. The Christian estate, though exhibited to us under two forms in the Sacraments, is, like the double vision of Pharaoh, strictly one; its series of actions and duties is one, though consecrated, as it were, to different purposes by these two ordinances respectively. Every Christian duty would appear to have, or to be capable of, a distinct relation to either Sacrament; it has a lower or a higher standing, ascends to a lower or a higher sphere, and so is in some sense a different

[a] See, in note G, quotations from the Apostolic Epistles.

thing, according as it is viewed in connection with the one Sacrament or with the other. The selfsame phenomenon has been already pointed out in reference to our Lord's actions. And as they appertained, under one aspect, to His Incarnation, and under another to His Priesthood; as they were, in one character, in order to the renewal of humanity, and in another in order to its acceptable presentation: so is it with our actions also. Viewed in connection with Baptism, they are the carrying out into action all that Baptism implies; the making good of the estate and condition of death to sin and new birth to holiness; of the renunciation of the dominion of sin, and obedience to the laws of God's kingdom; of putting off the spirit of bondage, and putting on the adoption of the sons of God; with whatever else Baptism involves. In a word, the whole Christian life, in all its parts and acts, is, from the baptismal point of view, a persistence in that condition of renewing and sanctifying union to the perfected Humanity of our Lord, in which the essence of Baptism consists. And this aspect alone, it is needless to say, can the Christian life possess for those who have as yet been made partakers of but one Sacrament only, that of new birth, renewal, and adoption. Whatever aspect or colour the having been made partakers of the other Sacrament may impart to the actions of a Christian, for *them*, at present, no such second aspect exists.

But for those who *have* been made partakers of the other Sacrament, the Christian life, in all its parts, owns a second and a superadded aspect. Viewed in connection with that rite, it is now the carrying out into act of those priestly and sacrificial relations which Eucharistic celebration and participation involve, as before of those re-creative ones which belong to Baptism. Life is no longer merely a continual dying and rising, a daily putting off the old man and putting on the new, an estate of adoption and sonship. Though it is still all this, it is now, over and above, a continual sacrifice of that which dies and rises again; a reiterated, life-long oblation of the renewed man; and partakes, as the means of its sustentation in this elevated condition, of peculiar effluxes of the Divine Nature[x], by feeding on a sacrifice. It has become, in short, an estate of priesthood unto God, involving functions and powers derived immediately from the one perfect Priesthood, as were those former ones from the one perfect Manhood, of Christ.

Now the ordinance of Public Worship is only one particular instance of that development of the Sacraments, that carrying out of them into detailed action, which has been here spoken of. Were those ordinances of such a nature as to terminate in themselves; did they convey a gift and a position of which no subsequent account was to be rendered by the receiver; or were sacramental participation the whole matter; then doubtless there had been, besides and beyond the Sacraments, no other duties of direct service and ritual towards God. It is because the deeds of a life, as well ritual as ordinary, are potentially wrapped up, as the oak within the acorn, in the reception of either Sacrament,—it is therefore that, by the necessity of the case, there must be other Christian rites continuative of these. The being of

---

[x] 2 Pet. i. 4: "Whereby are given to us" (have been bestowed upon us, δεδώρηται,) "exceeding great and precious promises," (rather, "the most exceeding precious promised gifts," ἐπαγγέλματα,) "that by these ye might be" (become) "partakers of the Divine Nature."

man stands in need, for its maintenance in those refined spiritual relations to God, upon which in the Sacraments it enters, of some more spiritual and ritual media than the ordinary actions of life supply. Whatever in the way of direct mutual communication between God and man, is compendiously transacted in the Sacraments, has to be done in a more developed and leisurely manner by actions of a corresponding and kindred nature.

The actual celebration of the Sacraments, accordingly, has ever been accompanied, at the very time, by such actions,—spiritual exercises of *detailed* prayer and profession of faith on the one hand, and of intellectual reception of Christian mysteries, as contained in Holy Scripture, on the other. These, though not [y] essential to the validity of the Sacraments, (which are both transacted, as to their essentials, with certain short ordained formulæ of words,) are the proper development of what is contained in them; and they serve for the germ, and furnish the pattern, and in some degree the substance, of more ordinary offices of worship.

Is there, as the common feature of both Sacraments, entire union to Christ,—a union which supposes, on the part of man, repentance, faith, love, and other Christian graces; and consists on God's part of an essential Presence vouchsafed? Those graces must be provided with a fitting vehicle and expression. There must be prayer of some sort. That Presence must be sought there, where it is specially promised;

---

[y] The essential formula for valid Baptism is known to be very brief: for proof that the essential formula for Eucharistic Consecration is proportionately compendious, see below, vol. ii., chapter on Primitive Form of Liturgy.

viz. in the common prayer of the many members of the One Body. Does the same union extend to all the saving actions of Christ, and must these be severally apprehended by the understanding, and embraced by faith and love with the heart? A necessity arises for knowledge, to be attained by adoring meditation of the whole economy of grace. And this too must be sought more especially there (viz. in the Church's public assemblies) where He who is "our *Wisdom*[z]" as well as "our Righteousness" is especially present in the one character no less than in the other. Has, again, either Sacrament its own proper gift; the one regeneration and renewal, the other priestly acceptableness and privilege? These estates obviously require, for their continued maintenance "after their kind," suitable ritual media of action and reception. For both purposes, *ascendat oratio ut descendat gratia*[a]. 1. That the renewed estate may be persevered in, recourse must be had not only to the other Sacrament, which is the high festival of its being, but also, (since that by its ordained nature cannot be continual), to more ordinary means of growth and perfection. For daily renewal, daily prayer must be made; that it may be according to knowledge, there must be daily exercise in the law of God; that the functions of the new estate may be duly performed, there must be praise, which is the life of the divinely conformed. That all these things, again, may be done in their perfection, the prayer, the meditation, and the praise, must be those, not of the single member, but of the Body, the Church.

---

[z] Compare the Eastern exclamation at the bringing in of the Gospels, "Wisdom: stand up." Supra, p. 134.

[a] St Augustine.

2. Still more, if possible, is public ordinary worship the necessary complement and filling up of that Christian priesthood which is supremely exercised in the Eucharistic act. For this purpose there must be "prayer set forth as incense and the lifting up of the hands as sacrifice," the "pure offering" of praise and self-dedication, by resorting to the highest vouchsafed Presence after the Eucharistic; there must be full and varied reception, by hearing of the mysteries of divine knowledge; lastly, there must be ever-renewed pleading, in the Church's great secondary method, and with detailed application to her needs, of the merits of the One Sacrifice.

Thus, then, Public Worship, as discharged by the Ordinary Offices of the Church, is far indeed from being, as some have imagined, an act of merely natural piety. Neither is it, as others perhaps conceive it, a Christian function indeed, yet an isolated thing, having no particular relation to the Sacraments, or occupying ground for which no provision is made, compendiously or otherwise, in those ordinances. The account to be given of Christian Public Worship—of the existence of such a thing at all—is, that it is strictly complementary to the Sacraments in the sense above explained. Complementary to them, I say, as filling up their idea; not supplementary, as if adding anything to it. To refer to the never-failing archetypal analogy of the Body of Christ: as "it pleaseth Him in mercy to account Himself incomplete and maimed without us[b]," the Church being the necessary "filling up" or "complement" of Him

[b] Hooker, V. lvi. 10.

"Who filleth all in all;" so is the Christian life in general, but Public Worship in particular, and in an especial degree, the "filling up" of the scheme or idea of the Sacraments. And of both Sacraments: not, as a third opinion would make it, of one only, that of Baptism; a view which is often more or less explicitly put forth, even in the improved theological teaching of the present day. That it is the acting out of that Sacrament, and may at all times be most properly used as such, has been fully admitted, and is to be most earnestly maintained. But its aspect towards the other Sacrament must be no less clearly held and contended for. To disallow a close connection as capable of existing between ordinary worship and the Eucharist, must appear on the slightest reflection most unsatisfactory. Of the two, indeed, it stands in more obvious connection with this than with Baptism; the work of prayer, praise, and of receiving knowledge of divine mysteries, being more strikingly akin to the Eucharistic action of conscious and active oblation and participation, than to that more passive and often unconscious process of renewal, of which Baptism is the instrument.

The Ordinary Worship of the Church, then, to state briefly the conclusion from our premises, is an eminent means of discharging the obligations and functions imposed, and of receiving the benefits guaranteed, in both the Sacraments. But its peculiar character is, that it is an exercise, in a lower way, of that Christian priesthood which we have in Christ, which is given to us in a measure in Baptism, but only bestowed in its fulness, or exercised in its highest form, in the celebration of the Eucharist.

The practical bearing of this view upon the mind

with which Ordinary Worship is to be joined in, is obvious.

There is a natural impulse, in the case of any one who has recently participated in the Eucharist, to view prayer, praise, and other devotional actions in connection with that great rite; as modes of realizing and carrying out the Eucharistic frame and position. The Church, by her Daily Offices, both recognizes and formalizes this rightful conception. Her ordinary public devotions are designed to be, to those who are in a position to use them as such, an expansion and carrying on of the Eucharistic functions and relations. To such, the general act of public worship is but a further cementing of the eucharistically imparted union with Christ and with His Body, the Church;—praise and thanksgiving, whether in Psalms or other forms, are as a tributary stream falling into the ocean of the Church's Eucharistic praise and oblation of herself in Christ;—the hearing of Divine mysteries of Scripture is an "eating[c]," as it were, "of the crumbs that fall" from the holy table; a continuation of the act of receiving into the soul Him who is the Eternal Word, and in Whom are hid all the treasures of wisdom and knowledge;—prayer and pleading are a keeping hold of the horn of the altar[d]. A view, it may surely be said, which dig-

---

[c] Compare St. Aug., Sermon vii. p. 85, vol. xvi. "Library of Fathers:" "What I am handling before you now" (i.e. the Scriptures) "is daily bread; and the daily lessons which ye hear in church are daily read."

[d] Hooker has briefly expressed the converse of this view: "Instruction and prayer," (by means of ordinary services of the Church,) "whereof we have hitherto spoken, are duties which serve as *elements, parts, or principles,* to the rest that follow; in which number the Sacraments of the Church are chief." (V. i. 1.)

nifies, while yet it duly subordinates, the act of Ordinary Worship.

In other respects, too, I venture to hope not only that the general correctness of these views will be admitted, but that they may prove the source to not a few of solid and enduring satisfaction, by exhibiting all the great lines of Christian ritual working unitedly and harmoniously together.

Such an adjustment between the Church's greater and lesser acts of worship would seem to be the proper antidote to a tendency which has begun to appear here and there amongst us, to depreciate the Church's Ordinary Worship, if not to desire even the partial abolition of it. There are those who, rightly impressed with the transcendent excellence of the Eucharistic rite, and possessed with a proportionate desire for more frequent celebration of it, are inclined to look upon the Church's Ordinary Offices with toleration at best, and as impeding rather than promoting the highest kind of spiritual life and growth. They see not why the ordinary Daily Offices, or the Morning Office at the least, might not be dispensed with, and daily celebration of the Eucharist be put in its place. The rest of the Western Church is known to have even substituted, in practice, *non-communicating* attendance at the celebration of the Eucharist, for her nominal Morning Offices; which have accordingly, as has been already [e] pointed out, ceased to exist as the vehicle of the people's devotion. And some among us would perhaps advocate our following even this extreme example [f]. But at pre-

[e] Compare ch. i., sub fin.

[f] On non-communicating attendance at the Eucharist, see the last chapter of this volume.

sent I have in view the case of those only who would desire the substitution of a daily and genuine congregational Eucharist for our ordinary Office of Morning Prayer. This view, as expressing a zeal for the one act of worship instituted by our Lord Himself, is naturally engaging to devout and reverent minds. But it leaves out of sight, on the one hand, certain limiting and restraining facts adduced above, which render it likely—nay, which prove with the force of a moral demonstration—that daily Eucharistic celebration was not the intended rule for the Church's observance;—such as the absence, acknowledged by all learned men who have examined the subject, of such frequency during apostolic and early times; the declension of Christianity under the condition of daily celebration; and the high festival character of the rite itself. And again, on the other hand, this expression of zeal for the Eucharist ignores the position, dignity, and powers of the Ordinary Worship of the Church; its position as being, under one view, the indispensable instrument for the carrying out of the Eucharistic idea; its dignity in virtue of that connection; and its powers, in virtue both of our Lord's express and separate promise to it, and of the quasi-priestly and sacrificial character which, in its degree, it shares with the Eucharist.

Others, again, without concurring in the desires and aims of those just alluded to, yet are impressed, more or less consciously, with the sense of there being a kind of rivalry between the Eucharistic and the Ordinary Worship of the Church, rather than that perfect compatibility and harmonious connection which in reality, as has been here shewn, exists between them.

Nor are such views of the whole field of Christian ritual less necessary for those—including, perhaps, the vast proportion of the English Church, both lay and clerical—whose danger lies in the opposite direction; who are even too well satisfied with the ordinary Services of the Church. Nothing short of an entire and radical misconception as to the Apostolic idea of Christian Worship and Service as a whole, could have brought in that generally prevailing acquiescence in infrequent celebration of the Holy Communion which characterizes the English Church at the present day. I say *acquiescence* in such infrequency; for that is the peculiar character of our shortcoming in the matter. While other Churches, to secure Apostolic frequency, have resorted to unapostolic and unjustifiable modes of celebrating, we have secured Apostolic and genuine celebrations, but Apostolic frequency we have, speaking generally, been careless of. This subject will be treated of hereafter; I will only point out here, with reference alike to Sunday and week-day Ordinary Offices, that in Apostolic times, the idea of their standing alone, or superseding the weekly Eucharist, was absolutely unknown.

There is, again, an important theological difference in the present day, about which the views contained in this chapter would seem to open the way towards something like an agreement. The assertion of certain real priestly functions as peculiar to the clergy, and specially of a commission to consecrate and administer the Holy Eucharist, is the distinguishing note of one large and influential school within the English Church. The assertion, again, of a Christian priesthood as appertaining to the laity, has been taken up as an antagonistic truth in other quarters. But surely the two positions, far from being antagonistic, not only may be harmonized, but must both of them be most firmly and fully maintained, if we would hold the true Christian doctrine in perfection. Each of these two great and earnest parties may, in fact, learn somewhat from the other. The one, in maintaining the power, undoubtedly pertaining to the clergy, to consecrate and administer the Holy Eucharist, have perhaps been too little careful to represent them as, (1) essentially and entirely ministerial under the Great High-Priest, whose Hand, as it were, they are; and as also (2) needing the concurrent action of the people; *not without whom*, as necessary consentients and coadjutors, they perform that sacred function. Such is unquestionably the view of the early Church as expressed in her Liturgies. "Be present, be present, O JESU, Thou good High-Priest, in the midst of us, as Thou wert in the midst of Thy Disciples," (i.e. at the original institution,) "and sanctify this Oblation, that we may by the hands of Thy holy Angel receive that which is sanctified," are the words of one very ancient Communion Office[g]; and correctly represent the mind of all. And again, it is priest and people united that make the solemn oblation of the Elements, call down the grace of the Holy Spirit upon them, and plead the merits of the One all-prevailing Sacrifice. It is in the plural number, in the congregational form, that these great transactions between heaven and earth take place. Above all, it is in the presentation, yet more by themselves than by the clergy, of an acceptable people,—acceptable[h] in Christ, and as the

[g] The Mozarabic, or ancient Spanish. Vide Neale, Tetral. Liturgic., or Gen. Introd., p. 545. On the joint action of priest and people in the consecration, see also Note G.

[h] Compare Jer. Taylor, Golden Grove, (Works, vol. xv. p. 61): "That

Body of Christ,—that the glory of that great Offering consists. The holocaust that flames on the altar, "the sweet savour acceptable to the Lord," is "themselves, their souls and bodies, a reasonable, holy, and lively sacrifice." In the power thus concurrently with the clergy to offer and plead, and finally to participate, the Christian priesthood of the people formally and essentially consists; nor can any of these functions be denied to them without abridging the gifts and privileges which are theirs in Christ. And these functions of the people as "priests unto God," thus chiefly and supremely exercised in taking part in the Eucharistic Rite, they do in a lower degree, as has been represented in this chapter, discharge also in joining in the Ordinary Services of the Church. Nay, even in their common life, they part not with these powers, but carry on the same work: it is their privilege acceptably to present to God in Christ every action and every hour of their lives; and what is priesthood but the power to present acceptably? Only this priestlike action, as we may venture to call it, is to be ever and anon gathered up for more formal and ritual presentation in the Services, both Eucharistic and ordinary, of the Sanctuary.

It is then in the more habitual recognition of *a* priesthood as appertaining to the people, that, as I conceive, the one of the two schools of theological opinion referred to may take example from the other. It may be questioned whether such recognition appears so distinctly, prominently, and broadly in their teaching as might be desired, and as it certainly appears in every line of the ancient Communion Offices,

she may for ever advance the honour of the Lord Jesus, and represent His Sacrifice, &c., &c., and *be accepted of Thee in her Blessed Lord.*"

P

and of our own. So long as we stipulate for the indispensableness of a duly (i.e. an apostolically) commissioned ministering priesthood in order to the effectual celebration of the Holy Communion, it would seem to be almost impossible to insist too strongly on the people's position as "priests unto God." For it may truly be said that all other priesthood, yea, the very Priesthood of CHRIST Himself, exists but for the sake of this, as the means exist for the sake of the end. Not for His own sake, but "for their sakes" did He "sanctify Himself[l]," i.e. consecrate Himself as a Priest and Offering unto God, "that they also might be sanctified," and become prevailing priests, and an acceptable sacrifice. Nor is there, perhaps, any truth which the laity generally have greater need to be taught, than the existence and nature of these lofty privileges of theirs, and how the exercise of them is involved, in different degrees, in the higher and lower kinds of attendance in the Sanctuary.

Those, on the other hand, who are so earnest in maintaining the existence and the rights of Christian priesthood as pertaining to the people, are in general very far from entertaining any just or adequate conception of what priesthood is. For this they must have recourse to the ancient teaching of the Church, embodied in her Communion Offices, and thoroughly confirmed by Scripture[k]. They must in their turn be willing to learn much on this point from those whom they now look upon as enthusiasts or upholders of priestcraft. Let them accept and realize, first, the verity of the PRIESTHOOD of CHRIST, and especially its intimate connection with the original institution of the Eucharist; next, the continuation of that priestly

---

[l] St. John xvii. 19.   [k] See Part II.

operation of His on earth by the hands of His ministers, as in heaven by His own; and lastly, the priestly character of even the people's part in that most exalted function of humanity, the great Eucharistic Transaction. Then, but not till then, they will believe in a "lay priesthood" worth upholding. At present, it must be plainly said, their view is for the most part a purely rationalistic one; a mere negation of the gifts and powers of the Gospel; a casting down of the ladder between heaven and earth, with all its array of ascending and descending ministries, in order to substitute for it the efforts of all but unaided natural piety. Those who entertain this view, while professedly looking to the grace of God, do in reality seek to cut the Church off from the guaranteed reservoirs and channels of that grace: those reservoirs being the Incarnation and the Priesthood of Christ; those channels, the Sacraments ordained by Him. Would that such could be brought to see that, in their zeal against a ministering priesthood, they really arrive at a position which evacuates the Gospel, for clergy and people alike, of its best gifts and privileges; and that it is through the instrumentality of such a duly empowered priesthood, and no otherwise, that the Christian scheme provides a true and worthy priesthood for the people of God.

It is obvious to remark upon the illustration which the views here expressed receive from the contents of the Church's Ordinary Offices, which are to some extent derived from the Baptismal Office on the one hand, and from the Eucharistic on the other. One feature of our own morning offices, from St. Gregory's time downwards, has been, there can be little doubt[1], that

---

[1] See above, chap. i. p. 97.

Creed which is the peculiar note of Baptismal profession. That symbol of our faith having had a place in the ancient Prime Office for near a thousand years, was maintained in a corresponding position in our present Morning Office. Thus is the Baptismal position day by day taken up, by profession of the Baptismal Creed: whether, as in the case of the merely baptized, setting forth the whole of their Christian position; or, as in that of communicants, recalling to their recollection these first and earlier vows. The Lord's Prayer, whether primitively or not, has certainly for many hundred years been in use, both in the Eastern and the Western Church. This may be viewed indifferently, either as imparting a Baptismal or Eucharistic character to the office: that prayer having so signal a place in the offices proper to both Sacraments; in the one, as the prayer of the adopted; in the other, as the perfect verbal compendium[m] of the great Eucharistic actions of Oblation, Participation, and Pleading.

But again, the Ordinary Offices of the Church, in the East and West alike, have ever, as we have seen in the first chapter, embodied some portion of the Eucharistic Offices. It may suffice now to advert to one or two signal instances of this. The "Collect for the Day," which has always formed part of the English Morning Offices, is manifestly designed to import into it the entire spirit and essence of the *variable* part of the Eucharistic Office; being, as a general, if not a universal rule, the concentration into a prayer of the spirit of the Epistle and Gospel. Nothing can more clearly, or in a more practical form, mark the desire of the Church that the Daily or Ordinary Offices should not lose sight of

[m] See Part II., Primitive Form of Liturgy.

the Eucharistical, but be considered as ancillary to it. We have a recognition, in this adoption of a Eucharistic feature in Ordinary Worship, of that lower kind or degree of Priesthood which has been above spoken of as attaching to the latter.

In the Eastern Church, again, we have discerned a kindred phenomenon to the Western Collect, only on a yet broader scale. The Ectenes, or supplications, too, used at the Ordinary Offices are borrowed entire, with much besides, from the great Liturgies[n]; sometimes from the very Consecration Prayer itself.

But it is much to be observed, that while the Church draws thus freely upon her Eucharistic Offices for the materials of her Ordinary Worship, she is careful to reserve to the exclusive use of the former certain high and transcending ideas and expressions; thus vindicating to the Eucharist its proper character as the supreme channel of intercommunion between God and man, and as having certain aspects and privileges of which no more than the shadow or faint image is communicable to lower forms of worship. Thus, though praise of any kind may not unjustly be called a sacrifice, and the application of this term even to Ordinary Worship might reasonably plead the sanction of St. Paul's words in Heb. xiii.[o], yet we find that in the practice of the Church, the expression is generally restricted to directly Eucharistic Offices. Our own Daily Office is an instance of this.

[n] Instances may be seen in Neale's Introd. to Hist. of Eastern Church, vol. ii. p. 897, compared with vol. i. p. 381; at p. 901, with p. 595; p. 902 with 442. See ch. i. s. 6.

[o] "By Him, therefore, let us offer the sacrifice of praise to God continually, that is, the fruit of our lips, giving thanks to His Name." It may of course be maintained that this is a strictly Eucharistic injunction.

In the General Thanksgiving we desire grace "to shew forth God's praise, not only with our lips but in our lives; by giving up ourselves to His service," &c.; thus following closely upon the steps of the apostolic injunction, and of the Eucharistic Offices. Yet we forbear to take into our lips the expression, "sacrifice," and use only those of "praise" and "service." Very different is the holy boldness with which, in a single Eucharistic prayer, we three times use the term "sacrifice;" "entirely desiring God's fatherly goodness to accept our sacrifice of praise and thanksgiving," presenting "ourselves as a reasonable, holy, and lively sacrifice," and acknowledging our unworthiness, yet our bounden duty, to offer such "sacrifice."

The same is observable in the Eastern Offices. A remarkable instance occurs in the adaptation made of a portion of St. James' Liturgy to ordinary use. It is part of the solemn intercession immediately after consecration, and we find all that modesty, so to speak, in making use of it, which becomes the inferior Office. While the things prayed for are the same, the form of prayer is in one case the high and solemn Eucharistic phrase, "Remember[p];" in the other it is lowered to the more ordinary form, "We pray for."

A comparison of our Baptismal and Eucharistic Offices in like manner, exhibits very strikingly the discrimination to be made, in the Church's view, between Baptismal and Eucharistic powers and functions. The ideas which pervade the Baptismal Office are purely those of renewal and regeneration; death

[p] "*Remember*, Lord, them that bear fruit and do great deeds in Thy holy Churches," &c. (Lit. S. James, Neale, vol. ii. p. 594). But, "We *pray for them* that bear fruit and do good deeds in this holy Church," &c. (Eastern Vespers, ibid., p. 601).

to the old man, and rising again in newness of life. The particular aspect, that is to say, of the saving actions of our Lord, into which the baptized enters, is that which belongs to them as the direct working out of the Incarnation. Though the baptized necessarily partake of the benefit of the Death of Christ as a Sacrifice, and are admitted by Baptism to the *rights* of active Christian priesthood, yet their position and duties are described without reference to these ideas. The dedication of them to God is spoken of as a passive thing ("Grant that whosoever is here dedicated to Thee by our office and ministry," &c.) even in the case of adults; they are not exhorted to "present themselves a reasonable sacrifice," or the like; because, although in some true sense they are capable of doing so, yet for the highest and truest measure of that capacity they must await their entering, by Eucharistic attendance and participation, on the actual discharge of the priestly or sacrificial functions of a Christian.

# CHAPTER III.

## ON THE STRUCTURE AND SIGNIFICANCE OF THE ANCIENT ENGLISH OFFICES.

### SECTION I.

"And these words, which I command thee this day, shall be in thine heart; and thou shalt teach them diligently to thy children, and shalt talk of them when thou sittest in thine house, and when thou walkest by the way, and when thou liest down, and when thou risest up."

THE earliest phase of our Offices of Ordinary Worship, discernible in the corresponding ritual of the Eastern Church, has been dwelt upon at some length in the first chapter of this volume; with a minuteness, indeed, which may at first sight seem disproportionate. Yet I know not to which of the two classes of readers into whose hands this work may fall, any apology on the score of such minuteness is likely, on consideration, to seem necessary. Such as possess much previous acquaintance with the Daily Offices either of the East or the West, or of both, will, it may reasonably be hoped, be interested in the line of research here pursued; this department of Eastern ritual having never before, I believe, been investigated, or only cursorily and unsystematically, with a view to elucidating the Western Offices. The feeling which naturally accompanies such an investigation and comparative analysis, is surely not unlike that with which the modern astronomer studies the constellations of another hemisphere, and finds in them ever new illustrations of the sidereal truths familiar to him in his own; or even elaborates, by the help of them, a more comprehensive and sounder conception of the entire science. Those, again, to whom such researches are more or less new, will find their account in this somewhat full inquiry into the earlier condition of the Church's ritual :—

"Lorsqu' on veut exposer," says a methodical and effective writer on a very different subject, "une science peu connue, le moyen le plus simple consiste à en faire l'histoire. Les connaissances s'introduisent alors dans l'esprit du lecteur, comme elles se sont formées dans celui des générations; on suit, pour ainsi dire, la science pas à pas; et l'on passe avec elle de ses élémens les plus simples à ses théories les plus complexes [a]."

Now, as Mr. Palmer, in his invaluable "Dissertation on Primitive Liturgies," or Communion Offices, has once for all elevated that branch of ritual study from a mere empiricism and guess-work to the dignity of a regular science, having its fixed laws and its classified phenomena; so is it a part of my endeavour, in this volume, to perform a like service for the study of the Ordinary Offices of the Christian Church: and it is in a clear and detailed conception of their earlier successive stages and aspects that the foundations of a correct apprehension of them can be most easily and securely laid. But so it is, that in the annals of the Ordinary Offices of the *East*, and there only, can we study that succession. We there obtain a

[a] Paul de Remusat, sur une Revolution dans la Chimie (vid. Revue des deux Mondes, 1855).

view, not of the result merely, as in studying the corresponding Western Offices, but of the process also. Their stratification, if I may be allowed to borrow an illustration from modern science, is distinctly seen in the order of its occurrence. The successive deposition of a first, a second, and a third formation go on almost before our eyes in the ritual history of the first few ages in the East. We have first the primary and simple twofold structure, composed in a great measure of the *detritus* of the elder Jewish formation, and comparatively little organized. This passes, within the first three or four centuries, into the threefold and far more elaborately organized structures of what we may call the second period. And we shall presently be called upon to witness the leisurely superposition of an entirely novel group, completing the series. The Western scheme, on the contrary, forged or recast as it was by a single process, (so to speak,) out of the Eastern materials laid ready to hand, presents no such leisurely and progressive phenomena to the eye of the student.

But again, the nomenclature, and to a certain extent the nature, of the elements entering into certain of the Western Offices, and those the great and principal ones, have meanwhile been gradually brought to view by this method of proceeding. The invitatory; the hymns; the various modes of using the Psalms,—whether continuously and without selection, or by selecting them with adaptation to particular purposes;—the different number of them appropriated almost universally to the different services,—as 12 to Matins, 6 to Lauds, 5 to Vespers;—the nature of Antiphons, and the various classes of them; the complex system by which the Psalms, on festivals more especially, were interwoven with the Lessons in one great musical scheme of mingled meditation and praise; the Responsories entering into that scheme; the Canticles forming another important feature of it; the Versicles and Responses, the Capitula, the Collect, the Confession and Absolution;—all these we have discerned in their rudiments, and, as it were, in the very course of formation. And even of our existing ritual not a few particulars have been examined by the way, and the view to be taken of them in a great measure suggested. So that not only the general purpose of this work, to investigate the universal principles of Christian worship, but its more particular aim of fixing the ideas proper to our own forms of service, have been more materially advanced in our first chapter than might at the time appear.

The object, however, with which we set out, was, it will be remembered [b], to ascertain the earlier history of the entire body of Offices of ordinary worship which reached our shores at the end of the sixth century; not merely of those principal, and, as it appears, more primitive ones, which have alone come under our observation hitherto. We have yet to complete our survey, therefore, by including within it those other and secondary Eastern Offices, which, though neither of apostolic nor early post-apostolic date as Church Services, had nevertheless probably existed in a rudimentary form, as private or household devotions, from a very early period, and had been received into the number of recognised public formularies previous to the re-organization of the Western ritual after the Eastern model.

The Offices in question are those called in the East

[b] Chap. i. sect. 1, p. 41.

the Offices of the first, third, sixth, ninth hours, and the Office for "after supper," (ἀπόδειπνον); afterwards known in the West by the names of Prime, Tierce, Sext, Nones, and Completorium, or Compline, (the *completion* of the day's services). That these services were without exception of later date in the East than those of the early morning and evening, has been sufficiently proved by Bingham [c]. Let us now briefly inquire into their nature and contents; and in what points they furnished a model to the corresponding Western Offices.

First, as to the Office for Prime. Cassian (circ. 420) expressly records the setting up of the service of the First hour as a new thing which had taken place in his time [d], having been first introduced in St. Jerome's monastery at Bethlehem, of which he himself had been a member. It was quickly adopted, probably through his influence, in many parts of the West. The contents of this " novella solemnitas," as he calls it, were chiefly three Psalms, v., xc., ci. These were evidently selected as practical Psalms to commence the day with. The first and third of them contain professions of stedfast duty; the 90th brings to view the entire condition of man, but is perhaps chiefly selected for the sake of ver. 14: " We have been filled with Thy mercy, O Lord, in the morning;" and ver. 17: " Prosper Thou the work of our hands upon us." To these were added a few verses from the latter part of Ps. cxix.: " Order my steps in Thy word," &c., (vv. 133—135); and Ps. lxxi. ver. 7: " O

---

[c] XIII. ix. 8.
[d] Instit. iii. 4: "Hanc matutinum functionem nostro tempore in nostro quoque monasterio primitùs institutam." See the interesting note of Gazaeus *in loc*.

let my mouth be filled with Thy praise, that I may sing of Thy honour and glory all the day long." And with some brief hymns the Office concludes. There is, however, attached to each of these "day-hours" a "mid-hour" Office, ($\mu\epsilon\sigma\omega\rho\iota o\nu$[e],) to be said midway between each hour and the next. The "mid-hour" attached to Prime contains especially two prayers of St. Basil, formed upon the Psalms just mentioned.

Now the Western Prime is, first of all, entirely of the same practical tone as the Eastern. While rejecting the particular Psalms used in the East, it adopts and carries out in the fullest manner the use of the 119th as a practical Psalm; the Benedictine and other uses all agreeing in transferring it from its ancient place in Nocturns to the Prime and other day-hours. (We have already noticed[f] other features for which the Western Prime was indebted to the Eastern Nocturns; as, e. g. the Creed, the Preces, the Confession, &c.) Some other correspondences with the Eastern Prime are still more striking. Thus it has among its versicles the last verse of Ps. xc.; "The glorious majesty, &c.; prosper Thou the work of our hands upon us," &c.: and ver. 7 of Ps. lxxi., (as above); "O let my mouth," &c. And again, this is combined with ver. 14 of Ps. xc. in a prayer peculiar to the English Office: "In this hour of this day fill us with Thy mercy, O Lord, that we may rejoice in Thy praise all the day long." Another prayer is literally translated from St. Basil's: "Almighty God, direct our acts according to Thy good pleasure, that in the Name of Thy beloved Son we may be found worthy to abound in good

---

[e] Goar, p. 107; Neale, p. 932, &c.  [f] Chap. i. sect. 5, pp. 98, 103.

works [g]." But the following prayer more especially, which has descended to us as our third morning Collect, and which in the Sarum Prime Office differs materially from the Roman form, has every appearance of having been derived from the two prayers of St. Basil attached to the Eastern Prime, and founded chiefly, as has been said, on the Psalms of that Office, though partly also on Ps. xci., used at noon:—

| PRIME PRAYERS OF ST. BASIL. | OLD ENGLISH COLLECT AT PRIME. |
|---|---|
| Ὁ Θεὸς ὁ αἰώνιος, τὸ ἄναρχον καὶ ἀΐδιον . . . (Ps. xc. 1.) χάρισαι ἡμῖν ἐν τῇ παρούσῃ ἡμέρᾳ εὐαρεστεῖν σοι, διαφυλάττων ἡμᾶς ἀπὸ πάσης ἁμαρτίας καὶ πάσης πονηρᾶς πράξεως, ῥυόμενος ἡμᾶς ἀπὸ βέλους πετομένου ἡμέρας καὶ πάσης ἀντικειμένης δυνάμεως. | Domine Sancte, Pater Omnipotens, *Eterne Deus*, qui nos ad principium *hujus diei* pervenire fecisti tua nos hodie salva *virtute* (δυνάμεως) et *concede* ut *in hac die* ad nullum declinemus *peccatum*, nec ullum incurramus *periculum*, |
| (From Second Prayer.) | |
| τὰ τῶν χειρῶν ἡμῶν ἔργα, . . . πράττειν ἡμᾶς τὰ σοὶ εὐάρεστα καὶ φίλα, εὐόδωσον. | sed semper ad *tuam* faciendam *justitiam* omnis *nostra actio* tuo moderamine dirigatur. |

The Latin form, as usual, is more terse and compact, but the opening address, the order of topics, and to some extent the expressions, are closely similar.

The service of the third hour, or nine o'clock, as used in St. Basil's time, contained the 51st Psalm, in reference partly to its being the penitential hour of our Lord's crucifixion [h], partly to the descent of the Holy Spirit, to which the verse, "Renew a right spirit within me [i]," was applied. The Office for the sixth

---

[g] Ὁ Θεὸς ὁ αἰώνιος, . . . τὰ τῶν χειρῶν ἡμῶν ἔργα πρὸς τὸ σὸν κατεύθυνον θέλημα, ἵνα καὶ διὰ τῶν ἀναξίων ἡμῶν, κ.τ.λ. Prayer of St. Basil, Mesorion of the first hour, Horolog., p. 114.

[h] Ap. Constit. viii. 34.  [i] St. Basil, Regul. Maj., ix. 37.

hour, or noon, in like manner contained the 91st Psalm, on account of the verse, "Thou shalt not be afraid for the sickness" (or the evil one) "that destroyeth in the *noonday;*" and the 55th, for the sake of the verse, "Morning, and evening, and at *noonday* will I pray." The Offices for these hours contain the very same Psalm still. We have no similar evidence for the antiquity of the Ninth hour Office, as now used in the East; nor indeed is there, apparently, the same peculiar fitness in the Psalms appointed for it, as in the case of the two preceding Offices. Yet the hour was certainly of very ancient observance in the East, since a canon of the year 360[k] prescribes the same prayers to be used at it as at Vespers. This was however, probably, a new and merely local arrangement.

The Western Offices for these minor hours bear a general testimony to the existence of the Eastern ones, either for public or private use, in the fifth century, by having adopted the Eastern number of three Psalms; while they differ, both among themselves and from the East altogether, as to the particular Psalms used[l]. This perhaps indicates that these Offices had not yet obtained universal recognition in the East as Church services; so that the Western framers felt at liberty to choose their own Psalms, only observing the traditional number. It was natural, as before observed, that they should make use of Ps. cxix. for the purpose, not only on account of its practical character, but as having been of most

---

[k] Concil. Laod., can. xviii. Bingham (vol. iv. p. 378) thinks the ninth hour service may have been in public use in St. Chrysostom's time.

[l] The Rom. Sar., &c., used three sections of Ps. cxix. daily at each of those hours, (third, sixth, and ninth,) as did the Benedictine on Mondays and Tuesdays; but three "gradual Psalms" on other days

ancient use in the East, (viz. in the Night Office,) and perhaps in the West also.

The date of the Eastern Compline, the last office of the day, is abundantly testified to by the universality with which the West has adopted, not the number only of its Psalms, but the very Psalms themselves. It is a common opinion, indeed, that St. Benedict was the actual inventor of this office; but with the facts of the case before us, this is absolutely incredible. It is true that the actual name Completorium seems to have been unknown in the East; but the thing, and even the name, in a rudimentary form, doubtless existed there long before St. Benedict's time, (530,) and evidently furnished the basis of all the Western varieties of the office. St. Basil, (370,) to whom we are indebted for so many particulars respecting the ancient services, appoints in his "Rules[m]" certain observances for the close of the day, making use of the very expression answering to the Latin Completorium ($\pi\lambda\eta\rho\hat{\omega}\sigma\alpha\iota\ \tau\grave{\eta}\nu\ \dot{\eta}\mu\acute{\epsilon}\rho\alpha\nu$.) He enjoins a giving of thanks for whatever benefits have been received in the day; confession of sins, voluntary and involuntary; and prayer to pass the night without offence, disturbance, or sin; and desires that Psalm xci. ("Whoso dwelleth," &c.) should be said. Now a prayer bearing the name of "the great Basil," and embracing precisely these topics, to a great extent in St. Basil's very words, is *subjoined* to the conclusion of the Eastern *Vespers* at this day[n]. It is not, however, part of the service; and the saying of it is optional. The 91st Psalm, again, is among those appointed for the following office of Compline. Surely

---

[m] Bas. Regul. ix. 37; ap. Bon., ubi supr.
[n] Horolog. Vesp. ad fin.

then we have in the aforesaid injunction of St. Basil the rudiments and earliest outline of Compline. It is probable that other suitable Psalms, as the 4th, (ending with "I will lay me down in peace," &c.,) had been customary for private use at bed-time; and that in the interval between the date of St. Basil and that of Cassian or Benedict the Eastern Compline office, very much as it now exists, was formed and introduced into the Churches, just as the other minor hours had already been. St. Benedict[o] also places Compline expressly after supper-time; thus recognising the Eastern nomenclature of ἀπόδειπνον.

There are now two or three forms of Compline in the East, varying in length. But the later additions, chiefly penitential Psalms and prayers, are easily discernible from the essentials of the Office, which are such as fully to establish the derivation of the Western Compline from it. We have, in the fuller form, Psalms iv. vi. xiii. xxv. xxxi. xci.; a very grand choral ode[p] on the Incarnation, based on Isaiah viii. 12—18, ix. 1—6, the burden being, "For God is with us;" a hymn of three stanzas to Christ, giving thanks for preservation during the day, and praying to be kept during the night without sin, scandal, or disturbance,—the very topics prescribed by St. Basil; a great hymn of praise, the manifest original of much of the Te Deum[q]; the Nicene Creed, the Trisagion, and the Lord's Prayer; a short prayer in the form of a hymn for illumination and protection during the night; followed by longer ones, and a prayer of St. Basil, all to the same effect, and all founded on the Psalms which have preceded. Subsequently, after

[o] Rule, ch. 42.     [p] See note D.
[q] Comp. above, p. 65, &c., and see note D.

some penitential Psalms and prayers,—apparently a later insertion,—we have the Gloria in Excelsis, Preces, or versicles and responses, for protection; Psalm cl.; a short thanksgiving for redemption; and, as at Nocturns, an interchange of confession and absolution, and a litany.

I have here selected, out of a service of immense length, (divided, in fact, into three great portions by the usual threefold invitatory,) such features as seem to be characteristic, as being common to the greater and lesser forms of the Office; or, again, such as have visibly passed over to the Western, more especially to the English Compline Office. It will be seen that we have, with great fulness, all the elements suggested by St. Basil for the close of the day,—viz., praise and thanksgiving for preservation and other benefits; confession and prayers for protection, &c.; and also Ps. xci. In the West, out of the six Eastern Psalms, three (iv. xxxi. 1-6, xci.) were adopted for Compline, with the addition of Ps. cxxxiv. borrowed from the Greek Nocturns, (St. Benedict omitted Ps. xxxi.) In lieu, as it would seem, of the great "Emmanuel" Ode, (by which the Eastern Compline Psalms are followed, just as the Nocturns, Lauds, and Vespers Psalms are by the midnight hymn, the Canticle, and the "Joyful light" respectively), the West subjoins to its Compline psalmody the Nunc Dimittis, instead of using it at the Vespers. And it is perhaps worthy of notice, as completing the resemblance, that the West has in this part of Compline a passage of Scripture (viz. the Capitulum, from Jerem. xiv.) on the dwelling of God with men: ("Thou art in us, O Lord; and Thy Name is called upon us; leave us not, O Lord our God,") accompanied by its song — that of Simeon — on the Incarnation, and followed closely by a hymn of three stanzas for protection. The theme, in a word, is the same, and the manner of treating it, though more brief in the West, entirely parallel. It may be mentioned here, that the old English Compline differed widely from the Roman both in the order of its parts, and in possessing no less than twenty-two varieties for different days and seasons, while the Roman is nearly unvarying. Among the variations are seven hymns; and these are manifest translations, though with much of compression, of various hymns or prayers in the great and protracted Eastern Compline Office.

But now follow, in the Greek Office, features which render absolutely certain the derivation from it of the Western Compline, of the English form more especially; and which moreover possess peculiar interest for us, from our having so fully inherited them in our existing evening Service. We have first, with the Lord's Prayer accompanying it, the Creed; a feature which, it will be remembered, has its place in Nocturns after the Psalms, but is not found again in the Eastern Offices we have been surveying until its occurrence here in Compline. Precisely the same is the case in the West: at Prime only and at Compline,—the first and the last offices, in one point of view, of the day,—is the Creed said. This correspondence cannot be accidental. And while it is a proof of communication between the East and West in the matter, it is also a disproof of the ordinary but intrinsically improbable assertion, that the Creed was not used in any Church Service until the beginning of the sixth century. It shews that in the East it certainly had place early in the fifth, when the service was imported thence; whilst its occurrence in Prime indicates, as has been already said, that it had from time immemorial been used in some part of the morning service, probably in the East and West alike.

But the Creed and Lord's Prayer in the Eastern Compline are followed shortly by a prayer-like hymn for illumination and protection. Now about this, two things, both of deepest interest, are to be remarked. The first is, that the hymn or prayer is distinctly based on the Psalms of the Office which have preceded. It is as follows.

"Lighten my eyes, O Christ my God, that I sleep not in death: lest mine enemy say, I have prevailed against him," (Ps. xiii. 4, 5.) "Be Thou the helper of my soul, O God, for I walk through the midst of snares; deliver me from them, and save me, Thou that art good, as being the lover of men," (Ps. xxxi. 1, 3, 5; comp. Ps. xci. 2, 3.) The latter part of the hymn in particular is a curious cento from the Psalms indicated.

| | |
|---|---|
| ἀντιλήπτωρ τῆς ψυχῆς μου | Ps. xci. 2. ἀντιλήπτωρ μου εἶ ὁ Θεός μου. |
| γενοῦ ὁ Θεός. | Ps. xxxi. 2. γενοῦ μοι εἰς Θεὸν ὑπερασπιστήν. |
| ὅτι μέσον διαβαίνω παγίδων | Ib. 4. ἐξάξεις με ἐκ παγίδος. |
| ῥῦσαι με ἐξ αὐτῶν. | Ib. 1. ῥῦσαι με. Ps. xci. 3. ῥύσεταί σε ἐκ παγίδος. |

The second thing to be remarked is, that this same hymn-like prayer, thus formed out of the Compline Psalms, is the original, as seems unquestionable, of the English Compline prayer, "Illumina quæsumus Domine Deus tenebras nostras," &c., so familiar to us as our third evening collect, "Lighten our darkness," &c. The characteristic commencement, "Illumina," (with only the substitution from Ps. xviii. 28 of "tenebras" for "oculos,") and afterwards "noctis hujus insidias," with the concluding "a nobis repelle propitius," (ὡς φιλάνθρωπος,) seem sufficiently to make good the connection. The Roman Compline has a different collect, but it is equally based on the Psalms of the Greek Office; especially on Ps. xci. 1, 3, 11, and Ps. cxxxiv. 4. It will be remembered that we found our English Prime Collect, in precisely a parallel manner, based on the prayers of the Eastern Prime, and through them on the Psalms of that Office. The result of this investigation is surely most satisfactory, as tracing our third Collects at morning and evening prayer to their very sources in the heart of Eastern antiquity. There are other resemblances between the Eastern and Western Compline; above all, the confession and absolution, resembling that which we have seen the Western Prime form borrowing from the Nocturns of the East, and occurring towards the close of the English, (as of the Greek,) though in the beginning of the Roman Prime.

Such then is the supplementary group of the Eastern Church's services, by which her eightfold (or, reckoning the *Mesoria*, her twelvefold) scheme was completed; and such the connection between it and the corresponding Offices of the West. Nothing is more clear than that the whole of these additions were imported out of the private closet, or the household or monastic oratory, into the public sanctuary. The hours from first to ninth, and Compline, were the growth of the private and household devotions of the earlier ages in the East, probably those of the very first ages. This view is entirely corroborated by our finding features of these Offices enjoined as matter of private prayer by early Eastern writers. Thus Athanasius [p], the Apostolical Constitutions, and St. Chrysostom, agree in recommending the Gloria in Excelsis (which was only used on Sundays in the public services, viz. at Lauds) for daily use in private. The Constitutions set down part of the Gloria in Excelsis, together with the Nunc Dimittis, for *evening* use. The former hymn, accordingly, we find in the Eastern Compline; and the occurrence of the latter in the Western, (not in Benedict's, however,) instead of at Vespers, is best accounted for by supposing that it held that place in some parts of the East, as a matter of private use. That as private forms these services are of immense and perhaps primitive antiquity, is indicated by the Psalms used in them, which are in most cases so singularly adapted to the time of the day for which they are prescribed, (as e. g. Ps. iv. to Prime, Ps. xci. to Compline,) that it is inconceivable but that they would have been adopted as part of the public daily services from the beginning, had they not been already allotted to private use: for which indeed, from the personal nature of them, they are more peculiarly suited.

One remark connected with the English Revision is suggested by this review of the supplementary Offices, so to call them, of the Eastern scheme. Of the expediency of introducing them as entire Offices into the sanctuary, I have ventured already to express a doubt. Not, of course, that the public ritual was not enriched and adorned by the addition of formularies so devoutly and beautifully conceived, and breathing so refined a spirit of meditation on Holy Scripture.

[p] Bingham, XIII. x. 9.

The objection is not to the adoption of new features, but to the inconsiderate accumulation of offices, without any such fusion or adaptation as might render the service, as a whole, still practicable for the members of the Christian body. There may indeed have been temporary reasons, such as the presence of Arianism and Pelagianism, which called for or justified at the time such an enlarged exhibition of public devotion. But the after-experience of the Church testifies that she would have done more wisely, had she been content to transplant within the bounds of that narrower τέμενος, which apostolic wisdom seems in a general way to have defined, the spiritual plants which personal, or household, or monastic piety had nurtured, instead of thus enlarging its border by taking whole tracts of service into it. And this is surely the very thing which the English Church, long and long after, but not too late, nor yet without signal results,—whether with perfect wisdom, and in the best manner that could have been, is not the question,—essayed to do. She retained the essence of the several Offices, as represented by certain of their features; an example which the West had already set her in some instances, e. g. by concentrating the whole spirit of the Eastern Prime into her Collect for that Office, founded on St. Basil's prayer. The Eastern Church might have done the same; she too might have invigorated, not have overlaid and crushed, her daily ritual. But, already possessing in her offices selections of Psalms, hymns, prayers, and litanies, she accumulated, without the smallest attempt at accommodation, system upon system, added more selections of Psalms, more hymns, prayers, and litanies, aiming in the main at the selfsame objects. And such an undigested mass, absolutely incapable of being really used as it stands, either by clergy or people, and only got through at all by a variety of senseless expedients, the Eastern hour-system continues to the present day[q]. The course pursued in the West was on the whole the same. Not content with enriching—a task which she executed most admirably—her older framework with elements drawn from every region of the East, she multiplied her services at the same time; thus piling together a structure which from its cumbersomeness has fallen into utter decay, leaving but a single fragment erect amid its ruins.

I must not take leave of the Eastern Offices without briefly summing up the *doctrinal* character which was visibly, though not always strongly, impressed upon them respectively. To Nocturns, then, belongs more particularly the idea and the doctrine of Christ's second Coming to Judgment. This has passed into our Matins in the form of the latter part of the Te Deum. In Lauds is expressed, rather in the broad characteristics of the Office than by direct allusion, the idea and the doctrine of the past Resurrection of Christ, and of our own hereafter. In Vespers, the Incarnation, being the coming in of the true Light in the eventide of the world, is commemorated; and the allusion is preserved to us in the Nunc Dimittis. This idea, again, easily combines with that of our Lord's giving Himself, at the institution of the last Supper, for our salvation. It was probably partly from a desire to complete this doctrinal scheme by the commemoration of other facts or truths of Christianity, that the later group of offices was adopted into the Church. Thus in Prime, the idea of the Resurrection is resumed

[q] See note II.

in the hymns; and at Compline that of the Incarnation is still more distinctly expressed, as we have seen, than at Vespers. And throughout all these Offices there runs more or less of reference to the Passion. Thus at Prime on Wednesdays and Fridays there is a special prayer or hymn for the aid of the Cross of Christ; and the hymn on which our evening third Collect is founded evidently alludes to the " snares" (insidiæ) laid for our Lord in His betrayal and crucifixion.

The Western Offices carry out these ideas in various degrees, as we shall have occasion to notice hereafter. In Prime, more especially, the Eastern reference to the Passion was rendered with great fulness, Pss. xxii.—xxv. being appointed to be used on Sundays; all of them probably, but the 22nd certainly, in this connection. It is remarkable that Ps. xxii. alone is appointed for the Prime Office of the Armenian Church; to which St. Benedict, too, appears to have been indebted, through whatever channel, for much of his scheme. These five Prime Psalms were subsequently distributed in the Roman ritual (by Pius V.) over the other days of the week, Ps. xxii. being appropriately allotted to Friday, and Ps. xxiii. to Thursday. Our own third Collects at morning and evening, as being based on Pss. xc., xci., and xxxi. 1—6, (see p. 228,) necessarily recal, according to the profoundest conception of them, those sorrows and perils of our Lord, and that triumph over them, which are at once the type of our daily condition, as the members of His Body, the Church, and the assurance of protection and deliverance.

## SECTION II.

"Arise, shine, for thy light is come, and the glory of the Lord is risen upon thee . . . And the Gentiles shall come to thy light, and kings to the brightness of thy rising . . . Who are these that fly as a cloud, and as the doves to their windows? Surely the isles shall wait for me, and the ships of Tarshish first."

THE most obscure chapter in the ritual annals of the Western Church is confessedly that which embraces the period from the first introduction of Christianity till the beginning of the fifth century. At this latter epoch, tradition, rather than history, begins to shed a feeble and uncertain light upon the past. The information that we obtain, even then, is chiefly of a negative kind. We discern, that is to say, the inauguration of a new and different era, in ritual matters, from that which preceded it. But wherein the difference consisted, and what consequently was the character of the superseded state of things, we are still left for the most part to conjecture. All that we know is, that by the hands of some persons, either traditionally named, (as St. Ambrose at Milan, and St. Jerome and St. Damasus at Rome,) or plausibly conjectured from their writings and known history, (as Cassian in the south of France,) the older forms were laid aside or remodelled, and new ones introduced; of which, while some have been swept away, others survive in some form or other to the present hour.

In this dearth of historical testimony, the internal evidence, which the Western ritual on examination supplies, of its derivation from Eastern sources, comes most opportunely to our aid. For if the arguments be well founded, by which I have endeavoured, in the first chapter, to make good the claims of certain of the Eastern Offices to represent in the main, and even as to some details, the apostolic manner of ordinary worship, it will follow, almost as a matter of course, that similar forms of service must have been widely if not universally diffused throughout the Christian world. Following the analogy of the ancient Communion Services or Liturgies, this more ordinary kind of worship would be likely to retain in all lands, as those certainly did[r], the same leading features, with only such variations as might arise from the differing mental or spiritual constitution of the first evangelizers, or from other accidental circumstances. If such services existed at all in the Church at the first, they would be likely, by the time the faith began to be preached to the world at large, (which was not until twelve years after the Ascension[s],) to have acquired a tolerably settled form. And then both habit, and reverence for apostolic institution, would conspire to secure a considerable uniformity in the ordinary worship of all Churches.

This conjecture is entirely confirmed by such notices as we have in ancient writers of the Church's ordinary service. Inhabitants of the most widely separated regions render, in the main, the same account of it. St. Basil in Cappadocia, St. Chrysostom at Constantinople, Origen in Egypt, Tertullian in Africa, Justin Martyr at Rome (probably), bear witness that it took place partly by night and partly by day. That its staple contents were Psalms and hymns we learn

[r] Vide Palmer's Dissertation on Primitive Liturgies.
[s] Vide Burton's Eccl. Hist., lect. v.

from the same writers, and indirectly indeed from others, as many as speak of Psalms and hymns as having been in use in the Churches, since we know that the Communion Offices were otherwise constituted. In the third and fourth centuries particular writers positively affirm the general prevalence of such services: as Origen and St. Basil in passages already quoted [t]; and Epiphanius, bishop of Salamis, circ. 370, "Morning hymns are used continually in the Church, and morning prayers; and evening (lychnic) Psalms and prayers." When the Church of Malabar [u], said to have been founded by the apostle St. Thomas, was discovered by the Portuguese in the year 1501, "The priests," it was found, "performed the Divine Office twice daily, at three in the morning and five in the evening;" a striking testimony, as it should seem, to the general correctness of the view which we have been led to, as to the ancient practice in this matter. Particular features of the Office, again, are occasionally testified to by remote and independent witnesses: as the 51st Psalm, and the prolongation of the Night Office into the daylight, by Tertullian and Basil; the invitatory of the Constantinopolitan Office by Athanasius in Egypt; "Before the beginning of their prayers, the Christians invite and exhort one another in the words of this Psalm (95th [x])." Arnobius, an African, in the fourth century, writing a general apology for the devotions of Christians, enumerates the topics of prayer as nearly as possible in the order, and that a somewhat peculiar one, which is found in the Litany sub-

---

[t] Supr., ch. i. sect. ii. Add S. Aug. Conf., ix. 4. "Toto orbe cantantur."
[u] For an interesting account of this Church, see Neale, p. 145.
[x] Athanas. De Virginitate.

joined to the Eastern Nocturns, viz., "for magistrates, the *army*, kings, friends, *enemies*, the living, the departed." That the Office was universally devoid of lessons from Scripture, is both negatively testified by the absence of any mention of them; and positively by the council of the fourth century at Laodicea, which provides for their introduction as a new thing.

In the West, although, as I have said, direct historical testimony is all but wanting, the conclusions arrived at by the best informed and most cautious of Western Ritualists represents ordinary worship as having probably exhibited the selfsame general aspect as in the East. Grancolas, to whom I refer, conceives its leading characteristics previous to the fifth century to have been abundance of Psalms and entire absence of lessons.

"Je ne fais pas même difficulté d' avancer que le Pseautier distribué par le semaine était l'ancien Office Romain, dont on a conservé le titre à la tête du Breviaire; 'Psalterium dispositum per hebdomadam;' et que comme le Pseautier faisait le Breviaire des Juifs, l'Eglise n' eut d'abord que les Pseaumes avec l' Oraison Dominicale... Il n' y avait à Rome de Leçon dans l' office, ni d' Hymne, ni de Collecte. A l' egard des Lectures, elles ne se firent pendant long-tems qu' à la Messe.... Ce sont les Moines qu' ont les premiers inseré les leçons dans l' office<sup>r</sup>."

These views of a very learned member of the Gallican Church, at the beginning of the 17th century, are thoroughly coincident, as to their main tenor, with those to which we are conducted by our investigations into the Eastern ritual, and into the relations between it and the Western. Only it is probable that the earlier Western ritual was more organized than Grancolas supposed, and already possessed the basis of those arrangements which it afterwards adopted in

[r] Grancolas, Comment. sur le Breviaire, i. p. 23. Compare Milman, Lat. Christianity, p. 28.

fuller measure from the East. The Churches of the West, if there be anything in the hypothesis we have proceeded upon, can hardly but have received, at their first planting, some kind of Nocturnal Office of Psalms and hymns. The testimony of Justin Martyr and Hippolytus[z], accordingly, is, as we have seen, as far as it goes, to this effect; the one speaking of nocturnal worship, the other of Psalms and hymns as its contents. And, indeed, independently of this presumption, and this degree of testimony, such a supposition seems almost necessary to account for the facility with which these Churches accepted Eastern arrangements and details at the hands of Cassian or others. It is most improbable that they would throw away entirely all their established usages; most natural, that, having a common basis with the Orientals, they should accept and incorporate their improvements or enlargements upon it. The same supposition is again confirmed by a certain independence with which, after all, and notwithstanding the vast deference they paid to Eastern arrangements, they of the West acted in the reconstruction of their Offices. We observe this in their incorporating the continuous psalmody with their first and Nocturnal, and not (as the Orientals since Basil's time) with their second or Matutinal Office; in their free rejection of some Psalms, as e. g., some of those of the hexapsalmus, while retaining others; in their different appropriation of the canticles to the several days of the week; and in their superseding some of the Eastern canticles themselves in favour of other claimants. All this was probably the result of adherence to their own usages. And in one or two particulars we seem to possess

[z] Supr., ch. i. sect. ii. Milman (Hist. Lat. Christianity, p. 27.) considers that the Roman ritual for three centuries was Greek. So also Wiseman, Bunsen, &c. This would fall in with the view in the text.

direct evidence of their having inherited certain ritual ways, some coinciding with, some differing from the Eastern. Thus Cassian testifies[a] that all the Churches of Italy in his time had Ps. li. at the end of their Matins Psalms or hymns; exactly as the East has always had it (vide p. 112) after theirs, and as the West has retained it in effect ever since, viz. on the confines of Matins and Lauds[b]. Again he says, still speaking apparently of the West before the introduction of the new services, that they had the 63rd Psalm in the early morning, and also the 119th[c], as the East had. Their Te Deum, judging from its universality in the West, and from its unvarying responsive position, they had probably wrought out some time before, out of ancient elements common to them with the East. Other features they seem to have inherited from Jewish times. For example, it is very singular that the West should unanimously, alike in the monastic and in the other uses, sing the Venite entire; the East, no less universally, using only an invitatory formed out of it. It was most likely a Western habit from the first so to use it[d]. Still more striking is it that the whole West should have one of the Songs of Moses (Deut. xxxii.) and also Ps. xcii. on the Saturday or Sabbath (at Lauds), this usage being a feature

[a] Instit., iii. 6.

[b] Mr. Palmer (i. 215) supposes that Cassian meant the end of Lauds, or even of Prime, and makes this a note of *difference* between East and West.

[c] Instit., iii. 3. In matutinâ solemnitate decantari solet "Deus Deus meus," &c., et "Præveniunt oculi mei in diluculo," (Ps. cxix. 148.) Now the latter of these passages is nowhere used now in the West in the morning. If Cassian then is speaking of the West, we have proof that Ps cxix. was used there, as in the East, in the antelucan service. The Te Deum has been ascribed to Hilary of Poitiers, circ. 354.

[d] See note B.

of the Jewish Temple service, and yet one which they cannot have received through the Greek Offices, since these have them not on that day. These considerations, indeed, suggest the possibility that in some few other instances they may have been retaining usages which they already had, and not—as I have for the most part assumed to be the case—borrowing them from the Greeks for the first time in the fifth century. It is of no importance for our present purpose, in what proportion the West inherited or adopted her existing forms. That all the more elaborate features of them, however, are due to the latter cause, we have, I think, seen abundant reason for believing.

If then it be asked, what was the ordinary service of the Church of this country from the first introduction of Christianity, down to the time of St. Augustine's arrival, it may be answered that here, as throughout Western Christendom, it was most probably a service of Psalms and hymns; performed, originally at least, partly at night, partly in the early morning, and again in the evening; possessing perhaps the same fixed Psalms as the Eastern Nocturns and Vespers, with a considerable addition of continuous psalmody; that it commenced possibly with some kind of penitential preparation, or else with the Venite; was devoid of Scripture Lessons, the Psalms being used for the purposes of meditation as well as of praise; but contained responsive Canticles, among them the Te Deum, the Magnificat, and Nunc Dimittis. The 51st and 63rd Psalms were also probably used in the Morning Office at day-break, with more Canticles, such as the Benedictus, the Songs of Moses, &c. Such, in their general outline, we may fairly presume, were the offices used by the Church of St. Alban and St. Amphibalus. The change to the offices introduced by St. Augustine, though considerable, would thus be no greater than the other Churches of the West had experienced in the century or two preceding; and would be rather of the nature of a development than of an actual substitution.

The next question is, How came this earlier and simpler state of things to be innovated upon and altered throughout the West? through what agency, or by what men, was so serious a change effected? Now there is a story[e], dating no further back however than the ninth century, and founded on a letter supposed to be spurious,—that Pope Damasus, in the end of the fourth century, at the suggestion of the Emperor Theodosius, commissioned St. Jerome to distribute the Psalms, fix the Lections, and otherwise re-arrange the old Roman Office after the Eastern model. And though this tradition is valueless so far as it rests on the letter in question, we shall see presently that it contains a substratum of fact; the letter, indeed, was probably forged to fill up a blank in a history substantially true. But rejecting the story as it stands, to whom can we point as likely to have originated the Western Offices? Now the fact that CASSIAN, so often alluded to already, dwells much[f] upon the number of *twelve* Psalms as prevailing in the Egyptian monasteries, joined to the almost universal prevalence of that number as the characteristic of Nocturns in the West, and to his known zeal in founding monasteries at Marseilles,— has procured him the reputation, by the general voice, of having been at least a principal agent in introducing the newer ritual. And whatever share he may

[e] Durandus, V. ii. 2; Grancolas, i. p. 22.    [f] Instit. ii. 5, 6.

have had in originating the Ordinary Offices of the rest of Europe,—a point which, from our imperfect information as to their contents, we are not in a position to decide,—it may, I think, be shewn that of his having been concerned in the construction of the Roman Office and of our own, there is very great probability indeed.

Those who, rejecting the account of St. Jerome's or St. Damasus' authorship, have gone furthest back in search of the origin of the Roman Office as a whole, have not ventured to carry it higher than the date of St. Benedict, circ. 530. It has been discussed "whether the Roman Offices were taken from the Benedictine, or the Benedictine from the Roman[g]." To this question we may confidently answer, Neither. Notwithstanding their general similarity, the internal structure of the Offices differs in such important points, that even without any knowledge of a common source to which their peculiarities may be traced, we could hardly resist this conclusion. Thus the number of Nocturns in the Benedictine (two); of Psalms in a Nocturn (six); of Antiphons (one to every Psalm); of Lessons in a Nocturn (four),—is quite different from the Roman. So are the selections of Psalms for Prime and all the other minor hours except Compline. And when in the rites of the East, we read a full and satisfactory account, as well of their resemblance as of their irreconcilable discrepancies, this conviction as to their independence amounts to certainty. Examples have from time to time been given in this work. With these facts before us, it is as incredible that either of these rites can have come from the other, instead of from the East as a common source, as it is that

[g] Palmer, i. 215.

the French language can have been derived from the Italian, or *vice versa*, and not both alike from Latin. St. Benedict refers (Reg. cap. 13.) to the Roman rite as furnishing the rule for his own in a single point, viz. the appropriation of the Canticles for each day. This affords a presumption of his independence of it in other respects, as well as a proof that the Roman was a rite then existing. It has been supposed that the Roman use in its turn borrowed Compline from St. Benedict: but for this opinion there are, as I have shewn, no grounds whatever; Compline having come to both rites alike from the East. I will only add that the *Armenian* variety of the Eastern Offices appears in several respects to have furnished the type of the Benedictine; having *two* sets of Psalms sung continuously at Nocturns, and followed by *four* homilies with responsory hymns. And that St. Benedict had the Armenian rite before his eyes, we have this curious indication, that in his Rule he speaks of it as the practice of monks in former days, which he would fain have imitated, to go through the whole Psalter every day. Now this was precisely the practice of the Armenian monasteries; while the Churches distributed it over the week [h]. It is very conceivable that monachism and monastic ritual may have passed over from that or any other part of the East to the southern parts of Italy [i], and supplied the foundation of St. Benedict's Offices.

Setting aside, then, the Benedictine scheme of ser-

[h] Bona, ib. 10.

[i] St. Equitius, an Abbot of Abruzzo, was about a contemporary of St. Benedict, (S. Greg. Dial. i. 4). It has been supposed by some that St. Gregory and St. Augustine were of his order. That they were Benedictines, though volumes have been written to prove it, (vide Rayner's Benedict. in Regno Angliæ,) is infinitely improbable; their ritual sympathies flowing, as we have seen, in quite another channel.

vices as having certainly not been the parent of the Roman, we may next observe that those of the various European Churches, as far as we are acquainted with them, are such as may very well have owed their origin to the impulse first given by Cassian to the spirit of ritual reconstruction. They exhibit, indeed, in very different degrees the peculiar characters of Cassian's revival; and all bear the marks, more or less, of connection with the East through other channels, besides what they owe to the Cassianic movement. Thus we find the Church of Arles[k] having *two* Nocturns; agreeing herein with the East and St. Benedict, while differing from Cassian, who fused the two Nocturns into one of twelve Psalms. The same Church had the Magnificat[l] at *Lauds*, adding the Gloria in Excelsis on Sundays; and the Kyrie eleison, on occasion, *twelve* times repeated; all features, as we have seen, of the Eastern Offices, though not adopted in the Roman. The authors of these Oriental arrangements were Cæsarius and Aurelian[m], at the beginning of the sixth century. Again, both the French and Spanish Churches go back to the Council of Laodicea as of great authority; and they may have derived their Psalm and lection arrangements, (as has been already suggested,) in a great measure at least, from that source[n]. The Church of Spain has been supposed to have differed[o] from all the West generally, in having little or no psalmody in its ancient Nocturns. But this is manifestly an error. Isidore of Seville prescribes for Nocturns, first, "the three regular Psalms," (meaning probably Pss. iii. xcv. li.); then three *services* (or *sets*,—

[k] Mabill. Curs. Gall., p. 406.
[m] Mabillon, p. 406, quotes their rules.
[o] Mabillon Curs. Gall., p. 391: Palmer, i. p. 224.
[l] Vid. supr., p. 112.
[n] Supr., ch. i. sect. vi.

Missæ) of Psalms; a fourth of Canticles; a fifth consisting of the Matins (i. e. Lauds) Office [p]. This is plainly the meaning of the passage, which Menardus, and after him Mabillon, misunderstood, taking "Missæ" to mean "Collects" connected with the Psalms. But its use in the sense of a "service," almost of any kind, is familiar to the readers of Bingham and Mabillon [q]. The rule of Fructuosus confirms the fact that there were numerous Psalms in the Spanish night Office. It may be observed, too, that one of St. Benedict's Nocturns on Sundays consists of Canticles, exactly as is here prescribed. That the Spanish Church had also Scripture lessons in their daily Offices is affirmed in the same passage of Isidore. The Church of Milan, once more, though manifestly Oriental in many of its provisions, and according with the Roman to a great extent as to the minor hours, is singularly independent in its arrangement of Psalms, and in various other respects: especially it pays no regard to the Cassianic number of twelve Psalms; spreads the Psalter over a fortnight; and has but two "festivals of nine lections" (viz. Christmas-day and Epiphany) in the year [r].

The Orientally-derived Western rituals hitherto enumerated, manifest, together with much of affinity, a marked independence of the Roman and of each other. There are, on the other hand, two which coincide so nearly, that it is hardly to be wondered that their coincidence has hitherto been taken, on a superficial view of them, for actual identity. I mean the ROMAN and the ancient ENGLISH rituals. Of the correspondence of these it is unnecessary to speak.

---

[p] Isid. Hispal. Reg. 7, apud Mabillon, ut supr.; and Fructuosus, ibid.

[q] Bingh. xiii. 4; of Mabillon, p. 406.

[r] Bona, Psalmod. xviii. 10.

The number of their Psalms in the several Offices, the selection and appropriation (with very few exceptions) of the Psalms themselves, the position of the Antiphons, the structure of the complex Psalm-lection-responsory-and-canticle system, the number of lessons, the prefixing of benedictions, the *arrangements* about the hymns, Capitula, Creed, Lord's Prayer, Preces, Collects, and countless other particulars, are for the most part, though not always, precisely the same. No such resemblance can be predicated of any two Western rites that we are acquainted with. The two sets of Offices, in a word, are cast unquestionably, as to all essential points, in the same mould. Yet that they are not identical, but only very closely akin, after all,—sister-rites, as it were,—a careful examination of them, combined with historical evidence, no less certainly evinces. In the first place, the two books which contain these two rites are totally different,—as different as their names of Breviarium Romanum and Portiforium (also Breviarium) Sarisburiense. The one is mostly in four volumes, the other in two; the one has the Psalter at the beginning, the other in the middle. The rubrical structure and phraseology is widely different: the Roman knows nothing of the English "Rules called the Pie," (Pica); the English nothing of the "*Rubricæ generales.*" The English has a peculiar title for the series of lection-responsories, viz. "*historia*[s];" and by the change of this the character of the day is in a great measure determined. It also distinguishes between *memoriæ* and *commemorationes*, and has many other rubrical peculiarities. But there are also great differences,

---

[s] Vide Pica de Dom. i. Adv. Brev. Sar. "Portiforium appears to have been adopted only in England." Maskell, Diss. vol. I. p. lxxxviii.

both of structure and contents, even in the body of the Offices themselves. First, of *structure*. The Roman use has the *Gloria* after every Psalm, unless the contrary is specified; the English only at certain specified places: the English had no absolutions whatever before the lessons; the Roman has a very elaborate system of them: the Roman *substitutes* the Te Deum for the last responsory on Festivals; the English *added* it, and *repeated* the responsory where the Te Deum was not used: the English prefaced Lauds with a *Versus sacerdotalis*, quite unknown, name and thing, to the Roman: the English had a full responsory to the Vespers Capitulum on Festivals; the Roman none. The Preces at Prime and Compline, (including the Apostles' Creed, and also the Creed of Athanasius,) were said all the year round in the English Church, though only on certain days in the Roman. She had also a special addition to these Offices, entitled, "For the peace of the Church," including Ps. cxxi. at Prime, and Ps. cxxiii. at Compline. And while the Roman use has but *one* form of Compline, the English has *twenty-two*. It would be easy to add to these differences. The variation of *contents*, again, between the two Uses, is on occasion very great, even where the structure is identical. The *particular* antiphons, benedictions, lections, responsories, hymns, Capitula, Preces, versicles and responses, are to a great extent, especially at particular seasons, quite different from the Roman. Sometimes, too, the number even of the Psalms is different. Thus on Low Sunday the English use had but three Psalms and lessons; the Roman, nine.

These diversities as clearly establish the *distinctness*, as the correspondences before mentioned do the close *affinity*, of the two rites. For that the variations of the English use from the Roman are of the essence of it, and not, or rarely, the effect, as might be supposed, of a gradual departure from the forms at first received, appears in various ways. Some of them, as e. g. the Compline and Prime peculiarities, have every appearance of having come direct from the East. The whole rite is by many degrees more Oriental than the Roman. How should the English Church develope such Orientalisms? Again, it is well known that the Roman Church, on more than one occasion, used considerable efforts to assimilate the English use to her own; as, e. g. at the Council of Cloveshoo[t] (748), and probably did so to some extent. Grancolas, who probably never had seen the English rite, hastily concludes hence that it was originally the same as the Roman: whereas it proves exactly the contrary. The fact that such material variation remained after all, argues the essential and invincible irreconcilableness of the two rites.

But further, some of these peculiarities are shared by certain other rituals otherwise of the Roman type, and thus tend to class the English rite in a particular *variety* of that species to which the Roman belongs. It is a curious fact, that the ritual of the Church of Lyons[u], otherwise agreeing with the Roman in all essential points, even more closely than the English does, departs from it in several of the selfsame respects as the English. It adds the Te Deum to the ninth responsory, prefixes a *versus* to Lauds, and on Sexagesima and following Sundays substitutes Ps. xciii. for Ps. cxviii. at Prime; which same thing the English did, only beginning on Septuagesima. But another French rite,

[t] Concil. Clovesh., can. 24.     [u] Bona, Psalmod. xviii. 6.

still existing,—that of the Premonstratensians[x],—coincides still more exactly with the English in its variations from the Roman. It had, 1, no absolutions before the lessons; 2, it prefixed a *Versus sacerdotalis* to Lauds; 3, on the first Vespers of great Festivals it had a responsory to the Capitulum; 4, finally, on Septuagesima Sunday it began to make the substitution just mentioned at Prime. Bona, who notices these peculiarities, adds that the Premonstratensians maintain "that theirs is the original Roman Breviary, which they have preserved in its purity, rejecting later alterations and reforms."

The English rite, it would seem from hence, may properly be classed with the Gallican variety of the family to which the Roman belongs. The only question is, how did two varieties so similar, yet so distinct, originate? and how came the French variety to be imported into England by St. Augustine? Now as to the first point, Cassian was singularly in a position to originate two rites thus circumstanced, as a brief glance at his history will shew[y]. A Thracian or Scythian by birth, he seems to have spent his earlier years as an inmate of St. Jerome's monastery at Bethlehem, and afterwards lived at least seven years in Egypt, in diligent study, as well as practice, of the peculiar monastic system, both disciplinary and ritual, of that country. Returning to his native region, he

[x] Vide Bona, ibid., 6. This order was founded by St. Norbert, an. 1115, at Premontrè, near Rheims. It was, however, only a reformation of the order of Regular Canons of St. Austin, already settled at Laon, in that neighbourhood, and so might very well be in possession of the ancient French variety of the Roman rite. Vide Butler, Life of Norbert, June 6; Helyot, Ordres Monastiques, tom. ii. ch. 23.

[y] See Life of Cassian, prefixed to his works, by Gazæus; and Butler's Lives of the Saints, note on St. Victor, July 21.

was ordained deacon by St. Chrysostom at Constantinople, circ. 403, (some think that he was his archdeacon[a],) and was sent by that Church, during Chrysostom's exile, on a mission on his behalf to Pope Innocent[a]. It was probably in consequence of the destruction of St. Jerome's monastery by the Pelagians, in the year 416, that he removed to Marseilles. Here he founded two monasteries, and wrote his "Institutions of the Cœnobitic Life," describing minutely the Egyptian monastic ways and ritual. In this work he dwells especially on the number of twelve Psalms, which the Egyptian monks alleged had been fixed by revelation; and on the reading of two lessons of Scripture, one from the Old Testament and one from the New, (both from the New on Sundays[b],) in their daily office; a thing unknown, as we have seen, to the rest of the East. He was also requested by St. Leo, then archdeacon of Rome under Pope Celestine, (422,) to write against Nestorius on the Incarnation. This must have been between the years 422 and 433, soon after which Cassian died. Leo became pope in 440.

Cassian then lacked no qualification, either of date, position, knowledge, influence, or inclination, for the chief authorship of these two rituals. Imbued from his youth with the Eastern ritual system, and especially with that expanded form of it which had recently grown up in the monasteries; equally well acquainted with the Egyptian monastic offices, and so

[a] Gazæus, ut supra.      [a] Innocent. Ep. ap. Hieron.

[b] It is curious, and indicates the influence of the Egyptian monastic ritual system, probably through Cassian, upon the Spanish Church, that its rule was to have lessons out of the Old and New Testament on week-days, but on Sundays from the New only. Isidor., ap. Mabillon, p. 393.

habituated to the number of twelve Psalms, and to the daily reading of Scripture; (which are the characteristics of the Western family of offices as compared with the Eastern); a diligent propagator of Eastern monastic ways on Western ground; holding a position in the south of France, yet reaching by his influence to Rome through one of the greatest of her Popes, to whom, as well as to Rome generally, he probably became known on the occasion of his embassy; the representative, in a manner, of the mind of St. Jerome, to whom the arrangement of the Roman Offices is traditionally ascribed;—there is hardly any feature or circumstance belonging to these Offices which is not accounted for on the hypothesis of his authorship. St. Jerome may perfectly well have been consulted by Damasus, as tradition represents[c], and have performed through his disciple Cassian the task commonly ascribed to him. He died in the very year (420) commonly named[d] for the reconstruction of the Roman ritual, the very same time at which Cassian must have been engaged on that of the French Churches. And as Leo is known to have been the originator of a particular feature in these offices, viz. of the Collects, and also the writer of a large proportion of the homilies used as lessons, we shall probably be not far wrong in ascribing to him, conjointly with Cassian, the authorship, in the main[e], of the existing Roman Daily Offices.

Again, as to the formation of the French variety of

[c] Vide supr. St. Gregory says (Ep. vii. 19.) that St. Damasus adopted some Greek usages at St. Jerome's suggestion. He died, however, in 384.

[d] Grancolas, ubi supr.

[e] Milman observes, (Hist. of Latin Christianity, vol. i. p. 20, 29,) that Leo was the first distinguished writer among the popes.

the Roman rite, and its transmission to England. Cassian would naturally draw up for the use of his own or neighbouring monasteries or Churches, a scheme of service after the Oriental model, grafted on the older and simpler forms of the West, combined with such methods as Lyons or other Churches had already derived from the East. The Church of Marseilles, of whose ritual we know nothing[f], may have adopted this. He would be free here to copy the Eastern model more closely, than when acting as the counsellor and assessor of Leo. The result would be such a service as that which England inherited, really independent of the Roman, and more distinctly Oriental. Neither is there any difficulty in understanding how Cassian's scheme of service found its way to England by the hands of St. Augustine. Here, too, authoritative history furnishes a most reasonable account of the matter. When St. Augustine was sent by St. Gregory on his mission to England, "they took ship," says St. Augustine's most recent biographer[g], "at one of the Italian ports, and landed probably at *Marseilles*." He was well received by Arigius, the bishop, by the neighbouring bishop of Aix, and by Stephen, abbot of Lerins. Returning to St. Gregory for further instructions, he received from him letters[h] to both the bishop of Marseilles and the abbot of Lerins, commending him to their counsel and guidance in the matter of evangelizing England. He was to acquaint the bishop[i] more especially with the occasion of his journey, and seek help from him. He was also to take with him some French presbyters[k], to assist him in his undertaking. Moreover,

[f] Mabillon, Curs. Gall.     [g] Lives of the Saints.
[h] Ep. Greg., vi. 51, &c.    [i] Ib., vi. 52.    [k] Ib., vi. 58, 59.

he afterwards returned from England to Arles to obtain consecration, and spent about two years there, from 596 to 598. Add to all this, that having sought from St. Gregory directions as to what ritual he should adopt, he was instructed "that whatever he found, either in the Roman Church, or in the Church of Gaul, or in any other, which might be more pleasing to Almighty God, he should most carefully (*sollicitè*) select, and should thus introduce into the English Church, as being new to the faith, (and therefore a fit subject for a special ordinance in the matter of ritual,) what he had been able to collect from many Churches[1]." St. Augustine would be fulfilling these instructions most *equably*, by introducing into England the Communion Office of the Roman, and the Ordinary Offices of the southern French Churches. The commonly-received hypothesis, that he merely adopted into the Roman Office some variations derived from French sources, is manifestly untenable. The English variations bespeak an Oriental hand, and extend to the whole structure of the rubrical part of the Office, and to not a little of the Office itself. Some alterations, tending to assimilate it to the Roman, such as certain of the Gelasian or Gregorian adjustments in respect of the Collects or antiphons, St. Augustine may have introduced; though I think it more probable that even these had reached the French Churches previously. But in any case, the stock upon which he grafted them was indisputably, I conceive, not the Roman, but the French, or pure Cassianic ritual.

[1] Bed. Hist. i. 27. "Mihi placet, sive in Romanâ, sive in Gallicanâ, seu in quâlibet Ecclesiâ aliquid invenisti, quod plus omnipotenti Deo possit placere, sollicitè eligas, et in Anglorum Ecclesiâ, quæ adhuc ad fidem nova est, institutione præcipuâ, quæ de multis Ecclesiis colligere potuisti, infundas."

The contents and character of the English Office, whose history we have now investigated, will form the subject of the next section. But some remarks on the result of our inquiry will not be misplaced here.

In the first place, then, it is deeply interesting to observe, that it was ordained that the whole West should, in the fifth and sixth centuries, brighten afresh the torch of her public devotions at the same Eastern fount of sacred fire at which she had at the first kindled it. "The isles waited" once more, for their portion in spiritual things, upon the more favoured and more fervid regions upon which "the light" had first risen[m] of old: and the East dictated, for a second time, the ritual of the world. It is, I conceive, as well ascertained as any fact of the kind can be, that the later Western ritual, in all its known forms, is universally derived from the Eastern. It is as clear from internal evidence, that St. Benedict's Offices, and the Roman, and the Milanese, and the Spanish, and the French, and the English, were largely indebted to the Greek Offices, as it is that the Italian, the Spanish, the French, and the English languages were indebted to the Latin, or Latin and Greek to Sanscrit. The notion, for example, that St. Benedict invented this scheme of services, though believed in Europe for a thousand years, and contributing largely to the extraordinary reverence in which he was held, is a fable and a dream. We of the West must be content to speak of the greater part, and of all the more striking features of our rituals, as of things which we have received from others, not struck out for ourselves.

Now this consideration may well moderate the contempt with which the West has so long looked upon the

[m] Isa. lx. 1, 9.

ritual, as well as the position in other respects, of her Eastern sister; that is to say, of sixty millions of Christians. There was a time when she as teachably sat at the feet of the Eastern Church in the matter of ritual, and even (too much so, indeed,) of doctrine also, as she now loftily affects to ignore her existence, except on condition of receiving her homage. The Churches of the West in the fifth and sixth centuries vied with each other in importing into their own simpler and perhaps declining ritual, the features and arrangements with which the East had enriched hers. They found that, while they had been content to keep the deposit of apostolically-derived service unimpaired,—if indeed they had so kept it,—the Eastern Church had laid out the same to usury. "We know certainly," says Mr. Palmer,—though it is astonishing that, with his information, he followed out the clue no further,—"that the Eastern Churches at an early period devised many improvements in the celebration of Divine Service, which did not occur to the less lively and inventive imagination of their brethren in the West; and that the latter were accustomed to imitate the former in their rites and ceremonies[n]." Stimulated, apparently, by the necessity for making a stand[o], in the shape of a more elaborate and attractive ritual, against the rising Arian heresy, the East had drawn off into more diversified channels the reservoir of ritual which in common with the West she inherited. Hence, in the earlier stage of her development, her splendidly conceived Morning Office; and her Vespers, less grand,

---

[n] Orig. Lit., vol. i. p. 310. He only instances alternate chanting,—the Kyrie eleison, the Nicene Creed, litanies and processions, and the position of the Lord's Prayer in the Roman Canon.

[o] See Bingham, XIII. x. 12; Socr., lib. vi. 7.

but even more refined in conception. Hence, a little later, the multiplication in number, as before the augmentation in bulk, of her services. Thus, when she sought "to water abundantly her garden-bed, her brook became a river, and her river became a sea." And from that deep and broad fount of waters it was that the West drew her later ritual conceptions and arrangements; nor can she deny her obligations, however she may desire to forget them.

But it is still more to the purpose of this work to observe, that the facts which have here been pointed out furnish a complete answer to that favourite theme of declamation against the English Church; viz. that in the full and fearless Revision she made of her ritual in the 16th and 17th centuries, she committed an act unprecedented, singular, and schismatic. I have already had occasion to allude to the condemnation which has been freely and confidently pronounced upon particular features of her revised Offices; as, for example, upon the penitential commencement and the thanksgiving close. We have seen how entire a justification those features receive from the primitive condition of our Offices, and indeed from the general principles, recognised in the East and West alike, of Christian worship. But, as is well known, this sentence of condemnation is by no means limited to details, but extends to the act of Revision itself, in all its parts. Now it is certain that neither the Western Church as a whole, nor any particular branch of it, is in a position to judge us in this matter; "for she herself, that judges, has done the same things." Of all the points in which Rome and the West have sat in judgment on the English Church, there is not one in which they have not set us the example.

To confine ourselves here to the Daily Offices. Did the English Church, in the 16th century, re-adjust the whole scheme of her services? All the Churches of the West in the fifth and sixth centuries did the same. Did England add new features? Rome and the West imported new offices. Are we accused of fusing together offices originally distinct, by the omission of some things, and the transposition of others? They dismembered the great Morning Office of the East, and divided its spoils between their Lauds and Nocturns. Did our revision involve the rejection of the then existing scheme of Psalms, omitting the fixed and re-arranging the continuous psalmody? The West revolutionized hers no less; rejecting, we can hardly doubt, the 119th, and perhaps other anciently fixed Nocturns Psalms, and substituting for the free course of Psalms[p], which followed, a fixed daily portion. Was the number of Psalms thus used in the English Church greatly reduced? So was it, in all probability, by the Western revision. Is it an unheard-of thing for a Church to be for three centuries without antiphons? The whole West had probably had few or none for four or five. Did we, again, put our lection system on a new footing? Rome and the West devised the system itself. Did we increase the amount of Scripture used? They brought in the reading of Scripture into their Daily Offices for the first time. Did Ridley and Sanderson compose Collects? Leo invented them. Or, lastly, was the sin of the English Church in this, that she acted for herself as a national Church, and not in concert with the whole West? Nay, all the Churches of the West acted

[p] Vide Grancolas, ubi supra.

with the same independence, revising, as we have seen, each one their own ritual; and that not even simultaneously, but in the course of two centuries. And the real "composers and compilers" of services, after all, were Leo and Gregory, Isidore and Fructuosus, Cæsarius and Hilary.

It is in no spirit of recrimination that these things are pointed out. On the contrary, as I have said at the outset, I conceive that the Churches of the West were not only justified in the main principle of thus revising their ritual, but were, so far as we can judge, fulfilling therein a great and general law of the Church's growth and progress. All I desire to do is to point out this as a signal exemplification of the saying,

"Quam temerè in nosmet legem sancimus iniquam;"

and to claim for the English Church of the 16th century the benefit of that weighty truth, which, though she was the first to enunciate it, the whole West had accepted and acted upon a thousand years before, viz. that—

"The particular forms of divine worship, and the rites and ceremonies appointed to be used therein, being things in their own nature indifferent; it is but reasonable, that upon weighty and important considerations, such changes and alterations should be made therein, as to those that are in place of authority shall from time to time seem either necessary or expedient q."

Freely, too, is it admitted, as was indeed noticed in the first chapter, that the changes effected in the West, though very great, were after all sufficiently conservative of the old landmarks to ensure ritual continuity. Only we claim no less for the English Revised Offices, as compared with the older forms,

---

q Preface to the Book of Common Prayer, 1662.

that (to adopt again the language of the document just quoted) this Church did indeed,—

"Upon just and weighty considerations her thereunto moving, yield to make such alterations as were thought convenient; yet so as that the main body and essentials (as well in the *chiefest materials, as in the frame and order thereof,*) have still continued the same until this day."

## SECTION III.

"When ye come together, every one of you hath a Psalm, hath a doctrine, hath a tongue, hath a revelation, hath an interpretation. Let all things be done to edifying."

WE have now seen what was the history, and made some acquaintance with the materials, of our ancient Services. But before we can appreciate the character which our present Offices derive from their relation to these older formularies, and the mind with which they should be used in consequence, we must endeavour to gather more exactly what was the characteristic spirit of each of them. For though it is exceedingly instructive to contemplate the earlier and Eastern phase of our Services, it must be borne in mind that it is from the *Western* ordinary ritual, from the English variety of it in particular, and from no other, that our own is immediately derived. Not a few, indeed, of the characteristics of the West have unavoidably come before us in connection with the Eastern Offices, whose spirit, together with their contents, it to a great extent inherited. Still the Western, and specially the English ritual, had a character of its own; and to offer a brief and summary view of this[r],

[r] For the scheme and contents of our older Offices, see the tables below, ch. iv. sect. 1, p. 288.

will be the design of the present section. For a full appreciation of it, it will be necessary that the reader should combine those former notices with what is here set down.

I have already remarked, that multitudinous as are the commentators, ancient and modern, on the ritual of the Western Church, they are of very little service indeed for our present purpose. They are mainly occupied with minute observations, and fail to appreciate broad general characteristics; nor do they dream of having recourse to Eucharistic sources or Oriental forms for purposes of illustration. From these causes, they constantly miss the true character, the most striking beauties, of their own ritual. Much greater weight is attached to a pious reflection, or suggestion of some ingenious writer, than to the manifest intent of an office as indicated by its structure and contents. It is rare, indeed, to find a simple and real, because historical account given of anything; or if there be, it is set side by side, and on a level, with a variety of mere conjectures, some of them, perhaps, far-fetched and preposterous. Thus, for example, Durandus suggests that the three Nocturns into which the Psalms of the old Matin Services on Sundays and Festivals were divided, are intended to remind us respectively of those who lived before the Law, under the Law, and since the Law; or of faith in the Holy Trinity; or of the thrice three orders of angels which theologians discern in the Holy Scriptures, and together with whom we sing to the glory of God. It may be so: but who would place speculations such as these at the same value, as helps to enter into the nature and spirit of the Matins Office, with the certain and leading fact that these "Nocturns" preserve in their name the traces of the ancient intention and use of them; viz. to serve as "songs in the night," as a high chorus of praise in the still and undisturbed hours of darkness; or, again, with the probability that they originated with the ancient watches, already consecrated to sacred uses in the days of David? Still less can any such co-equal importance be properly attached to the more minute, not to say trivial, speculations and analogies in which the Ritualists indulge: as when, for example, it is remarked that the Psalms precede the Lessons, just as the angels were elect before men, (for whose benefit the latter were written); that the twelve Psalms in a Nocturn correspond in number to the twelve Patriarchs or Apostles; the quaternary of Psalms repeated under one antiphon to the four cardinal virtues, of which the patriarchs are presumed to have been the example; the first quaternary representing, moreover, Abel, Enos, Enoch, and Lamech; Abel being an example of the first Psalm, "Beatus vir;" Enos of the second, because in his times (qu. Seth's?) "men began to serve the Lord in fear." The second quaternary is assigned, with the like fanciful applications, to Noah, Shem, Eber, and Terah; the third to Abraham, Isaac, Jacob, and Joseph. In like manner, the three Psalms which form the second Nocturn on Sunday are made to represent three orders of saints who lived under the Law,—Lawgivers, Psalmists, and Prophets; or Priests, Judges, and Kings. The three Psalms of the third Nocturn are to remind us of the faithful in the three parts of the world,—Asia, Europe, and Africa; of the three orders of saints under the Gospel, Apostles, Martyrs, Confessors[a]. The application here made of the Psalms is, however, apt enough: Ps. xix., "Cœli enarrant," is for the Apostles, because "their

[a] Durand., in loc.

sound is gone out," &c.; Ps. xx., "Exaudiat te," for the Martyrs, because "the Lord heard them in the day of trouble;" Ps. xxi., "Domine in virtute," for the Confessors, because "God hath not denied them the request of their lips."

In the following sketch of the nature and object of the old Services, my endeavour will be to catch the real and essential features of them, passing by, or placing in a very subordinate rank, such views of them as seem rather suggested by pious ingenuity, than to have any proper connection with them.

The old Matins then is, as we know, originally and properly a nocturnal, or even a midnight, Service. This character of our ancient Matins is marked by the ordinary[t] versicle and response after the first Nocturn on Sunday,—"I have remembered Thy Name, O Lord, in the night season." The ordinary[u] versicle after the second Nocturn is, "At midnight I will rise to give thanks unto Thee," &c. It may be observed that both verses are from Ps. cxix.; and their use countenances the supposition which we have already seen reason for entertaining, viz. that that Psalm was, before the Cassianic revision, used in the West at Nocturns. The versicle and response of the third Nocturn have reference, not to the time, but the character, of the Service, considered as a service of singing praises more especially. V. "Be Thou exalted, Lord, in Thine own strength. R. We will sing and utter Psalms of Thy power." The adoption of this versicle and response is again thoroughly Oriental.

[t] Viz., except in Advent. The Roman Use had it not either in Lent, Easter, or Advent.

[u] The Roman has instead a verse from Ps. xviii.: "Thou shalt lighten my candle." These are instances of a lower degree of Orientalism, or of less tenacity of tradition, in the Roman rite.

It is the last verse of Ps. xxi. which has just been sung, and the desire to include which seems[*] to have dictated the number of the Western Sunday Psalms; it having been the key-note of the Matutinal psalmody, which was about to follow, in the East, and perhaps in the West also. The contents of the Service are entirely Psalms and Lessons; the Psalms being accompanied by glorias, antiphons, versicles and responses, and the Lessons by responsories; the Psalms and Lessons changing with the day; the antiphons, versicles, and responsories with the season. The Te Deum was added on Sundays and Festivals, except in Advent and Ember weeks.

The idea under which this character was given to the Nocturns Office in the West may be easily conjectured. The day brings with it the works, the wants, the interests of man; but the night may well *vacare laudibus et meditationi*,—spend itself in pure praise and meditation. The soul of the Church rises free and unencumbered by earthly things to God. She confines herself at this season to singing God's praise and meditating upon His works and Word. Other associations belong to a Nocturnal or Midnight Service, and may have influenced its contents; e. g. the symbolical character which night bears in Holy Scripture, representing the deeds and thoughts of darkness, against which we are to strive by occupying ourselves in praises and meditation; the association of night with the deliverance from Egypt, with our Lord's betrayal and sufferings, and that of midnight with the coming of the Bridegroom. The beautiful character which this Office possesses, as distinguished from the rest, when thus viewed

---

[*] Supr., ch. i. sect. 4.

as a great tide of elevated and unmingled praise and meditation, seems to be entirely lost upon the commentators on the Western Ritual. Baronius, however, has applied with some felicity the words of St. Paul, 1 Cor. xiv. 26, as a sort of motto descriptive of this Office: "When ye come together, every one of you hath a Psalm, hath a doctrine, a revelation, tongue, interpretation." For there are Psalms, lessons for doctrine, responsories for revelation, (considering them as an expository key-note,) readings of the Gospel for a tongue, (on Sundays and festivals,) and of a homily for interpretation. The festival Te Deum is, of course, a noble descant of praise upon the whole of the preceding topics, whether of praise or meditation. The extraordinary uniformity with which it occupies this position in all Western Offices (including St. Benedict's) whose structure is known to us, while it is, at least in its complete form, unknown to the East, leaves no room to doubt either of its great antiquity, or of its responsorial intention.

The Lauds Office is at once seen to be in a far less degree a Service of broad and general praise and of meditation. First of all there are fewer Psalms by far;—only six, (including the canticles, and reckoning Psalms cxlviii.—cl. as one,) instead of twelve or eighteen. Then the lessons for meditation are reduced to a single text; and collects are introduced towards the close. And when we inquire for the positive characteristics of the Office, they are easily discoverable, and accord well with the hour to which it properly belonged. That hour, as in the East, was sunrise; the first breaking forth of light upon the earth: "Ad Auroram, seu luce incipiente canebantur[y]." Hence

[y] Martene, quoting S. Benedict.

in Benedict's time the Service was called *Matutinæ* and *Matura;* the night service being called *Vigiliæ*. And the Nocturnal Service was only completed on this condition, "nisi forte aurora interveniens hoc distulerit." Hence the characteristics of the Office. Instead of the quiet, continuous praise of Matins, taking the Book of Psalms in order, we have first of all Psalms, &c. selected on purpose for a keen burst of lauds at the return of daylight. This we have in the unvarying 63rd, and jubilant 148—150th, in Benedictus, and (generally) in the "song" from the Old Testament, one for each day in the week. But the return of man's portion of time, the day, brings with it penitential[z] associations also; hence the 51st Psalm was used every day but Sundays, and on Sundays also from Septuagesima to Palm Sunday. This double character of Lauds was further marked, as has been pointed out elsewhere[a], by the selection made of other appropriate Psalms besides the unvarying 63rd and 51st. This mixed aspect extends in a measure to the "songs" used one each day of the week. The joyful Song of the Three Children on Sunday, of Isaiah on Monday, and of Hannah on Wednesday, combine well with the jubilant Psalms appropriated to those days, (viz. xciii., c., lxvii., v.; and lxv.). The more subdued or even mournful strains of Hezekiah on Tuesday, (very similar to the appointed Ps. xliii.,) and those of Habukkuk on Friday (with Ps. cxliii.), and Moses on Saturday, both telling of the terrors of God, leave the balance evenly suspended between "mercy and judgment;"—the other song of Moses, on Thursday, striking it in favour of mercy.

[z] Comp. Hugo ap. Gavanti, in loc.; and Durandus: "Dies feriales recolunt peregrinationes sanctorum et pœnitentiam."
[a] Ch. i. sect. 6.

The Lauds Office, according to the English use, has also a feature peculiar to itself, in which the two-fold character belonging to it is clearly brought out. The *Versus sacerdotalis* already mentioned, on Sundays expresses praise, and on the week-days penitence: being, on Sunday, "The Lord is high above all people, and His glory above the heavens;" on week-days, "O Lord, let Thy mercy be shewed upon us. As we do put our trust in Thee." This latter versicle and response seem to be a sort of residuum and representative of the Te Deum, (which was not used on week-days,) being the penultimate verse of it. This Office has also, in virtue of its numerous morning allusions, a near affinity to the topic of the Resurrection[b].

In the same connection it is that Collects now for the first time appear, having reference to man's estate in Christ. The Collect for the day, from the Communion Office, is of this kind; as are the Memorials. This marks the care of the Church to place the first prayers, which her children utter in the day, in connection with the One all-prevailing Sacrifice, and with the Eucharistic Oblation and Communion.

Lauds, therefore, differs from Matins, on the one hand, in that it makes a different use of the Psalms, aiming at specific objects by the selections made of them, viz. the praise of God for the return of light, and the fallen but restored estate of man. As compared, on the other hand, with Prime, we shall find that its characteristic is, that it *has* Psalms of praise, selected as such; which Prime has not. But in those of its Psalms which respect man, we shall see that

---

[b] Durand.: "Officium Laudum Domini Resurrectionem significat; quae jam completa in capite, scilicet in Christo, adhuc est in membris complenda."

it is less pointedly practical than Prime; not dealing so much with the particulars of duty, as with the general fact of man's feebleness, as set forth in the penitential Psalms, such as the 51st and 143rd. Its Collects in like manner have respect to the general condition of man, not to the specific wants of the day. Compare the Collect for Peace in this Service, or the Communion Collects generally, with those that occur in the Prime Service, e. g. our third Collect, for defence during the day, &c.

In Prime, again, we have pre-eminently what may be called a practical service[e]. It is the Office for the first hour of the day, as its name implies:—a time when the world and its concerns are now a whole hour on their way, and consequently the whole business and needs of man are in a manner before the Church, and call for the prayers of her members. And to these human wants the whole structure of the Service is manifestly directed. The unvarying hymn, "Jam lucis orto sidere," is against the temptations of the world and the flesh. The Psalms are not taken in course, as at Matins, but selected; yet neither, as in Lauds, as Psalms of praise for the opening of the day, but of direction and guidance; e. g. Ps. liv. and part of cxix. The idea with which, on Sunday, Psalms xxii.—xxv. were used, has been remarked upon (p. 233) in speaking of the Eastern Prime; viz. in reference to our Lord's Passion. On Sunday, too, Ps. cxviii. was added, carrying on the idea of Christ's Resurrection, contained in Lauds; indeed, that Psalm was transferred to Lauds, from Septuagesima to Easter. The Prime Capitulum on week-days is practical; Zech. viii. 19, "Love peace and truth," &c.: the Collects,

[e] Compare above, sect. i. See also Durandus in loc.

as already observed, are on the actual wants of the day. It is in the same connection that certain features now appear for the first time for unvarying use. In this Service, in the English form, there are *preces* for daily use throughout the year. Now these are, chiefly, earnest petitions for pardon and guidance. The occurrence of the Lord's Prayer (twice) is also a new feature of the same character. Such also are the two Creeds, daily used, one aloud. It was obviously fitting that Christian men at the threshold of their day should thus make open profession of the God in Whom they believe. We have seen the Eastern Office introducing it similarly at the close of their Night Office. Next we have the Confession, with the interchanged Misereatur and Absolution, the petitions for pardon and direction, and Psalm li.; and the practical Collects,—among them our third Collect. The Office concluded with this benediction: "In the Name of the Father, and of the Son, and of the Holy Ghost. Amen."

We may well pause here in the consideration of these daily Morning Services, now wrought up into our own, to pay a just tribute of admiration to their beauty and fitness in the abstract, according to the original conception of them. If we have not erred in our attempts to interpret their meaning and design, there is a grandeur at once and a correctness in the theory of them, an adaptation to the real state of the case, if we may so speak, between God Almighty on the one hand, and His redeemed and sanctified creatures on the other. There is Matins, with its simple Nocturnal idea, its philosophic as well as religious recognition of night as the season for sacred meditation[d]; with its

---

[d] Compare the Greek εὐφρόνη.

broad, deep, and unceasing river of praise and meditation, flowing ever onwards in tribute to the ocean of God's perfections. There is Lauds, with its peculiar aspect of care for man's redeemed yet still sorrowful estate,—a grateful yet humbled " song of mercy and judgment ;"— a daily fresh-springing fountain, morning by morning, of sweet waters and bitter, both awakened to life by the touch of light, by the return of new present mercies, and of new memories and hopes of resurrection ; not without its gleam, too, of Eucharistic light and strength from the central orb of the Church's high act of Offering and Communion. There is Prime, with its more varied face of " Quidquid agunt homines;" reflecting in detail the particulars of man's estate towards God, such as he is " in Christ." Man therefore appears in these two later Offices as a supernaturally-endowed creature, reconciled and saved, baptized and eucharistized ; baptized into a Triune Name, and " going forth to his work and to his labour until the evening," with the sense of a baptismal vow upon him, and the facts of a baptismal Creed surrounding him ; sustained in act or desire, by present or recent participation, with super-substantial food, and himself offered and accepted in a continual Eucharistic oblation ; though reconciled, yet needing daily reconciliation for daily falls, by the healing virtue of Confession and Absolution , having the Spirit, yet requiring daily fresh supplies of it for guidance, to be sought for in set prayers, through the all-prevailing Name; finally, passing through a circuit of days, which, by the ordinance either of God or His Church, " are distinguished, some of them made high days, and hallowed, and some of them made ordinary days," and which receive their commemoration accordingly.

The Offices of Terce, Sext, and Nones carry on, as it were, the proper work of the Prime Office through the day; and by continued use of the same instrument, the 119th Psalm, that "paradise of fruits and storehouse of the Holy Spirit, on which the Church therefore feedeth and ruminateth through the hours, as on sweet spices of the Garden of Eden, that she may be as a sweet aroma to God."

Of this Psalm, the first four sections, according to our division, are used daily at Prime; the remaining eighteen are assigned to these Offices, — six to each. And it may be observed that herein lies the bond of union between these four hours; a bond which, from their common nomenclature of first, third, sixth, ninth hours, (whereas all the others are named either from the season of their occurrence, as Matins, Vespers, or from their contents, as Lauds, Compline,) one would expect beforehand to find existing somewhere. The ritualists, as Durandus, suggest various mystical applications, in connection with the acts of our Lord's Passion, of the contents of the Psalm to the various hours of the day; but it is evident that, though frequently apposite, they must be accidental: no such application can have been in the thoughts of those who arranged these Services, since this Psalm is taken in its natural order. They have themselves, however, introduced some allusions of this kind into each hour, in the form of antiphons before, or versicles and responses after the Capitulum. And in the Capitula thus accompanied we detect a further characteristic of these three Offices. There is a different one assigned for each of the three hours, for Sundays and week-days. The Sunday Capitulum is in each case doctrinal, setting forth the doctrine of the Holy Trinity in a text from the Epistles; and the antiphon ascribes glory to the Holy Trinity accordingly. Nor only so; but by the selection made of the text and antiphon, and the adaptation of a Versicle and a Response taken from the Psalm, the three Persons of the Holy Trinity are severally honoured at the third, the sixth, and the ninth hour; not, however, in their theological order, but the reverse. The Sunday Capitulum at the end of the third hour, the only one on which our existing services lead us to dwell, is 2 Cor. xiii. ult., "The grace of our Lord Jesus Christ," &c. This text, relating to the Holy Trinity, would seem to be selected for this hour on account of its being a prayer for the indwelling of the proper grace of each of the three Persons in man, and especially for the full communication of the Holy Spirit, which naturally belongs to the third hour, as the hour of His Pentecostal descent. With this exception, Terce, Sext, and Nones, add no new feature to those of the preceding Offices; they do but sustain and prolong certain elements of them. The same is, to a certain degree, true of Vespers and Compline; we shall find that, besides their actual brevity, no new methods of worship make their appearance in them. Yet there are here, in Compline especially, as there are in some degree in Vespers also, new and beautiful applications of the same or similar elements to the associations and needs of eventide.

The Vespers Office will be found to be, in its elements and structure, a copy or reflection, in reduced proportions, of two of the Morning Offices. I say of two Offices, not of one of them only; for though the ritualists, ancient and modern, are agreed in limiting the resemblance to *Lauds*, a little consideration will shew that it is otherwise, and that Vespers reflects the structure and spirit both of Matins and Lauds, in at least equal proportions [e].

The characteristic of Matins, we have seen, is its continuous flow both of praise and meditation; for which respectively the Psalms (taken in course, and without selection,) and reading of Holy Scripture in considerable proportions, supply the medium. Now Vespers for the first day of the week resumes this continuous and unselected saying of the Psalms at the point (Ps. cix.) where it is left by the Matins Office of the seventh day. The number of Psalms used on each evening is however reduced from twelve to five; the reading of Scripture, beyond a text, is laid aside altogether. But the Office, as far as the Psalms are concerned, evidently proceeds upon the Matins idea. It is important to remark this, because in virtue of this correspondence of its idea with that of Matins, the Vesper Office serves to dedicate the whole of the latter portion of the day to Divine praise, just as Matins does the earlier portion. It does not seize on special topics or associations as subjects of praise, but sends up general, irrespective adoration; the incense of man's existence to God's glory. Though in volume far scantier than its great morning prototype, it is evidently in idea and intention parallel. But the remaining features of the Office not less certainly bespeak it, as far as they are concerned, a parallel Office to Lauds. In fact, it is a combination of the Matins and Lauds types. In what may be called its numerical structure, i.e. the number of elements contained in it, it is parallel to the latter; it has five Psalms, hymn,

[e] See above, chap. i. sect. 7; and the tables and analysis below, ch. iv. sect. 1.

Capitulum, Canticle, (reckoned as a sixth Psalm,) Collects, and "memorials."

Vespers then, considered as the Lauds of Eventide, breathes, like Lauds itself, (chiefly in virtue of its Magnificat and Collects,) a spirit of remembrance of man's redeemed estate through the Incarnation.

Finally, Compline, like Prime, with which it has so much in common,—viz. Psalms and Collects for guidance, Creed, Lord's Prayer, Confession and Absolution, Petitions and Intercessions,—is an eminently practical and personal Office. It carries on, too, in virtue of its Capitulum (Jer. xiv.—see p. 226) and Nunc Dimittis, the Vespers allusion to the Incarnation; and by its Collect and Psalms (xxxi. xci.) rests the Christian's hope of protection on the sorrows and victory of Christ.

---

It will not be uninteresting to endeavour briefly to discriminate in this place the genius of the East and of the West, as exhibited in their respective forms of Ordinary Worship which we have now passed under review; more especially as our present Offices combine, in a measure, the temper and characteristics of both.

The East then, if we leave out of the account those enrichments which her ordinary Offices derive from the Eucharist on Sundays and Festivals, and take her, so to speak, in her every-day dress, is more uniform and unchanging; the West more multiform and variable. Witness the single, changeless Invitatory and Benediction[f] of the one Church, and their endless varieties in the other. While the West rings countless

[f] pp. 75, 114.

changes, according to the season, on the same essential idea, the East prolongs it in one unvaried and majestic toll, from the beginning to the end of the year. The East, again, is more rapt, the West more intellectual. The East loves rather to meditate on God as He is, and on the facts of Christian doctrine as they stand in the Creed; the West contemplates more practically the great phenomena of Christian psychology, and the relations of man to God. The East has had its Athanasius, and its Andrew of Crete[h]; the West its Augustine and Leo. Hence Psalms and hymns in more profuse abundance characterize the Eastern; larger use and more elaborate adaptations of Scripture, the Western Offices. The East, by making the Psalms all her meditation, seems to declare her mind that praise is the only way to knowledge; the West by her combined Psalm and lection system, that knowledge is the proper fuel of praise. While the East, again, soars to God in exclamations of angelic self-forgetfulness, the West comprehends all the spiritual needs of man in Collects of matchless profundity; reminding us of the alleged distinction between the Seraphim, who love most, and the Cherubim, who know most. Thus the East praises, the West pleads; the one has fixed her eye more intently on the Glory-throne of Christ, the other on His Cross. Both alike have been dazzled and led astray by the wondrous accidents of the Incarnation[i]. Finally, the East has been more inquisitive and inventive in the departments both of knowledge and praise: the West, more constructive, has wrought up, out of scattered Eastern materials, her exhaustive Athanasian Creed, and her matchless Te Deum.

[h] The author of some of the finest odes [i] See note A.

# CHAPTER IV.

### ON THE STRUCTURE AND SIGNIFICANCE OF THE ORDER FOR MORNING AND EVENING PRAYER.

#### SECTION I.

"The living, the living, he shall praise Thee, as I do this day: the father to the children shall make known Thy truth. The Lord was ready to save me: therefore will we sing my songs to the stringed instruments all the days of our life in the house of the Lord."

In turning now at length to take a more connected view of our existing services, seen in the light of the preceding inquiry, we are met by one very practical and indeed paramount consideration. It is this; that, as far as the Western Church at least is concerned, we herein take off our eyes from an extinct and buried past, to fix them on a living and an energizing present. Whatever the abstract difference between our ordinary service and that of all other Churches of the West; however to our disadvantage, in point of largeness, beauty, or the like;—in practice the great difference is this,—that the one speaks, the other, (with exceptions not worth naming, either as compared with the bulk of the services as a whole, or with the extent of Western Christendom,) is silent. To what purpose is it, as regards these services themselves, that I or any other should dwell on their glorious proportions, or trace their old and ennobling descent[a], or exhibit the exquisite skill with which they are harmonized to express the emotions or inform the life of Christian men? The goodly edifice is in ruins; the noble race is extinct; the exquisite harmony has ceased. Though the eloquence of a Chrysostom or a Bernard should be expended on these topics, it would answer no spiritual and practical purpose whatsoever: no one's devotion, speaking broadly, would be the better for it. The life, that is, the living use, of those once animated and still beautiful forms has passed away, apparently for ever. Some of them, as the Gallican and the Spanish, have been extinct for a thousand years, and survive but in the merest fragments. Others, as the Roman and the Milanese, exist as the devotions of the clergy, but of them alone. The Churches, whose devotions they nominally are, have long given over the struggle which for ages, with whatever success, they maintained, against the tendency to decay innate in services so numerous and complex, as well as unvernacular, and therefore uncongregational and unpopular. In truth, as we have already seen, the Offices of the Western Church, such as they continued from the sixth to the sixteenth century, were by their origin, and also in the general cast and scheme of them, monastic, and bear the marks of this deeply impressed upon their structure. St. Basil in the East, Cassian in the West, were earnest advocates of the monastic way of ritual, and indeed in a great measure the authors of it. The sevenfold scheme of service, whatever may be said, was not the Church's

---

[a] "Stemmata quid faciunt? Quid prodest, Pontice, longo
    Sanguine censeri....
    Si coram Lepidis malè vivitur?"

originally, but was urged upon her by the influence of a few, rather animated by monastic zeal than endued with apostolic and practical wisdom. And the ritual history of the centuries referred to, and of the English Church not least, presents the spectacle of a ceaseless, and it must be added a fruitless endeavour to coerce a service so originated and constructed, into a popular and universally used formulary; to make it, in practice as well as in theory, the ritual of the whole body of the faithful. Some indeed in the present day have ventured to maintain that the Church never intended these services for the use of the people, but for that of the clergy only; and defend their desuetude in modern times on this ground. No assertion could be more unfounded. Mabillon was not mistaken when he affirmed[b], speaking of the French Offices, "publicarum precum institutionem non minus in gratiam populi quam cleri factam fuisse."

"St. Basil, St. Chrysostom, St. Ambrose, St. Augustine, all speak of this important duty, and press the fulfilment of it. And in succeeding ages we find frequent exhortations to the same purpose. It is indeed a certain thing, that the Divine Office was not instituted solely for the clergy, but for all men who called themselves Christians[c]."

The writer just quoted gives accordingly[d] a most interesting series of decrees of bishops, and canons of councils, in this country, from Abp. Egbert downwards, urging the attendance of the laity on these services. By the middle of the sixteenth century we have a most striking indication of the practical abandonment in other countries of the system as a popular scheme of services, in the revision made of it by

[b] Curs. Gall., p. 405.   [c] Maskell, Mon. Rit., vol. ii. p. xxx.
[d] Ib., pp. xxv.—xxxi.

Cardinal Quignon in 1535. In the elaborate preface to this breviary—which was sanctioned for thirty or forty years—there is not, as far as I have observed, the slightest allusion to the use of it by the laity: it plainly assumes that the clergy, and they alone, were concerned in the matter. In this country, however, and probably in others also, attendance on some parts of the Daily Office on Sundays or Festivals—I have found no instance of other days—certainly survived in some degree[e];—to what extent it is very difficult to ascertain. There has therefore been no inconsiderable declension, even since that period, until at length the state of things described in an earlier chapter of this work prevails throughout Europe.

Let it be understood, then, that the noble scheme of services we have been contemplating is a thing of the past; and of which none, that we know of, desire or attempt the revival. Other aims engross the mind of the continental Churches; as 'Benediction,' or other newly-devised services; not Matins or Lauds, Prime or Compline. Even Vespers, the sole relic of the great system, is the object of earnest and uncompromising attack[f] by the most advanced section of Romanists. The study, therefore, of the Western scheme of Offices in its old form, is the study of a dead language. The inquiry into it is strictly an antiquarian one. Regarded as a public Service of the Church, there is, it may be said, no such thing anywhere now. Let this be distinctly realized: it is of the utmost mo-

[e] For interesting illustrations of this, see Maitland's Essays on the Reformation, pp. 275, 277, 281. Compare Preface to Prayer-book, "Concerning the Service of the Church."

[f] See "Oratorianism and Ecclesiology." (See above, ch. i. fin.) It is, I am informed, a rule with the Oratorians never to say the daily Offices together, for fear of bringing back a system so obnoxious to them.

ment, in its influence upon the spirit in which we approach the subject of the present chapter. Let it be clearly apprehended that the Churches, the congregations of Christian men and women, who use these ancient and grand services, nowhere exist. *Sundays or week-days*, no such tide of psalmody as we have been contemplating flows to the glory of God; no such adoring meditation on Holy Scripture occupies the hours whether of night or day; no Te Deum sums up the meditation or the praise; no Lauds salute the return of day with mixed notes of penitence and joy, or awaken Resurrection memories or hopes; no Prime pleads for pardon, or prays for guidance; no Creed is uttered as with one voice and heart; no Collect gathers into it the Eucharistic association of the passing week or season. The curious and exquisite devices of ever-varying Invitatory, Antiphon, and Responsory; the several doctrinal associations beating as pulses through the different offices,—these no longer quicken or guide the devotions of any. All this was done once, we hardly know when: all we do know is that it is not done now. In one country alone, in one form alone, does the ancient Western Office really survive. Psalmody, Scripture, responsive Canticles, Preces, Collects, the media of Europe's ancient worship, banished from all other lands, have taken refuge in the Churches of the English Communion. The English Church is in this matter the heir of the world. She may have diminished her inheritance; but all other Western Churches have thrown it away. The question is really between these ordinary offices and none:—

"Quod quærimus, hic est,
Aut nusquam."

"Roman controversialists," says a recent and well-informed

writer, "not unfrequently compare the poverty of our two offices with the richness of their seven. I know that in comparison they are poor; but every word in them, which our people have, is just so much more than they give to their own. The priests of that Church keep these seven Offices to themselves, convents and cathedral choirs alone excepted; and yet that exclusive use is a burden to them; nay, it is so from its very solitariness . . . . . Offices moulded for joint or common use are muttered over in private; and even when sung in choir are *never listened to* or *joined in*, by the people; with the exception of Sunday Vespers in some countries,—but not even these in Italy . . . . . The laity are absolutely ignorant of the Psalms. The Psalter, which always formed the chief manual of devotion of Christians in former days, so much so as to have been called 'the Prayer-book of the Saints,' and which is so largely used for devotional purposes amongst ourselves, is entirely unknown to the Roman Catholic laity, especially in Italy. The seven Penitential Psalms are all that are known among them. In France and England the Sunday Vesper Psalms are also known[g]."

It is this, then, which lends a life and an interest of its own to this part of our inquiry. The forms which we discern in the English Offices of Morning and Evening Prayer, with whatever degree of correctness they represent the older ones, are at any rate living forms; they animate the religious life, and transact the spiritual concerns, of tens of thousands of congregations, and of millions of Christians. Far from being devoid of vitality, they never manifested more of vigour, or of expansive power, than at the present moment. Wherever, from Canada to China, the English Church has taken root, they are enshrined as its choicest possession, as the palladium of its existence; they are the living language which all Churches of the English Communion speak. And though, as week-day and continual services, they have in times past been suf-

[g] "Divine Service," by Rev. W. Perceval Ward, 1855.

fered to fall into grievous desuetude, yet even in this character they have never ceased, were it only in Cathedral churches, to breathe representatively, by however scanty a delegation, the breath of the Church's collective and corporate life. And this use of them is continually on the increase, and bids fair, if it receive no injurious shock from ill-advised substitution of other forms, instead of the well-managed use of those which we have, to realize to a considerable degree the entire design of such services.

Whatever, therefore, of added light or heightened beauty may accrue to *these* Offices from investigations like the present, will serve a nobler object than that of awakening a merely speculative admiration; it will inform and invigorate a present and a living religion, not merely illustrate a past one.

It is first to be observed, and borne in mind as a leading principle of the utmost importance for the due appreciation of our Services, that all things of price, whether of Divine or human workmanship, are subject to this law,—that they cannot be estimated from any single point of view. This is more especially true of such things as are the work of long time, or of many and various influences. Thus, among works of the human mind, poetry, to be thoroughly appreciated, requires the heightened and perfect exercise of as many faculties and kinds of knowledge as there were concurrent causes in the production of it. The thought, the language, the rhythm, the figure or the classical allusion involved, all are so many aspects of the one thing; and it is the complex of these, and no one of them singly, that makes up the poetical character of the whole. And it may require much knowledge of past modes of language and thought, besides other accomplishments, to be equal to the due apprehension and enjoyment of such poetry. Can it be otherwise with a thing which has been so pre-eminently many-sided and historical, so truly a growth of ages, and a product of divers influences, as we have seen that our ordinary ritual is? Granting that our services are level, as happily in their first aspect they are, to the commonest apprehension; it must still be admitted that so to use as to do entire justice to them, requires that many distinct lines of thought, many separate fields of inquiry, be held under view. Nor, perhaps, will the best-instructed mind be able to grasp *simultaneously* the several aspects which belong to them; these will, for the most part, have to be appreciated and acted upon by turns. But it is in the possession of such varied aspects, and such multiform relations, that the wealth and glory of a ritual really consists: it is in exhausting, or at least using these to the best of our power, that the most elevated realization of worship is attained; simply because each such aspect or relation is an enriching element in man's service, and so enters as a fresh item into the sum of what is offered to God's glory.

Out of the mass of facts and considerations, however, which have now been presented to the reader in connection with our Services, we may disengage three principal aspects belonging to them. These are, 1. their Eucharistic aspect,—that which appertains to them in virtue of their relation, in part essential and unavoidable, in part express and designed, to the holy Eucharist; 2. what may be called their structural aspect,—the character which they derive from their having inherited certain general features of structure, and so preserving traits of modes of service once carried out in a fuller and more artificial manner; and, 3. their implicit or representative aspect; that which they possess as condensing into a comparatively brief compass large tracts of ancient service, Eastern or Western, apostolic or mediæval.

1. We have seen that, in what we have reason to believe were the earliest forms of ordinary worship, there was little indeed of express allusion to the Eucharistic rite, or of marked connection with it. The primitive Office was not, that we can perceive, avowedly framed after the Eucharistic as a pattern; it was merely a body of Psalms, hymns, and prayers; organized, indeed, but not, discernibly, after this model. It lacked one leading element, inseparable, as far back as we can trace, from solemn Eucharistic celebration; viz. the reading of Scripture. But we may be quite sure that this ordinary worship was none the less, in the sense above explained [h], a eucharistic, or rather eucharistically based and connected act. The whole life, the ritual action more especially, of a Christian, was deemed of by Apostles and apostolic men as a thing rising out of Baptism and the Eucharist, and owning no other root. That they were "in Christ," first by baptismal union, and next, more intimately still, by eucharistic offering and participation, —this was manifestly, as appears [i] from the apostolic Epistles, their entire idea of what, as Christians, they were. And the absence of any marked and artificial connection or parallel between the *form* of their daily devotions and the structure of the weekly Eucharistic rite, (if we except the Creed and Lord's Prayer, which connected it both with that and with baptism,) is in reality an indication how entirely it was taken for

[h] Chap. ii. sect. 3.     [i] See passages referred to in note G.

granted that all acts of worship and intercommunion with God *must* be of this character,—must spring from sacramental roots, and own sacramental relations; since only through Sacraments did they know of themselves as having attained to the Christian position at all. Our knowing that the Eucharist was with them a thing of weekly, or not much more frequent occurrence,—a point, I must be allowed to remind the reader, which all learned inquirers have conceded,—of itself might satisfy us that this was so. There is, we may say, in those primitive forms, a beautiful unconsciousness of there being any necessity for proclaiming the eucharistic character of a Christian's worship. All praise was for them, by the nature of the case, oblation in Christ, all knowledge was reception of Him, all prayer was pleading of His Sacrifice. It was in later ages that, by expedients tending to reflect[k] back upon the preceding Offices, (as e. g. by the Eastern 'prokeimenon' and Western Capitulum,) or forward upon them, (e. g. by our weekly Collect,) the mind of the current Eucharistic Scriptures, the two kinds of office were visibly linked and allied to each other. These later methods are doubtless merely the translation into outward form of the older apostolic habit of looking back or forward to the Eucharistic Scriptures as ruling the meditation of the week.

Thus too, then, should our offices of ordinary worship be used. The general aspect of them, first of all, is, as I have already had occasion to point out[l], that they are a great act of Praise. Now herein they reflect the most general conception of the Eucharist, according to the ancient and undoubtedly true view of it. The name it most anciently[m] bears is Εὐχαριστία,

[k] Supr., ch. i, sect. 6.     [l] p. 155.
[m] St. Ign. ad Philad., c. 4; ad Smyrn., c. 7.

"giving of thanks, or praise;" thankful memorial being the basis and essence of the rite, out of which both its oblationary and its receptive characters grow. This aspect of praise belongs to our Services in virtue of their derivation from the older forms, both Eastern and Western. From the very beginning, and all along, as we have seen, and as various authors have remarked, the ruling idea of ordinary worship has been praise by means of Psalms and hymns, Psalms more especially. Of the East it is unnecessary to speak. The West marked the same view by the most usual title of her Office-book, namely, 'Psalterium[n],' no less than by its plan and contents; the whole inclusive of lections, being one great musical scheme of praise, to which all else was subordinated. The Psalms were the *dominant*, as well as the unfailing element. The one Western rite, the Spanish, which has been hitherto supposed[o] to be an exception to this rule, has been above shewn to be conformable to it; and the very phraseology usually applied to the whole act of ordinary worship[p], notwithstanding its varied contents, is grounded upon this view, that the singing of praise is the essence of the whole action.

In the East and West alike, therefore, and in our own existing Offices, the key-note is correctly pitched, for the whole of the ordinary Service of the day, by means, 1. of the Invitatory and 95th Psalm; 2. of the single preliminary "Glory be," &c. By these we are admonished that the idea of praise claims to subordi-

[n] Grancolas, ch. iii. sect. 2. Compare Bona, Psalmod. ii. 2, on the various titles of the Daily Offices.

[o] "Cum in *toto orbe* psalmi tam in nocturnis quam in diurnis fidelium conventibus caucrentur, ita ut *primus, medius et novissimus esset David*, teste Chrysostomo: apud Mozarabes, saltem recentiores, non ita," &c. So Mabillon, Curs. Gall. But see above, ch. iii. sect. 2.

[p] Thus Mabillon always speaks of it as "psallendi ritus;" Bona derives the term *cursus* from "quia legendo et cantando percurruntur."

nate and appropriate, in a manner, any other element and conception belonging to our Service, whether confession, hearing, prayer, or whatsoever it may be. It is the very triumph of grace over nature; it is the higher element fusing by its native fervour, and assimilating to its own more ethereal essence, the lower and more human accidents of our being.

Now this is a very elevated and ennobling view to take of our Services. Thoroughly to realize it in the use of them is to take up the standing-ground nearest to heaven on earth that man can habitually attain. For whereas some features in our service towards God are notes of our imperfection and low estate,—such as the receiving of knowledge through hearing of the written Word, and the act of prayer;—praise is confessedly that which approximates our worship to that of the angels. Of angelic service we know but two things; the heavenly Ritual is revealed to us as having for its substance praise, and for its manner, joint action, and mutual exhortation: "Thou art worthy, O Lord, to receive glory, and honour, and power;" and again, "Hallelujah," and again they said "Hallelujah." And when the spirit of collective and mutually sustained praise so enters into *our* service towards God as to fuse and harmonize all, even to its lesser elements, into one homogeneous action of this kind, we seem most nearly to ascend to the height of that condition, in which intuition will have superseded knowledge, and fruition prayer.

It should be remarked, again, in connection with the Eucharistic bearing of our Services, that there is not improbably an intended parallelism, up to a certain point, between them and our Communion Office, as they now both of them stand. The revision of 1552, which prefixed our penitential commencement to the Daily Office, placed a similar act of confession before the Communion Office, where the Confession and Absolution had anciently been. At the same date the *Gloria in Excelsis* was placed after the Communion, instead of at the beginning of the rite. And to this entirely corresponds the subjoining of a thanksgiving to the entire Daily Office (in 1662) for the means of grace. The beginning and end, then, of the two Offices agree in character. Nor are these the only indications we have of a design thus to conform the lower to the higher Office as to outward form. Our present prayers for the Queen, Clergy, and people, &c. were first added to the Litany in 1559, and ultimately, in 1662, removed to their present place, as a substitute for the Litany on ordinary days. The intention most probably was to supply, by means of the ordinary office, that intercession which heretofore had been made daily, or on most days, by means of the Communion Office[q]. The scheme was further completed in 1662 by the addition of the "Prayer for all conditions of men," together with the "General Thanksgiving," as before mentioned. Whether so intended or not, however, these correspondences of form between our Ordinary and our Communion Office may well assist us in using the former as a means of carrying out the spirit of the latter.

2. But we shall be better able to appreciate this aspect of our Offices, when we have considered their structure and contents somewhat more in detail. The following scheme will exhibit more clearly than a lengthened description their structural connection with the older ones, from which they were immediately derived.

[q] Canon Missæ Sarisb., &c. init. "Pro Ecclesia tua sancta Catholica ...papa,...antistite nostro,...et rege nostro et omnibus orthodoxis."

| Ancient English Offices. | | | Revised Office. |
|---|---|---|---|
| Matins. | Lauds. | Prime. | Morning Prayer. |
| In the Name .. | Vers. and resp. | In the Name .. | Sentences. |
| | | | Exhortation. |
| (Priv.) | | [See below] | Conf., Absol. |
| Our Father | . . . . . . . | Our Father | Our Father |
| O Lord, open | . . . . . . . | . . . . . . . | O Lord, open |
| O God, make | O God, make | O God, make | O God, make |
| Glory be | Glory be | Glory be | Glory be |
| Alleluia | Alleluia. | Alleluia | |
|   or, Praise be | or, Praise be | or, Praise be | Praise ye |
| Invitatory. | | | The Lord's Name |
| Response | . . . . . . . | . . . . . . . | |
| Ps. Venite | . . . . . . . | . . . . . . . | Ps. Venite. |
| Hymn. | | Hymn. | |
| 12 Pss. 6 Ant. | 5 Pss. and Ant. | 3 Pss. 1 Ant. | The Psalms, |
| (S. 18 Pss. 9 Ant.) | (S. Jubilate,) | (S. 9 Pss. 1 Ant.) | (in course). |
| 9 Glory's | 4 Glory's | 1 Glory | Glory's. |
| Benedictions | | | |
| "A lesson of" | | | "Here begin- |
| 3 or 9 lessons | . . . . . . . | . . . . . . . | neth". 1st Les- |
| O.T., N.T., Hom. | | | son, O.T. |
| Responsories | | | |
| (S. Te Deum) | . . . . . . . | . . . . . . . | Te Deum |
| | Canticle. | Athan. Creed. | or |
| | (S. Benedicite) | . . . . . . . | Benedicite. |
| | Short chapter. | Short chapter | 2nd Less., N.T. |
| | Hymn. | | [Anthem.] |
| | Benedictus | . . . . . . . | Benedictus. |
| | [See above] | | Jubilate. |
| | | [See above] | Athan. Creed. |
| | | [Ap. Creed.] | or, Ap. Creed. |
| | | [The Lord be] | The Lord be |
| | | Short Litany | Short Litany. |
| | | Our Father | Our Father |
| | Petitions | Petitions | Petitions. |
| | | Conf., Absol. | |
| | Comm. Collect | . . . . . . . | 1st Collect. |
| | Coll. for Peace | . . . . . . . | Coll. for Peace. |
| | | Coll. for Grace | Coll. for Grace. |
| | | Intercessions | Intercessions. |
| | | | Thanksgiving. |
| | | Benediction | Benediction. |
| | | | "The grace." |

Short chapter, 2 Cor. xiii. Sunday, 3d hour "The grace"

NOTE.—In these tables the dotted lines will shew from which of the old Offices the parts of our own are derived. Any features transposed for the sake of comparison are included in brackets. S. signifies Sunday.

## MORNING AND EVENING PRAYER. [SECT. I.]

| Ancient English Offices. | | Revised Office. |
|---|---|---|
| *Vespers.* | *Compline.* | *Evening Prayer.* |
| In the Name | In the Name | Sentences. |
| | Turn Thou us | Exhortation. |
| (Priv.) | [See below.] | Conf., Absol. |
| Our Father | Our Father | Our Father |
| | | O Lord, open |
| O God, make | O God, make | O God, make |
| 5 Pss. and Ant. | 4 Pss., 1 Ant. | The Psalms. |
| 5 Glory's | 3 Glory's | Glory's. |
| Short chapter | | First Lesson. |
| Hymn | | Ps. xcviii., *or* |
| Magnificat | | Magnificat. |
| | Short chapter | Second Lesson. |
| | Hymn | Ps. lxvii., *or* |
| | Nunc Dimittis | Nunc Dimittis. |
| | [Ap. Creed] | Ap. Creed. |
| Short litany | Short litany | Short litany. |
| Our Father | Our Father | Our Father |
| Petitions | Petitions | Petitions. |
| | Conf., Absol. | |
| Comm. Coll. | | First Collect. |
| Coll. for Peace | | Coll. for Peace. |
| | Collect for aid | Coll. for aid. |
| | Intercession | Intercessions. |
| | | Thanksgiving. |
| | Benediction | Benediction. |

Confining ourselves for the present to the Morning Office, we may observe, first of all, that with the exception of the Sentences, Exhortation, and Thanksgiving, there is not a single feature which does not either actually come from some one of the older offices, or find its parallel and counterpart there. And at the primary Revision of 1549, whatever might be omitted, nothing new was introduced; only the brief lessons at Matins, and again, the "short chapters" of Lauds and Prime, were expanded into an entire chapter of the Old and New Testament respectively; the Te Deum made permanent; and the Benedicite classed with it as a responsive Canticle. So truly and *bonâ fide* was the new scheme redacted and developed out of the older. It will be found, moreover, that, with an exception to be mentioned presently, and that rather apparent than real, the old *order* of the retained features was in the original Revision [r] strictly preserved. And, to the last, nothing was added *in kind* but the Sentences and Exhortation at the beginning, and the General Thanksgiving at the close.

The most general way of characterizing the process thus performed upon the older offices, is perhaps to say, that it was an endeavour to return to first principles, preserving, meanwhile, as far as might consist with that design, the existing organizations. The Revisers had before their eyes, on the one hand [s], an ideal which they knew, by her own testimony, that the Church had aimed at by the general institution of such offices, viz. the public devotional use of the Book of Psalms at large, and no less broad knowledge of, and meditation on, Holy Scripture. On the other hand, they saw in operation a system, which, however designed, and whatever its other merits, certainly was in practice utterly subversive of that ideal. But few of the Psalms were said, chiefly owing to the substitution for the daily portion of some few and almost unvarying ones on the plea of a "festival of three or nine lections." Of the Scriptures, only the few earlier chapters of the different books were really in use. And, besides all this, the language of the services excluded the people practically from all share in them. Here, then, was a broad, general aim, and surely a correct one, to be carried out; viz. to bring back the

[r] It can hardly be necessary to recommend to the reader, as indispensable for studying the successive Revisions of the Prayer-book, Mr. Keeling's valuable "Liturgiæ Britannicæ," exhibiting them in parallel columns. See also Procter on the Prayer-book, L'Estrange's Alliance of Divine Offices, &c.

[s] See their Preface "Concerning the Service of the Church."

Psalms and Holy Scripture, the great features of ordinary worship, to real and effective use as instruments of praise and divine knowledge. But how was this to be attained, consistently with preserving sensible continuity between the old and the revised forms? Now whether the first Revisers debated previously of any other method of doing this than that which they in fact adopted, we are not informed. It is not improbable that they did so, but perceived that any attempt to retain either the old express division into three offices, or certain complicating features of their contents, would be fatal to that practicability for congregational use which they desired to bring about. On determining, then, to reduce the three offices to one, they would at once perceive certain phenomena in them favourable to such a design. The commencement of all of them, to a certain point, (see the table,) was all but identical. A single such commencement would therefore entail no loss of ritual elements. Next, the order of parts in all was so far the same, that, in each, Psalms were followed up by Scripture, however different the treatment of both Psalms and Scripture in each case might be. At the same time, the first office, that of Matins, took a decided lead and preponderance in respect of these elements. It contained, theoretically at least, the great mass of the psalmody and reading for each day. A body of Psalms and Scripture, then, standing first, and as the staple of the new office, would serve to give the old Matins conception its due place; while yet the psalmody and Scripture of the other offices would not be left unrepresented, since the whole of the Psalms, and every part of Scripture, were to enter by turns into the office. Next, they would observe that each of the offices possessed, chiefly *towards its close*, certain features peculiar to itself; viz. Matins its Te Deum, besides (at the beginning) the "O Lord, open," the Invitatory, and Venite; Lauds its Canticles, Benedictus, and Communion Collects; Prime its Creeds and Lord's Prayer, its Collects, petitions, and intercessions. These completing portions of the offices might therefore preserve, in a single service, the same order relatively to each other, and to the psalmody and Scripture, which they had always stood in. And thus, by retaining *once for all* such elements (e. g. the introductory part, and the Psalms and Scripture) as were common to all, and subjoining, in their natural order, features peculiar to the several offices, a single whole would result, recalling sufficiently, for the purposes of continuity, the older forms. It would only be necessary to combine, in one or two instances, the ritual methods observable in different offices; as for example, by imparting to the Benedicite (an unresponsive Canticle, retained from Sunday Lauds in its proper relative place,) the responsive character towards the reading of Scripture which the Te Deum already possessed. The Benedictus would not need even this degree of modification as to its use, since it already stood in a truly responsive position to the "short chapter" from the New Testament at Lauds. The adaptation of the Jubilate, from the same office, as another responsive Canticle to the *second* Lesson, as before of Benedicite to the first, was a natural afterthought, at the second Revision in 1552. In these cases, then, kindred features of the several offices were made to coalesce and conspire towards one purpose. The Collects of the two later offices fell easily, in like manner, from their natural affinity, into one group. The ordinary Sunday Capitulum at Terce, or 9 A.M., (2 Cor. xiii. 13: "The grace of our Lord," &c.,) performing the function of the final Prime benediction, would fitly conclude the office.

Such, in general terms, was the nature of our great Revision, as to the *facts* of it; such the mechanical process, so to speak, of which our present Morning Office is the result, preserving in its features a certain correspondence with three of the older offices, and even a slight memorial of a fourth. The next question is, how far may we consider the idea of them severally to have survived intact? Is the resemblance which remains merely an external and mechanical one, not extending to the inner mind and spirit of the offices? Has this been really transfused, or has it perished in the process?

In endeavouring to answer this question, we shall do well to bear in mind that, so long as certain elements and media of service are retained at all, there is not much fear but that the essential thing designed by the offices of Matins, Lauds, Prime, &c., will be really preserved. With what distinctness this is done is a further, and comparatively secondary, though not unimportant point. A review of the Church's past history in this department of ritual, and the earlier stage of it especially, shews us that the great matter, after all, from the very beginning, was "to sing praises with understanding." That axiom, taken in its widest, deepest sense, as including completest Christian adoration, and profoundest Christian knowledge, is the prescript of all ordinary worship. The manner of carrying it out, though far from indifferent, is secondary to the broad design itself. And that manner has, within certain limits, varied in all ages. No Church that we know of performs it now exactly in the same manner as the apostles did. Nor can any Church, under whatever variations of form, have really introduced any *principle* into this kind of service which the simpler apostolic method did not involve. All distinctive ideas of Matins, Lauds, Prime, and the like, necessarily existed, with all essential completeness, in apostolic worship. It is one and the same primeval light, only parted into manifold hues, that appears in the more gorgeous systems of later ages. These distinctly elaborated and discriminated offices were but as the prism interposed. And when, as in the instance before us, the decomposing media are in a measure withdrawn, it may surely be maintained, 1. that neither the essence of the act performed is in any way affected, nor any of its varied aspects really done away with; and, 2. that enough of the old methods may remain to assist greatly in the realization of that distinctness of hue which it was their purpose to impart to the services; more especially when we call to our aid the knowledge that we possess of what those methods in their completeness were.

The bearing of these remarks is more especially on the new treatment of the *Psalms* in the Revised English Office. How far such compensating considerations were in the mind of the Revisers, when doing away the distinction between Matins Psalms, Lauds Psalms, &c.; and again between the continuous psalmody of one office, and the selection made in others, we are not actually informed. But seeing that they preserved, with no less than reverent care, and in untouched order, as many of the other distinctive features of each office as their leading aim allowed,—it seems a fair inference that their hope was, that not in these features only, but in the use of the Psalms also, now thrown open to varied applications, the old ideas would in a great measure survive and be expressed. There is in their original preface, as was observed in the Introductory Chapter, a most remarkable unconsciousness of having effected any change in the purpose or nature of the services.

If this principal point then be conceded, viz. that the continuous and unselected psalmody of our service was probably intended to represent, not the old Matins Psalms merely, but also those of Lauds and Prime, we shall have less difficulty in recognising in the remainder of it the reality of all three offices, briefly indeed, but not inadequately represented, and surviving in a genuine though condensed form. Our Morning Service will then assume for us the following aspect, as the result of its derivation from the older offices. As being a day-office, and the first in the day, it not unfitly draws its penitential prelude from the Prime (or First Hour) Office; which itself commenced with Ps. li., and also, towards its close, provided a confession and absolution, especially in regard of imperfections in the service[1]; and so sent forth the worshipper, humbled and reconciled, on the duties of the day. The commencement of the service proper, until the Venite, is due to all the Offices alike; excepting only the "O Lord, open," peculiar to Matins. With the Venite the great Matins Office begins to assert its prerogative, and continues to be the dominant element as far as the Te Deum inclusive; nor is its force fully spent until the end of the second Canticle. Considered as continuous, the whole psalmody is of Matins character; while yet in virtue of

[1] See supr., p. 103.

such Psalms as are allied by their tenor to Lauds or Prime, it breathes from time to time the spirit of those Offices. The Psalms, Lessons, and Canticles, again, viewed as woven up into one complex act of praise and meditation[u], still wear the Matins aspect throughout. But meanwhile, in the Benedicite (if used), in the Lesson from the New Testament, and in the Benedictus or Jubilate, Lauds has gradually come to view; at first with faint streaks, as of the dawn, afterwards with a steadier and more certain light. Prime in like manner may claim some connection with both our Lessons, in virtue of its Capitulum,—which was indifferently from the Old Testament or the New[x]. But it is at the Creed, Apostolic or Athanasian, that the Office fairly modulates into the key of Prime. From thence throughout, the peculiar practical[y] character of that Office is maintained: Matins has ceased to contribute anything to the idea of the service. From Lauds alone the two kindred Collects gravitate towards this part of our Office, and are naturally absorbed and assimilated by it. Lastly, as has been already observed, Terce contributes a Capitulum, taking the form of a dismissal Benediction.

An interesting and pertinent illustration of the process by which our present form may have evolved itself, in the mind of the Revisers, out of the older ones, is furnished by a parallel and in a great degree independent revision of the older forms of *private* devotion, which was going on side by side with that of the public services from the year 1545 to 1575[z].

[u] See p. 129.

[x] The ordinary Sunday Capitulum at Prime was 1 Tim. i. 17; the week-day, Zach. viii. 19.

[y] See pp. 221, 267.

[z] For these forms see Cardwell's Three Primers of Henry VIII.;

In the former year, as is well known, Henry the Eighth's Primer, superseding all former ones, was published. Like them, it provided devotions (founded on those of the Office for Festivals of the Blessed Virgin Mary, only revised) for the several hours of Matins, Lauds, &c. This book was published in Edward the Sixth's reign, 1547, and again, with progressive revisions, 1549—1552. It appeared again in Elizabeth's reign, both in English and Latin, (entitled *Orarium*,) viz. in 1559 and 1560, and even in 1575; still exhibiting the old divisions of Matins, Lauds, &c. But meanwhile (viz. in 1564) appeared a highly modified form of it in Latin[a], expressly reducing the services to two, under the titles of *Preces Matutinæ* and *Vespertinæ*. As might be expected, it proceeded, in the main, on the same revisionary principles as had guided the construction of the Prayer-book Offices. Yet it was markedly independent in many points; and, what is very much to our purpose, belongs, so to speak, to an earlier stage of evolution. Thus the Morning Office, commencing much in the same way as our public one as far as the Venite, only with a prayer of Absolution, has then a Hymn, three Psalms (viii., xix., xxiv.) with one Antiphon; a first lesson (Prov. i., &c.) not preceded, as in the book of 1560, by a benediction, but ending with "Thus saith the Lord," &c.; and the Te Deum. At this point the transition to Lauds is *announced* by prefixing that title, and the prefatory "O God, make speed, &c.," "Glory be," &c.; but

Mr. Clay's valuable and learned volume of "Private Prayers put forth by authority in the reign of Queen Elizabeth," Parker Society, 1851; and for a complete and careful *resumé*, Procter, chap. iii. App. 2.

[a] "Preces privatæ, in studiosorum gratiam collectæ, et Regia authoritate approbatæ." Parker Society, ubi supr., p 115.

there is no Lauds versicle preceding, as in the older Primer of 1559, nor any Alleluia. Now commenced the Lauds Psalms, or rather Pss. c. and cxlviii., with the Canticle Benedicite; all of them, it will be observed, genuine Lauds features, and *two* the same as we have retained in our Office; only that here they appear simply in their old characters, not as responsive to a Lesson. Then a second Lesson, (St. John iii. 10—22, iv. 11, &c.) hymn, and the Benedictus; Creed, short Litany, Lord's Prayer, one versicle, a Collect, (second Sunday after Easter,) one prayer for the Queen, second and third Collects, blessing and Litany. It will be seen that this Office keeps much closer to the older ones; as, e. g. in having an express recognition of Lauds, though not (as in 1560) of Prime; antiphons, though but one to each group of Psalms; an actual set of Lauds Psalms, used as such, though no Prime ones, (the Orarium of 1560 had one Prime Psalm, cxviii.); hymns, and in the old places. We could almost imagine that the Office had been framed on the basis of an earlier project entertained by the Revisers of 1549; so entirely is it transitional towards the plan which they adopted. Of course the fear of complexity which confessedly operated to the rejection of certain features, as e. g. antiphons, from the public Office, would have less place here, where the office was to be unvarying.

Nor can I forbear to remark, that if any revision of our Morning Office were undertaken, on the principle of enriching it, with the least possible amount of disturbance, or increase of complexity, from the older forms, the Office which we have just reviewed would suggest one effective method of accomplishing this object. The weak points of our present Office, so to speak,—those in which it fails to render, with as much *fulness* as could be desired, the mind of the older forms,—are, 1. the small amount, quantitatively, of psalmody; and, 2. the absence of any expression, by means of *selected Psalms*, of Lauds or Prime ideas. The expression of these is thrown upon other features, as Canticles, (or Psalms used as Canticles,) Collects, petitions, &c. Now by introducing, immediately after the Te Deum or Benedicite, a small group of Lauds and Prime Psalms, exactly as is done in the private Office before us, this defect would be in a measure remedied. *Two* unvarying Lauds Psalms, as e. g. the 63rd and 148th, both of universal use in East and West, might suffice; with *one* of the Prime Psalms (118th, on the Resurrection,) for Sundays, and *one* (the practical 101st, or part of 119th,) for week-days. A single and fixed Antiphon, as here, or varying only for the Sunday or other Festival, might be added. This group of Psalms then, following the Te Deum or Benedicite, (itself a Lauds feature,) would precede the Second Lesson; and thus the ancient alternation of Psalmody and Lessons be in a very simple manner restored. But the great purpose answered would be the increased fulness of expression hereby given to the Lauds and Prime ideas. What has here been pointed out is, however, intended less as a suggestion, than as an illustration of the near approach which our present Offices make to the older forms; as is proved by the simplicity of the means required for bringing about a greatly increased resemblance between the two.

An analysis of our Office for Evening Prayer will make good in like manner its claims to be a genuine representative of the older ones of Vespers and Compline. Only there enters in, to a certain extent, in this case, a manifest design of equalizing and assimilating the Evening to the Morning Office, which exercises no inconsiderable influence on the general appearance of the service. This is chiefly discernible in the entire theoretical equality of the two offices in respect both of the number of Psalms, and of the amount of Scripture; though on careful examination it proves that a clear preponderance is given, even in these respects, to the Morning Office[b]. And the Canticles being also shorter, while the Litany is never appointed to be added to Evensong, the result is that the latter is always perceptibly shorter than the former. This approximate equalization, in point of length, of the ordinary Morning and Evening Office, is somewhat peculiar to our Church. But it must be borne in mind, that the greater length universally accorded in other rituals to the *morning* offices originated in times when they were chiefly ante-lucan, and so could realize such greater length without trenching unduly on the works of the day. In times when the services are diurnal, as in practice they have long been throughout the Church generally, there would seem to be no reason for any great disparity; the breathing times between rest and labour in the morning, and between labour and rest in the evening, being theoretically of much the same length[c]. On Sundays and other days

---

[b] The entire number of Psalms, reckoning each of the twenty-two portions of Ps. cxix. as one Psalm, is 171: of which 91 are allotted to Matins; 88 to Evensong. The disparity in amount, reckoned in verses, is however but slight; the number in the morning being on an average but a few more than in the evening. The Gospels and Acts are also longer than the Epistles, in the proportion of about 10 to 7.

[c] The subject of practical adaptation of our services to the various

of note, when it seems natural to throw the stress of our devotion on the earlier acts of it, while it is yet in its freshness, we, like the rest of the world, add other offices accordingly, whether the Litany, or the Communion Office, (or the earlier portion of it,) or both together.

The *assimilation* of the two services, as to the nature of their contents, yet still without rendering them by any means identical, is entirely in the spirit of the older offices. We have seen that both in East [d] and West [e], the Vespers Office reflected the features of the Nocturns and Lauds conjoined. The East, for example, used the same intercessions at Lauds and at Vespers; in which we now resemble it [f]. In the West, these two Offices, besides that they both had Canticle, Collects, Petitions, and "Memorials," as already pointed out, had to some extent the *same* things; the same Communion Collect and Petitions, and some of the same Memorials [g]. Compline again accorded in the East with the Nocturnal Office [h], in the West with Prime, in having the Creed and Lord's Prayer, Petitions, Confession and Absolution, and Collects for protection.

Thus the close parallel, for it is no more, which exists between our Offices of Matins and Evensong, is due partly to principles of equalization acted upon by the first Revisers, and carried out by subsequent ones; but mainly, after all, to correspondences inherent in the two sets of ancient Offices incorporated into them respectively. For the rest, the reader will

---

circumstances, in point of leisure, &c., of different persons and classes, is a distinct question.

[d] pp. 134, 272.  [e] p. 136.  [f] Vide Neale, pp. 901, 916.
[g] See Transl. Sar. Psalt., pp. 175, 292, &c.  [h] Supr., p. 214, &c.

easily trace in the table (p. 288) the operation of the same methods of evolution as before. It will be seen that Vespers, as corresponding up to a certain point with Matins, takes a similar lead in the structure of our Evensong, viz. as far as the Magnificat. Compline features then begin to enter in, and engross the rest of the Office; only, as in the morning from Lauds, so here from the Lauds-like portion of Vespers, Communion Collects are derived. The only points of difference are that our First Evening Lesson arises out of a single "short chapter" of Vespers, instead of, as in the morning, out of the threefold set of Matins lections; and that the alternative Canticles provided, are not drawn, as in the morning, from the older offices; but one (Ps. lxvii.) from another known source, the other arbitrarily, or from some source unknown to us. The "O Lord, open Thou," at the beginning, is borrowed from Matins, and is peculiar to the English Evensong.

Here then, on the same grounds as before, we may safely consider that the mind of the entire Vespers and Compline was intended to be preserved in the consolidated Office. The Psalms, though used in the main with the general idea of continuous praise, as in the old Vespers, will on occasion harmonize with the confessed Compline features of the Office, and breathe the spirit of devout retrospect and commendation, or the like. It will be perceived, too, that the introduction of the few and short Compline Psalms (iv., xxxi. 1—6, xci., cxxxiv.), or of some of them, before the second Lesson, would have the same effect of bringing back the outline of the old twofold Offices with the least possible disturbance, as in the case of the Morning Offices. And in both these instances the resolution of each of the existing Offices, when desired, into two well-constituted parts, would be greatly facilitated by the arrangement suggested.

I will only further remark on the comparative structure of the older and newer offices, that there is one apparent exception to that strict preservation of the old *order* of parts, which the original Revisers—scarcely by a conscious effort, but rather as the natural course to pursue—sedulously observed elsewhere. In the old Prime and Compline Offices the short Litany and Lord's Prayer *preceded* the Apostles' Creed, whereas now they follow it. But it must be borne in mind, that from the short Litany to the end of the Collect for grace,—including the Lord's Prayer, Apostles' Creed, Petitions, Confession and Absolution, and sundry Versicles and Responses,—was all reckoned as one group, following the "short chapter," under the title of Preces. And this group, as a group, was strictly kept in its place at the Revision; the transposition of the Apostles' Creed and Lord's Prayer within it was a very secondary matter. But, in truth, there was a special reason for such transposition. The Athanasian Creed, it will be observed, had a place earlier than that of the Apostles' in the Prime Office, viz. after Psalms, and before the short chapter; a position which it could not now retain without disturbing the whole of the proposed order. It was natural, however, on this account, to give as early a place as might be, after the Lessons, to the Creed element. Hence, probably, this transposition. The Athanasian Creed had heretofore been publicly said daily[1], not, as in the Roman Church, on Sundays only. The Apostles' Creed was now to take its place

---
[1] Brev. Sar. Rubr ad Prim.

in this respect, having hitherto been said privately, except the two last clauses; and thus it naturally obtained an earlier position than heretofore.

It is curious, and a fresh indication of the Oriental origin of our older Offices, that in them (viz. in Prime) the Athanasian Creed occupies precisely the same position as the Nicene Creed does in the Eastern Nocturns, (p. 107,) viz. immediately after the Psalms; and, indeed, after the selfsame Psalm, the practical 119th. This circumstance may well suggest to us that we should use our daily Creed as summing up, or rather as rounding up and completing, of *all* Divine truth that has come before us in the previous part of the service, in the Psalms no less than in the other Scriptures. It speaks, too, of that basing of all Christian practice upon Divine facts, which is the very *differentia* between the Gospel and all mere philosophy or morality.

On the whole, I conceive that we may, without any unreal assumption, or any straining of the facts of the case, deal with our Offices as designedly and consciously representing the ancient ones; to whose position as national Offices of ordinary worship, they have in all respects succeeded. In virtue of that real and genuine descent, they inherit a finely-conceived general structure, as well as a profound significance of details, which a newly-originated office, unless dictated by almost superhuman or apostolic wisdom, would be very unlikely to possess. To speak at present of general structure only. The chief points to be borne in mind in using the services under this aspect are such as the following. That the whole offices are in their primary conception an act of praise, of worship of the Great King, of which the key-note is struck by the Invitatory Psalm of the morning. That, however, this act of praise is very varied in its expression, character, and topics. That, accordingly, while Psalms, Canticles, and Invocations are the more immediate vehicles of it, it yet waits to be duly chastened, informed, and directed to particular objects, by particular provisions in the service: chastened by confession, and other penitential features, informed by Holy Scripture, directed to single Divine truths or attributes, or to the whole body of truth; and again, to circumstances in man's condition, special or universal. That in the older offices, from the earliest and apostolic down to the latest forms of them, and those of our own Church in particular, distinct provision was made for all these various *accidents*, so to speak, of the essential action, praise; as well as for due accompaniments of prayer and intercession. That the functions, however, of Matins, Lauds, and Prime, and again of Vespers and Compline, being not in their nature separated from each other by rigid lines, nor so discriminated in early times, are capable of being exercised together or by turns in one whole, such as our Matins Office, or, again, our Evensong; containing actually or representatively, and for the most part in the same order, the elements of the older ones.

3. The third aspect under which I proposed to consider our Offices was that which has just been referred to, and which belongs to them as representing in a brief compass whole tracts and departments of ancient service. It is a result of their connection with the ritual of former times, that while, owing to their comparative brevity and simplicity, their treasures lie strewn in abundance on the very surface of them, so that they can hardly escape the notice even of the

most careless, and may be appropriated by the simplest of worshippers; yet for those who are led by devotion, and qualified by knowledge, to enter into their depths, they open out into "a deep that lieth under," into vast fields of ritual and spiritual wealth. Our ritual, in short, is a microcosm,—I had almost said a system of microcosms. Both as a whole, and in its several parts, it reveals, on careful inquiry, a fulness and minuteness of organization, which go far to render its brevity a matter of secondary importance.

In this consideration is to be found, to a great degree, the true answer to objections which have been alleged, from directly opposite points of view, against the existing *status*, in point of fulness, of the English Offices. I speak not now of the different degrees of leisure of different persons, but of the varying ideal which they entertain of this kind of service. Our Offices are by many deemed far too long, by others far too short. There are those who, in spite of themselves, find them formal and wearisome. But this is, doubtless, in most cases, because they have not a sufficient conception of the full and interesting mental and spiritual occupation which every part of them, rightly understood, supplies. As St. Jerome says: "Breve videbitur tempus, quod tantis operum varietatibus occupatur." And the same consideration may well redeem these services from the charge of essential perfunctoriness or brevity. For so great is the range of topics concentrated into them; so pregnant are they with baptismal, and above all with Eucharistic associations; so linked on by their contents to the whole Church of the past and of the present, of the East and West, and by their tenor to the whole contexture of the Christian life; that, looking to the inner reality of things, they leave little in point of essential fulness and largeness to desire. Time, indeed, may sometimes well be craved for dwelling more at length on their varied contents, and for drawing out at greater leisure the fulness of their deep-lying significance. But even this is in a great measure supplied, wherever, as at our cathedrals, and now in not a few parochial churches, the musical presentation of our services is more or less fully given. Among other high purposes which that mode of performing them answers is this, of prolonging as well as deepening the mental act whereby we enter into their meaning. Thus does a brief but anciently connected ritual, such as that of the English Church, expand with the desires of those who use it; like the tent of oriental fable, which might at pleasure be grasped in the hand, or spread out to be the covering of a multitude of nations.

## SECTION II.

"Receive ye the Holy Ghost: whosesoever sins ye remit, they are remitted unto them; and whosesoever sins ye retain, they are retained."

"Now then are we ambassadors for Christ, as though God did beseech you by us: we pray you in Christ's stead, be ye reconciled to God."

It only remains to pass under review the details of our Offices of Morning and Evening Prayer. In so doing we shall in part be recapitulating the results of the preceding investigation, but shall also touch upon various points not included within it.

I will first remark, that the *simplest* view to take of the distribution of our Office into parts is that which makes it to consist of one introductory and three substantial portions; the introductory extending from the sentences to the end of the Absolution, or to the Lord's Prayer; the first division of the service proper, from the Lord's Prayer to the end of the Psalms; the next, from the First Lesson to the second Canticle, inclusive; the last, from the Creed to the end. But this, though the simplest and most convenient division, and in one point of view a correct one, must not be so entertained as to keep out of sight the real blending into one whole, which properly belongs to the service. There are in reality no hard and rigid lines of separation and demarcation in it. We may, indeed, for convenience' sake, group the service into Psalms, Lessons, and Prayers, and take these groups as embodying in a more especial manner the three great ideas of Praise, Knowledge, and Pleading, respectively. But, as we have seen, neither are the Psalms, the chief instruments of praise, to be dissociated from knowledge, nor the lessons or the prayers from praise. The older forms, again, of Matins, Lauds, &c., suggest altogether another way of looking at the service. What is desirable, therefore, is that the mind be kept open to these various modes of conception, without being absolutely tied down to any. We shall do well to avail ourselves of them, in so far as they conduce to clearness, but lay them aside when they tend to deprive the services of that play and freedom which is proper to them.

On one portion of the services, however, it will be necessary to speak somewhat more at length than on the rest. Of the PENITENTIAL INTRODUCTION, as such,

I have already had occasion to speak[k], and to point out that it is in full accordance with the ancient Eastern phase of these services, and possibly with that which originally prevailed in this country[l]. The form of it, however, its origin, and the purpose which it was intended to answer, are points which call for more particular consideration. The germ, then, and indeed the substantial part of it, is, I conceive, beyond all question, traceable to the older forms of the English Church. First, as to the CONFESSION and ABSOLUTION. Those of the old Prime and Compline Offices had, by Cardinal Quignon, whose revision of the Roman Offices in 1535 furnished in a great measure the idea of our own, been prefixed[m] to the Matins Office. There was, therefore, sufficient precedent and suggestion for commencing both daily Offices with a similar form. Next, the old formulary was, as has been already pointed out, (p. 104,) primarily a deprecation of God's judgment in respect of any imperfection in the performance of the service, whether on the part of clergy or people. Now such, too, is expressly the more immediate design of our form: "Though we ought at all times to acknowledge our sins before God, yet ought we most chiefly so to do when we assemble and meet together," &c. And again, the particular thing desired by the whole is, "that those things may please Him which we do at this present;" i.e. doubtless the service we are offering[n], or about to offer. If our form

---

[k] p. 72.      [l] p. 240.

[m] This, which was done in his second edition, appears to have escaped general observation. For a brief account of Quignon's revision, see Palmer, i. p 228; Procter, p. 22.

[n] The Prayer-book translated into French for the use of the Channel Islands, (in 1549 and 1552; see Procter, p. 33,) well renders "le *culte* que nous lui offrirons." So Comber, in his paraphrase: "That is, our

is also, by its tenor, of wider extent,—"Let us beseech Him to grant us true repentance and His Holy Spirit, that, &c., and that the rest of our life hereafter may be pure and holy,"—such also is the tenor, and such, we may say, the very words, of the older form: "Spatium *veræ pœnitentiæ*, gratium et consolationem *Sancti Spiritus* .... tribuat omnipotens et misericors Dominus." Our form adds, "so that at the last we may come to His eternal joy." The old form had already said, "et ad vitam perducat eternam. Amen." But besides this identity of purpose and language, we may observe one or two other indications pointing to the same conclusion. The full expression, "absolution and remission of their sins," is exactly the "absolutionem et remissionem .... peccatorum vestrorum," and would of itself suffice, perhaps was designed, to identify the new form with the old. Again, the old form was said interchangeably, with the exception of the last clause, by priest and people[o]. Now to this there is, I conceive, a clear allusion in the title of the Absolution, "to be pronounced *by the priest alone*." This is very commonly, but without the slightest reason, supposed to design the exclusion of a *deacon* from saying the Absolution. It is infinitely improbable that the possibility of his doing so ever crossed the

absolution, our prayers, and all the other duties which we do at this present perform in His house."

[o] The outline of the entire form was: "*Priest.* 'I confess to God ... and beseech ... you all to pray for me.' *Choir.* 'Almighty God have mercy upon you,' (*restri*, Sar.; *tui*, Rom. Vide Maskell, Anc. Lit. p. 6,) 'and forgive you all your sins, deliver you from all evil; preserve and confirm you in what is good, and bring you to eternal life. Amen.' *Choir.* 'I confess,' &c. *Priest.* 'Almighty God have mercy, &c. ... eternal life. Absolution and remission of all your sins, space for true repentance, amendment of life, the grace and consolation of the Holy Spirit, may the almighty and merciful God grant unto you. Amen.'"

Revisers' minds. It refers, doubtless, in part, as Wheatly, &c., take it, to the preceding rubric, ordering the Confession to be said by *all*. But it is improbable that it would have been thought necessary to add, in this place only, the word "alone," to the title, "Absolution, &c., to be pronounced by the priest," but for some risk there was, or was conceived to be, of a misunderstanding. Now such was very likely to arise in the minds of those who knew and were accustomed to the old Offices; for there, as has been said, the people (or choir rather) had been used to desire pardon for the priest, no less than he for them. It would not have comported with the congregational aims of the Revisers to retain the old *choral* interchange of acknowledgments; they therefore expressly provided against the continuance of it by this word in the rubric.

To the same cause is probably to be attributed a peculiar expression in the original and proper form of our Absolution: "Wherefore we beseech Him," &c., (and so the Primer and Orarium, 1559 and 1560,) altered at the last revision to "let us beseech." As it stood at first, it would preserve in a measure the old community of action and mutual intercession between priest and people. It has been thought by some that our present form cannot be intended to convey a pardon, but merely to announce the existence of such pardon, and to invite the people to pray for it. Had this been its intention, however, it would doubtless have been followed by a prayer to that effect, which it is not. And in truth we see that originally no such invitation was expressed. It was rather a wish or desire arising out of what went before, equivalent to "may God therefore grant us true repentance," &c.;

and so corresponded precisely to the latter part of the old form: "God grant you .... space for true repentance, ... amendment of life, and the grace of His Holy Spirit." Only with us it assumes in the priest's mouth the plural form, herein returning to the Eastern original of all: "God have mercy on us, and pity us all through His grace." (See p. 102.)

The two great clauses into which our Absolution falls are in themselves some evidence of its derivation from the similarly constituted older formula; only there has been some interchange of ideas and expressions. All objections which have been urged against the possibility of our form being intended for a genuine absolution, on the ground that the latter part of it goes on to desire the gift of "true repentance," &c., would lie equally against the older form, which desires the same things in the same position, viz. after the precatory and absolving portions. The truth is, that what is desired in both cases, after absolution prayed for or pronounced, is the grace of perseverance, and of genuine fruits of repentance.

Thus does the older form, in those points in which our own is indebted to it, throw great light upon the latter, instructing us in what manner we should understand a portion of it, otherwise somewhat ambiguous. It may be added, that the more elevated turn given to the last clause, "may come to His eternal *joy*," as compared with the old "ad *vitam* perducat eternam," not improbably represents the joyful interchange of versicles and responses which followed the old absolution:—V. "God, Thou wilt turn again and quicken us." R. "And Thy people shall rejoice in Thee," &c.

But while our Morning and Evening Absolution is

distinctly traceable to this extent to the old Prime and Compline form, it is no less plain that it differs from it in the mould into which the absolving part is cast: the old form being throughout a prayer or desire; while the significant part of ours is an announcement or declaration. There is little difficulty, as it would seem, in pointing either to the source whence this changed form was derived, or the motive for adopting it. As to the former point, there is in a Latin Service-Book published for the use of the German refugees in this country, about the year 1550[p], a declaratory absolution which we can hardly doubt suggested the phraseology of our own; though this is probably the only point in which this introduction was indebted to foreign reformers. In it occur the expressions:—

". . . desirest not the death of a sinner, but rather that he should be converted and live . . . . [and that] He may entirely *pardon and abolish all their sins for all them that truly repent* . . . : *to all of you, I say, who are thus minded, I pronounce* (or declare, *denuncio*) *on the faith of the promise of Christ*, that all your sins are forgiven in heaven by *God our Father* . . . We beseech Thee that Thou wouldst give us Thy Holy Spirit . . . that Thy holy law may in all our life be expressed[q]."

We may especially note, besides the pervading resemblance in other respects, the irregularity of

[p] By John a Lasco the Pole, an intimate friend of Cranmer. See Procter, p. 44; Clay, ut supr.: Laurence, Bampton Lect., p. 210.

[q] See the original Latin, Procter, p. 44. This form was, it is true, as we shall see presently, based throughout upon certain *old* formulæ of confession and absolution: which is the secret indeed of many resemblances between our forms and those of foreign bodies;—but its order and phraseology are so singularly those of our own form, that I cannot doubt, after the fullest consideration, that it was here that our Revisers found the old elements put together for them in the shape which they adopted.

construction, which required the insertion, "to all of you, I say;" strongly reminding us of our very similar suspended clause: "Almighty God ..... Who desireth not .... *He* pardoneth," &c. But the most important point is the authoritative pronunciation of pardon based on Christ's promise to His Ministers that His Father in heaven would ratify their acts of this kind. For there is a plain and unquestionable allusion, in the words, "that your sins are forgiven in heaven by God the Father," to St. Matth. xviii. 18, 19: "Whatsoever ye shall bind, &c..... of my Father which is in heaven." This Absolution, then, somewhat stronger and more distinct in its terms than our own, but otherwise a twin formula with it, most clearly, and as it were authoritatively, (if our obligation to it be admitted,) interprets for us the *earlier*, as the old Latin forms do the *latter* part of our absolution. And it entirely bears out the view entertained by Comber and others as to the construction of it. According to them, there is first the opening of the ministerial commission, "Almighty God .... who hath given power," &c.; equivalent merely to the assertion that "God hath given such power<sup>r</sup>," &c. Next, a solemn exercise of this power towards all present and duly qualified persons, (compare a Lasco's, "To all of you I say who are thus minded, I declare,") by a minister understood to be so commissioned<sup>s</sup>; and then lastly follows the wish or recom-

---

<sup>r</sup> So Comber in his paraphrase: "Be it known unto you .... that Almighty God .... He whose prerogative it is to acquit or condemn, hath solemnly sworn .... and to confirm this, hath given power."

<sup>s</sup> Comber: "Know ye, therefore, that *we are authorised* in God's Name, to bring to such this message of absolution .... and by virtue of the power and in obedience to the command given us by God, *we do now proclaim*," &c.

mendation, already illustrated out of the old forms, on the subject of persevering repentance. Thus from two widely different sources, but both alike familiar to our Revisers, we seem to obtain a firmly based construction, in lieu of any merely conjectural one, to put upon our daily Absolution.

The only remaining question is as to the object of thus departing from the older structure. With what view did the Revisers, while taking the old forms as a guide, thus innovate after the example of the foreign form just examined, upon the previous cast of the absolution? Now, that it was not through any shrinking from the old precatory form, is manifest from hence, that in the Communion Office they translated and adopted, with little variation, the very form in question. The reason then of the change probably was, that they desired to give to the *public daily* absolution that form which would most completely adapt it for superseding, in all ordinary cases, *private* confession and absolution. The particular thing which would need in the first place to be set forth for the satisfaction of persons accustomed to that practice hitherto, was that the Divine pardon was capable of being effectually and sufficiently conveyed to all truly penitent persons confessing their sins to God ("to His people being penitent"), through the public ministrations of a duly commissioned order of ministers; without insisting on that private laying open of the heart to man which had hitherto been deemed necessary. The preamble then of our form of absolution was designed, as it should seem, as a protest against a favourite opinion with Roman canonists, that public absolutions do not reckon for much, or are applicable only to venial sins. And it was only a natural sequel to this, that the absolving formula should take the authoritative and declaratory, not the precatory form. For that was exactly the distinction as to form between the public and private absolutions then in use, as we shall see presently. It will at the same time appear, that for making such public and general use of the private and authoritative forms, there was already a distinct precedent in the usages of the English Church.

This is not the place for vindicating at length the view upon which our Revisers would thus seem to have proceeded. It may suffice to remark, that it was undoubtedly the tendency of the later ages of the Church, in the West more especially, to narrow, in a manner unknown to earlier times, the application of pardoning grace to the soul of man through the Church's ministrations. There is not the slightest appearance, in the most ancient rituals, of the dependence of man, as a condition of the Divine forgiveness, upon the entire privity of his fellow-man as to the state of his heart. The ancient view manifestly was that which speaks in the absolutionary form which we have been considering; viz. that while the message of pardon has from the beginning been committed to mortal lips, the bestowal of it by them was meant to be free as the breath of heaven itself. It is *therefore* committed to them that they may fling it abroad, not jealously narrow and husband its application. The lightest word spoken in His Master's Name by such a duly commissioned ambassador, is with power,—his every prayer for his fellow-men has a peculiar promise of being accepted and ratified. Whether this ministration of his be public or private, whether in the form of a desire, a petition, or a declaration, matters nothing to its efficacy; for, in all forms alike, it waits on the same heavenly ratification. All that is needed is that there be fit, i.e. truly repentant recipients of it; that secured, wheresoever it touches, it blesses and heals. Not as though the private opening of griefs and receiving of assured pardon has not its own peculiar power for comfort, as the Exhortation in our Communion Office fully recognises; but that that is the extraordinary and occasional, this the ordinary and indefeasible ministration. The following prayer of absolution from an ancient Eastern Communion Office will at once exemplify the views here stated, and supply an illustration and almost a paraphrase of our present form:—

*Prayer of Absolution to the Son, in the Coptic Liturgy of St. Basil*[t].

"O Lord Jesu Christ, the Only-Begotten Son, the Word of God the Father, Who by Thy salutary and life-giving passion hast burst in sunder all the chains of our sins; Who didst breathe on the faces of Thine Holy Apostles, saying unto them, 'Receive ye the Holy Ghost: whose sins soever ye remit, they are remitted unto them; and whose sins soever ye retain, they are retained;' Thou hast also, O Lord, made choice, by the same Thine Apostles, of those that should always discharge the Office of the Priesthood in Thy Holy Church, to the end that they may remit sins upon the earth, and bind and loose all the bonds of iniquity. We pray and beseech Thy goodness, O Thou lover of men, for Thy servants our fathers, our brethren, and our own infirmity, who now bow down our heads before Thy holy glory: shew us

---

[t] Neale, Gen. Introd., p. 389. It is curious, as completing the parallel suggested in the text, that by the same arbitrary distinction as in the West, this form "was not considered," at one time, "of sacramental efficacy, but simply as designed for the remission of venial sins: till auricular confession was for a time abandoned; and then this prayer was supposed to supply its place." Neale, ibid.

Thy loving-kindness and burst all the chains of our sins. And if we have offended against Thee by knowledge or ignorance, or by hardness of heart, by word, by deed, or by weakness, do Thou, O Lord, which knowest the frailty of man, which art gracious, and the lover of men, give unto us the remission of our sins: bless us and purify us, absolve us and all Thy people: fill us with Thy fear, and direct us into Thy holy and gracious will; for Thou art our God, and to Thee, with Thy good Father and the Holy Ghost, all honour and glory is now and evermore to be ascribed."

The same design of substituting in all ordinary cases public for private confession and absolution, which we have seen influencing the cast of the latter, would naturally suggest the working up of the well-known contents of the private forms as materials for the public ones. This accordingly appears to have been done to some extent. Thus the ancient and customary form of private absolution was (as has been already remarked) authoritative and declaratory, as follows:—

"Our Lord Jesus Christ of His great goodness absolve thee," &c., and "I by the authority of the same God and Lord Jesus Christ committed unto me, absolve thee from all those sins which, being contrite in heart, thou hast confessed to me[u]." Compare "Almighty God, the Father of our Lord Jesus, who desireth not, &c., and hath given power and commandment to His ministers to declare and pronounce to His people, being penitent, absolution . . . of their sins. He . . . absolveth all them that truly repent," &c.; together with the exhortation to "confess our sins with a penitent heart."

The only addition in our form (viz. "who desireth not," &c.) is supplied by one of the customary prayers preceding private absolution: "Who hast said I

[u] From the Manuale Sarisb., a form of very ancient use in the English Church. It will be found with others here referred to, in Lumley's "Companion to Confession and Communion," translated from the English Sarum Offices, p. 21, &c.

would not the death of a sinner, but rather that he should be converted and live[x]."

Our Confession, again, is emphatically entitled "A *general* confession to be said of the whole congregation," probably in contradistinction to these private forms. One of them, called the "Orison of David," &c., opens with the same idea as ours: "O Lord .... be intent unto us, who all as sheep have gone astray, who are all dying creatures." Now this seems to fix for us in a deeply interesting manner the allusion intended in "we have erred and strayed like lost sheep." It is not a mere quotation from Ps. cxix. ult., or Is. liii. 6, but rests, as those passages themselves probably do, on the archetypal fact of David's sin in numbering the people, which is the subject of this "Orison," ("I have sinned, and I have done wickedly; but these sheep, what have they done?" &c.; see 1 Sam. xxiv. 17;) and this is the probable key to the profoundly penitential character of our confession; viz. that it is thus based upon a private form of such deep intensity. To this too may possibly be traced in part the adoption of such strong language in the Exhortation, as "manifold sins and *wickedness;*" for the prayer alluded to proceeds: "It is I who have sinned: it is I who have done *wickedly:* O Lord, lay not to heart my *wickedness*. I acknowledge my sin," &c.

The next few clauses of our Confession seem plainly based upon Rom. vii. 8—25; perhaps as an expansion of the idea which comes next in the "Orison of David," as above given, ("we are all dying creatures.") The parallelism will be best seen in the following comparison :—

[x] Vide Lumley, p. 11.

| Confession. | Romans vii. 8—25. |
|---|---|
| We have followed too much the devices and desires of our own hearts. | Sin ... wrought in me all concupiscence. |
| We have offended against Thy holy laws. | The law is holy, .. But I am carnal, sold under sin. |
| We have left undone those things which we ought to have done; | The good that I would I do not: |
| We have done those things which we ought not to have done; | But the evil which I would not, that I do. |
| And there is no health in us. | In me dwelleth no good thing. O .. the body of this death. |
| But Thou, O Lord, have mercy upon us, miserable offenders. | O wretched man that I am! who shall deliver me? |
| According to Thy promises, declared unto mankind in Christ Jesu our Lord. | I thank God through Jesus Christ our Lord. |

The idea of sin as death, or as "the body of death," (Rom. vii. 24,) is the central one alike in the passage of Romans and in the Confession. The division of sins into those of omission and commission, the former placed first, and the whole taking the form of a confession, is found in this place of Scripture alone. The epithet "miserable," or "wretched," (ταλαίπωρος,) applied to man as sinful, is also peculiar to this passage, and was hence adopted in the old private forms: "Have mercy upon me, and be favourable to me a most miserable sinner ʸ." It may be added, as

---

ʸ Orison, &c.: Lumley, p. 11. Compare the whole context. "If sick, Thou canst heal me; if dead and buried, Thou canst quicken me ... Regard not therefore the multitude of my iniquities, but have mercy upon me, and be favourable to me a most miserable sinner. Say unto my soul, I am thy salvation, Who hast said, I would not the death of a sinner, but rather that he should be converted and live."

corroborating the view that this part of the Confession is a paraphrase of a whole passage of Scripture, that the particular phrase towards the close of it, "But Thou, O Lord, have mercy upon us," was the customary and universal one all over the West, at the end of the short passages of Scripture which formed the lections at Matins, ("Tu autem, Domine, miserere nostri;") unless they were taken from the Prophets, when the phrase was, "Thus saith the Lord." And we have proof of a habit existing in the English Church long before, of framing *private* prayers, at any rate, by paraphrasing Scripture, in the "Orison of David;" and indeed in the other forms I have referred to. Finally, the remainder of the Confession, "Spare Thou them, O God, which confess, .... restore Thou them that are penitent, .... that we may hereafter live a godly, righteous, and sober life," finds its counterpart in another private form, called the "Orison of the Priest and of the Penitent [z]," just as our Confession is "to be said of the whole congregation after the Minister." It concludes, "Spare Thou them that confess; that by Thy help ... returning from the ways of error to the paths of *righteousness*, they may possess what Thy grace hath bestowed, and Thy mercy hath *restored.*"

It may be well, by way of answer to different classes of objections, no less than for the sake of a juster conception of this Confession, thus to have pointed out how it is based to all appearance, 1. on ancient and usual forms of the English Church; and 2. through them, on an extensive and profound combination of Holy Scripture. And it is by taking these passages of Scripture along with us in using the Confession,—

[z] Lumley, p. 19.

more especially the searching and humbling expressions from Rom. vii., in their order,—that we shall most fully enter into the mind of it.

Of the SENTENCES and EXHORTATION a slightly different account must be given. Yet these too represent, in a far greater degree than is generally imagined, old established devotional ways and forms of the English Church. First, two of the old English Offices, (not of the Roman,) one in the morning and one in the evening, viz. Lauds and Compline, commenced with a single penitential verse[a] of a Psalm; only in the form of a versicle and response, coming before the usual opening, "O God make speed," &c. It is just possible that this may have suggested the idea of the Sentences. Next, a form of exhortation to confession and repentance, preparatory to absolution, was a regular part of the old English Visitation of the Sick; and it would have been perfectly analogous to the general design of our Revisers (as above described) in this part of the office, had they on this ground alone introduced such an exhortation in this place. But in truth a *public* Exhortation, *in English*, followed by a form of confession and absolution, and forming an introduction to a Service of the Church, (viz. the Communion,) was already in use, apparently whenever there were communicants, in some parts, at least, of the English Church[b]. And while the earlier part

---

[a] Viz. Lauds, on week-days, "Let Thy mercy, O Lord, be upon us," &c. And Compline, "Turn us, O God our Saviour, and let Thine anger cease from us." This was never omitted but on Easter-eve and Easter-day.

[b] The form is given by Maskell, vol. iii. p. 348. The earlier part ran thus: "Good men and women, I charge you by the authority of holy Church, that no man nor woman that this day proposes to be communed, (communicated,) go not to God's board, unless that he believe stedfastly, &c., and that he be of his sins clean confessed, and

of it is the manifest original [c] of our present Exhortation before Communion, the few concluding words no less clearly shew that from hence, and not from any novel or foreign source, the whole idea and method [d] of our daily Exhortation was derived. For it thus concludes: "Furthermore, ... that he be of his sins clean confessed, and for them contrite. Also ye shall kneel down, *saying after me....*" Next came a confession in English; then (in Latin) the ordinary public Misereatur and Absolution, and the *authoritative* form used in private absolution, as above given: "Our Lord Jesus Christ of His great mercy absolve you .... and by the authority .... I absolve," &c. It hence appears there was already actual precedent in the English Church, with reference to the Communion Office, for that bringing into the sanctuary of the private and authoritative form of absolution, and that conversion of it into a general and public ministration, which at our Revision was adopted in the daily services.

For the materials, again, of such an Exhortation to penitence, it would be natural to turn to the offices for Ash-Wednesday, and for Lent. Now on that day, by an arrangement peculiar to it, a regular address or exhortation on the topics of the season—not, as was often the case, a passage from a homily—formed the three lections at Matins. It commenced, as was indeed very usual, with "Dearly beloved brethren,"

for them contrite. Also ye shall kneel down upon your knees, saying after me, 'I cry God mercy.'" &c.

[c] Maskell, ubi supr.

[d] One turn in it is traceable to Abp. Hermann: "It is agreeable to godliness, that as often as we appear before the Lord, before all things we should acknowledge and confess our sins, and pray for remission of the same." (See Procter, p. 187.) Yet compare too the Lenten homily from St. Leo, to be quoted presently.

("Fratres charissimi, *or* dilectissimi,") and was mainly a cento of suitable passages of Scripture. On the next Wednesday, reckoned the first Wednesday in Lent, (as indeed on other days of the season,) there was a very similar homily from St. Leo. In it occur the following expressions, which seem the manifest original of a part of our Exhortation. "For although, dearly beloved, there is no time which is not full of the divine gifts; and we have always access afforded us, through God's grace, to His mercy," (compare "accompany me to the throne of the heavenly grace,") "yet now ought all our minds to be moved, .... more zealously, .... when," &c., &c. Other prominent features of the Lent services, were the fixed Capitula, daily said at the hours from Lauds to Vespers; and the penitential Psalms also, said every day, one at each office. Now on these hints there is considerable appearance of our Sentences and Exhortation having been framed. The Lenten Capitula were all penitential texts from the Prophets. So also are the Sentences, so far as they are taken from the Old Testament. And with a single exception, they are all but identical with those Capitula; or else are taken from the penitential Psalms. Thus we have for the first of the Sentences, as they stood originally, a composition, rather than a quotation, from Ezek. xviii.: "At what time soever a sinner doth repent him of his sin from the bottom of his heart, I will put all his wickedness out of My remembrance, saith the Lord." (Ver. 27 was substituted for this in 1662.) Now this same chapter of Ezekiel (ver. 20) furnished the fixed week-day Capitulum at Vespers throughout Lent[e]. The Capitulum for the sixth hour was nearly

---

[e] Brev. Sar. Fer. ii. Hebd. i. Quadrag.

the same; viz. "Let the wicked forsake," &c. Our next Sentence from the Prophets (Joel ii. 13, "Rend your hearts," &c.) furnished the week-day Capitulum at Lauds through the same season, and also the responsory to the second lesson on Ash-Wednesday[f]. Another, from Jeremiah x. 24, ("Correct me, O Lord,") is nearly identical with the well-known "Domine ne in inâ[g]," the responsory at beginning of this season. The remaining Sentence from Dan. ix. is probably due to some similar association. Passages are added from the penitential Psalms, especially three from the great central one, the 51st; and others follow from the New Testament. These Sentences then being prefixed, the Exhortation which follows is in its earlier part little else than a cento formed out of them in the order of their occurrence; just as the Ash-Wednesday address is out of similar passages on repentance. For we have represented to us in the beginning of the Exhortation, as in the earlier Sentences, "our sins and wickedness," (Ezek. xviii., Ps. li. 3). Next, that we should not "hide them from the face of God," (Ps. li. 9,) but "confess them with contrite hearts," (Ps. li. 17; Joel ii. 13,) in order to obtain "forgiveness through His goodness and mercy," (Joel ii. 13; Dan. ix. 9). This, then, and not any design of meeting the wants of various classes of penitents, as Comber imagined, seems to be the probable rationale of these Sentences. The remainder of them, being from the New Testament, are perhaps intended to represent in a general way the necessity of repentance under the Gospel dispensation. The last, from 1 St. John i.,

---

[f] Ib. Fer. iv. in capite Jejunii ad Laud.; fer. ii. hebd. i. quadrag. ad sext.

[g] Brev. Sar. Dom. i. post Oct. Epiph.

is specially to this purpose; that from St. Luke ("I will arise,") seems aptly to represent the desire of the adopted to retain their place, by forgiveness, in their Father's house [h]. In the rest of the Exhortation occasion is taken to set forth, as a means of steadying and methodizing the thoughts of those present, the several purposes which are proper to all acts of ordinary worship, and for which due provision is made in that which follows. These are correctly characterized as, 1. to render thanks and praise to God; a description applying in truth to the whole service, but especially to the compound scheme of Psalms, Lessons, and Canticles; 2. to hear His Holy Word, which is done at the saying of Psalms and the reading of Lessons; 3. to make request for all temporal and spiritual needs.

On the whole, the Sentences and Exhortation may be viewed in the light of a varying Capitulum or Text, followed by a brief and unvarying homily on the parts and objects of ordinary worship, especially on the necessity of repentance as a preparative for it. It should accordingly be listened to as suggestive of mental prayer or desire for what may be called the proper graces of Divine Service. And its effect as designed to awaken a penitential feeling in particular, will be greatly promoted if either the eye is allowed to glance over the passages of Scripture on which it is founded, or the mind be duly trained habitually to associate those passages with it. When thus used, far from being a superfluous feature in our Offices,

---

[h] This same sentence was prefixed as a versicle and response to the ancient Spanish Communion Office, (Neale, Tetral., p. 3,) and indeed seems to be the basis of the Western *Confiteor*, especially "I have sinned *against heaven and before Thee.*" Compare "I confess to God ... and to you, that I have sinned," &c.

much less an objectionable one, or alien to their proper spirit, it may well be deemed a help to devotion, than which nothing more effective, or more true to the mind of the Church, has in these later ages been devised: it is an exact and well-weighed invitatory to the act of public worship, such as would not have discredited the thoughtful pen of St. Leo, (from which indeed it seems partly to have proceeded,) and is in singular accord with the ritual mind of the earliest age. (See p. 73.)

I have only to add, that we possess in these Sentences, or variable Capitula, as we may call them, one of the few appliances which remain to us for setting the tone of the service according to the season or day. For this purpose, however, they are capable of becoming far from inefficient instruments, thus compensating for the absence of variety in our Invitatory. Their position at the very outset of the service gives them perfect command over the whole of it, enabling them to fix its character from the very first. They can indeed only mark different degrees of penitence; nor, all things considered, and looking especially to the example of the Eastern Church, can we wisely desire that, even on Sundays or Festivals, the Office should altogether part with this character. The Sentences from the Prophets, then, as being old Lenten features, and again those from the penitential Psalms, will fitly characterize penitential seasons or days. The one exception is Dan. ix. 9, 10, "To the Lord our God," &c., which, differing in origin, is also of a more cheerful tone. This, therefore, with the New Testament Sentences, is suitable for Sundays and Festivals, or ordinary days; St. Matthew iii. 2, perhaps, to Advent.

## SECTION III.

"O sing praises, sing praises unto our God; sing praises, sing praises unto our King. For God is the King of all the earth; sing ye praises with understanding."

THE LORD'S PRAYER, which follows the Absolution, having first become a feature of the public Office at the Revision, it may be considered somewhat doubtful whether we ought to reckon it in the introductory portion, or as the commencement of the service itself; which certainly was anciently held to begin with[1] "O Lord, open," &c. In the Eastern ordinary offices (p. 66) it was also part of the introduction. It is perhaps best, therefore, so to consider it still. The design, however, with which it was first made to preface all ordinary, and perhaps all Communion Offices[k] also, was probably not so much (like the penitential prefaces) by way of preparation, as (1) to pay due honour to our Lord's own Prayer, and (2) that it might serve as a *summary* of all the succeeding acts of worship. For such would seem to be the original character of it[l]. It is a matter of ancient observation that this Prayer furnishes in a measure the outline of Eucharistic Service[m], having its act of praise and thanksgiving, and also its act of pleading and prayer; the mention of "daily bread" serving to

---

[1] Brev. Sar. Mat. de Adv. Dicat sacerdos Pater Noster et Ave Maria. Postea sacerdos incipiat servitium hoc modo, Domine labia, &c.
[k] See Part II. chap. on Primitive Liturgy.
[l] See Note K.
[m] Greg. Nyssen, de Orat. Domini 2.

complete the parallel[n]. It would no less fitly take its place, as a summary, at the beginning of ordinary Offices. It may well be used therefore with this reference. The first three clauses are a great act of praise, corresponding to and representing all that is more fully done afterwards by Psalms, Canticles responsive to reading, and the addresses at the commencement, or doxologies at the close, of collects and prayers. The central petition, " Give us this day our daily bread," will have special application to the reception of Divine knowledge through the Lessons and Psalms. The remaining petitions will be a summary of all prayer and intercession. The doxology at the close, used here only in the office, is greatly to be prized, as possessed by us alone among Western Churches. It also serves to impart to this Divine summary of our worship, as the General Thanksgiving does to the Office itself, the dominant and pervading aspect of praise.

The opening versicle and answer, "O LORD, OPEN," &c., should be used (see p. 116) as the link between our penitential preface and the act of worship itself; its humbling character, as being taken from Ps. li., being also duly remembered. The next, "O GOD MAKE SPEED," &c., has a no less penitential connection with Ps. lxx.

With the "GLORY BE," &c., the Praise of the Office commences. There is no reason whatever to suppose with Mr. Palmer (i. 220) that, as occurring here, it was originally no more than the termination of the 70th, or some other introductory Psalm; since it has the same independent position at the beginning of the Eastern Offices, (pp. 66, 112). Far from being a mere

[n] See St. Augustine, referred to in note G.

appendage to something else, and the result of accident, it is designedly set on high to proclaim the object of our entire act of worship, as the Lord's Prayer is to sum up its contents.

It has already been explained ° that our versicle and response, "PRAISE YE, &c., THE LORD'S NAME," &c., represents for us both the Alleluia and the Invitatory. The entire dropping out of the former, in its Hebrew form, from our services, is much to be regretted. Of the latter I have spoken in the place referred to.

The VENITE itself, as an Invitatory Psalm, it is difficult to estimate too highly, whether on the score of the antiquity and universality with which it has ever supplied throughout the Christian world the keynote of all ordinary worship, or for its perfect suitableness to answer that purpose. Its claims on the latter score have for the most part been but partially realized. It is not merely that, in common with many other Psalms, it invites to the worship of the GREAT KING; but that it goes on to exhibit so perfect a portraiture, in terms of Israelitish history, of the frail and erring, though redeemed and covenanted estate of man. It is this that fits it to be a prelude to the whole psalmody and worship of the day, whatever its character; since it touches with so perfect a felicity the highest and lowest notes of the scale, that there is nothing so jubilant or so penitential as not to lie within the compass of it. The Church of old time was not insensible to this, as has been before observed[p]. It may appear from hence that nothing could be more ill-advised than any idea of rejecting or omitting, under any circumstances, this feature of our Morning Office. I may add, that it is some com-

[o] p. 76.     [p] p. 74.

pensation for whatever loss we sustain in the generally unvarying character of our Invitatory Psalm, that this tends to put a singular degree of honour upon the one Day in the year on which we lay it aside, the great and supreme Festival of Easter. It is not that at other times we fail to acknowledge CHRIST as the Great King, One with the Father and the Holy Spirit; but that the one piece of heavenly tidings which we recognise as making Christian praise itself more Christian still, and so claiming to supersede our ordinary Invitatory, is that "Christ is risen from the dead, and become the first-fruits of them that slept[q]." The omission of the Venite as an Invitatory when it occurs in the ordinary course of the Psalms, which has sometimes been animadverted on as a novelty, was customary throughout the West[r]. It anciently occurred as a proper Psalm for the Epiphany.

The chief thing to be borne in mind in the saying or singing of the PSALMS is, that we are now fairly embarked on our great enterprise of Praise. With that thought in the mind we can scarcely go wrong; only let us at the same time bear in mind the lesson which the Eastern Offices in various ways so significantly teach us, (as e. g. by the absence of all other Lessons, and by following up the Psalms with the Creed,) and which St. Basil points out as one use of

[q] A perfectly analogous usage prevails in the East. On Easter-day alone, the Morning Office commences (see the Pentecostarion) with the anthem or hymn, "CHRIST IS RISEN FROM THE DEAD;" the wonderful effect of which is described by a modern traveller (vide Neale, p. 878, note). Hence, doubtless, was directly derived our old Easter-day usage; the Matins being prefaced by the anthem, "Christus resurgens, non jam moritur," &c., with response and collect. Hence, finally, our present usage referred to in the text.

[r] In Brev. Rom. the Psalm was still treated Invitatory-wise, but in Sar. not so.

the alternate method of singing or saying, viz. that they are *also* great media of knowledge, as well as of praise, though that is doubtless their first function. And with a moderate degree of thought and attention we may also appropriate the advantages which the older services possessed in their distinct and varied treatment of the Psalms. Considered as flowing onward and onward still in praise to God, all will have a Matins or Vespers character. The *want* which can scarcely fail to be felt here, is that of a greater body and abundance of psalmody. Such Psalms, again, as speak more especially of meditation on the Divine law, of judgment, or of other topics associated of old time with Matins and the nocturnal hour, may be used in the same feeling still. Psalms of the Incarnation, occurring in the Evening Office, will waken up the spirit of the old Vespers, and anticipate the Magnificat. Whatever Psalms, again, bear upon topics[s] proper to Lauds, as the morning hour, the works of Creation, the Resurrection; or, again, the low estate of man, and the penitential side of his being: all these may be used accordingly. As many, once more, as are practical and personal, Psalms speaking of Divine guidance, or of human temptation and struggle; of faith resting in God; of the sorrows, Passion, and deliverance of Christ; all such may be to us, to all intents and purposes, Psalms of Prime or Compline.

Of the degree of importance that can fairly be attached at ordinary seasons to the absence of Antiphons from our Office I have already spoken[t]. It is commonly represented that the Antiphon at all times brought out, as a key-note, the meaning of the Psalm. But this, especially in the case of the Matins and

[s] pp. 131-2, 266.   [t] pp. 120—123.

Vespers Psalms, was far from being the case. The antiphons for these offices were for the most part totally incapable of answering any such purpose. A fragment of the first verse; an echo of the last; some ordinary devotional sentiment applicable to any Psalm whatever; or a verse, well selected enough in its application to some one Psalm, but pointless when applied (as on Sundays or at Compline) to some three or four; such are the most usual types of these much coveted antiphons. And at speical seasons even, it was to the *season*, not to the Psalms, that the antiphons were really harmonized and adapted. This of course was desirable enough, considered as merely calling to mind ever and anon the associations of the season; but it is quite another thing from a skilful bringing out of a given Psalm in its real application to such and such a season or doctrine.

Yet the antiphon system, like the larger scheme of services, is in a high degree suggestive as to the manner of using the Psalms. It spoke of meditation on the words used; it recognised, though often it but very ill brought to view, a leading significance as belonging to each, and doctrinal references as underlying all. Whether it could ever be made a very effectual instrument for the two former purposes may be doubted; for the last-mentioned it might, as I have already ventured to suggest[u], be found valuable at the greater seasons. But the truth is, that the antiphon idea, as to the essence of it, may become a powerful instrument for stimulating and guiding the devotional use of Psalms, without our having any recourse to the introduction of the antiphons themselves. A large proportion of the Psalms have visible

[u] p. 123.

and determinate Christian associations, in virtue of references made to them by our Lord Himself or by His Apostles[x]; others are associated, by traditional usage which has descended to our own Church, with doctrinal or other conceptions[y]. From these two causes, there are about fifty Psalms which, in the mind of any person fairly acquainted with Scripture, and trained in the ways of the Church, wear a distinct Christian aspect, and will without any effort be used as such; and the number may easily be added to. To a fairly catechised and instructed people, in a word, the greater part of the Psalms are nobly and effectually antiphoned already. It may be added, that an ill-catechised one will remain blind to these bearings of them, though provided with the most perfect system of antiphons that could be devised.

And here we may remark on some compensating advantages belonging to the cycle for saying the Psalms which is peculiar to the English Church. Owing to their revolving, not with the week, but with the month, the Sundays, or other days of observation, on which there is naturally the greatest attendance of worshippers, come in for all parts of the Book of Psalms in turn: whereas in the old Western cycle the same Psalms were said at Vespers and Matins, as a general rule, on all the Sundays of the year; and those not by any means selected, though many of them (as ii. iii. viii. xv—xxi. cx—cxv.) were appropriate enough, and the Lauds and Prime offices added others equally so. But admitting this to the utmost, it still remains that the Sunday psal-

---

[x] See Bp. Horne on the Psalms.

[y] See the table of proper Psalms for certain days; the Offices for the Visitation of the Sick, Matrimony, Burial of the Dead, Churching of Women, Commination.

mody was narrow and confined in point of range. Whatever of Eucharistic, or Resurrection, or other high doctrinal allusion is scattered through the Psalms at large, was absolutely excluded from use on the great high day of Christian worship and assembly. The same remark applies to the Saints' days: the Psalms chosen were suitable enough, but never deviated from a narrowly selected few. The English Church then, taking the year round, now feeds the mass of her children in far wider and freer pastures than of old, as regards the use of the Psalms, for doctrinal purposes more especially. Her application of them knows no other limit than that of the Psalter itself. Her manner of treating the Psalms, if less pointed and directly didactic, is more comprehensive; and, it must be added, doubtless in that degree more apostolic. The Eastern Churches, by similar fixed applications, suffer the same kind of loss as the Western, though not in the same degree, since their weekly cycle varies at different seasons of the year[z]. The English Revision then thoroughly succeeded in one of the objects proposed by it[a], viz. that of bringing the whole Psalter into general use. One minor improvement was also effected at the same time, by bringing back the ancient Western usage[b] of saying the "Glory" at the end of every Psalm, instead of, as in the Eastern use which the English Church had inherited, at certain intervals only in the Psalmody.

It has been thought, again, a disadvantage in the present English method, that the "penitential Psalms,"

---

[z] Vide Neale, Gen. Introd., p. 856.
[a] See the Preface "concerning the Service of the Church."
[b] Cassian.

technically so called, are not removed, as in the old Western scheme, from ordinary, and more especially from Sunday and Festival use; but have their place, if it so chance, on those days, like any other Psalms. The same remark is made on the use of the Lauds or other jubilant Psalms on penitential days. But the truth is, that the design of eliminating either the penitential or the jubilant element from the Book of Psalms, by way of adapting them to festival or penitential use, is alike impracticable and undesirable, and indeed was only partially attempted even in the West. It is impracticable by reason of the constitution of the Psalms themselves, which, like that of human nature, even under the conditions of grace, whose language they speak, is necessarily and inextricably mixed as to its elements. The East knows not—the Apostolic Church, we may with some confidence say, never knew—of any such elimination. On the contrary, as we have seen, the selection of the Lauds Hexapsalmus[c], in equal proportions of jubilant and penitential, (followed in a measure by the West,) marks the ancient sense of what the character of Psalmody must ever be. Nor, in the East, are even those Psalms which are selected for particular purposes, on that account omitted in the continuous psalmody. While, therefore, it might be well, as I have already expressed[d], that we had some few Psalms selected for doctrinal or practical application, in addition to our continuous course, we at the same time have no reason whatever to deprecate the free entrance, in turn, into it, of all the Psalms without exception. Unless on the highest festival or most deeply penitential days,—for which provision accordingly is

[c] p. 119.     [d] See above, sect. i.

made,—there is no one of the Psalms, sorrowful or jubilant, which can really be out of place.

It only remains to speak of the Psalms under their highest aspect. The Psalms then, from the Eucharistic point of view, are the carrying on of that great act of Thanksgiving, Praise, and Oblation, by obedient dedication of the entire being to the glory of God, which is supremely and most effectually performed in the Eucharist. By means of them the tones of the Tersanctus, the Gloria in excelsis, and similar features of the Communion Office, are prolonged, and re-echo through the Sunday and the week: a continued presentation of "ourselves, a reasonable, holy, and lively sacrifice."

## SECTION IV.

"And when He had taken the Book, the four beasts and the four-and-twenty elders fell down before the Lamb, saying, 'Thou art worthy to take the Book, and to open the seals thereof.'"

THE LESSONS and CANTICLES should, in accordance with the ancient ideas and modes of service which they represent, be considered primarily as carrying on jointly the work of Praise begun in the Psalms: the former supplying fresh matter for it by continually advancing our knowledge of God, and of His work on behalf of man; the latter descanting on these great subjects, and rendering due acknowledgment for them. It is while doing this, and making this our primary aim, that we shall most effectually attain to the other great purpose of hearing, viz. the gathering of Divine counsels for our guidance and instruction. The first reason for desiring to know

God is that we may glorify Him when known. "The fear of God," too, after all, "is the beginning of wisdom, and the knowledge of the Holy is understanding e." Nothing can be more instructive on this point, or more significant of the *order* in which these two uses of Scripture have ever been estimated, than the astonishing universality with which, in all offices, all Churches, and all times, the reading of it has used to be followed by a burst of praise in the form of canticle, or hymn, or responsory f, sometimes of all three g. In the East the Psalms, in the West the Lections, have ever been so attended. The petitions for practical guidance, &c., always followed later; sometimes, as in the West, in separate offices: the Matins being devoid of prayers altogether, the Vespers nearly so.

It is in this ancient and rightful conception of the leading purpose with which Holy Scripture is read in the Church at all, that our large and ample use of it finds its fullest and most unanswerable justification. If that purpose be the knowledge and adoration of God as revealed by Divine history and fact, and the history be of great extent, and the body of fact large, as confessedly they are,—how else than by taking cognizance of them on a scale of some magnitude, can the object be effected? Why was the Book of the Divine wisdom and doings written at large, but that at large it should be "read and known of all men?" why made

e Prov. ix. 10.
f See pp. 107, 112, 134, 226. In the Vespers Office, (p. 134,) it will be remembered that the hymn "Joyful Light" follows the entrance of the Gospels.
g See the old Offices *passim*, and the table supr. p. 288. Prime is the one apparent exception; yet even it had its *Deo gratias* after the short chapter.

various and multiform in its contents, but that men might know and adore "the *manifold* wisdom," the πολυποίκιλος σοφία, of God? Why was Redemption a world-wide history, but that it should be historically apprehended? It has become necessary to insist on these obvious truths, because a notion has been taken up and earnestly entertained by members of the English Church, that we read too much of Holy Scripture in our Services. The undoubted truth, that short passages of Scripture, commented on or otherwise emphasized, (as e. g. by short responses, or the like,) are capable of being made a valuable instrument of Christian knowledge, is urged to the prejudice of all reading of Scripture in larger portions. The old Capitula, consisting of a single verse, and yet more the old lections, containing at most three or four, with responsories subjoined, are pointed to and regretted, as furnishing the true model for the reading of Scripture in the Church. Now I have no desire to set below its due psychological value this particular treatment of Holy Scripture, and I should gladly[b], as I have already implied, see the revival of the genuine Capitulum in particular, could it be accomplished by any simple adjustment. But I would also observe, 1, that we already have, to some extent, the principle of the Capitulum in operation in our services, and have retained some genuine specimens of it, though not under that name. Whether the principle of the Capitulum be defined to be the repetition and inculcation of some short text of Scripture, varying or variable with the season, we have in our "Sentences," as I have shewn, variable Capitula, for the most part anciently selected, followed by a brief homily pressing

[b] See p 140.

home their argument. We have in 1 Cor. xiii. ult. another old and familiar Capitulum[1]. I will add, what is the main thing after all, that these Capitula or texts do the proper work of such ritual provisions upon the common mind of the English Church. The familiar tones of some of them more especially, such as, "To the Lord our God belong mercies," &c.; and again, "The grace of our Lord Jesus Christ," &c.;—live, and not in vain, on the ear, and wind themselves about the heart, of Christian millions. Or if the Capitulum idea be conceived of as either the anticipation or the carrying on through the week of the Sunday's Eucharistic Epistle[j], all this we have in our first Collect. And again, what are the Sunday Epistle and Gospel, appointed to recur in the week whenever the Communion Office or any part of it is used, but brief lections with their responsory, "Glory be to God on high," emphasized by repetition, and brought home, when the Church's evident design is carried out, by expository comment? The essence, too, of the responsory system, nay, its highest realization, we have, as will be more fully shewn presently, in our ordinary Office, in the form of the Canticles. But I would remark, 2, that the desire of *superseding* our larger reading of Holy Scripture, by returning to the old system of brief lections and responsories, proceeds upon more than one misconception, and would, if carried into effect, be as ill-advised a measure as could be conceived. It proceeds, first, upon a misapprehension of the nature of the old responsories. The responsory was not, as is commonly supposed, a brief and pertinent reflection or meditation introduced at intervals in the course of the reading. It was mostly

[1] See table, p. 288. [j] p. 137.

a totally independent and very complex anthem, as we should now call it, two or three times the length (including its versicle, repetitions, &c.,) of the portion of Scripture read, rarely adapted to it, often of most widely diverse import. The adaptation, in truth, was either to the *season* in a general way, or to the lesson, by the repetition of some sentence of it. In the former case the thought of the season lived on in a manner theoretically beautiful; but in practice struck in at such random intervals, as to confuse, rather than to steady and guide the mind. In the other case no idea was added; and as the same series of responsories was made to serve for several chapters, they became an element of merest confusion. Thus, e. g. on Sexagesima, when St. Leo's homily is on the parable of the sower, the responsories are on the building of the ark. The same responsories, again, would recur every Sunday in a season, and partly on weekdays, without the slightest adaptation to the change of lesson. In Advent, the responsory would be about the first Coming of Christ, when the lection was about the second, and *vice versâ.* In the Epiphany season, again, in our Church, the responsories were verses, varying with the day, selected from Psalms vi. to lxxxvi., one or two each day, but absolutely devoid of any particular reference to the passages of Scripture they were appointed to. The aspect, in fact, which, owing to these provisions, the lectionary part of the office assumed, was that of a long and elaborate piece of music, interrupted at intervals by a very brief recitative out of Holy Scripture as a homily [k].

---

[k] Specimens illustrative in some degree of these statements, may be seen in Leslie's Portiforium Sarisb., *Pica*, pp. 1—36. See also Bennett's Principles of the Prayer-book, p. 85, &c.

It is, again, an entire misconception to suppose, as many would seem to do, that prolonged reading of Scripture is a modern device, and foreign to the mind of the Church of the first ages. It were strange indeed,—supposing there is any truth in the grounds above alleged for such reading,—if it were so. And in point of fact, all the records and indications that we possess of the early practice in this matter point to large and unstinted use of Scripture in the Sunday assemblies. The author of the Apostolic Constitutions gives apparently a very wide scope to the lessons which were to be read on the same day: two (at least) out of the Old Testament, one from the Acts, from the Epistles, and from the Gospels; or possibly two from each of these[1]. Little reliance indeed could be placed on his representation, if isolated, or contradicted by other testimony. But Justin Martyr gives a similar account of the Sunday service in the second century, saying that the memorials of the Apostles, or writings of the Prophets, were read "as long as the time permitted[m];" after which the minister exhorted the people to the imitation of these good deeds;—a proof that it was not a mere verse or two which was read. And the ancient Liturgy of St. James (circ. 200) confirms all this to the letter; saying, "Then are read *at very great length* (*ΔΙΕΞΟΔΙΚΩΤΑΤΑ*, literally, "through and through"), the oracles of the Old Testament, and of the Prophets; and the Incarnation of Christ is shewn forth, and His Passion, &c. . . . and this is done on all occasions in the holy celebration, and after this reading and instruction[n]," &c.

---

[1] Constit. Ap., 57. Bingham supposes but four lessons to be meant; but the only question is, whether the author did not mean *many more* than I have assumed in the text.

[m] Apol. i.       [n] Neale, Tetral., pp. 31, 39.

This rubric has the air of the most primitive antiquity, since it seems to belong to a time when the old Scriptures only were in existence, and the facts of the Christian Creed were as yet taught by word of mouth only. Relics of this multitudinous reading have survived, on certain days, both in the East and West. In the East on Maunday Thursday evening are read *twelve* Gospels[o], some of them of great length, besides an Epistle, and four long passages from the Old Testament in the morning. On Easter-eve and Whitsuneve, in the West, *twelve* long prophecies[p] are read.

The only difference between the English and the primitive Church, then, in this matter, is that whereas the former set the Scriptures with great fulness before her children on the Sunday only, doubtless designing them for the meditation of the week, the latter spreads this ample reading over the other days also. The West, at the time of our Revision, had for many hundred years abandoned the ancient use of the Scriptures at large, and doubtless had suffered proportionate loss. It was rare indeed for an entire chapter to be accomplished in a week,—a state of things which loudly called for redress. And it is remarkable that on English ground, a quarter of a century before our Revision, and long anterior even to Quignon's reform, an attempt at amendment had been made. An edition of the old Offices published in 1516, and again in 1531, exhibited Lessons[q] of double the old length, and assigned them for every day in the week, instead of for some days only. It also went on the plan of finishing a chapter when begun; and in all respects was a manifest instalment of our existing lesson-

---

[o] Occupying forty columns of the Triodion.
[p] Occupying sixteen columns of the Missale.
[q] See Leslie's Portiforium, second edition, notes, p. 6.

system. But it remained for our Revisers to bring back the apostolic largeness of Scripture reading, and to restore to the people something of that historical knowledge of Divine things which must, after all, be the basis of all other. It may be added, that as the Psalms, more especially under the old Matins conception of them, are a type and foretaste of future unceasing Praise, so are our full Lessons of future untiring contemplation.

It is not my purpose to speak in detail of the particular cycle of Lessons adopted at our Revision. The appointment of them from the Old and New Testament alike, in accordance with an ancient Western usage[r], is an arrangement beyond all praise, and well worthy of the meditative mind of that old Egyptian Christianity from which it first emanated. In our own ancient lection system, it was the Old *or* the New Testament that was read, never *both* on the same day: except that when the lections were from the former, there would follow on Sundays a few lines from the Gospel, by way of text to the Homily; and again, the Capitula, chiefly from the New Testament. We may remark the more *equable* conception which such a method as ours tends to generate and maintain in the mind, as to the importance of studying all parts of Holy Scripture. It may safely be said, that either the Old without the New Testament, or the New without the Old, were equally an enigma. The two are mutually interpretative on a basis of perfect equality. And if in other points of view the New Testament challenges superior importance, this is fully recognised by its being *thrice* read through in the year, the Old but once.

[r] Supr., p. 250, note.

Of the advantage of reading such large portions, viewed as historically informing the mind in Divine things, and so qualifying it for rightly directed acts of praise, I have already spoken. Of its value as an instrument of ethical and spiritual formation, I would venture, in accordance with the old psychological views, to speak no less confidently, in opposition to the almost universal disposition of later ages, and of the present day more especially, to depreciate its effectiveness for this purpose: some (whom Hooker has long ago answered [s]), confiding rather in the effect of sermons, others in that of *short* passages of Scripture. The process by which mental and spiritual formation takes place, though generally assumed to be obvious, is in reality one of the least-probed mysteries of our being. One thing bearing upon the present point is certain, viz. that the *passing before the mind of realized images* has a *tendency* to conform it, apart from any conscious effort, to an attitude or position correspondent to the ideas so excited. The mind is not what it was previous to such apprehension. Its world, so to speak, has become enlarged or varied by the entering in of a new feature; and its own recognition of this newly apprehended fact has made *it* also, *pro tanto*, and for the time being, different. And when, as is universally the case in the hearing of Holy Scripture, the objects set before the mind are such as it must entertain some disposition towards either of approval or disapproval, sympathy or distaste,—growth (i. e. variation), of a *moral* kind, ensues. We admit this freely as regards evil; we speak of hurtful and defiling images passing through the mind or soul. And doubtless the same is the case with the images of good, with the repre-

---

[s] L E. P., v. 22.

sentations, narrative or didactic, which Scripture brings before us. The faith, e. g. of Abraham in offering up Isaac,—a faith, be it observed, in its nature Christian; —or again, the direct admonitions of the Prophets;— these, looked on, approved, sympathized with almost unconsciously, are directly formative of the mind, because of their throwing it, *pro tempore*, into such attitudes of approval and sympathy. Of course the sympathy, and the consequent profit, are in proportion to the Divine grace given and attained; but there is no reason to doubt that that grace acts through universal mental laws, such as that just enunciated. And the spiritual profit of hearing is probably to be measured, not, as is so often imagined, by the amount of knowledge, historical or moral, that we consciously have carried away, and are able to call up before us at will; but by the degree of faithful and loving sympathy which we at the time exercise on the things divinely submitted to us. Improved mental and spiritual action, as far as it results from hearing, is comparatively seldom due to particular precepts recalled at the moment: as a general rule, it flows rather out of strengthened and improved tone and character, itself formed by sympathetic conformity to the good propounded to us. Spiritual growth on this principle of course finds its highest realization in the devout and loving contemplation of Christ Himself, the Image of the Invisible God. "We all, with open face, *beholding as in a glass the glory of the Lord, are changed into the same image*, from glory to glory, even as by the Spirit of the Lord [t]."

In reference to the old system, we may remark

[t] 2 Cor. iii. 18. Comp. 1 St. John iii. 2: "We know that when He shall appear, *we shall be like Him, for we shall see Him as He is*." For a singular testimony to our Lesson-system, see note L.

that our first morning Lesson has somewhat of the Nocturns character, as succeeding (p. 288) to the position of the Scripture read in that Office. The second stands similarly related to the "short chapter" of Lauds. Their selection in this point of view is appropriate; for "by Matins that are said in the night is understood the old Law, that was all in figures of darkness; and by Lauds that are said in the morning-tide the new Law; that is the light of grace [u]."

The cycle according to which Scripture is read on week-days in the English Church has this incidental advantage, that it produces a variety of instructive combinations. The self-same chapter of the New Testament appears at three periods of the year in conjunction with as many different chapters of the Old Testament; and a watchful and well-trained eye will continually discern beautiful correspondences or contrasts, of the same kind as are often so finely worked out and stereotyped for us in the old Offices. That system, however, excluded these fortuitous combinations between Lesson and Lesson; the configuration of Scripture, for a given day, being fixed. Our Sunday cycle, in which one Lesson is regulated by the season, the other by the day of the month, presents a still more varied field for such combinations. The Proper Lessons are a finely conceived addition to our ritual possessions; while deferring in a great degree to the old mind of the Church, and taking counsel of it, they are as a whole perfectly original in conception, and proceed mainly on the principles above traced out, of presenting large tracts of the Divine doings in old time, wrought up, as far as the case

[u] The Myrroure, ap. Maskell, ii. 39.

admitted of, into a harmonized picture of the elder Economy. For the Festival cycle, unless when there were Lessons especially proper, the principle was adopted of selecting them from the didactic books, as Job, Proverbs, and Ecclesiastes, and the apocryphal ones of Wisdom and Ecclesiasticus. Such Lessons could hardly fail to illustrate appropriately the general idea of the saintly character, and had further the advantage, compared with historical chapters, of being intelligible each one by itself. And it may be remarked here that a somewhat excessive anxiety has of late been manifested for the possession of precisely and minutely adapted Offices for particular days. While some degree of character is of course desirable, the advantages of largeness and freedom in such arrangements are also, as I think we have seen reason to admit, very considerable.

Among the old accompaniments of the Lessons in the West, we miss chiefly, and cannot but regret, the Benedictions. The universality of this religious feature of service has been before pointed out [x], and it were much to be wished that some one or more of our old forms of it might be restored to us. The Absolutions, which in the Roman rite are prefixed also, were never possessed in this country [y]. Our present manner of commencing the Lessons was retained, with slight variation, from that which was used before the exposition of the Gospel at Matins on Sunday; "a Lesson of the Holy Gospel," &c.

I have only to point out, lastly, that the hearing of the Lessons is, from the Eucharistic point of view, a most true and real reception of Christ, closely akin to that which takes place in the Holy Communion.

[x] p. 113.     [y] Notes to Leslie's Portif. Sar.

Though His indwelling in us is effectual to the sanctification of the whole being, in body, soul, and spirit; yet is knowledge and apprehension of Him by the understanding, the will, and the affections, the chief purpose of it. And while, in the reception of the Holy Communion, the soul is, we may not doubt, informed and illuminated in a peculiar manner, transcending the processes of natural knowledge; yet are these too accredited media of supernatural illumination, and as such to be resorted to diligently. The condition of our perfection through sacramental reception is, that we keep the subject-matter of it, which is no other than Christ Himself, continually before us; "feeding on Him," as our formula for communicating well expresses it, "by faith with thanksgiving." Such is our Lord's own instruction to us in His prayer to the Father immediately after imparting to the disciples the Eucharistic gift of life in Him[a]: "As Thou hast given Him power over all flesh, that He should give eternal life to as many as Thou hast given Him. And *this is eternal life, that they may know Thee the only true God, and Jesus Christ* whom Thou hast sent." That passage is the Church's warrant to the end of time, for making much of Divine knowledge, as the proper complement, the involved accessory, to sacramental reception of Christ. Eucharistic celebration, accordingly, has ever had its Lessons of Holy Scripture; in early times very full and large, as we have seen. And the daily lessons are but the prolongation of these. The Eastern recognition [a] of Christ as the "Wisdom" of the Father, as enshrined in a

[a] St. John xvii. 2. See Sermon on Eucharistical Offices, by Rev. J. Keble.
[a] pp. 135, 148.

manner in the Scripture, the Gospels especially, will be remembered. As "Wisdom," He waits continually to enter into the soul in the public hearing of Scripture, illuminating, conforming, assimilating it to His own Divine Manhood.

Among the Canticles responding to the Lessons, the TE DEUM challenges the first place, as in order, so also as furnishing in some degree the type of the rest. A Canticle has been defined[b] as "a Song of Thanksgiving for some great benefit." And of the intended character of the Te Deum as a thanksgiving for the knowledge of God revealed in the Scripture, there would seem to be no doubt, from its universal position at the end of the Nocturns or Matins lections[c]. In the English Church[d] this was further marked by its being substituted, when used, for the customary repetition of the responsory to the last lection. The whole of the responsory idea is indeed gathered and summed up into this most noble hymn. And the guiding thought for the due use both of it and all the other responsive canticles, is that whatever of Holy Scripture has preceded it (inclusive, be it borne in mind, of the Psalms,) is not read for its own sake alone, or even chiefly, nor for the sake of the particular lessons it may convey; but as a sample and specimen of the vast whole to which it belongs,—a single streak of the "cloudless depth of light" which beams from the great orb of Scripture. It is therefore that this great Canticle is ever in place; never, with all its grandeur and depth of

---

[b] Ricard. Abbas, ap. Bona, Psalmod. xvi. 2.

[c] Even in the East, in its rudimentary forms, it universally followed Scripture. See pp. 107, 225. See also the Eastern Lauds, Neale, p. 924.

[d] Transl. Sar. Psalt., p. 53.

meaning, speaking a word too much for the thought which the Lesson is meant to convey or suggest. Whether what we have heard be some shewing forth of God's power, some ray of His wisdom, or some foreshadowing of His promised redemption, it suffices to set the whole before us, and thus fully justifies the most exalted and angelic forms of adoration. Yet particular circumstances contained, or Christian events foreshadowed, in the Lesson just before read from the Old Testament, may be kept in view. We may add, that whereas, in the old Offices, the use of the Te Deum was fitly limited to those days on which, besides the lections, the Gospel, or part of it, and the martyrology, had preceded; it was with equal reason now appointed for continual use, when the Gospels and Epistles had become a constant feature of the Office. Though said when the reading of the New Testament is yet to come, it may well be used with anticipative reference to it.

It has been sometimes felt to be a note of inferiority in the Te Deum, that it is not, like other Canticles, taken from Scripture. But though this is so, a glance at its structure and essential character will serve to establish for it a strong claim, even on scriptural grounds, to occupy the position assigned to it. The essential part of the Te Deum, out of which all the rest grows, is the angelic hymn, "Holy, Holy, Holy." This accordingly is the one feature which is common to all, even the briefer and more rudimentary Te Deums[e] of the East. Now the angelic hymn is found once in the Old, and once in the New Testament, (Is. vi. 2, Rev. iv. 8,) with certain variations. The Western Te Deum adopts nearly the Old Testament theme,

* For these, see note D; and above, pp. 101, 225.

"Holy, Holy, Holy, Lord God of Sabaoth; the whole earth is full of His glory." But it leads up to this invocation by declaring who they are that use it, viz. the whole earth, the Angels, Cherubim, Seraphim; thus combining, after the Eastern models referred to, the features of the two passages, in the former of which only the Seraphim, in the latter only the Cherubim, (the "living creatures," or "beasts,") are mentioned. It then takes up the subject in the New Testament development, according to which, "when those beasts," themselves representing the worship of the universal Church [f], "give glory .... to Him that sat on the throne .... the four-and-twenty elders [g]" also "fell down and worshipped," &c. This is expressed by the "glorious company of the Apostles, the goodly fellowship of the Prophets, the noble army of Martyrs praise Thee; the Holy Church throughout all the world," &c. And then the Three Divine Persons in the Holy Trinity, shadowed forth [h] in "Which was, and is, and is to come," in the Revelation, appear more distinctly as "the Father of an infinite Majesty," &c. So much is there of faithfully rendered Scripture in the entire tenor of the Te Deum.

But the conception under which it was so universally subjoined to the revelation of God as *contained in Scripture*, and *made known to the Church by reading*, seems to be based on a yet further passage in the Revelation of St. John. In those which we have

---

[f] See Mr. Isaac Williams' beautiful exposition. Apocalypse, p. 68.

[g] "The number being twelve of the Law and twelve of the Gospel, may serve to comprehend the twelve Prophets and the twelve Apostles .... or the Church of the Jews and Gentiles combined." "With the Priesthood of the Elders the natural accompaniment is the whole body of the elect, gathered from the four winds."—pp. 58 to 68.

[h] Williams, ibid.

already considered, both from the Prophet and the Divine, the adoration of the created universe is offered to the Triune God as the Holy, and Almighty, and Eternal Creator: "Holy.... Almighty.... Which was, and is, and is to come.... Who liveth for ever and ever;.... Thou hast created all things." Nor does the Te Deum, though associating Prophets, Apostles, and Martyrs, and the whole redeemed Church, in the adoration, thus far speak anything of the process of redemption which gave them a part in it: they appear as "equal with the angels," and as "the children of God[j]," without any hint that it is as "the children of the Resurrection[k]" that they became so. But in the next chapter of the Revelation, "He that sat on the throne" has a sealed Book in His right hand; and "no man in heaven or earth, neither under the earth, is able to open it.... No man is found worthy to open and to read the Book, neither to look therein[l]." But "in the midst of the throne, and of the four beasts, and of the elders, stood a Lamb, as it had been slain.... and when He had taken the Book," they all "fell down *before the Lamb*, having every one of them harps, and golden vials full of odours, which are the *prayers of the saints:* and they sang a *new song*, saying, "Thou art worthy to take the Book, and to open the seals thereof, for Thou wast slain, and hast redeemed us unto God by Thy blood, out of every kindred, and tongue, and people, and nation, and hast made us unto our God kings and priests, and we shall reign on the earth (for ever and ever, xxii. 5). And I heard the voice of many angels .... and every creature which is in heaven and earth .... saying, Blessing ... to Him that sitteth on the

[j] St. Luke xx. 36.  [k] Ib.  [l] Rev. v. 4.

throne and to the Lamb." This time, then, the universal adoration is also of the LAMB; of God the REDEEMER, as such; and that not for Redemption only, but also, and more immediately, for the *Revelation* of it by opening of the Book; evidently the Book of that Redemption, which none but He could open. This wondrous scene, then, it is that the Church throughout the world, as it should seem, has sought to enact, or however to perform her own part in, in accordance with this Divine prescription, by the acclamation of praise with which she has ever saluted "the opening of the Book<sup>m</sup>" by Him Who alone has power so to do, and Who still opens the sense of the Scripture to the Church "in the reading of the Old" and the New "Testament<sup>n</sup>." But it is in the angelic language of the Te Deum, and in the Western form of it, that she chiefly, and with the most exact imitation of the revealed pattern, does this. The angelic hymn, as said in the Eucharistic Office, is rather on behalf of the redeemed estate itself, and the Eucharistic gift of it, than immediately and directly for the written Revelation of it, though this is included. But in the Ordinary Office throughout the world, it is Christ as opening the Book, Christ present as "Wisdom" in reading of Holy Scripture, that

---

[m] Compare Berengaudus (quoted by Williams) on the words, "When He had taken the Book," &c. "They fall before the Lamb, when through meditation of the Divine Scriptures, considering the boundless mercy of God, they humble themselves in the sight of their Creator." "Thus the vision of this chapter is in fact being fulfilled from the Resurrection until the end of the world. Christ began to open at His Resurrection, and is opening still, . . . . and in His opening the Church is in spirit giving thanks. And this worship is with 'harps and golden vials of incense;' which are *Psalms and Liturgies and prayers*. And it is a new song they sing, for in the Gospel," &c. Williams, p. 79.

[n] 2 Cor. iii. 14.

is specially and immediately in view in the singing of the Te Deum. And accordingly the rest of this great Canticle, from the point up to which, as we have seen, it is an act of irrespective adoration, takes up (in the words, to a very great extent, of the passage in Revelation,) a "new song," the adoration of Christ as REDEEMER for His great work, and as King for His coequal glory. "Thou art the King of Glory, O Christ;" ("Worthy is the Lamb to receive ... glory.") "When Thou tookest upon Thee to deliver man, &c. ... When Thou hadst overcome the sharpness of death;" ("Thou wast slain." ... .) "Thou didst open the kingdom of heaven to all believers;" ("out of every kindred and tongue, &c. ... "). "Thou sittest at the right hand of God;" ("in the midst of the throne"). "Help Thy servants whom Thou hast redeemed with Thy precious blood;" ("Thou hast redeemed us unto God by Thy blood"). "Make them to be numbered with Thy saints in glory everlasting;" ("Thou hast made us kings . . . . and we shall reign" . . . . "for ever and ever." "And the number° of them was ten thousand times ten thousand, and thousands of thousands").

The exalted estimation in which it would thus appear that ordinary worship was anciently held, need hardly be pointed out.

The BENEDICITE, or Song of the Three Children, was in the older Offices the Lauds Canticle for Sundays. As a canticle then, and an honoured one, it was fitly enough at our first Revision appointed as an alternative for the Te Deum, to be used during

° This point of the parallel gives some countenance to the peculiar *English* reading, "Fac cum sanctis tuis *numerari*," (Rom. *munerari*).

Lent; at which time, and perhaps in Advent too, it would seem most fitting still to use it; to the laying aside at those times the exalted tone of jubilant adoration which, as we have just seen, belongs to the Te Deum. At the same time it is by no means ill-qualified for the function assigned to it, and accordingly was used in the old French and Spanish Communion Offices as a responsory to the reading of Scripture. Though wanting the angelic hymn, and the grand structure of the Te Deum, it is in point of range no way inferior to it, summoning "all the works of the Lord," without exception, to praise Him: the Angels, the heavens, the Powers of the Lord; all nature, animate or inanimate, the children of men, the spiritual Israel, the Priests of the Lord, and finally "the spirits and souls of the righteous." It is to be regretted that its proper conclusion, "Blessed art Thou, O Lord, in the firmament of heaven, worthy to be praised, and glorified, and highly exalted for ever," was laid aside. It need scarcely be added, that though now adapted to a responsive use, the Benedicite still retains its Lauds character, which must always predominate in it, in virtue of its dwelling so largely on the works of Creation [p].

Its contents admirably adapt the BENEDICTUS to be the responsory canticle to the second Morning Lesson from the Gospels or the Acts, as it formerly was to the "short chapter" at Lauds. It there possessed, indeed, precisely the twofold character which has now been imparted to the Benedicite. In its Lauds aspect it gave thanks for the spiritual dayspring from on high; but yet kept in view the penitential side of things, as relating to St. John the

[p] p. 132.

Baptist, and speaking of the "remission of sins," and of "them that sit in darkness and the shadow of death." But this acknowledgment was called forth, as by a memento, by the text of Scripture, jubilant or penitential.

The JUBILATE, a Sunday Lauds Psalm, has been promoted, exactly as the Benedicite, to the position of a responsive canticle. Being throughout jubilant, it is scarcely fitted to be used in lieu of the Benedictus at Lent or Advent. But it would seem, as inviting all nations to the praise of God, to harmonize especially with the Epiphany period. And both from its tone, and as a feature of the old Sunday Lauds, it is not undeserving of that very general use into which it has been brought on that day; probably from an intuitive perception of the more mixed and less purely jubilant tone of the Benedictus.

In using the MAGNIFICAT, it will be well to bear especially in mind what has been said of the canticles generally, viz. that they are a descant upon the whole of revealed truth in all its extent. Though indeed the particular fact for which the Song of the Blessed Virgin was an acknowledgment, viz. the Incarnation, is in itself of sufficient compass to include, in some sense, the whole scheme of salvation. Used with this fact in mind, the Magnificat will interpret for us, as well as enable us with due thankfulness to acknowledge, the pregnant economy of the elder period of the Church, as set forth in the Old Testament, ever pointing on to the Incarnation of the Word. And, on the principle already enunciated, it may, like the Te Deum, be viewed as referring also to the Scriptures of the New Testament, about to be read. It has already been pointed out that this reference to the Incarnation[q] has always been a characteristic of the Church's Evensong; though the East did not employ the Magnificat for its expression, but the hymn of the "Joyful Light," instead;—a composed canticle, like the Te Deum.

To what ritual association, if any, the appointment of the CANTATE DOMINO, (Ps. xcviii.,) as an alternative canticle for the Magnificat, is due, I have been unable to trace. It may suffice that it abounds in striking parallels to the Magnificat; the phraseology of which, indeed, would seem in part to be derived from this very Psalm[r]. It is also called a "new song;" a title which especially consecrates it, (compare above on the Te Deum,) to the position of a Christian canticle responsive to the reading of the Scriptures. Its invitation to "all lands" fits it, like the Jubilate, for Epiphany.

The profound and touching aspect which belongs to the NUNC DIMITTIS, as the responsive canticle to the Epistles, will be best appreciated by studying its position in the Eastern Vespers[s]. It is true that, as a feature of the Western Compline, the last office of the day, it breathes, like the Psalms and Collect, the spirit of consummated work, and repose in Christ. But it originally occurred in an office in which the True Light had symbolically been brought in, in the form of the Gospels; the summary of the Eucharistic Epistle read; and other features of the great Rite im-

[q] pp. 135, 232, 273.

[r] Compare especially, "He hath done marvellous things;" "hath done to me great things:" "With His holy arm;" "hath shewed strength with His arm:" "He hath remembered His mercy and truth toward the house of Israel;" "He remembering His mercy, hath holpen His servant Israel."

[s] pp. 135, 140, 141.

itated or paralleled[t]. It was a thanksgiving, therefore, not for the Incarnation only,—which it was the more especial function of the hymn "Joyful light" to acknowledge,—but for the Eucharistic consummation, and the great eventide Offering; and for the Apostolic announcement to all nations, "by word or Epistle[u]," of the finished work of salvation. The Nunc Dimittis has a special fitness to discharge this office, more especially as compared with the Magnificat: not being addressed, like that, to the fact of the Incarnation merely, but to the offering also of Christ, now inchoate[x] by His presentation in the Temple. To His Passion, accordingly, the words of Simeon to the Blessed Virgin, recorded next after the Nunc Dimittis, pointedly refer (St. Luke ii. 34, 35). These great topics then, associated with the eventide of the world and of the day, may well be in our thoughts in using this Canticle, and not merely, or even chiefly, our personal repose in the thought of the Saviour; true as such feelings are to the spirit of the Nunc Dimittis. And in taking it with reference to the Passion in particular, we shall be in harmony with the entire mind of the ancient Compline, Eastern and Western, expressed in Pss. xiii., xxxi. 1—6, and preserved to us in our third evening collect for aid against all perils. Nor can we ever fail in the Epistles which are so largely commended, beyond the example of other Churches, to our evening meditation, to find abundant topics of thankfulness, general and particular, for the True Light which, specially through the preach-

[t] pp. 136, 147.  [u] 2 Thess. ii. 15.
[x] See note F, on the earlier manifestations of Christ's Priesthood; also Dr. Mill's invaluable volume of twenty-four Sermons, Serm. xxi. pp. 410, 412: e.g., "He Who was to interpose His precious Blood, ... was now presented as it were in earnest of His future all-perfect self-oblation."

ing of the great Apostle St. Paul, "lightens the Gentiles," and "is the glory of God's people Israel."

The DEUS MISEREATUR (Ps. lxvii.), the alternative for the Nunc Dimittis, is a feature borrowed from Lauds, but also familiar to the English Church in a bidding prayer[y] used every Sunday. There is nothing to surprise us in such interchange between Morning and Evening, the Offices having many ideas in common[z]. The East (and part of the West) had the Magnificat at Lauds, the Gloria in excelsis at Compline. The key to the selection in this case is probably the first verse of the Psalm, "Shew us the light of His countenance," and the summons, as in Ps. xcviii., of all nations to the praise of God.


## SECTION V.

*"If two of you shall agree on earth as touching anything that they shall ask, it shall be done for them of My Father which is in heaven."*

THE leading conception under which the CREED is to be used in our daily Offices, judging from its position in the old ones, is that it lays the foundation, and declares the object, of the act of *prayer;* with which it has always stood nearly associated[a] in the Services, and upon which we, for our parts, enter immediately after it. Using it as an act of faith, we by it severally avow, as the many members of the one Body, the profession made at our baptism in the

[y] See below, sect. v.

[z] In the revised Primer above described, (p. 297,) the second group of Vespers Psalms was borrowed from Lauds. Vide Clay in loc.

[a] See for the East, pp. 87, 277 : for the West, pp. 268, 288

matter of belief. It is therefore that this alone, of all publicly used formulæ, is conceived in the singular number. Nor only so, but we also recal and accept anew the position [b] then sacramentally given us as members of the body of Christ "by the washing of regeneration, and renewal of the Holy Ghost." And this is fitly followed by the prayer which none but the baptized are privileged to use; the symbol, by its plural form, of our common inherence in One, as the Creed of our distinct consciousness and responsibility. For this reason it is, probably, that baptisms were ordered to take place after the second Lesson; that so the admission of the newly baptized might be followed by *liturgical* avowal, so to speak, of that Creed, and saying of that Prayer, which, as a part of the rite, have already been avowed and used. It need hardly be added, that both of these all-important formulæ, as used by communicants, and with Eucharistic thoughts in view, assume a yet profounder meaning, and lay yet deeper the foundation of all prayer. With this Creed then—thus widely related to our whole position as Christians—on our lips, we go on to prayer, and thence pass forth [c] strengthened and armed to the Christian warfare of the day or night.

But while the Creed is thus primarily and emphatically a personal and practical, or, to speak the old language, a Prime or Compline feature, it stands also in an avowed relation to the preceding part of the Office. It has ever succeeded hearing, whether of Psalms or other Scriptures, or both; no less than it has preceded, or been associated with prayer. It is this that renders the transition to the prayers from the lessons and canticles,—to the Prime or Com-

[b] p. 212.   [c] Compare the remarks on Lauds and Prime, p. 269.

pline tone, from that of Matins and Lauds, or that of Vespers,—though sensible, by no means abrupt. We pass by a nicely shaded gradation out of the stage of service in which the objective is dominant, to that in which the subjective claims the larger part, though it can never rightly be the supreme consideration. This function is finely performed by the Creed; while it rounds up, fills in, and completes the cycle of Christian doctrine brought to view by the Lessons; it at the same time turns towards us its subjective and practical side, as the faith of living men; and admonishes that "praying is the end of preaching," and prayer, in this world, the condition and the instrument of the fruition of God. It has already been observed how completely the Athanasian and the Apostles' Creed changed places at our Revision, as to the manner, and partly as to the occasion of using them. The former had till then been said daily aloud[d]; the latter, only under the breath. In appointing the Athanasian for certain high Festivals, and some secondary ones, our Revisers approximated somewhat to the Roman use; which is to have it on Trinity Sunday and all ordinary Sundays.

The brief interchange of benediction between priest and people, "The Lord be with you: and with thy spirit," is of known antiquity, and seems to be alluded to in St. Paul's, "The grace of our Lord Jesus Christ be with your spirit," (Gal. vi. 18). St. Chrysostom remarks[e] that the people's rejoinder, "and with thy *spirit*," is a recognition of the absolute need the clergy had of the grace of the Spirit to effect anything. It is a desire for the "stirring up of the

---

[d] Mr. Palmer (in loc.), with very unusual incorrectness, says that it was used on Sundays only.   [e] Bingham, iv. 382. 1 Tim. i. 6.

gift," and spiritual power, "that is in them" by virtue of their Ordination. It was therefore, in the ordinary offices of the West, specially prefixed to the Collects; prayer being "the proper weapon of their ministry." In our first Revision it retained this place, together with the usual "Let us pray." At the second it was, by a slight departure from Western precedent, placed where it now stands. But as L'Estrange remarks, "it was of old used as a notice of transition to some new department of service," and is appropriate enough here, when we pass on, from other elements, to prayer. It may be remarked too, that this interchange between clergy and people of mutual prayer or desire for each other's good success in the spiritual work of the sanctuary, is entirely in the spirit, and to the purpose, of the old interchange of Confiteor and Misereatur. It is still to us, what that formula was designed to be, a touching recognition of the equal need, under difference of position, of clergy and people, and well illustrates the mutually sustaining character of their common worship.

The "short Litany," or threefold petition, "Lord have mercy," &c., ushering in the Lord's Prayer, Petitions, and Collects, is to the *prayer*, what the "Glory be" is to the *praise*, of the whole Office; a prayer setting the tone and fixing the object of all the rest, by being addressed to the Holy Trinity. It was triple, as with us, at its first occurrence in the old Eastern Offices [f]; in our own it was threefold before the Lord's prayer at Lauds, though ninefold at Prime [g].

It will already have been discerned that the LORD's PRAYER, at this its second occurrence in the service, wears a widely different aspect, and discharges quite

[f] p. 66.   [g] Transl. Sar. Psalt., p. 71.

other functions, from what it did as prefacing the whole Office. A preface, indeed, it still is, to all the coming acts of prayer, and the model and summary of them. But, 1, it has a peculiarly baptismal aspect in this place, from its connection with the Creed; and, 2, it is now used far less in reference to the remainder of the Office than to the needs of the coming day or night. In its position towards the close of Prime and of Compline, it very distinctly wore this character, as the first step in the closing stage of the long enterprise of morning or evening worship.

The PETITIONS, which follow, are a selection from the *Preces* used at Lauds and Prime, and again at Vespers and Compline. At the two later services of the morning and evening they occurred daily; at Lauds and Vespers only on week-days. They are taken in somewhat larger proportion from the earlier Office in each case. The number of them, however, (six, with answers to each,) is much the same as occurred in one group in Prime and Compline. But it would seem that the exact number, and the selection made, are to be traced to another source. On all Sundays and Festivals, according to the Sarum use, a Bidding Prayer, in English, was given out; then was said, in Latin, a Psalm (lxvii.) and the Lord's Prayer, followed by precisely this number of petitions; and, with one exception, the selfsame in topic, and nearly in expression, as those we now have. Whereas, to derive them from the hour Offices, we must gather them as they are strewed up and down there, as may be seen in Mr. Palmer's table of them. The exception referred to is, that for the last petition in the old Bidding Prayer, "O Lord, hear our prayer," &c., is substituted, "O God, make clean," &c.; "And take not Thy Holy

Spirit," &c.; representing, as it would seem, a collect which immediately followed the petitions in the Bidding Prayer, " O God, who through the power of Thy Holy Spirit," &c.

The *order* in which the temporal powers and the clergy were prayed for was here, as elsewhere in the old Western forms, the reverse of that which we now have, both in these petitions and in the longer prayers, and which has often been severely commented on as a note of Erastianism [h]. It is however, the old Eastern order, both in the Liturgies [i] and ordinary Offices [k]; and, indeed, we may add that it is the order prescribed by St. Paul himself [l]. The words of the form of Bidding just referred to bear a considerable resemblance to the earlier part of the Eastern Lauds [m], of which the ruling idea is prayer for victory on behalf of faithful kings, and for the good estate of the whole Church and clergy; and it was not improbably derived from thence. And thus the "petitions" before us would own a direct Eastern parentage, and one which well illustrates their character and design.

These Petitions are also important as having a designed reference, apparently, to the subsequent collects and prayers on the same topics respectively. This correspondence has been pointed out by Wheatly (in loc.). The first and two last, " Grant us Thy salvation;" " Give peace," &c.; " Take not Thy Holy Spirit," &c., correspond with the three Collects; which are respectively for salvation, peace, and grace. And that this is

[h] See "Loss and Gain." Compare Tracts for the Times, 86.
[i] Viz. St. Mark's; Syriac St. James', St. Basil's. The Greek St. James' does not mention "kings." St. Chrysostom's and the Armenian have the Western order.
[k] See the Eastern Lauds, Neale, pp. 915, 916.
[l] 1 Tim. ii. 1, 2.    [m] p. 112; and Neale, p. 915.

not accidental appears from hence, that the petition for "peace" is the old antiphon used at Vespers just before the Collect for peace [n], having been substituted at the Revision for the older petition, ("Grant them peace in Thy strength," &c.,) which formed the versicle and response to that Collect. The intermediate three answer to the prayers for the Queen, the Clergy, and for all Conditions of men. And it is by no means improbable, though we have no proof of the fact, that the filling in, at the later revisions, of the scheme of our collects and prayers, was suggested by the *headings* which these petitions furnish. Whether the correspondence, however, was designed or accidental, it legitimates our present intercessory prayers in reference to the old forms, as being a natural development out of them; though, indeed, as will be pointed out presently, the old Offices were by no means so devoid of detailed intercessions as is commonly supposed.

Of the THREE COLLECTS at Morning and Evening Prayer, it may be truly said that each one is a microcosm, revealing, on close examination, singular beauties of structure and contents. And the morning and evening group, though composed, as regards the two last, of different elements, are, even as regards these, perfectly parallel and in harmony, owing to their being drawn from parallel parts of the older system. It should be observed, however, that though all three of these prayers are alike called Collects, they are so in different senses. The two former only are connected with the Communion Office at all, and only the first with that of the current week.

No part of the ritual mechanism of the West is more worthy of admiration than the means by which

---

[n] Transl. Sar. Psalt., p. 298.

the ordinary Office is continually linked on to the Eucharistic. The chief medium for effecting this, and indeed the only one that is of continual application, is the weekly COLLECT. We have traced[o] in an earlier page the probable derivation of this element of service from the Eastern system. But it possesses such marked characteristics of its own, that it may nevertheless be said of it that *tota nostra est*. In its terseness and high finish, and in its *continual* use, it differs widely from its Eastern prototypes. In the East, the Vespers and Lauds preceding a Sunday or Festival are largely coloured by the infusion of a variety of hymns, many of them resembling prayers, and all referring to the Gospel of the coming day. In the West, though originally there were several[p], we have now (mostly) a single prayer, composed generally out of Epistle and Gospel taken together, or with some reference to both. And this, though specially used at the Vespers of the Eve, and characteristic of that office, is also continued throughout the week.

It is to be observed, then, that our FIRST COLLECT is not merely *a* bond of union between our common and our Eucharistic Office, but such a one as to present to us the appointed variation of that Office for the current week. The Collect, every one knows, varies with the week; but it is not so generally observed, or taken into account, that it is of itself no random thing, but a reflection of the mind and spirit of the Epistle and Gospel[q]. Here, then, is opened up a field of weekly study, really indispensable to a full

---

[o] pp. 141—147.  [p] p. 145.

[q] A valuable series of sermons, bringing out the design of the Epistles, Gospels, and Collects, has just been put forth by Mr. Isaac Williams.

perception and right use of a portion of our Daily Offices. At each Communion our Lord is presented to us, through the medium of the Epistle and Gospel, under some special aspect; or some particular duty or doctrine is set forth to us. Now such varying aspect of our Blessed Lord, such duty, or doctrine, is only appreciable in one way. If we would be faithful to the design of the Church for us in her Daily Offices,—I had almost said, if we use them as a whole in any intelligible sense,—it need scarcely be pointed out what our endeavour or desire in this matter should be. The Epistle and Gospel, and the Collect epitomizing them, were appointed and fixed with no other design in the world than that they should accompany Eucharistic celebration; that they should impart a certain colour, varying with the season or the week, to the one divinely-appointed memorial Offering and participation of Christ. It is when, by joining in that high act, we have taken home to ourselves, under circumstances of special supernatural aid, the lesson of those Scriptures; when it has blended itself with the most awful and absorbing moments of our spiritual existence on earth; it is then that we are fitted, in any true sense, to say with the Church her profoundly-related weekly Collect. The mere reading and hearing on the Sunday of the Epistle and Gospel, apart from Communion, though better than no hearing of them at all, and serving to set, to that extent, the tone of the week, is a feeble substitute indeed, as regards the purpose before us, for the use of them according to their proper intention. Used, on the other hand, after such celebration, the Collect is endued with a wonderful power for carrying on through the week the peculiar Eucharistic memories and work of the preceding Sunday, or of a Festival. Under whatsoever engaging or aweing aspect our Lord has more especially come to us then in virtue of the appointed Scriptures, the gracious and healthful visitation lives on in memory, nay, is prolonged in fact. Or in whatever special respect, again, suggested by these same Scriptures, and embodied for us in the Collect, we have desired to present ourselves "a holy and lively sacrifice" in that high ordinance, the same oblation of ourselves do we carry on and perpetuate by it. Through the Collect, in a word, we lay continually upon the altar our present sacrifice and service, and receive, in a manner, from the altar, a continuation of the heavenly gift.

The SECOND COLLECTS at Morning and Evening, both entitled "for Peace[r]," have a peculiar and deeply interesting origin. It should perhaps have been explained before, that in the old English Lauds and Vesper Offices certain features[s], called "Memorials," were introduced on week-days, varying with the season. Each "Memorial" consisted of a special antiphon prefixed to the Benedictus or Magnificat, a versicle, and a Collect; all bearing upon some one doctrine, such as the Incarnation, the Crucifixion, the Holy Spirit, the Communion of Saints. The Collect was mostly taken from the Communion Offices of the Festivals connected with these doctrines, such as the Purification, Whitsuntide, All Saints[t], &c. Thus was the Lauds Office,—the Office, as it may be called, of man's mystical estate in Christ,—and the

[r] Matins, rubric and title; Evensong, rubric.
[s] See Transl. Sar. Psalt., pp. 175, 181, for an accurate account of the Memorials.
[t] In a perfectly parallel manner were the daily Offices of the Eastern Church enriched with Theotokia, Staurotheotokia, Anastasima, &c. See the Octoechus, &c.

Vespers corresponding to it, enriched with *general* collects, bearing on the great Christian verities, besides the particular one for the week[u]. But besides these, there were one or two fixed memorials used daily. One of these was of the Holy Spirit, another of Peace. Of the Collects on the latter subject, one, (our Evening Collect for Peace) was used at Lauds and Vespers, the other (our Morning Collect) at Lauds only. They were from a special Eucharistic Office on the subject of peace. The Epistle for that Office was a suitable passage from Maccabees; the Gospel was St. John xx. 19, 24,—Christ giving His peace to His disciples after His Resurrection. But the Collects[v] are also full of allusions to the "Peace" similarly given at the Eucharistic Institution, and to our Lord's discourses and prayer at that time. These Collects, then, represent a whole Communion Office, designed to embody, and appropriate in the highest way, our LORD's Eucharistic promises of peace.

Though the THIRD COLLECTS at Matins and Evensong are found in the Sacramentaries or Collect-books of Gelasius and Gregory, there is no reason for supposing that they were ever part of any Communion Office[x]. They have in a former page been traced

---

[u] Miss. Sar. et Rom.

[v] Strictly speaking, the Collect and "Postcommunio." Compare more especially the words, "this is eternal life, that they may know Thee the only true God:" ("in knowledge of Whom standeth our eternal life"): "My peace I give unto you, not as the world giveth," &c.; ("that peace which the world cannot give"): "Let not your hearts be troubled;" "If ye love Me, keep My commandments;" ("that both our hearts may be set to obey Thy commandments . . . . and that by Thee we being defended from the fear of our enemies, may pass our time in rest and quietness.")

[x] The commencement of the former is however a part of the Western Tersanctus preface ("Domine Sancte, Pater omnipotens, æterne Deus.")

through our own Prime and Compline Offices to corresponding Offices in the East; and through them again to certain of the Psalms[r]. It will only be necessary by way of recapitulation to observe, that the third Morning Collect thus stands based (p. 222) on Psalms xc. and xci. From the former (ver. 1, 2,) it derives its contrasting of the pre-mundane Eternity —*ex parte ante*, as it seems to mean especially— of God, with the days of man (ver. 3—12); and its prayer, "That all our doings may be ordered," &c.; ("Prosper Thou the work," &c, ver. 17). From the latter Psalm it frames its petitions for bodily and spiritual protection, on behalf of the mystical members of Him, of whom the Psalm primarily speaks (ver. 11—16). The third evening Collect, again, (p. 228,) rests on Pss. xiii. 4; xviii. 28; "Lighten mine eyes;" "Thou shalt make my darkness to be light;" and Ps. xxi. 1—6: and in virtue of the latter reference associates us with our Lord in His commendation of His spirit into the hands of God.

The remainder of our Office consists almost entirely of intercessory prayers. It is not a little remarkable that at our last revision there should have been none such appointed for daily use. An impression has from hence arisen that there were no intercessions in the old Offices; and that consequently those which were added to ours at successive Revisions were an innovation on the old ways. But this is a misconception. On all week-days, as a general rule, there was in the English Lauds, immediately after the Collect or Collects, a short office of intercession for the Church, containing a fully developed prayer, that "being de-

[r] pp. 222, 228.

livered from all adversity and error, it might serve God in freedom and safety<sup>z</sup>." And there was another short office, with prayer of intercession, attached to Prime; only it was said in chapter, not in choir<sup>a</sup>: and this intercession was in behalf of the sick and afflicted: "Hear us in behalf of those Thy servants for whom we entreat Thy compassion, that so their health being restored to them they may," &c. So again there was the same prayer for the Church at Compline; and at Vespers an intercession of some length (comparatively), for "mercy and grace to the living, pardon to the departed, rest to the Church, peace and concord to the Kingdom." And thus our intercessions, though added in times when the old forms had been lost sight of, and probably rather designed to follow the pattern of the Communion Office<sup>b</sup>, yet had their counterpart in the former phase of our Ordinary Offices.

I will first remark on the structure common to the Collects and to these prayers alike. There is then in Western prayer-forms, as a general rule, first an invocation of God the Father, with some attribute, and the ascription, in the relative form, of some property or action (as, e.g., "Almighty and everlasting God, Who alone workest," &c.). Next follows the object—(as, "Defend us," &c.)—desired by the prayer; often with the addition of ulterior effects desired from it ("that we surely trusting," &c.). Lastly, is either an ascription of glory, or a pleading of the merits of Christ. This form is so familiar to us, that it may seem superfluous to dwell upon it. But yet it is, (1,) in its entirety, unknown to the East, and (2,) these characters of it are but imperfectly appreciated among our-

<sup>z</sup> Transl. Sar. Psalt., p. 71.   <sup>a</sup> Ib., pp. 124, 125.   <sup>b</sup> See p. 287.

selves. 1. It is in the *entire absence of any pleading of Christ's merits*, that all Eastern prayers, as far as I have observed, differ from those of the West. The ascription of glory, &c., is the usual termination: or if any intercession of merits be pleaded, it is uniformly those of the Virgin Mary or the Saints. It is not unnatural to conjecture that in all these instances the intercession of the Saints has been substituted for that of our Lord;—it seems otherwise very unaccountable that the East should retain no trace of a form and feeling so universal and so much valued in the West. It should be said, however, that pleading under other forms, as e. g. by invoking the power of the Cross, is common enough; and moreover, that the ascription, in prayers addressed to Christ, of power and will to save, is in reality to the same effect. But we may well be deeply thankful for the great frequency of direct pleading in our Western Collects and prayers. 2. The form in which these prayers are thus uniformly cast is full of deepest instruction, and must be duly appreciated ere we can use them aright. The invocation with which we commence them is, first of all, unquestionably an act of *praise*, and must be used as such. Even human titles are a vocative form of exaltation: much more Divine. The very mention of God cannot rightly be devoid of praise, much less the addressing of Him by Name. And how much of truest praise, and of delight in rendering it, there may be in such mere address, apart from the express offering up of any, need not be said. For it is, as Hooker says, "a joy even to make mention of His Name." And when, as is the case in most of our prayers, there is mention also of His attributes and doings, it were a prayer ill begun which did not give special praise for these also. On this view, then, our prayers do most truly contain in their measure this chief element of worship, besides that which it is their peculiar province to discharge. These invocations, thus used as ascriptions of praise and glory, are to a great degree a compensation for the comparative absence, in the West, of those lofty and joyous exclamations, or acclamations rather, which rekindle continually the flame of Eastern devotion. Of course, where our prayers have ascriptive terminations, these will, like our doxology at the end of the Lord's Prayer, renew the praise offered at the beginning. And it may safely be affirmed, that habitual realization of this sense of the addresses in our prayers casts altogether a new brightness over them, and goes far to redeem the entire Offices from that charge of defectiveness in the spirit of praise, to which comparatively they lie open. In this view is also to be found a valid *à fortiori* argument on behalf of the musical mode of saying our ordinary Offices. It can hardly have failed to occur to the reader, that in proportion as we recognise the *singing of praise* as the dominant idea of the *whole*, musical utterance, of however plain a kind, becomes natural. And if our very prayers are thus fitted to be sung, much more such parts of the Office as the Psalms, Canticles, &c.

It has been well observed [c], again, that these prayers, in virtue of their most usual structure, pay a several honour to the three Persons of the Holy Trinity. For since all gifts are specially from the Father, by and in the Holy Spirit, through the Son, the Holy Spirit is no less honoured in that which we pray for, than the

[c] Durandus.

Father by our addresses, and the Son by our pleading. And this, as the same writer observes, would seem to be the true reason why the Church addresses comparatively few of her prayers, though some, to the Holy Spirit; since He is emphatically the Gift, and the object of desire rather than of address.

It is the more to the purpose thus to remark on the structure of Western prayers, because the present English Offices, by universal admission, prescribe them in a far greater degree, both as to number and volume, than the old Western rituals. The spirit of praise, as expressed in the accessories of prayer, has far more vent with us than elsewhere. The addresses, too, in those prayers which are peculiar to us, are far more glowing and full than in the old Collects. The Western ordinary ritual may be searched through and through without bringing to light anything comparable, for sublimity of address, to the opening of our prayer for the Queen's Majesty, or for fervour of tone to our General Thanksgiving.

This greater length, indeed, and fulness of expression in the prayers peculiar to us, is very commonly dwelt on as altogether condemnatory of them; as a modern and Puritan characteristic. Now of the merits of the brief and terse Collects of the West, enough has been already said to mark the value to be entertained for them. But while, with Hooker, we duly estimate these, we surely carry our admiration for them too far, when we are led by it to seek the exclusion of ampler forms, which the Church, in some of her brightest ages of faith, and happiest moods of devotion, has not disdained but delighted in. The truth is, that the somewhat cold shade of the ritual mind of St. Leo, deep and exact, rather than lofty or genial, has rested, ever since his day, on the devotions of the West. There is a mean between unvarying brevity and unsparing prolixity; between the manner of St. Leo, and that of the worthy author of the Saints' Rest. Such a mean we find in the long and full, yet not lengthy prayers in the ancient Communion Offices of the East, and in those which, in the ordinary Office, bear the superscription of St. Basil.

Let me briefly illustrate what has been said by examining a single one of our prayers, that "for the Queen's Majesty." It has been lately pointed out that this prayer, though not placed in our Office until 1559, was contained in one of the earliest publications of the period of our Revision, only in a somewhat longer form [d]. No apology ought to be needed for that noble apostrophe or invocation, "High and Mighty, King of kings," &c., which, by the heaping up of all that is noblest and most exalted of temporal dignities, piles a footstool for the Throne of the Eternal. This is the true answer to objections to the titles of sovereignty, given (as of old) in this and other prayers, to the earthly ruler. Divine loyalty is but the sublimation of human, or at any rate is never more justly exhibited than when it is represented as transcending all duty that we owe to earthly government. The mystery of earthly government, in truth, is one of the most indefeasible, and also one of the most expressly sanctified conditions of our earthly estate; and the recognition of it in prayer, in all its fulness, far from interfering with right views of Divine government, throws us at once, and most effectually, into the true attitude of spiritual loyalty. And in the majestic *incessus* of this and some others of our prayers, we

[d] See Procter, p. 218.

seem to hear sounding in the Western climes of the Church the more rich and lavish orisons of the great Basil, or the unknown composers of Eastern Liturgies. Nor do I hesitate to say that it even excels in majesty both of thought and expression, anything of the same kind that Eastern antiquity can boast. The following prayer from the beginning of St. Mark's Liturgy, i. e. the Alexandrian Communion Office, will serve at once to justify the length and the topics of our prayer, and also—itself no ignoble form—to set off the exceeding beauty of ours.

"O Lord, God and Master, the Father of our Lord and Saviour Jesus Christ, we beseech Thee preserve our King in peace, valour, and justice. Subdue under him every enemy and every foe. Lay hold of the shield and buckler, and stand up to help him. Grant him, O Lord, victory, counsels of peace towards us and towards Thy holy Name; that we, in the peace of his times, may lead a quiet peaceable life, and in all godliness and honesty, by the grace, and mercy, and loving-kindness," &c.

And there is one feature deserving of our notice common to the principal among these prayers; those viz. for the Queen, the Royal Family, the Clergy and people, and for all Conditions of men. It is that in every one, no less than the gift of the Holy Spirit itself is desired on behalf of those prayed for. They thus fully illustrate a principle above mentioned. And while we may well feel some surprise that, together with the memorial Collect for Peace, that for the Holy Spirit was not retained also; we may also see in these detailed prayers to the same effect abundant compensation for the loss of it.

But all these Prayers and Collects, lastly, stand

in a distinct relation to the supremely solemn act whereby in the Eucharist we plead the Sacrifice of the Death of Christ. As usual, the Eucharistic Offices themselves set the example of naming before God the things which we desire for ourselves and others, as the fruit of that great interceding medium. Our daily prayers do but prolong that pleading by the usual form of their conclusion, and by bringing to the altar, in a manner, our daily and continual needs, with a never-ceasing importunity.

The immediate design of placing a GENERAL THANKSGIVING at the end of the Office, would appear to be not so much to supply a supposed deficiency of praise or thanksgiving in general, (which was the ground taken by those whom Hooker answered[e],) though this is included, as in order that praise may be given for the means of grace, with reference to the Office just concluded, and so for the whole economy of Salvation; just as the Confession is general, yet with the like special reference. It thus holds an entirely parallel position, as was before observed, to that of the Gloria in Excelsis in our Communion Office.

The old English LITANY, on which our present form is based, is remarkable for resembling, more closely than the ordinary Western Litany, that which was attached to the Eastern Nocturns, (p. 86.) The design with which it was appointed to supersede the intercessory prayers on three days in the week, seems to have been originally in part only penitential. By Edward's Injunctions of 1549, and Elizabeth's of 1559, it was ordered to be said immediately before the Communion Office. And in the first Revision, 1549, it was to be

[e] V. xliii.

followed, on Wednesdays and Fridays, and other days of greater observance than common, by the early part of that Office. It was therefore viewed as a great prelude of intercession in connection with the Communion. And as such on Sundays or Festivals it may still be taken; while on ordinary Wednesdays and Fridays, on which no part of the Communion Office is now used, it may retain its penitential aspect.

The PRAYER OF ST. CHRYSOSTOM, so called, seems by its contents to sum up, in a reverse or retrospective order, the features of the foregone Office, desiring, 1, the fulfilment of our *petitions*; 2, *knowledge* of God's truth; 3, life everlasting, the occupation of which will be endless *praise*. And, though this was perhaps not contemplated in appointing it, it is at least significant, that in its ancient Eastern position it was part of a *prelude*[f] to the Holy Communion.

The BENEDICTION which concludes our Office stands related in several ways to the ancient ritual, and will be best interpreted and used by keeping those relations in view. It represents, first, the closing Prime and Compline benedictions, of which the former was in the Name of Father, Son, and Holy Ghost. Again, it was the "short chapter" used at the Terce, or 9 A.M. Office, on Sundays throughout the West; and as such, and not merely as a suitable apostolic benediction, found its way to its present position. But the selection of it for that hour on the First Day of the week, (said to be due to St. Ambrose,) doubtless arose from hence, that it formed, throughout the greater part of the East, the introductory benediction to the more solemn part of the Communion Office; for the

[f] It was the prayer of the second antiphon to the hymn, "Only-begotten."

celebration of which, 9 A.M., the hour of the Descent of the Holy Spirit, was more especially set apart.

And the chief excellence, accordingly, of this conclusion is, that while it breathes the present peace of old apostolic blessing, it is nevertheless not an absolute conclusion at all, but points onward still to some better thing hoped for; and so leaves the spirit, which has most faithfully yielded itself up to the joys of this lower service, in the attitude of one unsatisfied still, and expecting a higher consolation.

# CONCLUSION.

"Hold fast the form of sound words."

GRAVE questions, bearing upon the interests of the English Church at the present hour, are suggested by the contents of the preceding chapters.

In the first place, it has pleased God to put it into the hearts of many, within the last half-century, earnestly to desire and diligently to labour for the greater efficiency of the Church of Christ in this country. Of the apostolic zeal and love which animated the earlier stage of that endeavour; or of the improved knowledge, directing and chastening a zeal and love noway inferior, which has on the whole marked its subsequent progress, it is unnecessary to speak here. Nor has this awakened vitality been without signal results. The practical energies of the Church, in every branch of her operations, are sensibly quickened; her real position and powers are, by the clergy especially, more truly estimated;—her own estimate of them being, in fact, through increased study of her Formularies and her Divines, more generally understood, and more frankly and *ex animo* accepted. And this return to a sounder condition in point of Christian *doctrine*, is ground for the deepest thankfulness. It is a great matter for a Church thus to have recovered, to have grasped, to be acting upon, the great doctrinal principles of apostolic days; and for harmony to have been thus restored between her written mind and her actual and living operation.

But next to the principles of doctrine come those of ritual administration; and these, in their turn, have naturally come to engage the Church's solicitude. Assuming her to have returned, in the main, to sound doctrinal principles of action, does her ritual administration, and specially do her Offices of Public Worship, need alteration, either in point of general theory, or of practical capability for dealing with the work she has to do?

These questions are more or less formally raised, both by practices which are here and there recommended and adopted among us, and by various plans proposed for a re-adjustment or retouchment of our Offices, or for additions to them.

By the general theory of a Church's services I mean the broad plan which they set out as that on which the Christian life, so far as it is regulated by public prescript, should be formed, and the Christian estate persevered in. This is a profound, and may well be an anxious question, for any Church, at any time. One main aspect which it necessarily assumes has reference to the measure to be observed in the frequency of Eucharistic celebration and reception, and to the relation to be maintained between that great Rite and ordinary worship. What the apostolic practice was in this matter has been pointed out in these pages; and in representing that it was to have Sunday, with occasional festival celebration, I am borne out by the concurrent opinion of the best-informed writers, of whatever communion. That the complement to this, again, was daily service, for as many as could attend it, I have also endeavoured to prove. And indeed, independently of all proof, it is the conclusion to which our estimate—undoubtedly correct—of the piety and holiness of those ages necessarily conducts us. For, as has been already observed, it is incredible that the apostolic Church, as a Church, was content to acknowledge and worship God publicly but once a-week. Now while we have no warrant for representing apostolic practice, in matters of ritual, as binding on all ages of the Church, it nevertheless is surely the part of Christian wisdom to defer in a great degree, in this as in all else, to the clearly and practically expressed mind of Apostles and apostolic men. The grounds upon which we depart from it should be weighty indeed. And we may throw into the scale the further consideration that, as a matter of historical fact, it has never gone so well with the Church, in the matter of ritual efficiency, since the day that she departed, with however good intention, on the right hand or on the left, from the Apostolic standard in these matters.

For, that in the Apostolic and immediately succeeding ages they *realized* weekly and probably festival Communion for all, is what none, I believe, in the present day will care to dispute; since the prevailing, though utterly unfounded impression is, that they communicated *daily*. That, for as many as possible, (though there must at all times have been exceptions,) daily attendance on ordinary worship was the rule also, will, for the same reason, hardly be disputed either. And these positions are entirely borne out by such glimpses, historical or ritual, as antiquity gives us of early practice. Now will any one for a moment compare, in point of desirableness, with this state of things—this actual realization, for all the members of the Church, of the degree of ritual privilege here described,—anything that has existed since? The Church in the third and fourth century began in places to devise or recognise a different standard. We now first behold the astonishing inequality of *daily* reception in some cases, *yearly* reception in others; vast polar and equatorial extremes of ritual condition, both alike unknown to Apostolic days. But the Church, as it would seem, disheartened at the neglect of privileges manifested by the many, grasped at a higher condition, as they deemed it, for the few. And thence dated the recognition of privileged classes in Christianity; of a redeeming few who *could*, and a vast multitude who *could not*, enter upon the high and supreme, but at the same time the *designed normal condition* for Christian men. The Apostolic system bore no trace of any such inequality. Its condition of sacramental privilege and practice was *equal* for all, as far as anything in this world can be equalized. With "one Lord, one faith, one Baptism," was conjoined one Lord's-day Eucharistic Festival; the last, like all the rest, made equal for all. This provision was indeed founded, as I have shewn elsewhere, on the solemn and festival nature of the rite itself; but this incidental result of it, viz. the glorious equality on which it placed, as a general rule, all the subjects of the heavenly kingdom, may well be dwelt on as an argument of its wisdom, and even of its Divine appointment.

To this Apostolic standard, then, neither less nor more, broadly accepted, and acted on in its general spirit, I would fain urge the English Church to return. For doing so she stands, in one respect, at a singular and immeasurable advantage. It is this:

that she has no need, in order to its full accomplishment, to alter an iota of her existing theory in the matter of ritual, but only to give practical effect to it: she has, though much to do, yet nothing to undo; no mutilated Sacrament[a] to restore, no abandoned or abolished ordinary worship to recal. She need not change her course by a single point, but only

> "Still bear up, and steer
> Right onward."

The theory of weekly Eucharist,—with tempered festival or other added celebration,—is significantly written for her, as indeed for Western Christendom generally, in her weekly-varying Collect, Epistle, and Gospel. The theory of twofold daily service, for the greatest possible number, is no less plainly written in her rubrics on that subject. And her practice, however defective, has all along tended, and tends increasingly at the present hour, towards the realization of these usages by means of her anciently derived Offices. Whatever of improvement or of growth has taken place, has been uniformly, or with exceptions that hardly call for notice, in this track and in this direction. All that is needed is that she should set before her more definitely than ever, and as her fixed and unswerving aim, the recovery of the entire ritual condition of apostolic days, by bringing back at least the bulk of her children to the great primeval practices of WEEKLY COMMUNION and DAILY COMMON PRAYER.

This aim will, I am well aware, be deemed by

---

[a] On the subject of the permission to use the earlier part of the Communion Office when there are no communicants, which some have imagined to come under this description, see Part II. See also p. 49, for an ancient precedent; and Bingham, as there referred to.

some low and unworthy; by others no less visionary and extravagant. I venture to affirm that it is neither. Those who would contend for a vastly greater frequency of Communion, as indispensable to the life of faith, I would remind, that the measure of it here advocated,—with only such occasional increase as our scheme of service also contemplates and provides for, —was that of Apostolic times; and that there are weighty reasons, already set forth, for believing that such is the safer, if not the ordained condition for the Church in all ages. And in reply to that far greater number, who look upon the restoration of these practices, with any sort of universality, as impossible, I would say, that I by no means underrate the difficulty. Difficult it unquestionably is, and ever must be, to win the world to Christian obedience and practice, in ritual matters no less than in practical,—difficult to gird on Apostolic weapons, and wage an Apostolic warfare. But the question for a Church, as for an individual, is not what is difficult or easy, but, as far as it can be ascertained, what is right or wrong: not what we think will succeed or not succeed, but what, on a wise and well-weighed investigation, it seems that the Church's Lord designed for her to do or to aim at. And surely success may better be expected in the attempt to recover a regimen known to be Apostolic, as compared with others which, however plausible in show, are the invention of later times, and have on trial been found wanting. I am persuaded too that we exaggerate the difficulty of bringing things back to the position here contemplated.

First, as regards Holy Communion. We have too much, it must be said, invested it with circumstances of discouragement. It has too much been represented as a provision for an occasional ecstatic state of sanctity; too little in its real character, as the ordained instrument of appropriating afresh, at *brief* intervals,—and those of scarcely less than Divine appointment, — the Christian estate of salvation, and of discharging its duties in their highest and only complete form. A solemn and a festival thing doubtless it is designed to be; but it is a solemnity and a festival of ordained weekly recurrence, at the least. It is this that we have need to realize; viz. that in apostolic days the return of the weekly Festival of Christ's Resurrection, and of the Descent of the Holy Spirit, without Eucharistic celebration and participation, would have been looked upon as scarcely less than an abandonment of the whole Christian position. Surely we should then be less disposed to acquiesce in such ideas as that of monthly Communion, as being a tolerably satisfactory measure of Christian privilege; and contend with more earnestness, from a more strongly fortified position, and with greater success, for the weekly practice. Is there any reason to doubt that the same kind of persons whom we now unhesitatingly and effectually invite to monthly reception, might with equal safety to their souls, and with equal success, be prevailed upon to become weekly Communicants? It is the habit, which in various ways (as e. g. by books containing a "week's preparation" for communicating) has been spread abroad, of viewing Communion as in its nature a rare event;—it is this, and not any unmeetness or disinclination for more frequent reception, at any rate in the case of the more devout members of our congregations, which makes the general restoration of weekly Communion appear so formidable and difficult. Let the practice, and the irresistibly strong grounds on which it rests, be fairly set before them, and there is no reason to doubt that the call would be responded to; more especially since monthly Communion has no definite standing-ground of recommendation, any more than quarterly, or the like. Both are, though in different degrees, a corrupt and unhealthy state of Christian privilege; whereas weekly reception has the claim and the strength of Apostolic sanction and example.

The fuller consideration of this subject must be reserved for the second part of this work. It was necessary, however, to treat of it in a measure both here and elsewhere in the present volume, because of the intimate relation subsisting between the Holy Communion and lower acts of service. Similar reservation must be made of another deeply important question, which is beginning to assume some prominence in the present day; viz. that of non-communicating attendance on the Eucharist. Not until the true nature and design of that Ordinance, as they are plainly written for us in the liturgical records of early and Apostolic days, are fully laid open, can it be shewn how utterly at variance such a practice is with the mind of those times, and of the Ordinance itself. It may suffice to observe here, that the main ground [b] upon which the upholders of it have hitherto relied, viz. the difficulty of imagining what the early Christians did at the daily celebrations if indisposed to communicate, is completely cut away from under them by the well-

---

[b] See Dr. Mill's well-known letter in "Tracts on Catholic Unity." The very partial countenance which that learned and lamented writer accords to the practice, was visibly extorted from him by the consideration referred to in the text.

established fact to which I have drawn attention, that such daily celebration did not exist. As a recent writer[e] has brought it as a weighty charge against the English Church, that she gives no countenance to this practice, it may be well to have pointed out thus briefly in this place, that such discountenance is in reality a note of apostolicity in her Eucharistic provisions.

It is, however, on the restoration of the Ordinary Offices of the English Church to greater efficiency, that the contents of this volume properly lead me to dwell. And in turning to speak of this, I find myself so far in a more advantageous position than when urging universal return to Weekly Communion, that in this desire and hope, at any rate, I do not stand alone. Little as such an event might have been expected, there has lately arisen, throughout the length and breadth of this Church and nation, from men of all minds, one accordant desire for improved efficiency in the ORDINARY WORSHIP of the Church. The zeal thus manifested is of long standing with some, of more sudden growth in others; welcome, surely, to the heart of the English Church from all. No question is made on any side of the desirableness of such Service, alike on Sundays and week-days; but only of how it may be made most efficient.

It will not be expected that I should discuss the countless schemes for this purpose which have been devised, whether in the way of revision and retrenchment of the existing offices, or providing supplementary ones:—for to these objects the aims of most, if not all, have been limited; the actual superseding or abolishing of the present forms none have ventured

---

[e] Wilberforce on the Eucharist.

to suggest. It is well known, however, that the alteration, however slight, of the existing *status* of the English Church's Ritual, is surrounded with difficulties; and that, in the endeavour to improve it, its very existence, or at any rate its integrity, might be seriously imperilled. And the question, I conceive, really before the English Church at the present moment, is not whether any improvement is theoretically possible, but *whether the advantages sought are such as can be set against the risk involved in seeking them.* Now I confess to sharing, for my own part, in the desire, could it be safely and skilfully accomplished, for certain improvements, and those on no mean scale, in our existing Offices. These alterations are not, it may be, exactly those which are most popular in the present day. The prevailing inclination is to reduce our services in various ways. I confess to wishing them, under certain conditions, considerably longer than they are. In the greatest part of our Offices, indeed, I discern nothing but subject for truest content. The penitential prelude, as of old; the ample scheme on which Holy Scripture is sounded forth in our worship day by day to a degree which has never been witnessed in any Church in East or West for more than a thousand years[d], and which was not surpassed even in Apostolic times[e]; the no less ample and Apostolic stream of prayer and intercession following; combined with the exquisite and profound structure of the whole Office, epitomizing all the great ritual conceptions of the past, yet answering, with the simplicity and ease of the most perfectly

---

[d] The Spanish and French Churches had numerous and apparently full Lessons of Scripture in their daily services. See pp. 128, 245.

[e] P. 343.

adjusted machinery, to the needs of the present hour:
—in all this I see nothing that, in the interests of the
Church of this land, I should greatly care to see
otherwise. It is only when looking back to the multitudinous and unstinted Praise of Apostolic times
—the vast volume of Psalms, hymns, and canticles,
that went up from the hearts and lips of the first
ages day by day ;—it is only then that, notwithstanding compensations involved in our Lesson and Prayer
system, I confess to feeling our measure of psalmody
and similar features somewhat scanty and unsatisfying. This, however, I only therefore mention, that
it may be seen that the counsel, towards which these
remarks are tending, is the result of no feeble optimism or blind admiration; but that I too, in sounding
the note of *quieta non movere,* have some sacrifice to
make of personal wishes.

It will perhaps be admitted that in the preceding
pages some fresh reasons have been added to those
which have long deservedly swayed the English mind
in favour of dealing in the spirit of tender and reverent conservatism with our present Offices. With
some, their purely English and Oriental descent, their
independence of the Roman ritual, will plead in their
behalf. With some, their affinity to the world-wide
family of similar Offices, and their consequent fitness
to stand as a symbol, a witness, and an instrument of
our oneness with the Church Universal : with others,
their mighty grasp of the breadth of Scripture, their
profound intuition into its depths, will be their recommendation. Some will value them for their Apostolic
origin, others for their re-moulding's sake in a later
age, a third sort for their sympathy with the period
of Europe's revival. I will add to these one further

ground. It has appeared in the preceding inquiry that these Offices are the last of their race. It is also generally conceded among us, that in their present form they have not existed in vain. Whatever of rugged or straightforward virtues, of simple loyalty towards God and man, is generally associated with the modern English character under favourable circumstances, may doubtless be traced in no small degree to the influence of these Ordinary Services. The Communion Office can claim far less share in it. And it is a task of the utmost responsibility, to take any part in destroying or impairing, by whatever means, a ritual representing such great influences of the past, and so probably rife with expansive and fructifying powers for the future.

Still it is frankly to be conceded, that if the present needs of the Church so require,—if any serious loss is being suffered for want of alteration, or some great gain is even probably to be achieved by it,—no reasons of antiquity or association, no theoretical excellence of structure, ought to avail against it. With such objects in view, even some degree of risk may reasonably be run. But it may confidently be asked, Has any such case been made out for the changes or additions advocated?

The main lines in which projected alterations run are these: 1, internal rectification; 2, retrenchment of the old, or substitution of shorter Offices; 3, addition of new Offices for special purposes.

1. It is represented that the services are in certain points not perfectly appropriate. The Lessons for certain days, and for one particular period of the year, (viz. when the Apocrypha is read,) might be better selected. Supposing this conceded to the ut-

most, it were a slender foundation indeed on which to base the re-organization, or jeopardy the existence, of our entire ritual. But the truth is, that the Lessons chiefly referred to are selected on a sound principle enough, as has been already pointed out[f]. And in one particular instance, that of Ash-Wednesday, it appears to have been by design, not accident, that no Proper Lessons were appointed. In the English Church it was always deemed that sufficient solemnity was given to that day by a special homily on repentance, and other methods; exactly as now by the Commination Service. Not, of course, that this binds us to have no Proper Lessons now; but it is an instance, among many, where arrangements have been found fault with, of which a fair account, to say the least, can be given. It has also been pointed out[g] in a general way, in a previous page, that while there are obvious advantages in a fixed and appropriate selection, so also are there in those freer cycles which were adopted at the Revision of our Offices. In this particular case of Ash-Wednesday, the First Lesson being in most years from the solemn pages of the later Mosaic books, can seldom fail to be appropriate; while it varies from year to year the Scripture combinations of the day.

2. The grounds alleged for retrenchment of the old Offices, or for the substitution, on week-days, and as an alternative, of new and shorter ones, are equally slight and unconvincing. *There is no one object proposed by either plan, which may not in the simplest way be accomplished without any alteration or substitution whatever.* We have seen in these pages how

[f] P. 348.  [g] P. 347.

truly and *bonâ fide* our existing Offices are a combination of the more numerous preceding ones. This alone might suggest the plan of once more, on occasion, and where need is, resolving them into their constituent elements. Owing to the structure thus belonging to them, they lend themselves with great facility to such a design. They all but suggest *pauses*, serving to reduce them in practice to more services than one, each short enough for all conceivable purposes. The Morning Office easily resolves itself into two, the one corresponding to Matins and Lauds, the other extending from the Creed inclusive to Prime; the Evening Office falls in like manner into two services, resembling Vespers and Compline: though indeed there is more than one way of dividing each Office intelligibly enough, without reference to the old arrangements. Thus in either Office the pause might well be after the Canticle to the First Lesson. All that is needed is, that such pauses be pre-arranged and understood, as occasions for free egress and ingress of worshippers; a bell, if necessary, being rung to give notice of the time. Such an arrangement seems to be contemplated by the frequent breaks in the old Offices; especially in the two Eastern Nocturns, each commencing in the same way. By this method then, which *has been found to answer its purpose most completely,* and is no less applicable to week-days than to Sundays, all necessity for any retrenchment, or substitution of shorter services, may be precluded; the English Church saved the apparent discredit of proclaiming that her services, already the shortest in Christendom, are yet longer than she knows how to use; and the setting up of rival Offices, which might here as elsewhere become the watchwords of parties, avoided. If it be said, that there is somewhat novel, and un-English, in such a plan, and that few will be at the pains to carry it out, or avail themselves of it: it is obvious to reply, that novelty of administration is less serious than that of substance; and that if those who plead for relief in point of length will not accept it in this form, it only shews that their alleged need is not very urgent.

3. The authorization of new and additional offices to meet special needs of the Church, stands on somewhat different ground from the two former proposals. That such offices are in themselves desirable, and have been provided in all ages, as they are still in a measure by the English Church, is unquestionable. The Euchologies of the East, the Missæ Votivæ, or special Communion Offices of the West, made somewhat ample provision of this kind. But it may still be questioned whether our existing ritual machinery, if worked with that moderate degree of licence which it is inconceivable that it was intended to exclude, cannot supply all that is absolutely required. One particular need alleged is that of an additional Evening Office of a simpler and less liturgical kind than our present Evensong. But such an Office is, in the first place, supplied by the method above described, of breaking the Evensong by a pause. A second method, which has been deemed by high authorities perfectly compatible with the Church's rubric, is to combine the Litany with a sermon. And further, a great and most desirable degree of freedom has ever been recognised in connection with sermons, as regards the use both of prayers and hymns. It would seem, then, that round the

combination here mentioned might be gathered, under due regulation and authorization in the several dioceses, the materials not only of such a popular Evening Service as is desired, but also of a minor kind of Office adapted to special occasions and emergencies. It may be added here, that in the free use of hymns, which has never been disallowed, but rather encouraged in various ways, in the English Church, lies one great resource for amplifying and enriching our ordinary Office.

On the whole, then, I conceive that no cause has been shewn, nor can be, for embarking at the present hour on so great and hazardous an enterprise as that of revising once more our Ordinary Offices, whether in the way of retouchment, retrenchment, or addition. No such second emergency and crisis has arisen now, as that which prompted and demanded the Revision of the sixteenth century. The English Church had sinned deeply *then*, had she failed to recognise the new duty which had come upon her by the breaking up of the great crust of the old mediæval condition, and to cast forth the bread of a vernacular and popular ritual on the rising waters of knowledge. It remains now to "find it after many days." What is really wanted is a better understanding and appreciation of what was done then, together with faith and love to give— what has never yet been given—full effect to it. Our need, in a word, is not of new services, but of a new mind and heart, in clergy and people alike, towards those which we have. The affection felt for them by this Church and nation, though deep, has surely been blind. Their powers as instruments of spiritual perfection, and as the exponents of religious feeling and worship, have been—if there be any truth in what has been here unfolded—underrated and unknown.

But above all, these Offices have not been duly *used*. As services reaching through the whole of life, and so, in due subordination to Eucharistic service, guiding, moulding, and elevating it, they are to the far greater part of our clergy, much more to the mass of the laity, utterly strange. Solemnly bound though the former are, by their ordination vow, to the daily and continual use of them, and to bring others to them to the best of their power, it is but lately that any sense of these obligations has begun to be manifested among us.

The causes which have led to this state of things cannot here be inquired into. One fertile source of it, and which must continue to have the same result until the evil shall in God's good time be remedied, is to be found in the strange and well-nigh incredible custom which has prevailed among us, and is only beginning in the rarest instances to be broken through, of our clergy being admitted to their holy Office without a shadow of training in the duties, but specially in the *mind* and *habits* proper to it, and essential to the well-being of the Church. All, however, that it falls within the scope of this work to point out is, that the responsibility and shame of such neglect, in clergy and laity alike, is tenfold greater in the case of the English Church than of any other. First, because in no other have the public Offices of Ordinary Worship been so sedulously and completely popularised, and fitted for the use of all in whom a spark of love or faith survives; and next, because, though a faithful use of these services, beyond the example of other ages and lands, will abundantly justify that reduction of them from their old grandeur to their present simplicity, and from an ideal to a practicable standard, nothing short of this can possibly do so.

END OF VOL. I.

# NOTES.

Note A.—p. 21.

The charge which, in no heated spirit of controversy, but in all sadness as well as soberness, is in the text advanced against the existing Roman Church of "treading, to say the least, on the very verge of polytheism;" and again, of sanctioning more or less formally a direct idolatry paid to various objects of sense,—is too serious a one not to demand some degree of substantiation. I shall confine myself to one strong instance of each kind. The following is from the Prayer-book of the Oratory of St. Philip Neri, p. 41. We may surely well ask what distinctive attributes or powers are reserved for Almighty God, when such prayers as this are addressed to one of His creatures. "O most holy . . . . . keeper of the treasures of grace, and refuge of us miserable sinners, we have recourse to thy . . . . . . love with lively faith; and beg of thee the grace ever to do God's will and thine; we give up our hearts into thy most holy hands, and implore of thee the salvation of our souls and bodies, and in the sure hope that thou who art our most loving . . . . . . wilt hear us, we say with lively faith . . . . . ."

The blanks in the original are filled up with the titles of the Blessed Virgin Mary; the last with three "hail Maries." The following is a prayer to St. Aloysius Gonzaga, ibid., p. 50:—"O holy Aloysius, beautiful for thy angelic virtues, &c., I recommend to thee in a particular manner the purity of my soul and body. I beseech thee . . . . to preserve me from all sin: never permit me to be defiled; and when thou seest me exposed to temptation, remove far from my heart all impure thoughts, and renew in me the remembrance of God;—imprint deeply in my soul the fear of God, and enkindle within me the fire of divine love . . . . . ."

These are the devotions, it is true, of an extreme section of Romanists; but they of necessity possess the sanction of the see of Rome. Throughout a great part of Spain, again, as we are informed by a candid and credible witness, (vide Meyrick's Church in Spain,) a very principal object of the popular worship is Saint Philumena; a person who, there is good reason to believe, never existed. It is difficult to see the difference between this and the worship of Ceres or Diana.

On the subject of idolatry, it may suffice to allege the following passage from the Roman Pontifical; bearing in mind the Roman definition, following the second Nicene Council, " Latria *solum Divinæ Naturæ* competit."—" Ille qui gladium Imperatori præfert, et alius crucem Legati portans, simul ire debent. *Crux Legati,* quod *debetur ei Latria,* erit a dexteris, et gladius Imperatoris a sinistris." Ordo ad recip. process. Imperat. Pontificale Rom., p. 672, ed. Rom. 1595. Pont. Rom. Urban VIII. pars iii. p. 109, Paris, 1664. Pont. Rom. p. 571, typ. Vat. 1745. I have selected these peculiarly flagrant instances, not as in the least admitting that the lower degrees of worship addressed to creatures in the Roman communion are in any way justifiable, but as conceiving the present instances, at least, to admit of no answer or palliation.

It is only just, however painful, to add that the existing Eastern Offices go to quite the same lengths as the Roman in ascribing to the Blessed Virgin the attributes of Almighty God: such as the government of the world and the Church, the disposing of the hearts of kings, the giving of victory, &c. " It must be confessed," says Mr. Neale, " that these troparia are at least as strong as any corresponding expressions in the Latin Church," (p. 833). Take the following instance, (Ib., Lauds, p. 915): " O Mother of God, confirm the state of the orthodox, preserve *those whom thou hast chosen to rule,* (!) and give them from heaven the victory; because thou, who only art blessed, didst bring forth God." More awful blasphemy it is difficult to conceive. Indeed there is strong historical ground (vid. Nicephorus) for believing that this and many like hymns were originally, or in their earlier forms, addressed to Christ, but have been perverted to their present purpose, simply by substituting the name of the Theotokos. In like manner, the intercession of Christ, which I do not remember to have seen pleaded anywhere in the existing Greek services, seems to have been obliterated to make room for the constantly recurring request for the intercession of the saints, and of the Blessed Virgin Mary especially.

If any one should think it absolutely improbable, either that so vital a corruption should for so long a period have infected the greater portion of the Church of God, without its forfeiting the very name and the being of a Church; or again, that a comparatively small remainder of the Church should retain the pure deposit of the truth, the far larger part holding it in a deeply vitiated form; let such ponder well the strikingly parallel case of the Church of the Elder Covenant.

From about the 6th to the 16th century of the Christian era, certain corruptions in doctrine and discipline had been gathering to a head. That they grew up as encroachments upon the old truth and the old prerogatives, has been again and again demonstrated. And there existed all the while, even to the last, a leaven and an element of protest. The two leading aspects of the innovations which had thus grown up had reference, 1, to the Headship of the Church; and 2, to the Object of worship. A claim had been gradually set up to an earthly headship, alike in things temporal and spiritual; and worship of the most exalted kind, trenching very closely, to say the least, upon that which is due to Almighty God, had been introduced, and was declared to be due to various created things. And when, in the 16th century, various events raised the momentous issue between the old ways and faith and the new, and compelled men to choose their side, the result was that a great preponderance adhered to the novel doctrines and discipline which had thus arisen in the course of several preceding centuries; while a comparatively small number refused to acknowledge any other supreme Headship than the Church had known from the beginning, or any other Object of worship than God Himself.

Such, stated in general terms, and drawn in its true colours, was the spectacle which was exhibited to the world in the 16th century. And it is singularly parallel, in all its main features, to the breaking off of the ten tribes from the theocratic commonwealth of Israel. It has been well pointed out by a writer of our own, (see Blunt's Hulsean Lectures,) that that disruption was only the result of tendencies which had long been in operation, —tendencies on the part of the great mass of Israel, 1, to form themselves into a separate confederation under the headship of the tribe of Ephraim; and 2, to worship God through forbidden media, as well as to worship other gods.

And the points that we are concerned to notice are these two: 1. That the body which broke away from its allegiance to the

Mosaic theocracy, and to the one Object of worship, was of the two by far the *larger* and more imposing in grandeur and populousness; while the far smaller body exclusively retained the pure form both of ecclesiastical polity and Divine worship; and yet, 2. that notwithstanding the deep degradation, and apparently hopeless apostasy, of the kingdom of Israel, it did not cease to be accounted a portion of the Church of God; that God still pleaded with it by His prophets; and that there were still, even in its darkest days, " seven thousand who had not bowed the knee to Baal."

We might, indeed, pursue the parallel further. While it is not for us to lift the curtain of the Church's yet future destiny, we cannot but be struck with the fact, that though Judah was scourged for her sins by the captivity, yet it was not upon her, but upon "backsliding Israel," that the curse of final excision and dispersion fell; that the true ark of refuge in those days was *not Ephraim, but Judah*, (see 2 Chron. xi. 13—16). Thoughtful men have deemed that even such a destiny as this, to be the one refuge of the faithful in the last days, may be reserved to the Church of the English succession.

### Note B.—p. 75.

It may be conjectured, though we have no positive evidence for the fact, that the Temple Service commenced daily with the 95th Psalm itself, or with some part of it. For it were surely most remarkable that a Psalm so peculiarly to the purpose, and bearing so expressly upon early Israelitish story, should find no appointed place in that Service. Now it is not among the seven Psalms allotted to the seven days of the week; which are said to have been as follows :—

On the 1st day of the week, our Sunday, Ps. xxiv.
"    2nd " " Monday, Ps. xlviii.
"    3rd " " Tuesday, Ps. lxxxii.
"    4th " " Wednesday, Ps. xciv.
"    5th " " Thursday, Ps. lxxxi.
"    6th " " Friday, Ps. xciii.
"    7th (Sabbath) " Saturday, Ps. xcii.

Is it improbable that the 95th Psalm, though the Jewish writers have preserved no record of it, was used also; viz. as

a fixed every-day Psalm, preparatory to the whole psalmody of
the day,—a purpose for which it is so entirely suitable? We
may take notice, as lending some countenance to this conjecture,
that the Psalms in the above scheme are numbered *backwards* in
two instances, viz. in the case of the 81st and 82nd occurring on
the fifth and third days; and again, in that of the 92nd, 93rd,
and 94th, which are allotted to the 7th, 6th, and 4th. Now
this is a thoroughly Jewish way of reckoning; an instance
of which in the Synagogue Service has already been referred
to (p. 71, note z);—the Sabbath, though last in order, being
reckoned the chief and leading day of the week to which it
belongs, and regulating its character in ritual things. Though,
indeed,—and it is another indication of the Jewish origin of the
Eastern ritual,—some weeks in the calendar of Constantinople
derive their name and character from the *following* Sunday.
Thus the six days preceding Palm-Sunday make up with it
what is called Palm-week; and so of others (vide Neale, pp.
743, 753). This feature in the Jewish scheme furnishes some
presumption in favour of its antiquity, which, though highly
probable, cannot be absolutely demonstrated. But our present
concern with it is to observe, that it seems to point to the 95th
Psalm as having had in some way, and in some shape or other,
a place in the Temple Service. For there is manifestly a principle, and the same principle, in the selection of these two
groups of Psalms. The 81st Psalm is an exhortation to stedfast adherence to the service and praise of God, grounded on a
review of the events in the wilderness: the 82nd, though differing in subject, is connected with the 81st as being a Psalm of
Asaph, the only two in succession that bear his name. In like
manner the 95th Psalm is the culminating point of the series
which commences on the Sabbath, or rather sets out from it.
The peculiar character of the *ninetieth* Psalm, as being probably
a genuine composition of Moses, widely separates it from the
next group of Psalms extending from the 91st to the 100th.
And of these the first five—among which are the Psalms now
under our consideration—possess a character of their own. The
whole group is thought by competent judges to belong to
the period just preceding the captivity[a]; probably to the last
national revival under Josiah[b]. But the first five are clearly

[a] Hengstenberg on the Psalms, Appendix II. p. 17, and pp. 156, 157.
[b] Ibid., p. 17.

discernible from the last five. The former set are emphatically national Israelitish Psalms; the latter contemplate prophetically the Divine rule as extended over all lands, though having its seat still in Sion[c]. The former, then, would be very likely to be adopted, at the time when they originated, as fixed Psalms for the Temple Service; and they would be reinstated as such by Ezra, with the rest of the national worship. Such, accordingly, is the place which tradition represents most of them as holding at the Christian era. One exception is the last, and in many respects the most remarkable, as well as the most deeply imbued with the pervading spirit of the entire series, viz. the 95th. A mighty and triumphant deliverance from the coming captivity, the anticipation of which seems to run through the four preceding Psalms, is here contemplated as actually come. In language based (just as in the 81st Psalm) on what befel the nation on their way to the promised land, and no less applicable to the captivity, with its seventy years of exile, they are exhorted to faithful adherence to the worship of God their King. It is hardly credible but that this Psalm, if our premises be at all correct, must have had its place somewhere in the restored Temple Service[d], the rather because its contents being such as we have seen, would have a tenfold applicability after the return from the captivity; since the exhortation, "to-day, harden not your hearts," &c., would rest upon a new and personal experience perfectly parallel to that of ancient Israel.

## Note C, on Chap. I. Sect. VI.

This Hexapsalmus, taken with the 51st, which follows, may possibly be the foundation of the "seven penitential Psalms" of the West; these do not seem to be known in the East. Origen appears to be the first to allude to them (Hom. Lev. xi.), and after him St. Augustine, both writing in Africa,—the stepping-stone between the East and the West. Of the seven Eastern Psalms, three (viz. xxxviii., li., cxliii.) belong to the Western Septett; a fourth (88th) is profoundly penitential, and a Psalm of the Passion in the West.

[c] See Hengstenberg, ubi sup., and Ps. xcvi. p. 172.
[d] Compare Hengstenberg in loc., p. 165.

### Note D.—p. 142.

In this note shall be given a few specimens of the Eastern hymns, &c., chiefly such as throw light on the origin of Western forms.

First, as to the original of the Western Te Deum. The legend of its having been composed, as by inspiration, at the baptism of St. Augustine by St. Ambrose, rests upon no higher authority, *that we know of*, than that of a spurious chronicle ascribed to Dacius, a successor of St. Ambrose, but in reality written 500 years later, (Vide Mabillon, Analect. ap. Bingham, xiv. ii. 9). It is however so singular a story for any one to have entirely invented, that it is just possible it may be founded on authentic traditions of some part taken by those two great Doctors of the Church, either in putting together the Te Deum, or in introducing it into the Church Services. It is worthy of note, in reference to this story, that the Te Deum has somewhat the appearance of a choral paraphrase on (1) the Creed and (2) the Lord's Prayer; which may be owing to its having anciently had some connection with baptism, or may have given rise to this legend.

Since Abp. Ussher's time it has commonly been ascribed to Nicetius of Triers, (circ. 555,) on the authority of a French MS. Psalter of about the year 1100. But another MS. Breviary of about the same date (1086, ap. Gavanti) entitles it "Hymnus Sisebuti Monachi;" a third, "Hymnus S. Abundii." Now these traditions, being found in ritual-books, are probably all alike of some antiquity, and go far to neutralize each other, and to prove that the real author of the Te Deum is unknown. Meanwhile, its universal appearance in all known Western Offices, in the same position, viz. at the close of the Nocturns (i.e. Matins), just after the Lessons, affords a strong presumption that it was a recognised feature of Church Service even before the fifth or sixth century. Mr. Palmer, (ii. 227,) supposes St. Benedict's rule, and that of Cæsarius of Arles, to assign it different positions: but they doubtless both meant the same; only the one calls the Night Office Nocturns, the other Matins. The earliest author ever named for it is Hilary of Poitiers, (circ. 354; vide Palmer, l. c.); and it may be as old, and cannot be much posterior to his time.

But however this be, one thing is plain, viz. that the rudiments, at least, of the Te Deum, are to be found in the Eastern

Offices, and that it is, as to its essence, an Eastern production, though probably cast into its present noble and inimitable form by some Western composer. In those Offices, though it is nowhere found entire, all the main topics and leading expressions of it are scattered here and there. Thus, first, in the Midnight Office, we have the "Holy, Holy, Holy," and again, (viz. in the Saturday form,) "Imitating the Powers above, we offer a hymn to Thee, Holy," &c.; and afterwards follows the expectation of Christ's coming to judgment. The same topics are found in the Sunday "Triadic" hymns at Nocturns, and the expression, "The Father everlasting." Again at Lauds, in the similar "Triadic" hymns for Lent, we have "The Father everlasting, the co-inoriginate (συνάναρχος) Son, the co-eternal Holy Ghost, let us like the Cherubim magnify; Holy," &c.; and again, "The Judge will come anon." And after the ninth ode, "For Thee all the Powers of heaven praise." Hymns of this kind are indeed of frequent occurrence. In the Typica, again,—a service subjoined to that of the sixth or ninth hour,—we have:—

"The heavenly company praise Thee, and say, Holy, Holy, Holy, Lord God of Sabaoth; heaven and earth are full of Thy glory:

"The company of the holy angels and archangels, with all the powers of heaven, praise Thee, and say," &c.

Again, in Compline:—

"The bodiless nature of the Cherubim with restless hymns glorify Thee.

"The six-winged Seraphim with endless voices magnify Thee.

"The whole army of the angels with Trisagion hymns worship Thee.

"For Thou art before all things—the self-existent Father.

"And hast Thy Son co-inoriginate with Thee.

"Also Thou hast the equally-honoured Spirit of life.

"All the choir of prophets and martyrs," &c.

Thus varied, and on the whole gradual, is the appearance of this hymn in the Greek Offices—nowhere put together, but diffused everywhere. It is probable that further inquiry would bring to light other portions of the Te Deum.

It may be added, that its very exordium is so peculiar as to indicate some metrical necessity as the cause of it,—"Te Deum laudamus;" and on turning to the Greek hymns we see exactly how this would originate. It is by no means uncommon for them to begin thus; as e.g. Σὲ τὸ ἀπόρθητον τεῖχος . . ἱκετεύομεν.

And do I not doubt but that the Te Deum is the translation, as to its exordium, of a Greek hymn beginning, Σέ τὸν Θεὸν αἰνοῦμεν, ὁμολογοῦμέν σε Κύριον, or the like. It is very remarkable that in the English Church a rudimentary or inchoate form of Te Deum was appointed as the ordinary Antiphon to the Athanasian Creed, (see Brev. Sar. ad Prim.; and Tr. Sar. Psalt., p. 112,) "Te Deum Patrem ingenitum, te Filium unigenitum, te Spiritum Sanctum Paracletum, sanctam et individuam Trinitatem toto corde et ore confitemur." Compare the Compline form as given above.

It is interesting to trace in like manner the manifest origin of a more mediæval composition, the "Stabat Mater," to Eastern originals. Short hymns on the same theme are very common in the East: and their language, metre, and rhyme have manifestly suggested those of the western hymns. Thus on ordinary Wednesdays and Fridays throughout the year the following is among the exaposteilaria (see p. 143):—

| Ἐν τῷ Σταυρῷ παρεστῶσα | Stabat Mater dolorosa |
| Ἡ σε ἀσπόρως τεκοῦσα | Juxta crucem lacrymosa |
| Καὶ θρηνῳδοῦσα ἐβόα. | Dum pendebat Filius |

Other hymns supply minor resemblances. See Compline, Monday in Holy-Week, Third Ode; and Tuesday in Holy-Week, First Ode; and Holy Thursday and Good Friday: where we have the "pendebat Filius" in Σήμερόν σε θεωροῦσα .. ἐν σταυρῷ ... ὦ Λόγε ἐξαρταμένον: and the "pertransivit gladius," in ἐτέτρωσο τὴν καρδίαν.

The following may serve as specimens of the collect-like hymns of the East:

"O Lord, who hast restored those who were cast out of Paradise at the first by eating of the tree, by Thy Cross and Passion, O God our Saviour, help us," &c. *Sunday of the expulsion of Adam.*

"O Lord, who at the third hour didst send down Thy all-holy Spirit on the Apostles; that Holy Spirit take not from us, but renew it in us who pray to Thee." *Monday in the same week at Lauds. See Andrewes' Devotions, First Day.*

"O Thou, who by Thy Cross hast strengthened us to fulfil the course of abstinence, of Thy good pleasure accomplish the same in us by sincere repentance, O Lord of mercy."

NOTE E, on Chap. I. Sect. V.- VII.

THE following passages from Palmer's "Dissertations on the Orthodox or Eastern Catholic Communion," which have come under my notice since writing this chapter, will furnish an interesting comment on the Services which are the subject of it.

"When .... in the catacombs, under some great city, or in the retired house of some brethren in the outskirts, the Hexapsalmus, or 'Six Psalms,' at the beginning of Matins, were read with a devout and meditative voice by the superior, containing the complaints and meditations of the Messiah, the perfect Man, under the sorrows and afflictions of His humanity, and the assaults of His enemies, all who were present know that this voice was not only from the Messiah, the Head, but also from the Church, His Body; and each of them in particular found his or her own spiritual application of the verses of those Psalms, according to the personal troubles and necessities of each; and his own comfort and strength in that mixture of more cheerful prayer and meditation with which one of these Psalms (ciii.) tempers the others."—p. 285.

"And at Vespers, after the reading of a Psalm (civ.) fit for the commencement of a day or a week, concerning creation and the renewal of creation; and after the singing of other Psalms (cxli., cxlii., cxxx., cxvii.), not unlike the Hexapsalmus of the Matins, in which 'prayer was set forth as the incense, and the lifting up of pure hands was an evening sacrifice;' having come to the setting sun, and seen the star of evening, and lighted the lights of the church, the clergy coming out, and standing in a broad curve eastwards, sang that glorious and most ancient hymn ('O cheerful Light,' &c.) to the eternal and consubstantial Effulgence of the Father, of whom the visible light is a symbol, glorifying Him, together with the Father and the Holy Ghost, one God;—a hymn full-orbed, mellow, calm, deep-toned, (as expressing the depth of the mystery,) slow, (as being contemplative,) rich with the splendour of vestments, accompanied by the gospel, and by incense representing prayer and praise; sung by the elders, the first half standing without, the latter half, after going up into the sanctuary; as the doxology of the Holy Trinity, begun in the Church on earth below, and to be finished and continued for ever in heaven."—p. 287.

"After the earliest and golden ages of the Church, during which she was subject to persecution, and during which her ritual worship, and the writings of her saints, like their lives, were almost wholly spiritual and practical, there followed in the fourth and fifth centuries another phase of character, in which the divine depth and earnestness of the ancients, without ceasing altogether to exist, is clothed in a garb of intellectual, rhetorical, and poetical cultivation."

"In the greater Compline there is a manifest relic of those primitive times when the Church was in the catacombs, under Jewish and heathen persecutors."—Ib., p. 289.

NOTE F, on Chap. II. Sect. I., p. 168.

*On the earlier manifestations of our Lord's Priesthood.*

BY one especial act of anticipative Priesthood, as it would seem, was the whole of the sinless life of our Lord solemnly presented and offered to the Father; viz. by His presentation in the temple. Yet that very act, while it implied and involved a priestly and sacrificial character as appertaining to the Life of Christ from its very beginning, implied also an abeyance of the actual priestly operation whereby it would be sanctified and rendered acceptable. For the presentation of first-born sons in the temple did not constitute or consecrate them priests, but was only an acknowledgment of their services in that capacity being due to God, ever since the sanctification of the first-born at the coming out of Egypt. Our Lord, accordingly, by His presentation, did in a mystery prefer His claim to the Priesthood of the world as the "First-born among many brethren." Yet not by this action did He enter upon His priestly office, but only on a certain lower kind or degree of dedication to God, and one possessing a passive rather than an active character. Passively, in a manner, if we may say so with reverence, He partook of the virtue of His own priestly operation yet to come. As the offering of the morning lamb was held to be secondary to that of the evening lamb,—incense being offered with the latter alone,—so was it here; it was the

Morning but not the Evening Sacrifice. The Priest was in Person the same, but not as yet in virtue, and in the nature of His action.

There is some appearance, again, of our Lord's receiving a yet more especial designation to His Priesthood on the occasion of His Baptism; for this event took place when "Jesus began to be about thirty years old,"—the priestly age: and St. John the Baptist, after His baptism, points to Him as "the Lamb of God which taketh away the sins of the world." And, doubtless, in entering on His prophetic office and ministry, He did enter also upon a course of actions more immediately pertaining to His Priesthood, and destined to be in due time gathered up into it as actions of especial power for man's salvation.

Note G, on Chap. II. Sect. I., II.

Subjoined are a few illustrations of the views contained in these sections as to the Priesthood of Christ, and that of Christians derived from it.

In the Old Testament we discern four great and recognised historic types or foreshadowings of the destined work of Christ towards man; and in each case *two* stages seem to be distinctly marked; the one of recovery or renewal, the other of priestly and ritual oblation and dedication of that which is restored or renewed. The four events—covering, with their antecedents, the whole period of pre-evangelic history—are, the flood, the call of Abraham, the bringing of Israel out of Egypt, the return from the captivity. By these four events the world, so many times lost and fallen away from God, was marvellously recovered, by the agency in each case of some single person,—Noah, Abraham, Moses, Zerubbabel,—who thus become, and are indeed recognised, as signal types of Christ in the work of restoration and recovery. But in each case presentation by means of sacrifice follows closely upon the work of recovery. Noah, on coming out of the Ark, makes his oblation and is accepted on behalf of mankind. Abraham on reaching the promised land does the same; and is yet more signally accepted through the ministry of Melchisedec, (see below, Part II., chap. on Theory of Eucharistic Worship). Moses completes the typical regeneration of the Red Sea by installing the subjects of it in the condition of "a kingdom of priests," and of full ritual presentation and acceptance through Aaronic ministration. The work of Zerubbabel, lastly, in restoring the people to their own land, is completed by Ezra and by Joshua the High-priest, through the rebuilding of the temple and re-instalment of the nation into its old ritual relations to God; a state of things which continued until the coming of Christ.

By these types it was not obscurely intimated, that the work of Christ would be twofold; first regenerative, and then oblationary. In the Apostolic Epistles the same view is fully maintained, and has influenced the structure of some of the most remarkable of them. The Epistle to the Romans is well known for the fulness of its declarations as to regeneration in baptism, (ch. vi.) It is less frequently observed, though it is equally clear, that the dedication and oblation by a subsequent and separate, though life-long act, of the creature thus restored to the Divine image, is most earnestly dwelt on as that in which the whole economy terminates and is completed in. After St. Paul has ended his great argument, chap. i.—xi., proving the admission of all alike to saving membership in Christ, his exhortation is, "I beseech you, that ye *present* your bodies a living *sacrifice*, holy, acceptable, unto God, which is your reasonable service." There is no more ground for dissociating this passage from the Eucharist than there is for disconnecting the other with baptism The Church has accordingly in all ages embodied these words or the substance of them, in her Communion Offices. St. Paul also,—after detailing the duties which go to make up this perfect and full act of dedication, (ch. xii.—xv. 15,)—speaks of it as his own crowning privilege to act as the ministering priest of this offering: "That I should be the minister (λειτουργὸν) of Jesus Christ to the Gentiles, ministering (ἱερουργοῦντα) the Gospel of God, that the offering up (προσφορὰ, i. e. either the offering up of themselves, or of them by him,) of the Gentiles might be acceptable, being sanctified by the Holy Ghost." In Ephesians, renewal is first spoken of as an argument for Christian living, (iv. 22): "That ye put off the old man, which after God is created in righteousness;" then follows (v. 9, 20,) the *ritual* aspect of the Christian position: "Giving thanks (εὐχαριστοῦντες, offering Eucharistic praise,) to God and the Father." And again, the same order is observed in the next four verses: "As Christ loved the Church, &c... that He might sanctify and cleanse it with the *washing of water* by the Word, that He might *present* it to Himself a glorious Church, not having spot," &c.; where, though the marriage idea is perhaps the prevailing one, the sacrificial certainly enters in, in virtue of ἵνα προσφέρῃ. In the twin Epistle to the Colossians (iii. 10, 17,) the order is the same. Finally, in the Epistle to the Hebrews, while the doctrine of baptism is laid down (vi. 1.) as among "the first principles of the doctrine of Christ" (or "the word of the beginning of Christ," marg.), and the danger of falling away from that estate duly insisted upon; something further and more mysterious is intimated, the full apprehension and thorough embracing of which is, as compared with the baptismal doctrine and position, a "going on unto perfection," (ibid.) What this higher and inner doctrine and position are, the rest of the Epistle declares: it is the Priesthood of Christ, supervening upon and added to His Sonship; and the Eucharistic position and function of Christians, superadded in a parallel manner to their regeneration and sonship. "Having therefore boldness," is the sum of his exhortation, the point of the whole Epistle, "to enter into the holiest by the blood of Jesus .. through the veil, that is to say, His flesh," (into which we are engrafted, and made mystical members,) "and having an High-Priest over the house of God; let us draw near, having [had] our hearts sprinkled from an evil conscience, *and our bodies washed with pure water*, (ἐῤῥαντισμένοι, λελουμένοι,) let us hold fast the confession of our faith," (ὁμολογίαν: Johnson understands it of the Eucharist, as Clemens Romanus seems to have done,) "not forsaking the assembling of ourselves together," &c. (Heb. x. 19—25). Without insisting upon Johnson's interpretation of ὁμολογία, it is still difficult to conceive what else all this can possibly refer to than Eucharistic approach to God. The First Epistle of St. Peter furnishes a striking parallel to those of St. Paul before quoted. In ch. ii. 1, the saints are first addressed as "*new-born* babes," who ought naturally "to desire the sincere milk of the Word, that they may grow thereby;" and then reminded of their still higher position as "a spiritual house, a holy priesthood," ordained "to offer up spiritual sacrifices acceptable to God by Jesus Christ."

It is further to be remarked, that almost every one of these cases, Christian duties, and the same duties, are based on *both* the stages or aspects of the Christian position; only the Eucharistic position is viewed as entailing a more intense responsibility. Thus we have the Christian life set forth to us baptismally in Rom. vi.; eucharistically in Rom. xii., &c.; and so of the rest.

The following citations from the Fathers will illustrate these positions.

### *Christ, and fellowship in Christ's Actions, given in Baptism.*

"Let no one then suppose that Baptism is merely the grace of remission of sins, or further, that of adoption. Nay, we know full well, that as it purges our sins, and conveys to us the gift of the Holy Ghost, so also it is the counterpart of Christ's sufferings. For for this cause, Paul, just now read, (Rom. vi. 3,) cries aloud and says, 'Know ye not that as many of us as were baptized unto Christ Jesus, were baptized, &c. Therefore we are buried," &c.

"These words he spake unto them who had settled with themselves that Baptism ministers to us the remission of sins, and adoption, but not that, further, it has communion also, in representation, with Christ's true sufferings."—St. Cyril, Catech., Lect. xx., Lib. of Fathers, vol. ii. part i. p. 265.

"Having been baptized unto Christ, and put on Christ, ye have been made conformable to the Son of God; for God having predestinated us to the adoption of sons, *made us share the fashion of Christ's glorious Body.* Being therefore made partakers of Christ, ye are properly called christs, (anointed ones,) and of you God said, 'Touch not My christs, or Anointed.' Now ye were made christs by receiving the emblem of the Holy Ghost, *and all things were in a figure wrought in you,* because ye are figures of Christ."—Ib., Lect. xxi. p. 267.

### *Baptism gives participation in Christ's Priesthood.*

"Ye shall receive proofs from the Old and New Testaments, how ye have been cleansed from your sins by the Lord, with the washing of water by the Word; *and how by being priests* ye have become partakers of Christ's Name."—Ib., Lect. xviii. p. 255.

"This is Jesus Christ, who is come an *High Priest* of good things to come, who out of the munificence of His Godhead *has imparted to us His own title.* For kings among men have a royal style which they keep to themselves; but Jesus Christ, being the Son of God, has counted us worthy to be called Christians," (alluding to the meaning of Χριστὸς, "anointed" as a priest).—Lect. x. p. 106.

"And 'they shall be priests of God and of Christ, and shall reign with Him 1.000 years,' is certainly not said of Bishops and Presbyters only, who are now *properly* called priests in the Church; but as we call all 'Christians' on account of their mystical anointing, so do we call all priests, *since they are members of the One Priest.*"—St. Aug., Civ. Dei, xx. 10.

*Participation of Christ by means of His Word, or Holy Scripture.*

"When we ask for bread, we thereby understand all things. There is a spiritual food which the faithful know, when ye shall receive it at the altar of God.

"Again, what I am handling before you now (i.e. the Scriptures) is daily bread; and the *daily lessons which ye hear in church* are daily bread, and the hymns ye hear and repeat are daily bread."—St. Aug., Serm. vii., Lib. of Fathers, vol. xvi. p. 85.

"Our daily food then in this earth is the Word of God, which is dealt out always in the Churches. Again, if by this daily bread thou understand what the faithful receive, what ye then receive after ye have been baptized, it is with good reason we ask and say, 'Give us this day our daily bread,' that we may live in such sort that we be not separated from the holy altar."—Serm. vi., p. 74, same vol.

*The Church's offering of herself an imitation of Christ's.*

"Christ is the Offerer and the Oblation, of which thing He designed the sacrifice of the Church to be a Sacrament, (or resemblance,) who, as being the Body of Him that is the Head, *learns to offer herself by Him;* of which one sacrifice the many and various sacrifices of the ancient saints were but signs."—St. Aug., ap. Johnson, U. S., ch. ii. p. 98.

"This is the sacrifice of Christians: in that oblation which the Church offers, *she herself is offered.*"—St. Aug., ibid.

Johnson adds:—"The bread represents the *Body of Christian people,* as well as the natural Body of Christ."

*The Eucharistic Offering made by all, not by the ministering Priesthood only.*

St. Augustine, &c., constantly dwell on this view: see Bingham, XV. iii. 12, 34. It is perhaps most interesting to observe, that the ancient Western Communion Office, including our own, distinctly recognised it not only by the plural form of the consecrating prayers, (e.g. "supplices rogamus, ut accepta habeas hæc dona, hæc sacrificia, quæ tibi offerimus,") but also by this address of priest to people : " Orate fratres et sorores (sic Sarisb.) pro me, ut meum *pariterque vestrum* (Id.), acceptum sit Domino Deo *sacrificium*." Nor were the middle ages, even, altogether forgetful of this great truth; e.g. Guerricus, a monk of Clairvaux, under St. Bernard: "Neque enim credere debetis, quod soli sacerdoti supradictæ virtutes sunt necessariæ, *quasi solus* consecret et sacrificet Corpus Christi. Non solus sacrificat, non solus consecrat, *sed totus conventus fidelium* qui astat cum illo consecrat, cum illo sacrificat."—Serm. de Purif., inter Op. S. Bernardi, tom. iv. p. 1896.

Of modern writers who have contended strongly for a universal Christian priesthood, while denying the existence of any priesthood ministerial, Dr. Arnold and M. Bunsen may be named as the chief:—the former in his Fragment on the Church; the latter in his " Church of the Future." See " Christian Remembrancer," No. 59, Jan. 1848. Mr. Maurice, while denying the atoning power of Christ's priesthood, and so leaving it without a foundation, has some eloquent passages on the oblationary personal priesthood of Christians. (" Doctrine of Sacrifice," sub fin.) See Moberly's " Sayings of the Forty Days," Disc. iii. p. 118.

NOTE H.—p. 159.

" AFTER the composition of the first ' Canons,' (which are sets of nine ' Odes,' to be sung with the nine prophetical and evangelical hymns,) that is, after the time of St. Andrew of Crete and St. Cosmas, we come to an *imitative* period ; . . . in which, for the sake of a certain uniformity or symmetry in the ritual, vast numbers of canons and other singings were composed for all the saints of the daily calendar throughout the year, on the model of the earlier compositions of the same sort; and the monastic ritual, calculated for communities which should employ one-third part of the twenty-four hours of the day and night in the Services of the Church, was introduced more or less into general use even in common churches. During this period, which we may fix from the end of the eighth to the end of the twelfth century, we find a great deterioration in the quality of the additions made to the ritual, and a vast growth of formalism and unreality in their actual use.

" In place of deep, warm, and just poetry, we have often cold, empty, and hyperbolical rhapsodies. And the readings and singings being felt to be too long for a full and proper performance of them, men commonly fell into a perfunctory and merely external performance of the ritual, or of many parts of it; an abuse which was in still later times brought to its climax by the gradual corruption and change of the Hellenic language into the modern Romaic; so that not only were the Psalter and Lesson Offices, instead of being read devoutly, gabbled over with heathenish rapidity; and the canons, or streams of hymns, instead of being sung, read or gabbled in the same manner; but all this was done, and the rest of the service was performed, in a language no longer familiar to the people, and only partly intelligible to them, nor to them only, but even to the majority of the clerks and singers."—Palmer's Dissertations on the Eastern Communion, p. 290.

" A stranger would notice, at least here at Athens, a too general neglect of attendance at Divine Worship, and the practice of coming in only about the beginning of the Liturgy, or a little before, so as to assist neither at Vespers nor at Matins . . . and numbers leaving the church almost as soon as the Consecration is over, without even waiting for the Dismissal."—p. 292.

The same writer adds, that certain parts of the daily offices are reverently performed: others in the most slovenly and profane manner.

" The above-mentioned defects and scandals, which would strike a stranger, are often freely admitted by members of the Eastern Church themselves, most commonly lightly, and as an excuse for irreligiousness and general scepticism; but sometimes with an appearance of serious desire that religion should again become a living reality instead of an external superstition. Such persons will commonly regret, and with reason, that the Services of the Church are too lengthy to be performed becomingly; and that though they are in fact shortened in actual use in the Church to suit the convenience of the people, this is still done in such a way as to leave the priests burdened with the duty of reading over all that is omitted; so that they who ought to lead the people out of formalism, are thus habituated to a profane formalism themselves."—*Palmer on the Eastern Church*, p. 293.

"On the other hand, from traditionary prejudice and habit, from a desire to approve themselves to the people, from regard to personal and pecuniary interests, and from a sincere dread of that Sadduceeism to which any admission of the ideas of criticism and reformation seems to lead, the greater number take the side of the Pharisees of old: and, without conceding an iota, defend honestly or hypocritically the whole existing system, dead, rotten, and crystallized though it be; and are deaf to all arguments or warnings pointing out the defects of their Communion, and blind to all consequences of their obstinacy."— p. 295.

### Note K.—p. 328.

The contents of the Lord's Prayer have been referred by some (see Wetstein on St. Matt. vi.) to forms of private prayer anciently in use, or supposed to have been so, among the Jews. But from a careful comparison of it with the "eighteen prayers" (see p. 65) of the Jewish Synagogue, I am strongly inclined to believe that it is no other than a summary or compendium of that public form, and not a mere collection of scattered and private fragments. The topics are the same, with the single and most characteristic addition of the clause, "as we forgive them that trespass against us," to which the Jewish prayer contains nothing parallel; and on which alone, accordingly, our Lord dwells and comments in giving the prayer, as if it were some new feature which needed to be explained or accounted for: "For if ye forgive men their trespasses, your heavenly Father will also forgive you. But if ye forgive not," &c. It would be impossible, without drawing out at length the greater part of the Jewish prayers, to do justice to the parallel in question; and I must therefore refer the reader to them as given by Prideaux, I. vi. 2.

## Note L.—pp. 337—347.

"But simply in this light, considered merely as a method of reading the Scriptures wholly, thoroughly, and frequently, the value of the Daily Service can never be sufficiently estimated. By what other plan are we likely to accomplish what it does, i.e. the reading of nearly every book and chapter in the Old Testament, including a good deal of the Apocrypha, once a-year; and every letter of the New Testament, except the Apocalypse, three times? What other plan has been proposed, what other practice has been adopted, that does not involve very serious omissions, or imply too long and protracted a period of time for its performance? Again, consider the manner in which the Scriptures are thus brought before us. Various portions, things new and old, are brought together for each day's meditation. Thus, besides that the attention is relieved by this very diversity,—by the remarkable difference of matter and style,—the Old Testament, the Gospels and Epistles, are daily made to throw light on one another. The infinitely vast and diverging parts of one vast plan are daily contemplated. Involuntary comparison suggests numberless mutual illustrations. The mind also expands, and adapts itself to the manifold character of God's dealings.

" And it is no little aid to the spiritual powers and aspirations, to hear the Scriptures thus read in the Church, rather than in the parlour or closet. It is in the Church that they are fulfilled. The place is holy and solemn, sacred in its heavenly realities and in its awful associations. Its tone is unearthly. We are there assembled, with the door of our hearts closed for fear of our spiritual enemies, and awe-struck and attentive, for the ground whereon we stand is holy. The Church is a refuge from the cares, the frivolities, and the sensualities of the world. Its felt and almost visible holiness and glory are a stay to the unstable, a repose to the wearied, a home to the wandering, a calm to the shaken and distracted. Very few people indeed have, as individuals, any place to call their own; very few have a place to sit down in, and read for half an hour without interruption. The Church supplies the want. Private *prayer* is possible to all; for the inward and spiritual operations of the mind and its *immediate* communications with the Father of Spirits, need never be interrupted by outward things; and the mind does in a sense enjoy perpetual solitude. But it is not so with religious *information*. Knowledge comes by hearing and reading, which are outward acts involving certain external circumstances; and generally, nay, almost universally, no circumstances can be so auspicious and kindly as the act of public worship in the house of God.

"The very fact of the Scriptures being read in the Church without break or comment, while of course it has its unavoidable disadvantages, has more than one recommendation. There is nothing to jar the tone, nothing to break the tenor. The letter is treated as a thing of sacramental power. Day by day, things are heard and heard again, till year after year their meaning dawns, and grows to a vastness of development and a fulness of maturity, which forced attempts at explanation might only have warped and stunted."—From the "British Critic," No. 65, Jan. 1843: a periodical not at that time disposed to look too favourably on English ritual practices.

www.ingramcontent.com/pod-product-compliance
Lightning Source LLC
Chambersburg PA
CBHW020539300426
44111CB00008B/724